Foundations in
SPORTS
COACHING

Anthony Bush • John Brierley • Sam Carr • Adam Gledhill • Nikki Mackay
Andrew Manley • Haydn Morgan • Wayne Roberts • Nicholas Willsmer

D0543201

ALWAYS LEARNING   PEARSON

Heinemann is an imprint of Pearson Education Limited, Edinburgh Gate, Harlow, Essex, CM20 2JE.

www.pearsonschoolsandfecolleges.co.uk

Heinemann is a registered trademark of Pearson Education Limited

Text © Pearson Education Limited 2012

Designed by Brian Melville

Typeset by Brian Melville

Original illustrations © Pearson Education Limited 2011

Illustrated by Pearson Education, Oxford Designers and Illustrators and Brian Melville

Cover design by Brian Melville

Picture research by Susannah Prescott

Cover photo © Getty Images: Rubberball

The rights of Anthony Bush, John Brierley, Sam Carr, Adam Gledhill, Nikki Mackay, Andrew Manley, Haydn Morgan, Wayne Roberts and Nicholas Willsmer to be identified as authors of this work have been asserted by them in accordance with the Copyright, Designs and Patents Act 1988.

First published 2012

14 13 12

10 9 8 7 6 5 4 3 2 1

British Library Cataloguing in Publication Data

A catalogue record for this book is available from the British Library

ISBN 978 0 435 04684 2

Printed in Malaysia, CTP-PJB

Websites

There are links to relevant websites in this book. In order to ensure that the links are up to date and that the links work we have made the links available on our website at www.pearsonhotlinks.co.uk. Search for this title Foundations in Sports Coaching or ISBN 9780435046842.

Contents

Author acknowledgements

Anthony Bush

To Beatrice, Charlotte, Nicolas, John, Patricia, Peter, Maria, Camilla and Hanna. Thank you.

John Brierley

For the two inspirational and guiding influences in my life - Pat and Kathryn.

Sam Carr

Thanks to my wife, Ira, and son, Alex, for their support during my various writing endeavours.

Adam Gledhill

Thank you to my family and Amy for all their support and patience throughout my writing of this book, and thank you to my nephew Jack whose smiles and giggles were a very welcome distraction.

Nikki Mackay

Thank you to my fiancé, mum, dad, sisters and wonderful nephews. To Bob next door for all his kind words and encouragement. Many thanks also to my friends and mentors Kate Randerson, Julie Hancock and Lynne Evans for your wisdom and advice over the years.

Andrew Manley

Firstly, I would like to thank my colleagues at the University of Bath for their help and guidance throughout the process, their constructive criticism and academic insight provided an environment that helped inspire and develop the chapter from its birth to completion. I would also like to thank my family who provided a useful platform to discuss and debate ideas both old and new.

Haydn Morgan

I would like to thank all those who have been involved in this project, which has been interesting and challenging but ultimately very enjoyable. Also, I would like to thank my family for their unabated support and inspiration every day.

Wayne Roberts

Dedicated to Jo, for making me believe anything is possible. Particular thanks go to Morph Bowes and Anthony Bush for constantly challenging my thoughts about coaching.

Nicholas Willsmer

I would like to acknowledge everyone who has contributed to where I am today, as you have all helped shape the contents of this chapter.

Acknowledgements

The authors and publisher would like to thank the following individuals and organisations for permission to reproduce material:

pp.16-17: The traditional sports development continuum, the modified model of the sports development continuum and the house of sport reprinted with permission of Taylor & Francis; pp.22-23: data from Active People Survey reprinted with permission from Sport England; p.70: Mosston and Ashworth's Spectrum of Teaching Styles reprinted with permission of Spectrum Institute for Teaching and Learning; pp.141-142: material on the Inclusion Spectrum reprinted with permission of Ken Black, Pam Stevenson and sports coach UK, sports coach UK's *Code of Practice for Sports Coaches* is free to download from the sports coach UK website: www.sportscoachuk.org. For further details of sports coach UK products, please visit www.1st4sport.com or call +44 (0) 113 201 5555; p.161: Overview of the development of psychological abilities reprinted with permission of The Crowood Press; p.168: material reprinted with permission of Youth Sport Trust (http://gifted. youthsporttrust.org); p.168-169: material reprinted with permission of the English Institute of Sport; p.172: Calculating basal metabolic requirements reprinted with permission of Nature Publishing Group; p.173: Physical activity levels for three levels reproduced under the terms of the Open Government Licence; p.174: Eatwell plate. Crown copyright, 2012. Reproduced under the terms of the Open Government Licence; p.189,191: examples of Dartfish tagging system and image of video analysis reprinted with permission of Dartfish Ltd.; p.203: Strength, speed and endurance relationship adapted, with permission, from T.O. Bompa and M.C. Carrera, 2005, Periodization training for sports, 2nd ed. (Champaign, IL: Human Kinetics), 7; p.204: Force velocity relationship reprinted by courtesy of Quintic.com; p.208: Review of agility reprinted by permission of Edizioni Minerva Medica from: J Sports Med Phys Fitness. 2002 Sep;42(3):282-8; p.208: Reactive agility test reprinted with permission of Elsevier; p.216: Coaches code of practice reprinted with permission of sports coach UK; p.219: Model of frustration in sport reprinted with permission of The McGraw-Hill Companies; p.219: Typology of sports violence reprinted with permission of John Wiley & Sons; p.248: Kolb learning cycle reprinted from Kolb, David A., Experiential Learning: Experience as a Source of Learning & Development, 1st Edition, © 1984. Adapted by permission of Pearson Education, Inc., Upper Saddle River, NJ. p.249: Gibbs' reflective cycle reprinted with permission of Oxford Brookes University; Diagram of review of agility reprinted by permission of Edizioni Minerva Medica from: J Sports Med Phys Fitness. 2002 Sep;42(3):282-8.

The publisher would like to thank the following for their kind permission to reproduce their photographs (Key: b-bottom; c-centre; l-left; r-right; t-top):

Alamy Images: Friedrich Stark 83; Anthony Bush: 252, 254, 255; Corbis: moodboard UO; Getty Images: AFP 27, Alistair Berg 118, Fuse 123, Jose Luis Pelaez Inc 133, Louis Fox 213, Philippe Marchand 218, Rubberball Productions 29, Thomas Barwick 65; Pearson Education Ltd: Gareth Boden 60; Photolibrary.com: Radius Images 9; Press Association Images: Tim Ireland / PA Wire 17; Rex Features: Back Page Images 37, Sipa Press 140; Shutterstock.com: AISPIX 52, Shutterstock/Andrey Bondurenko 139, Supri Suharjoto 82

Cover images: Front: Getty Images: Rubberball

All other images © Pearson Education

About the authors

Anthony Bush

Dr Anthony Bush is a lecturer in sports studies, education, and coaching in the Department of Education at the University of Bath. He is a former professional badminton player and has over 20 years of coaching experience. His research interests include the development of interpretive-critical research methodologies and engaging a cultural studies sensibility with sports coaching research, an ongoing project that democratises sports coaching research, opening it to critical conversations about social justice, cultural politics, violence and progressive futures.

John Brierley

John Brierley is currently Field Chair and Senior Lecturer in Sport, Coaching and Physical Education in the Department of Sport and Health Sciences at Oxford Brookes University. He currently teaches Sports Psychology, Training Science, Skill Acquisition and Applied Sports Psychology at undergraduate level and was previously involved in the design and teaching of the MSc in Sports Coaching at Brunel University. He is currently External Examiner at University of Wales Institute Cardiff on their HND in Sports Coaching and Development programme having previously served in the same capacity for the BSc in Sports Coaching. He is a former international athlete, coach, manager, selector and team leader for athletics in Scotland and England and has worked at four English Premier League football clubs as fitness coach and sport scientist. His research interests include psychological interventions in sport, plyometric training and the psychology of leading international teams.

Sam Carr

Sam Carr has 10 years of teaching experience in higher education and has recently published the monograph "Attachment in Sport, Exercise and Wellness" (October 2011).

Adam Gledhill

Adam Gledhill has nine years experience teaching sports and exercise sciences and sports therapy courses across Further and Higher Education. He has contributed to the development of a Foundation Degree in Sports Therapy that is currently accredited by the Society of Sports Therapists. Adam has co-authored ten publications within sport or sport and exercise sciences, works as an educational consultant for a national consultancy firm and is currently working towards a PhD in Sport Psychology.

Nikki Mackay

Nikki Mackay has her own Sports Injury Consultancy and Wellbeing clinic working with elite, professional and recreational sports people and clubs. She has recently been appointed as Chief Verifier Sport and Active Leisure for a lead education awarding body. She also works as an educational consultant, freelance lecturer and examiner.

Nikki is an assessment associate and writer, and an external examiner for leading educational awarding bodies. She has lectured across a range of programmes and module subjects, including lecturing on teacher training programmes, mentoring and contributing to staff development programmes. Specialising in Sports Therapy, she led the writing and validation of FdSc and BSc Sports Therapy programmes by the University of Northampton.

Andrew Manley

Andrew Manley is a teaching fellow at the University of Bath where he teaches courses in areas related to ethics, globalisation, sports policy and development and the sociology of sport. He has built up a wealth of teaching experience both in the UK and abroad, and both within a corporate environment and an academic setting. His key areas of interest involve analysing the sociological aspects related to sport. Having completed his PhD in Sociology and Social Policy at the University of Durham, he is looking to continue researching into areas surrounding identity, power and the development of elite athletes.

Haydn Morgan

Haydn Morgan is currently a Teaching Fellow in the Department of Education at the University of Bath. He has taught extensively on a broad range of sport-related foundation degrees and also teaches on honours degree programmes. Haydn has vast experience within the wider sports industry, having played professional cricket and worked in a variety of sport development roles, both in the United Kingdom and in New Zealand.

Wayne Roberts

Wayne Roberts is currently a senior lecturer in Sport, Coaching and Physical Education in the Department of Sport and Health Sciences at Oxford Brookes University. He has taught at universities for six years on a range of undergraduate and postgraduate degrees, as well as designing and teaching course content for Foundation Degrees. He is currently an active coach and holds his UEFA B Licence in Football, and has worked in both women's and men's football. His research interests include the construction of coaching knowledge, the development of narrative writing in sports coaching research and he is currently engaged in his doctorate, applying a cultural studies sensibility to the work of sports coaching.

Nicholas Willsmer

Nicholas Willsmer holds a degree in Sport and Exercise Science from Leeds Metropolitan University (Carnegie) and a Masters in Strength and Conditioning from Edinburgh University. Since 2006, he has been a teaching fellow for the University of Bath teaching on a variety of sports programmes. Nicholas has delivered Strength and Conditioning support to a range of different sports including football, rugby, judo and snowboarding. He is currently working with track and field athletes. His research interests include bridging the theory-practice gap in strength and conditioning coaching from an educational and performance perspective.

Introduction

Who is this book for?

This book is an essential guide for students studying a foundation degree in Sports Coaching and BTEC Higher Nationals in Sport and Sport and Exercise Sciences.

About foundation degrees

Your foundation degree should enable you to develop the intermediate higher education skills that characterise high-quality graduates needed in the labour market and should integrate academic and work-based learning. It is likely that your foundation degree will have been developed in collaboration with employers and have a focus on the development of work-related skills and knowledge and their direct application to the workplace.

As a foundation degree graduate you should be able to demonstrate the following in your field of study and also in a work context:

- knowledge and critical understanding of the well-established principles

- successful application of the range of knowledge and skills learned throughout your programme

- knowledge of the main methods of enquiry in your subject(s)

- the ability to evaluate critically the appropriateness of different approaches to problem solving

- effective communication of information, arguments and analysis, in a variety of forms, to specialist and non-specialist audiences

- qualities and transferable skills necessary for employment and progression to other qualifications requiring the exercise of personal responsibility and decision making

- the ability to utilise opportunities for lifelong learning, and should you wish to pursue it, a smooth transition route to an honours degree programme.

Your foundation degree will have been developed in line with relevant National Occupational Standards where appropriate. National Occupational Standards recognise established benchmarks of competence. They are developed by employers, academics and other sector experts and define the skills and knowledge required to undertake particular job roles.

As competition for employment opportunities grows most foundation degrees offer a bridge between learning and earning. Authentic and innovative work-based learning is an integral part of a foundation degree. The work-based learning aspect of your foundation degree should offer you the opportunity of relevant work and training.

In your foundation degree, academic knowledge and understanding should integrate with, and support the development of, vocational skills and competencies. It should enhance and extend your career prospects and foster the development of life-long learning. You should get the opportunity to work on real projects, making a real difference whilst picking up technical and practical skills needed for your chosen career path.

Assessment

Different foundation degrees will assess your work in different ways. The purpose of assessment is to determine your performance in relation to the learning outcomes of your award, level and modules. Assessment methods will include a variety of formal and informal, summative and formative techniques. The assessment strategy for your programme is likely to provide a good mix of competency-based assessments, examination and employer feedback that may include:

- case studies

- presentations

- project work

- examinations

- reports

- practicals or simulations

- observations and viva examinations

- peer and self assessment

- personal development plans and evidence portfolios.

You should understand the relationship between learning outcomes and assessment and develop your confidence in tackling different forms of assessment.

About BTEC Higher Nationals

BTEC Higher Nationals are designed to provide a specialist vocational programme, linked to professional body requirements and National Occupational Standards where appropriate. They offer a strong, sector-related emphasis on practical skills development alongside the development of requisite knowledge and understanding. The qualifications provide a thorough grounding in the key concepts and practical skills required in the sector and their national recognition by employers allows direct progression to employment. A key progression path for BTEC HNC and HND learners is to the second or third year of a degree or honours degree programme, depending on the match of the BTEC Higher National units to the degree programme in question.

The BTEC HNC and HND in Sport and in Sport and Exercise Sciences offer progression routes to membership of The Institute of Sport and Recreation Management (ISRM) and The Institute for Sport, Parks and Leisure (ISPAL).

BTEC Higher Nationals in Sport and in Sport and Exercise Sciences have been developed to focus on:

- providing education and training for a range of careers in the sector
- the education and training of those who are employed, or aspire to be employed, in a variety of types of work, such as in performance analysis, nutrition for sport and exercise, sports therapy, sports development, sports coaching, education, research and development
- opportunities for you to gain a nationally-recognised vocationally-specific qualification to enter employment in the sector or progress to higher education qualifications such as a fulltime degree in a related area
- an understanding of the roles of those working in the sector, including how their role and that of their department fits within the overall structure of their organisation and within the community
- opportunities for you to focus on the development of the higher level skills in sport, sport and exercise sciences and related areas
- the development of your knowledge, understanding and skills in the field of sport, sport and exercise sciences and related areas
- opportunities for you to develop a range of skills, techniques and attributes essential for successful performance in working life.

Assessment

For BTEC Higher Nationals the purpose of assessment is to ensure that effective learning of the content of each unit has taken place. Evidence of this learning, or the application of the learning, is required for each unit. The assessment of the evidence relates directly to the assessment criteria for each unit, supported by the generic grade descriptors. The process of assessment can aid effective learning by seeking and interpreting evidence to decide the stage that you have reached in your learning, what further learning needs to take place and how best to do this. Therefore, the process of assessment should be part of the effective planning of teaching and learning by providing opportunities for both you and your assessor to obtain information about progress towards learning goals.

The role of the Sector Skills Councils

Sector Skills Councils (SSCs) are independent, employer-led, UK wide organisations that are licensed by government to build skills systems relevant to employment. They have four key goals:

- to reduce skills gaps and shortages
- to improve productivity, business and public service performance
- to increase opportunities for skills development
- to improve learning through National Occupational Standards, apprenticeships and further and higher education.

SSCs make labour market information available to key stake holders. This information is at the centre of effective careers counselling. SkillsActive is the SSC for Active Leisure, Learning and Wellbeing. This sector covers everything from the grass-roots through to performance sport and they ensure the sector has suitably qualified employees and volunteers to support the delivery of sport and sport related activities. Find out more about SkillsActive at www.skillsactive.com.

How to use this book

This book is divided into chapters that cover the theory you will need to help you through your studies and chapters that cover the practical aspects of studying for a foundation degree or a BTEC Higher National. This book contains many features that will help you use your skills and knowledge in work-related situations and assist you in getting the most from your course.

Features of this book

Activities

There are different types of activities for you to do throughout the text that will help you to develop your knowledge, skills and understanding.

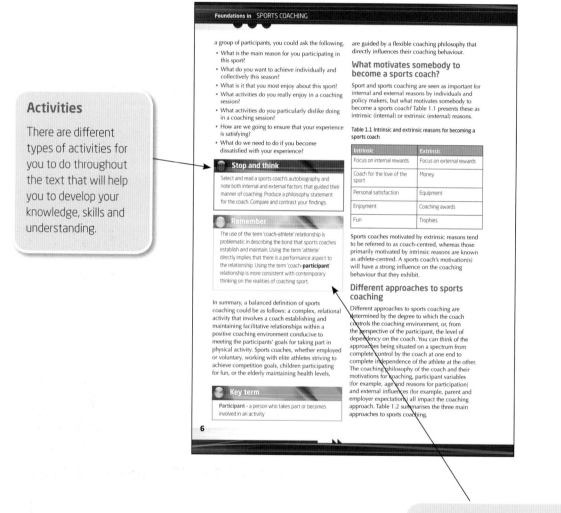

Useful information

Key facts that are crucial to the course or to professional practice are highlighted throughout the text

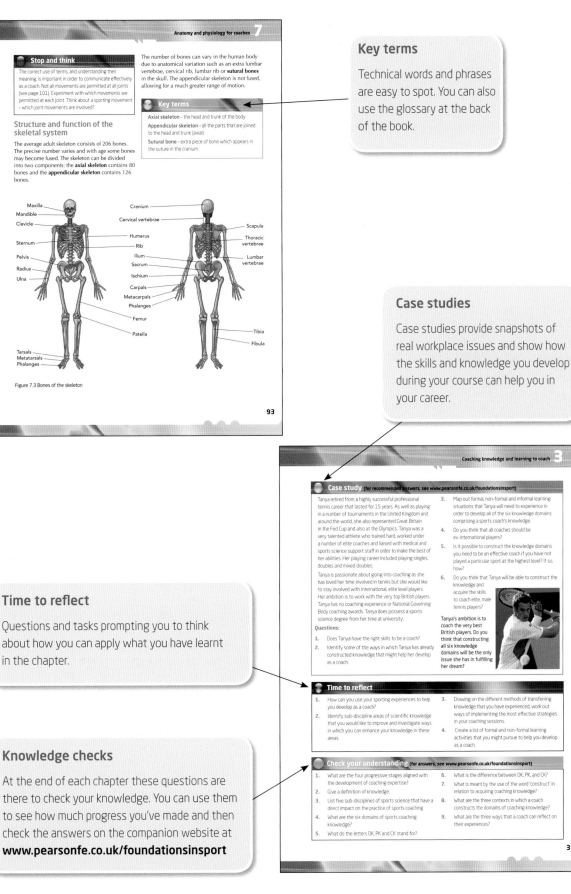

Anatomy and physiology for coaches 7

Stop and think

The correct use of terms, and understanding their meaning, is important in order to communicate effectively as a coach. Not all movements are permitted at all joints (see page 101). Experiment with which movements are permitted at each joint. Think about a sporting movement – which joint movements are involved?

Structure and function of the skeletal system

The average adult skeleton consists of 206 bones. The precise number varies and with age some bones may become fused. The skeleton can be divided into two components: the **axial skeleton** contains 80 bones and the **appendicular skeleton** contains 126 bones.

The number of bones can vary in the human body due to anatomical variation such as an extra lumbar vertebrae, cervical rib, lumbar rib or **sutural bones** in the skull. The appendicular skeleton is not fused, allowing for a much greater range of motion.

Key terms

Axial skeleton – the head and trunk of the body
Appendicular skeleton – all the parts that are joined to the head and trunk (axial)
Sutural bone – extra piece of bone which appears in the suture in the cranium

Figure 7.3 Bones of the skeleton

93

Key terms

Technical words and phrases are easy to spot. You can also use the glossary at the back of the book.

Case studies

Case studies provide snapshots of real workplace issues and show how the skills and knowledge you develop during your course can help you in your career.

Coaching knowledge and learning to coach 3

Case study (for recommended answers, see www.pearsonfe.co.uk/foundationsinsport)

Tanya retired from a highly successful professional tennis career that lasted for 15 years. As well as playing in a number of tournaments in the United Kingdom and around the world, she also represented Great Britain in the Fed Cup and also at the Olympics. Tanya was a very talented athlete who trained hard, worked under a number of elite coaches and liaised with medical and sports science support staff in order to make the best of her abilities. Her playing career included playing singles, doubles and mixed doubles.

Tanya is passionate about going into coaching as she has loved her time involved in tennis but she would like to stay involved with international, elite level players. Her ambition is to work with the very top British players. Tanya has no coaching experience or National Governing Body coaching awards. Tanya does possess a sports science degree from her time at university.

Questions:

1. Does Tanya have the right skills to be a coach?
2. Identify some of the ways in which Tanya has already constructed knowledge that might help her develop as a coach.

3. Map out formal, non-formal and informal learning situations that Tanya will need to experience in order to develop all of the six knowledge domains comprising a sports coach's knowledge.
4. Do you think that all coaches should be ex-international players?
5. Is it possible to construct the knowledge domains you need to be an effective coach if you have not played a particular sport at the highest level? If so, how?
6. Do you think that Tanya will be able to construct the knowledge and acquire the skills to coach elite, male tennis players?

Tanya's ambition is to coach the very best British players. Do you think that constructing all six knowledge domains will be the only issue she has in fulfilling her dream?

Time to reflect

Questions and tasks prompting you to think about how you can apply what you have learnt in the chapter.

Time to reflect

1. How can you use your sporting experiences to help you develop as a coach?
2. Identify sub-discipline areas of scientific knowledge that you would like to improve and investigate ways in which you can enhance your knowledge in these areas.
3. Drawing on the different methods of transferring knowledge that you have experienced, work out ways of implementing the most effective strategies in your coaching sessions.
4. Create a list of formal and non-formal learning activities that you might pursue to help you develop as a coach.

Knowledge checks

At the end of each chapter these questions are there to check your knowledge. You can use them to see how much progress you've made and then check the answers on the companion website at **www.pearsonfe.co.uk/foundationsinsport**

Check your understanding (for answers, see www.pearsonfe.co.uk/foundationsinsport)

1. What are the four progressive stages aligned with the development of coaching expertise?
2. Give a definition of knowledge.
3. List five sub-disciplines of sports science that have a direct impact on the practice of sports coaching
4. What are the six domains of sports coaching knowledge?
5. What do the letters DK, PK and CK stand for?
6. What is the difference between DK, PK, and CK?
7. What is meant by the use of the word 'construct' in relation to acquiring coaching knowledge?
8. What are the three contexts in which a coach constructs the domains of coaching knowledge?
9. What are the three ways that a coach can reflect on their experiences?

37

Chapter 1

Introduction to sports coaching

Introduction

Sports coaching means different things to different people.
For some, sports coaching is their job, for others it is a pastime that they
willingly give up their time to do on a voluntary basis. Some pursue
the academic study of sports coaching for personal attainment or for
sharing ideas and information; others pursue the vocational study of
sports coaching to acquire certification that demonstrates a particular
level of competence. Individuals and teams are the consumers of sports
coaching. Often coaching is all about improving individual or collective
performance; however, receiving sports coaching also offers the space to
enjoy participation in sport. This chapter will enhance your understanding
of sports coaching by challenging you to explore some of the assumptions
surrounding the study and practice of sports coaching.

Learning outcomes

After you have read this chapter you should be able to:

- understand the importance placed on sport in modern society
- appreciate the context in which sports coaching currently exists
- define sports coaching
- understand what motivates people to become a sports coach
- appreciate the different approaches to sports coaching
- understand why a humanistic approach to sports coaching is regarded as the
  benchmark in coaching practice
- explain why a humanistic approach is compatible with a performance sport culture
- understand what makes a good coach
- understand the multiple roles of a coach.

The importance placed on sport in modern society

As recently as the middle of the last century, there was a limit on the roles that an individual might fulfil in relation to sport. Involvement was restricted to participating, spectating, volunteering and consuming the sports news mainly in the newspapers or on the radio. The professionalisation and commercialisation of sport was yet to develop, and the relationship between television and sport was in its infancy (Houlihan, 2009). In modern society, sport touches the lives of many. It has been estimated that billions of people tune in to view global mega-events such as the Olympic Games or the World Cup finals.

In the United Kingdom, watching sport has never been easier with over 20 dedicated sport channels, and the British Sky Broadcasting Group alone transmitting in excess of 100 hours of sport on a daily basis to its ten million subscribers. Additionally, increasing press coverage of sport on the front and back pages as well as the iconic status of sports stars are indicators of the importance invested in sport. As a result of media coverage, few if any areas of public policy have the exposure offered by sport to policy makers and as such it is seen as a vital component in the delivery of a wide range of government objectives.

Sport can play key roles in contributing to wider government policy, such as improving the health of the nation, stimulating the economy, national pride in our elite success, national and international prestige, city regeneration and tourism. In addition, sport is inherently linked to community benefits; for example, improved educational attainment, reduction in crime rates and enhanced social cohesion; as well as being seen as having the potential to help redress the social divisions around class, race, gender and disability. **Instrumentalism** describes the way that the government's interest in sport derives from the way it helps to develop personal and social life. As well as being valued by TV viewers and consumers of other media, sport is also valued by participants because it develops personal skills, competition, friendships, fitness, health, psychological well-being and it's fun!

In England, 17 million adults participate at least monthly in sport and physical activity (Carter, 2005), and of these, almost seven million participate at least three times a week (Sport England, 2011). It is recommended that children engage in at least 60 minutes of moderate intensity activity on a daily basis, and it is estimated that 70% of boys and 60% of girls in England between the ages of 5 and 16, which equates to approximately five million children, meet or exceed this requirement (British Heart Foundation, 2011). Children meet this requirement through compulsory and extra-curricular physical education and school sport in combination with sport and physical activity away from the school setting.

Whether it is participation in sport for personal (internal) reasons or for broader (external) reasons, the environment in which sport takes place is very important. At the centre of this environment is the sports coach.

The context in which sports coaching currently exists

It is estimated that over six million people receive sports coaching in the United Kingdom (DCMS, 2002). Approximately 80% of the 1.2 million people involved in the practice of sports coaching contribute their time on a voluntary basis (SkillsActive, 2011); however, paid employment as a sports coach represents a significant part of the active leisure, learning and well-being sector workforce. Sport is categorised as a sub-sector of the active leisure, learning and well-being sector, with a total workforce of about 400,000 people employed on a full-time basis. Sport provides 2.2% of all jobs in the United Kingdom (Carter, 2005), where it is estimated that there are 240,000 paid sports coaches, of which 80,000 are employed full time (SkillsActive, 2011). Coaching contributes approximately 20% of the full-time workforce in the sub-sector of sport (SkillsActive, 2011).

Remember

SkillsActive is the Sector Skills Council responsible for Active Leisure, Learning and Well-being, which includes the following sub-sectors.

- Sport
- Fitness
- Playwork
- The outdoors
- Caravan

Sports coaches work with children and adults from the grass roots through to performance sport. In addition to improving an individual or team's **performance**, sports coaches are increasingly seen as playing an important part in working towards a wider social role for sport and the government's policy goals. The result of this is that sports coaches operate in a very exciting time. To capture the invaluable contribution that sports coaches can make, sports coach UK in 2008 launched the United Kingdom Coaching Framework as a focal point for developing a world-leading sports coaching system by 2016. Chapter 2 (Sports Development) explores these developments in the sports coaching system in the context of the broader sport policy influences in the United Kingdom.

Definition of sports coaching

The use of the term sport can be problematic. Sport is often defined in terms of team sports (for example, hockey, netball, football, rugby and volleyball) or individual sports (for example, tennis, badminton, golf, athletics and fencing). The definition is usually refined by adding that sport is normally associated with being physical, requiring skill, involving competition with clearly identifiable winners and losers, and that sport is played or performed according to set rules. This definition of sport often leads to intense discussions about whether or not a particular activity is a sport or not.

Stop and think

Consider whether or not the following are sports.

- Ballroom dancing
- Chess
- Darts
- Snooker
- Ice skating
- Archery
- Parkour
- Skateboarding

In adopting, and not questioning, this narrow definition of sport, we limit our understanding of what sports coaching is by restricting it to working with **athletes** in a selection of mainly games-based activities that meet a set of rigid criteria. This book embraces an understanding of sport to incorporate any physical activity that is undertaken for any reason (including competition but expanded to include other purposes such as enjoyment, social activity, weight management, friendships and developing self-esteem). Activities that are brought under the banner of a broader physical definition of sport, to sit alongside 'sports', include **exercise**, **health-related activities**, **exergaming**, dance and **activities of daily living**.

Key terms

Exercise – activity that maintains or enhances fitness

Health-related activities – activity aimed at improving the health and well-being of an individual

Exergaming – the term used for video games that also incorporate physical activity

Activities of daily living – the things that you normally do in your daily life at home or at work

Athlete – a person who competes in organised sporting events

An example of a widely accepted definition of sports coaching is that it 'centres on the improvement of an individual's or team's sporting ability, both as a general capacity and as specific performances' (Lyle, 2002, p.38). Similarly, Kidman and Hanrahan (2004, p.145) state that one of the primary roles of a coach is to help athletes improve their performance.

The main assumption surrounding these definitions is that the primary goal of any sports coach is to improve the performance of an individual or team in a competitive arena. However, there are a number of different coaching **contexts** in which it would be inappropriate for the coach and the participants to treat performance enhancement as the primary goal (for example, working with individuals exercising for health benefits). Contemporary thinking about sports coaching has suggested that the primary goal of any coach is to enable athletes to learn. Chapter 5 (Coaching pedagogy) unpicks this notion and develops a detailed account of theories and strategies to ensure that you will be able to maximise athlete learning in your sessions.

Coaching sport is a highly **contextual** act and there are a number of factors that directly influence the **coaching environment**. Coaching is primarily a social activity that involves the coach establishing and maintaining a number of coach–athlete **relationships**. Chapter 6 (Sociology for coaches) explores the sociological influences on coaching sport, helping you to develop an appreciation of coaching relationships at the micro-level and the broader societal influences on coaching at the macro-level.

Sports coaching is a **relational** activity. As a relational activity, the personal characteristics of both the coach and the individuals or teams have a direct influence on the coaching environment. The list below presents some of the personal characteristics of an individual or team that significantly influence the coaching environments with which sports coaches work:

- Age
- Gender
- Learning preferences
- Reason for participation
- (Dis)ability
- Personality
- Motivation
- Level of proficiency

Chapter 4 (The coaching process) looks at how these factors, amongst others, influence the planning, delivery and evaluation of a coaching session. Chapter 9 (Coaching special populations) and Chapter 10 (Coaching young performers) examine how sports coaches need to adapt their practice in order to ensure a positive coaching environment for a range of individuals and teams that might present a number of different challenges.

From a coach's perspective, the term **coaching philosophy** is often used to describe the guiding principles that shape a coach's behaviour in the coaching environment. These guiding principles can be internal to the coach, based on a set of deeply held beliefs, or externally imposed expectations from participants and employers or organisations. These guiding principles can collectively be referred to as the ethics of coaching. Morals, values and virtues combine to provide the sports coach with a framework against which reflection and choices are made. It is these choices in a particular context that shape the coaching philosophy. Chapter 14 (Ethics and good practice) explores these ethical tensions from a coach's perspective and highlights the challenges that face practising coaches on a daily basis.

Key terms

Performance – how well a person or team does an activity

Contexts – the situations within which something exists

Contextual – related to the specific situation within which something exists or happens

Relational – involving interaction with others

Relationships – the way in which the coach and athlete are connected

Coaching environment – the physical space in which sports coaching activities take place

Coaching philosophy – the guiding principles that shape a coach's behaviour in the coaching environment

A written record of a coach's philosophy is referred to as a **philosophy statement**. The following list of questions might be helpful in developing your coaching philosophy statement.

- How important is winning?
- Are you interested in the **holistic** development of your athletes?
- How important is playing by the rules?
- Are you comfortable with ceding control and power to your athletes?
- Do you want to encourage a coaching environment where athletes feel comfortable questioning you?
- Do you care if your athletes enjoy the session?
- Do you foster an environment that embraces respect for others?
- How would you deal with a 'pushy parent' in your coaching environment?

Key terms

Philosophy statement – the written record of a coach's philosophy

Holistic – considering someone as a whole rather than dealing with a part

Here is an example of an excerpt from a coaching philosophy statement. It lists aspects of coaching in order of priority. The statement could also be presented as a piece of continuous text. This is a coach working with a group of 20 county squad players of an individual sport. The players' abilities range from a competitive social standard through to national level and they are between 15 and 17 years old. There are equal numbers of male and female athletes in the group.

1. The sessions should be fun and the player should want to come back to the next session.
2. The coaching environment should be a safe space to be in.
3. All players will be treated as knowledgeable and creative beings who are able to think for themselves.
4. Players will demonstrate respect for all other individuals in the coaching environment.
5. Players will demonstrate high levels of motivation at all times.
6. Parents are welcome to observe the sessions but cannot interfere with the players during the session.

In striving to provide a positive coaching environment it is essential that there are no mismatches between a coach's philosophy and the expectations of the individual or team that the coach is working with. Any mismatch would result in conflict or tension in the coaching environment. This could mean that coaches decide to adapt their privately held values and beliefs in order to ensure that conflict is either removed, minimised or at least managed in the coach–athlete relationship. This means that sports coaches can present a very different public face in comparison to their privately held values and beliefs. There will be situations where compromise on certain core values and beliefs might not be an option for a sports coach and in these cases it is probably best for the coach to seek out another coaching opportunity that is consistent with their coaching philosophy.

There are approximately 240,000 sports coaches in some form of employment (SkillsActive, 2011). Employment can add a layer of complexity for sports coaches to negotiate. In addition to the expectations of the individuals and teams that they are working with, they must also consider their employers' expectations. For example, coaches working for a professional club need to treat winning as a priority, whereas coaches working for a school need to ensure that the holistic development of the child is central. It is a delicate balancing act for coaches in being flexible and adaptive in relation to the context presented to them, while remaining faithful to their deeply embedded set of values.

To avoid potential conflict between the coaches, participants, parents and, where applicable, the employers, the coach should attempt to establish a mutual direction that will guide what takes place in the coaching environment. This means presenting the public version of their coaching philosophy, and then asking questions to those with a vested interest in the coaching. For example, prior to working with a group of participants, you could ask the following.

- What is the main reason for you participating in this sport?
- What do you want to achieve individually and collectively this season?
- What is it that you most enjoy about this sport?
- What activities do you really enjoy in a coaching session?
- What activities do you particularly dislike doing in a coaching session?
- How are we going to ensure that your experience is satisfying?
- What do we need to do if you become dissatisfied with your experience?

Stop and think

Select and read a sports coach's autobiography and note both internal and external factors that guided their manner of coaching. Produce a philosophy statement for the coach. Compare and contrast your findings.

Remember

The use of the term 'coach–athlete' relationship is problematic in describing the bond that sports coaches establish and maintain. Using the term 'athlete' directly implies that there is a performance aspect to the relationship. Using the term 'coach-**participant**' relationship is more consistent with contemporary thinking on the realities of coaching sport.

In summary, a balanced definition of sports coaching could be as follows: a complex, relational activity that involves a coach establishing and maintaining facilitative relationships within a positive coaching environment conducive to meeting the participants' goals for taking part in physical activity. Sports coaches, whether employed or voluntary, working with elite athletes striving to achieve competition goals, children participating for fun, or the elderly maintaining health levels,

Key term

Participant – a person who takes part or becomes involved in an activity

are guided by a flexible coaching philosophy that directly influences their coaching behaviour.

What motivates somebody to become a sports coach?

Sport and sports coaching are seen as important for internal and external reasons by individuals and policy makers, but what motivates somebody to become a sports coach? Table 1.1 presents these as intrinsic (internal) or extrinsic (external) reasons.

Table 1.1 Intrinsic and extrinsic reasons for becoming a sports coach

Intrinsic	Extrinsic
Focus on internal rewards	Focus on external rewards
Coach for the love of the sport	Money
Personal satisfaction	Equipment
Enjoyment	Coaching awards
Fun	Trophies

Sports coaches motivated by extrinsic reasons tend to be referred to as coach-centred, whereas those primarily motivated by intrinsic reasons are known as athlete-centred. A sports coach's motivation(s) will have a strong influence on the coaching behaviour that they exhibit.

Different approaches to sports coaching

Different approaches to sports coaching are determined by the degree to which the coach controls the coaching environment, or, from the perspective of the participant, the level of dependency on the coach. You can think of the approaches being situated on a spectrum from complete control by the coach at one end to complete independence of the athlete at the other. The coaching philosophy of the coach and their motivations for coaching, participant variables (for example, age and reasons for participation) and external influences (for example, parent and employer expectations) all impact the coaching approach. Table 1.2 summarises the three main approaches to sports coaching.

Table 1.2 Approaches to sports coaching

Approach	Authoritarian	Power sharing	Humanistic
Who is in control?	Coach	Joint	Athlete
Dependence on coach	Coach dependence	Athlete/coach interdependence	Athlete independence
Characteristics	No decision-making responsibility	Shared decision-making	Self responsibility
Strengths	Safety and security Teaching skills	Sense of control	Personal autonomy Holistic focus
Weaknesses	Participant has no control	Confusion about who is responsible	Reduction in coach accountability

Stop and think

Using the information provided in Table 1.2, consider how you think that the following will influence the approach used by a coach:

- Age
- Performance level of participants
- Participants' reasons for participation (fun, health, competition)
- Employers' expectations
- The sport itself

Remember

Sport is any form of physical activity that is undertaken for any reason (including competition but expanded to include a myriad of other purposes such as enjoyment, social activity, weight management, friendships and developing self-esteem). Activities included in a broader physical definition of sport include: exercise, health-related activities, exergaming, dance and activities of daily living.

Key term

Empowerment – the control that athletes have over themselves to change things for the better

Humanistic approach to sports coaching – a person-centred approach focusing on the holistic development of an empowered individual

Why is a humanistic approach the benchmark in coaching practice?

The coach–participant relationship is at the core of the practice of sports coaching, and in order to ensure a positive coaching environment, the coach must be proficient at establishing and maintaining these, sometimes multiple, relationships. Therefore, to think that it is the coach who is solely responsible and in control of what takes place in the coaching environment, ignores the importance of the relationship dynamic that is present in all coaching contexts. This person-centred approach to sports coaching emphasises empowering participants to strive towards achieving personal goals within a positive interpersonal relationship and is widely accepted as being the benchmark for the majority of coaching contexts. Although there are a number of terms associated with this approach to coaching, such as an **empowerment** approach, a person-centred approach, a collaborative approach, a non-manipulative approach, a democratic approach and a holistic approach, it is most commonly referred to as a **humanistic approach to sports coaching**. The humanist approach is described as being the benchmark for sports coaching practice. Figure 1.1 presents the main assumptions on which a humanistic approach to sports coaching is based.

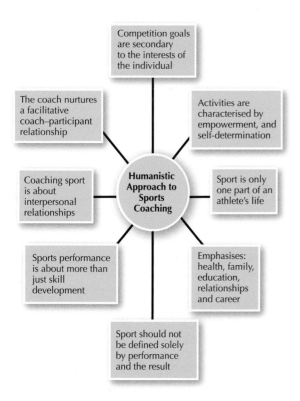

Figure 1.1 The main assumptions on which a humanistic approach to sports coaching is based (adapted from Lyle 2002, p.176)

(Text within figure:)

Competition goals are secondary to the interests of the individual

The coach nurtures a facilitative coach–participant relationship

Activities are characterised by empowerment, and self-determination

Coaching sport is about interpersonal relationships

Humanistic Approach to Sports Coaching

Sport is only one part of an athlete's life

Sports performance is about more than just skill development

Emphasises: health, family, education, relationships and career

Sport should not be defined solely by performance and the result

Why is a humanistic approach compatible with a performance sport culture?

Adopting a humanistic approach to sports coaching allows coaches to take the moral high ground; it is seen as 'good' coaching practice and the 'correct' way of doing things. However, just because something is viewed as the correct way of doing it, it does not necessarily mean that it is the most **effective** way of doing it. For coaches working with athletes with a performance agenda, a tension exists in balancing athlete welfare and competition success. Those coaches working with performance athletes whose jobs are secured on sometimes short-term measures of competition success sometimes argue that placing the interests of the individual before competition goals could be problematic for them. Additionally, in the current performance sport culture, an athlete's personal funding is fundamentally linked to competition success. The substantial level of funding available

for athletes can often be the difference between being able to pursue their competition goals in a sport or not.

> ### Key term
>
> **Effective** – achieving the results that you want

UK Sport terms the personal funding awarded to athletes on the World Class Performance Programme the Athlete Personal Award (APA). This is given to 'Podium' level athletes based on sports specific criteria relating to the level at which the athlete is capable of performing. For an Olympic or World Championship level athlete, this personal funding is approximately £27,000 per annum, dropping to £20,000 for a top eight finish in a major games, and falling to £13,500 for being a performer at major championships. The average APA payment is currently £18,500 for 'Podium' level athletes. In addition, each elite athlete following a performance programme could receive any (or all) of the following benefits that are termed collectively 'in kind' support.

- World class coaches
- Sports science support
- Medical support
- Warm weather training and acclimatisation
- International competition schedule
- Athlete development programmes
- Access to appropriate training facilities

For athletes performing at 'Podium level', this 'in kind' support could equate to a value around £55,000 per annum, and even for development level athletes on the World Class Performance Programme this could be worth in the region of £30,000 per annum. For elite athletes that are outside of the UK Sport performance programme, for example those in professional football, rugby, and cricket clubs, the financial pressures on performance are equally as demanding. The balance between athlete welfare and competition success is a tension that must be reconciled in the coach–athlete relationship.

Instead of falling into the trap of thinking that a humanistic approach to sports coaching is incompatible with a performance culture and is only effective for working with participants without competition goals, it could be argued that it is necessary for coaches to challenge the performance culture that exists in elite athlete development. Performance culture reduces an athlete's development throughout their career to a short-term focus on competition success and typically places an authoritarian coach at the centre of this process. Authoritarian coaches are sometimes referred to as prescriptive or autocratic coaches, and have mistakenly been located as an important part in achieving competition success. Kidman (2001, pp.12–13) identifies a number of issues with locating these prescriptive/autocratic coaches at the heart of a performance culture. These issues are summarised below.

- Autocratic coaches try to control athlete behaviour in both the sport and beyond the sport setting
- Athletes are coached as if they are on a factory assembly line
- The limited athlete learning is focused on memorising rather than understanding or solving problems
- Encourages athletes to be robotic in their actions and thinking
- Athletes feel that they do not have an active role in their learning
- Coaches tend to give athletes extraordinarily gruelling training sessions
- Coaches sometimes use dehumanising practices to enforce control
- 'Must-win' environment contradicts why many athletes are participating in sport
- Results in athlete **disempowerment**
- Reading a game is largely a prescription from the coach
- Coaches believe they need to be hard-nosed and discipline-oriented
- Coaches hold all the power in the relationship
- Coaches have license to 'exploit' their power
- Coaches expect unquestioned acceptance of their actions

Key terms

Disempowerment – to deprive the athlete of power or influence

When things go wrong, a coach can blame the athlete and indicate that the athlete was not motivated or did things that the coach didn't tell them to do, whereas the athlete can blame the coach for their poor performance and develop resentment over the way that they have been treated.

Coach in control: is this the key to achieving competition goals?

An alternative to this is achievable through using more democratic approaches to coaching performance athletes. A humanistic approach promotes athlete empowerment and independence, developing a high degree of self-responsibility. Athletes therefore exert a direct influence on the coaching environment and by taking ownership of their learning, competition and performance goals, it becomes more likely that these will be achieved.

Remember

Your (performance) athletes might not have been coached in a way that encourages empowerment before and so must 'buy in' to the approach for it to be fully effective. In these contexts, to introduce a humanistic approach to your coaching practice you will need to implement it in small steps.

What makes a good coach?

What do you think are the qualities of a good coach? Table 1.3 presents the typical responses of athletes, participants and sports students in response to being asked what they think makes a good coach.

Table 1.3 Qualities and characteristics of a good coach

Qualities and characteristics	
Patient	Flexible
A good player	Experienced
Not just a dictator	Uses different approaches
Sense of humour	Makes me feel good about myself
Motivator	Good time manager
Interested in other things in my life	Good listener
Good communicator	Creative
Knows what I like	Caring
Punctual	Knowledgeable
Appears to enjoy coaching us	Friendly

The qualities of a good coach include a range of roles, skills and responsibilities. The roles of a coach are explored later in this chapter, and the skills and responsibilities of a coach are covered in Chapter 4 (The coaching process) and Chapter 5 (Coaching pedagogy). The requirement of coaches to be knowledgeable is consistently ranked as one of the most important characteristics of a good coach. Chapter 3 (Coaching knowledge and learning to coach) illuminates the knowledge that a coach possesses. It is important to be able to identify the knowledge that a coach requires and to understand how you acquire that knowledge. Chapter 3 (Coaching knowledge and learning to coach) details where and how coaches learn to coach.

One area of knowledge that is referred to as being important to coaches is scientific knowledge. This book presents the key scientific knowledge that underpins coaching practice. Chapter 5 (Coaching pedagogy) considers the science of teaching, something which is sometimes referred to as the 'art' of coaching. In addition to this the following chapters explore the key science areas that underpin coaching practice: Chapter 7 (Anatomy and physiology for coaches), Chapter 8 (Psychology for coaches), Chapter 11 (Nutrition, exercise and lifestyle management), Chapter 12 (Analysis of sports performance), and Chapter 13 (Athletic preparation for sports performance).

The multiple roles of a coach

Academic and professional literature documents the **roles** of a coach as the functions carried out in relation to completing the coaching tasks in the coaching environment. Typically the roles of a coach are presented as the following.

- Motivator
- Friend
- Demonstrator
- Instructor
- Assessor
- Mentor
- Role model
- Organiser
- Leader

Documenting the coaching roles in this uncritical way ignores the essence of coaching. As coaching is relational and contextual, the potential roles that a sports coach could be faced with undertaking become readily expanded when considering what a coach must do in order to establish and maintain a series of relationships in a range of contexts. For example, a coach working with participants with weight management concerns might have to take on the role of nutritional advisor, or the role of travel agent in organising a trip for the participants. Sometimes a coach needs to interpret performance analysis data and so needs to be a statistician. A coach can sometimes be a taxi-driver, social worker, police officer, actor, teacher, pseudo parent and counsellor, amongst many others. Figure 1.2 presents the multiplicity of roles that a coach could be faced with undertaking. The central spine of the diagram represents the typical roles of a coach, whereas thinking about what coaching actually involves in reality results in additional roles being added to the left and right of the central spine.

In addition to these multiple roles of a coach, coaches require particular skills (for example, communication, organisation, problem solving,

Key term

Roles – the range of behaviours displayed by a coach in maintaining a positive coaching environment

evaluating and time management) in order to establish and maintain facilitative coach-participant relationships and a positive coaching environment. Chapter 5 (Coaching pedagogy) explains the different forms of communication that a coach can use in order to convey information to the participants. Chapter 4 (The coaching process) covers a range of additional skills that coaches possess that are relevant to organising and delivering a coaching session.

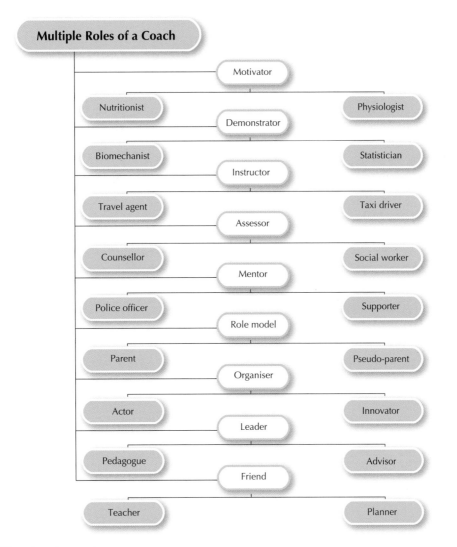

Figure 1.2 The roles of a coach

Case study (for recommended answers, see www.pearsonfe.co.uk/foundationsinsport)

Charlotte's coaching practice is characterised by a humanistic approach. She has recently been asked by a netball club to coach a group of children (aged 11–14) of mixed ability. Charlotte has sole responsibility for selecting a team to play in a local league. She knows that the previous coach left because a group of players and their parents were not happy with only finishing third in the league.

Questions

1. How could Charlotte present her coaching philosophy to her new group of participants?

2. To minimise future tensions, what questions would Charlotte need to ask the participants in her group before the first session?

3. What questions could Charlotte ask the parents of the participants before the first session?

4. How could Charlotte deal with participants and parents that disagree with her coaching approach before the first session?

5. All the children tell Charlotte that they are thoroughly enjoying the coaching sessions; however, the team that she has selected loses the first four matches of the season. What should Charlotte do?

6. Charlotte is informed that her 'star' player is struggling to manage her time between sport and education and is getting into trouble at school for non-submission of homework, late arrival at class, and not participating in physical education lessons. What should Charlotte do?

Check your understanding (for answers, see www.pearsonfe.co.uk/foundationsinsport)

1. Give a definition of sport.

2. Give a definition of sports coaching.

3. List five internal reasons why someone might participate in sport.

4. Why are politics and sport difficult to separate?

5. Why is sports coaching described as relational?

6. Why is sports coaching described as contextual?

7. What do you understand the term 'holistic coaching' to mean?

8. What is a coaching philosophy?

9. Write a coaching philosophy statement for a high profile coach of your choice.

10. Why is it thought that a humanistic approach to sports coaching is the correct way of doing things?

11. Is it only coaches working at the participation level that should be guided by a humanistic approach to coaching?

12. What do you think makes a good coach?

13. List ten roles of a coach.

Time to reflect

- Drawing on your coaching experience, develop a coaching philosophy statement for each of the contexts in which you coach. To do this, you might like to refer to the series of questions on page 5.

- Reflect on whether your coaching practice is person-centred. Investigate the ways in which your coaching does or does not align with the main assumptions on which a humanistic approach to sports coaching is based. Work out ways of implementing a humanistic approach in your coaching sessions.

Useful resources

To obtain a secure link to the websites below, see the Websites section on page ii or visit the companion website at www.pearsonfe.co.uk/foundationsinsport.

- British Cycling
- British Gymnastics
- British Heart Foundation
- Coachwise
- English Basketball Association
- International Journal of Sports Science and Coaching
- Skills Active
- Sociology of Sport Journal
- sports coach UK
- Sport England
- Sport England, Active people survey
- Sports Leaders UK
- The British Olympic Association
- The Football Association
- The Lawn Tennis Association
- The Rugby Football Union
- The Sport Psychologist
- UK Athletics UK Sport

Further reading

British Heart Foundation (2011). *Children and physical activity policy statement* [online]. See 'Useful resources' for source [Accessed 23 March 2011].

Carter, P. (2005). *Review of National Sport Effort and Resources*. London: Sport England.

Cashmore, E. (2000). *Making Sense of Sports* (3rd edition). London: Routledge.

Cassidy, T., Jones, R.L. and Potrac, P. (2009). *Understanding Sports Coaching: The social, cultural and pedagogical foundations of coaching practice* (2nd edition). London: Routledge.

Coalter, F. (2007). *A Wider Social Role for Sport: Who's keeping the score?* London: Routledge.

Cross, N. and Lyle, J. (1999). *The Coaching Process: Principles and practice for sport*. Oxford: Butterworth-Heinemann.

Department for Culture, Media and Sport (DCMS) (2002). *The Coaching Task Force: Final report*. London: DCMS.

Denison, J. (ed.). (1997). *Coaching Knowledges: Understanding the dynamics of sport performance*. London: A&C Black.

Hardman, A.R. and Jones, C. (ed.). (2011). *The Ethics of Sports Coaching*. London: Routledge.

Houlihan, B. (2009). *Sport and Society: A student introduction* (2nd edition). London: Sage.

Jarvie, G. (2006). *Sport, Culture and Society: An introduction*. London: Routledge.

Jones, R.L. (ed.) (2005). *The Sports Coach as Educator: Reconceptualising sports coaching*. London: Routledge.

Jones, R.L., Armour, K.M. and Potrac, P. (2004). *Sports Coaching Cultures: From practice to theory*. London: Routledge.

Kidman, L. (ed.). (2001). *Developing Decision Makers: An empowerment approach to coaching*. Christchurch: Innovative Communications.

Kidman, L. and Hanrahan, S. (2011). *The Coaching Process: A practical guide to improving your effectiveness* (3rd edition). Palmerston North: Dunmore.

Lombardo, B.J. (1987). *The Humanistic Coach: From theory to practice*. Springfield: C.C. Thomas.

Lyle, J. (2002). *Sports Coaching Concepts: A framework for coaches' behaviour*. London: Routledge.

Martens, R. (2004). *Successful Coaching* (3rd edition). Champaign: Human Kinetics.

SkillsActive. (2011). *Sport and Recreation* [online]. See 'Useful resources' for source. [Accessed 23 March 2011].

Sport England. (2011). *Active people survey 4* [online]. See 'Useful resources' for source. [Accessed 23 March 2011].

Chapter 2

Sports development: coaching in context

Introduction

The modern sport context is influenced by politics, economics and socio-cultural factors, where the identification and acquisition of money is crucial to resourcing coaching programmes and, consequently, ensuring survival as a coach. As coaching becomes more professionalised, coaches must find out where funding opportunities exist, which agencies provide funding, and in what aspects of sport this funding is available. To add further complication, the structure of sport provision in the UK is a complex network of organisations, with different remits and objectives. Some sports organisations have a UK focus (such as UK Athletics and UK Sport), while others have a 'home country' emphasis (such as Sport England, the Scottish Football Association, the Welsh Rugby Union and Netball Northern Ireland). A detailed understanding of the intricate nature of this network, and the context within which these organisations operate, may help to indicate to a coach where opportunities to access funding and resources to support coaching work exist. This chapter provides a broad overview of the UK sporting landscape and the various contributors to sport provision in this country. It highlights some of the key issues which face coaches in identifying opportunities to expand their coaching work.

Learning outcomes

After you have read this chapter you should be able to:

- define the work of sports development and its intentions
- appreciate how models of sports development contribute to an understanding of the role of sports development personnel
- comprehend the involvement of government and how this impacts on sports development work
- identify and appreciate the roles and responsibilities of key agencies in sports development
- understand the practice of sports development work
- appreciate the current state of participation in sport
- recognise the implications and opportunities that exist for coaches with the remit of sports development work.

Starting block

The sporting landscape in the UK is defined by a complex network of organisations with different remits but which have the shared focus of developing sport. List as many organisations as you can that contribute to the development of sport in this country. Choose one organisation and then consider the following questions.

- What is the geographic reach of this organisation (international, national, regional, local)?
- What is the main focus of their work (mass participation or elite)?
- Which other organisations do they directly work with?

Defining sports development

The philosophy and practice of sports development has two focuses: firstly, it provides a structure which affords more people greater access to sporting opportunities and, secondly, it provides a higher quality, positive experience of sport for those who participate. However, the aim of sports development is more complex than this and for those who work in sports development, decisions have to be made as to where to direct resources, such as coaches.

There are three distinct views as to where and how sports development work should be directed: development of sport, development through sport and a focus on both.

Development *of* sport

This view supports the notion that sports development is about providing sporting opportunities for their own sake with the intention of meeting sport-based objectives. Typically, the aim of this perspective is to benefit those who have good access to sport and are passionate about improving their performance in sport. Consequently, the structures in place are geared towards increasing **participation** in sport with the aim of improving the performance of participants so that they have a lifelong involvement in competitive sport and a minority can progress to elite levels of sport. Furthermore, those who reach the elite level then become the role models to initiate participation and provide inspiration for younger people to follow

them into sport. For many coaches, their view of sports development will align with this 'sport-for-sport's sake' focus. Many National Governing Bodies for sport set targets to increase the number of participants who transfer into elite talent groups, which is a good example of this type of sport development work.

Development *through* sport

In contrast, some believe that the development of sport should traverse the traditional boundaries of sport and sport should be a vehicle to address a variety of social issues and concerns. For example, there is growing evidence to suggest that participation in sport can be used to tackle issues related to health, crime, **social exclusion**, and other 'cross-cutting' social issues. Here, the emphasis is not so much on the development of sport and sports people, but rather on increasing participation in physical activity and providing opportunities for those who have difficulty in accessing sport by removing the **barriers to participation** (see also page 23). This 'sport-for-good' approach has been particularly welcomed by governments, given that this wider social role for sport can impact on a broader section of the population. A good example of this type of sport development work would be the Football Foundation's 'Kickz' initiative which aims to create stronger, safer and more respectful communities using football as the catalyst.

Key terms

Participation – involvement in an organised activity, such as sport

Social exclusion – a process where individuals or communities are prevented from accessing certain opportunities for social reasons, which results in being disadvantaged in some way

Barrier to participation – a social factor that limits or blocks access to involvement in a particular organised activity

Focus on both

A final view is that sports development work should encompass both positions and recognise that there is a need to provide for those in society for whom sport is central to their lives and self-expression, as well as facilitating opportunities for disadvantaged or socially excluded groups. On the surface, a dual-focus appears to be fair; however, one of the biggest constraints in sports development is funding, and so spreading resources across both areas can mean that neither focus is covered thoroughly or fairly.

Stop and think

In a group with some other coaches, discuss and debate your position on where sports development work should be aimed. How might this perspective change if you coached a different sport or worked in a country where poverty and social deprivation were significant issues?

Models of sports development

To assist the debate on where the focus of sports development should lie, several models have been proposed to distinguish the roles and responsibilities for sports development personnel at various levels of achievement. The most basic model (see Figure 2.1) views sports development provision as a hierarchical endeavour with provision necessary at four levels ranging between 'foundation' and 'excellence'. This simplicity allows sports organisations to make clear decisions about where on the pyramid to focus their efforts.

Figure 2.1 The traditional sports development continuum

The model is based on the assumption that some drop out from sport will occur between the levels

and that not all participants in sport can progress to the next level. The model also assumes that a broader base of sports involvement at the foundation level will ensure that a larger talent pool will materialise at the elite level. This possibly explains why many sports development initiatives are aimed at foundation level involvement.

An adaptation of this model (see Figure 2.2) identifies that participants in sport have different needs and aims in sport, and that not everybody wants to progress to the higher levels of involvement. This adapted model recognises that an individual's involvement in sport can fluctuate between levels, based on the various forces that impact on the degree to which an individual prioritises sport.

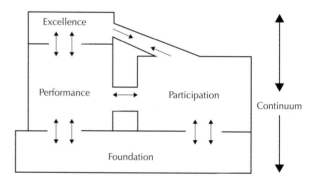

Figure 2.2 The modified model of the sports development continuum

A final model – the house of sport (see Figure 2.3) – is a more complex illustration of sports development. Again, it distinguishes between recreational and performance-oriented participation, and identifies sports development work to be messy and non-linear. The model assumes that there is no correlation between the breadth of the base at the foundation level and the size of the talent pool at the elite level, and that initial involvement in sport can occur at any point in the life cycle – not just in childhood. This suggests that the quality of the programmes and initiatives at each level is a better indicator of sustained participation, or improved performance, than merely increasing the quantity of participants in sport.

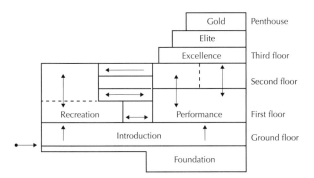

Figure 2.3 The house of sport

Government involvement in sport

The relationship between sport and government is ever changing. Within the last fifty years there is clear evidence of the growing importance of the role of sport in meeting government targets both within sport and wider society. However, sport continues to be a discretionary service for local authorities, with no legal requirement to provide sport facilities and programmes. An understanding of the changing political priority of sport and a history of sports development will help you to appreciate the present and future direction of sports policy and funding.

Sport is often touted by government as an important contributor to a functional society, but sport remains a discretionary service for local authorities.

Pre-1960

Before 1960, sport in the UK was largely organised and administered by amateur sports organisations and bodies and was seen as a private matter that required little or no government involvement. However, the commissioning of a report to examine the state of sport in the UK by the Central Council for Physical Recreation (CCPR, now the Sport and Recreation Alliance), which was published in 1960, changed the nature of the relationship between government and sport. The findings of the Wolfenden Report, as it became known, recommended a focus on young people's involvement in sport, the development of sports facilities to support increased sport provision and improvement in the coaching and administration of sport. Most significantly, the Wolfenden Report highlighted the drop-off in participation between school-based sport and club-based or adult sport participation, as a major concern. Addressing this gap has become the focus of many sports development initiatives since.

1960-1990

In response to the Wolfenden Report, this period saw an unprecedented increase in the development of sports facilities, in particular in the construction of local authority operated leisure centres and swimming pools. In addition, the first attempts were made to target particular groups which were not well represented in sport. Under the banner of 'Sport for All', the focus of sports development during this time was clearly focused on efforts to increase mass participation in sport. However, sport remained a low priority for government.

1990-1997: Major government

When John Major became Prime Minister in 1990, there was a renewed link between government and sport. As a lover of sport, Major saw the benefits of sport participation and competition, and was keen to identify ways of integrating sport more centrally into society. A significant factor was the introduction of the National Lottery which provided a fund that could be spent on 'good causes' – one of which was sport. The publication in 1995 of *Sport: Raising the Game* identified a clear policy for sport which deviated away from mass participation towards a focus on school sport and elite sport.

1997–2010: New Labour

The return to a Labour government saw a further shift in sports policy and a restoration of the previous focus on mass participation alongside a continuation of efforts to improve sport within schools and at the elite level. School sport, in particular, received unprecedented levels of funding to improve facilities and provision, and widen opportunities for young people in sport. The publication of *GamePlan* (2002) stressed the need for a more streamlined approach to administering sport and set specific targets for participation in sport and physical activity at the grassroots level and success at international events for elite performers. This period of government also oversaw the successful London bid for the 2012 Summer Olympic Games, which unlocked unprecedented funding and considerable opportunities for the development of sport in the UK. In response to the successful bid, the government published *Playing to Win* in 2008, which focused more on the development of sport (as opposed to physical activity) and identified three key agencies as the strategic leads in developing sport: the Youth Sport Trust for Physical Education and School Sport; the Home Nation Sports Councils (e.g. Sport England) for community sport; and UK Sport for elite sport provision. This period also saw government recognise the important role that coaching had to play in facilitating efforts to increase participation and achieve the targets set for sport. Uppermost in the development of coaching in the UK at this time was the need to professionalise coaching and devise a coherent strategy for developing coaching activity. Consequently, the UK Coaching Framework was developed by sports coach UK to provide a system whereby sport participants could receive support from coaches to enhance the quality of their sporting experience, and coaches could be supported to develop their coaching skills and sustain their involvement in coaching.

2010 to the present: Conservative/ Liberal Democrat Coalition

The current government has stated a commitment to continue to focus on school sport, community sport and elite sport up to and beyond the 2012 Olympic Games. However, it has announced cuts to spending on sport, in line with other similar measures being taken across government, and has requested a merger of the lead sports agencies to provide a unified voice for sport. Perhaps the most significant change in policy direction is the prioritisation of competitive sport in schools rather than a focus on widening access and opportunity in sport. The 'School Games' initiative aims to provide competitive sport opportunities for young people across four levels of competition ranging from intra-school competition through to national sports events.

Remember

An understanding of the involvement of government in sport will help you to consider where and how future sport policy may be directed.

Roles and responsibilities of key agencies in sports development

Department of Culture, Media and Sport (DCMS)

DCMS is the government department that has responsibility for deciding upon policy and strategic direction for sport in the UK. Moreover, it decides how tax payers' money is spent on sport. However, this is not the only government department to have an involvement in the development of sport. The Department for Education is key to the development of school sport and provision for young people, and many other government departments (for example the Department of Health) have related links to sport, particularly as sport and physical activity is seen as possessing a 'cross-cutting agenda' (see p. 15).

Youth Sport Trust (YST)

YST is a charitable organisation that aims to support the education and development of all young people through physical education and sport. The core work of the YST involves:

- improving the PE experience for every young person
- using PE & sport to inspire learning and achievement
- enabling every young person to enjoy competition and providing support to the most talented

- developing a new generation of coaches working in schools
- connecting school and club sport
- supporting the development of young leaders and volunteers.

Home Country Sports Councils

These bodies are responsible for the development of community sport and assisting sports clubs, coaches, facility development and volunteers, among others. In addition, the Sports Councils act as a conduit between school sport and the elite level. Separate councils operate in England, Wales, Scotland and Northern Ireland and work towards strategic aims that reflect the individual culture of each country and address the specific issues that face them.

Stop and think

Research the aims, objectives and initiatives of two Home Country Sports Councils making comparisons between the two. How do these aims, objectives and initiatives reflect the specific sport and physical activity issues faced by the two countries you have identified?

UK Sport

This organisation has full responsibility for investment in and development of elite sport. Its core work aims to maximise the opportunity for predominantly Olympic and Paralympic athletes to win medals at major international competitions. Essentially, this involves investment in high-class coaching and sport science support, as well as effective talent identification and talent development systems.

The World Class Performance Programme is the vehicle for much of UK Sport's investment and focus. This programme supports three separate levels of elite competitors and operates to assist athletes in all Summer Olympic and Paralympic sports, as well as selected Winter Olympic sports. The three levels of performance are:

- **podium** – consisting of athletes with realistic medal winning capabilities at the next Olympic/Paralympic Games
- **development** – comprising athletes whose

performances have suggested that they are demonstrating the ability to be competitive by the next Olympiad

- **talent** – consisting of athletes who have been identified as having the potential to progress through the World Class pathway with the help of targeted investment.

As part of the World Class Performance Programme, UK Sport adopts a 'no compromise' approach, whereby the development of elite talent involves taking no short-cuts; investment is strategic and targeted to ensure that athletes are surrounded by the best possible resources for coaching and sport science services. Therefore, UK Sport has also implemented the UK Sport World Class Coaching Strategy to address and develop the needs of elite level coaches.

National governing bodies

These organisations are independent, self-appointed bodies that govern specific sports through the common consent of that sport. Examples of NGBs include: the Football Association; the England and Wales Cricket Board; UK Athletics; and the Lawn Tennis Association. They have responsibility for the development of their sport at all levels of participation.

sports coach UK

This organisation is the central **agency** for coaching in the UK and supports the recruitment, development and retention of sports coaches. It does so by:

- providing a central source of coaching expertise
- implementing cross-sport coaching initiatives
- sharing good practice between sports
- minimising inconsistencies in coaching across sports.

Key term

Agency – an organisation that is responsible for the promotion and administration of an activity, such as sport.

Central to the work of sports coach UK is the implementation of the UK Coaching Framework, a single, cohesive, ethical and valued coaching system that allows coaches to support the development of sports participants, regardless of their age, skill level or aspiration in sport. In addition, this framework hopes to support a clearer career structure for coaches, including the professionalisation of coaching as a vocation. As noted in Chapter 14, the implementation of the UK Coaching Certificate aims to assist this process by standardising coaching competencies across sports and ensuring that safe and equitable coaching practice is delivered.

Stop and think

Research some other agencies and organisations that are involved in sports development work in the UK and design a structure that charts the relationships between these sporting bodies and the ones highlighted above.

Practice of sports development work

Community sports development

This aspect of sports development work largely correlates with the focus of Home Country Sports Councils – increasing and sustaining participation in sport. Evidence suggests that good coaching is a fundamental aspect of prolonged sports participation and, therefore, coaches are increasingly being employed as vital resources to achieve community sports development aims. However, at a structural level, efforts to increase participation involve removing the barriers to participation that exclude various community groups from enjoying the benefits of sport. In practice, this occurs through two broad approaches: top-down and bottom-up.

Top-down approach

The top-down approach involves central organisations deciding on the design and implementation of sports development programmes and rolling them out across a designated geographic area. Consequently, these programmes are externally driven and require manipulation of the local community in order for them to be successful. Moreover, the participants who are targeted by such programmes have little say in their development or implementation, which suggests that a top-down approach imposes the aspects of the programme on a community. The benefits of this approach are that experienced or expert people are usually involved with the design and implementation of these programmes and that, because these ideas are driven from a central organisation, they usually are well funded and resourced.

Bottom-up approach

In contrast, the bottom-up approach is driven by the local community with the design and implementation of development programmes being initiated by local people who understand the specific needs of their community. Such an approach offers ownership of programmes to local people and may empower them to make the programme a success. However, despite these obvious benefits, this approach may lack professional co-ordination and may not link with the strategic direction of key agencies – making these programmes susceptible to lack of funding or resources.

Key terms

Top-down approach – externally-driven sports development programmes that are implemented by a centralised organisation who offer expertise and experience

Bottom-up approach – community-led sports development programmes that are better aligned to the specific needs of a local community

Irrespective of the approach taken, Coalter (2002) offers some recommendations for good practice in community sports development projects. These include the following.

- Partnerships and agreed aims – effective sports development programmes consist of partnerships between various, related organisations which share a vision and have mutual aims.
- Transparent aims and objectives – these partnerships need to communicate clearly and openly with each other to ensure that all partners involved in a programme understand and agree on the intentions of the programme.

- Staffing – all individuals who are involved in a programme need to fully understand the intentions and practical delivery of the programme.
- Identity and status – programmes should be professional and taken seriously to have impact. This may involve working in collaboration with recognised key agencies.
- Long-term commitment – the programme should have sustainability and a long-term focus rather than being concerned with quick fixes.
- Innovation – the programme design and delivery needs to be creative and distinctive to ensure that the experience of the programme is memorable and has impact.
- Empowerment and ownership – at some point within the life cycle of the programme, those who benefit most from the programme should be given ownership of it and decide how best to develop the initiative further.

While the aim of sports development is to increase participation and involvement in sport, good practice in sports development work suggests that programmes need sustainability to ensure that participation is lifelong. How can this be achieved?

Elite sports development

For many coaches, performance enhancement is at the heart of what they do. Often, coaching success is measured in terms of the number of athletes who move through the hierarchy of sports development towards the performance and elite levels.

In order to facilitate elite development, research clearly indicates some key characteristics of effective elite sports development systems. For example, Beamish and Ritchie (2006) identify four features of effective systems drawn from the success of the former Eastern bloc countries:

- systematic identification and selection of young people for particular sporting activities
- immersion of these identified people into high quality systematic programmes involving the best coaching, sport science support and facilities
- development of research that is relevant to the enhancement of human physical performance
- concentration of efforts into a restricted range of sports that usually offer multiple medal potential at major games.

Many elite sports development systems across the globe now integrate aspects of the former Eastern bloc approach. This has led Bloyce and Smith (2010) to observe three aspects that are common to elite sporting success:

- funding that is provided and prioritised for elite sports development
- an emphasis on systematic talent identification and talent development
- provision of facilities, professional coaching and sport science support.

The work of UK Sport provides the talent identification and development programmes as well as the support to elite athletes in terms of facilities and human resources. In addition, funding from the National Lottery is prioritised for the elite sport system, which suggests that the base-blocks of elite success can be found in this country. However, this funding is not endless and it is necessary for National Governing Bodies to ensure that the money spent on elite development is worthwhile and accountable. As such, four criteria have been set by which UK Sport will judge performance at elite level. These same criteria are also used to inform future funding decisions:

- medal potential – assessing the likelihood of medal success in future major competitions using indicators such as world rankings and success in junior competitions
- evidence of a performance system that will produce high numbers of talented athletes – National Governing Bodies are required to produce a pathway and programmes for athlete development and performance enhancement from grassroots to the elite
- track record – the level of success that a sport has produced in recent years using quantity of

medals at major competitions, among others, as an indicator

- significance of the sport – the public perception of a sport and its relative importance in comparison with other sports.

These criteria certainly benefit those sports that consistently perform to a high standard in major competitions, such as cycling and rowing. However, it also benefits those sports that have perhaps enjoyed moderate success in competition but have significant public support. For example, athletics is one of the most prestigious sports at the Olympic Games, and therefore will attract significant funding – despite the results of British athletes at recent major competitions not being as strong as in some other sports.

Stop and think

Consider the elite sport funding criteria and assess whether this offers a fair method of rewarding NGBs and athletes. What alternative criteria could you use to make judgements on the funding of elite sport?

Participation in sport

Accurately measuring the rate of participation in sport is difficult to determine, but surveys that indicate the proportion of the population who do participate in sport are useful in offering guidance as to where and how efforts to raise participation should be focused. Sport England initiated the Active People Survey (APS) in 2005, the broadest and most detailed study of participation rates undertaken in England. The survey measures the number of people aged 16 and over who participate in at least 30 minutes of moderate intensity sport at least three times per week. In reporting the results, the APS provides breakdowns on participation based upon demographic factors such as gender, age, ethnicity, disability, socio-economic background and geographic region (see Tables 2.1 to 2.3).

Stop and think

Consider the information presented in Tables 2.1 to 2.3 and comment on the figures, giving reasons to explain the levels of participation across different demographic groups.

Table 2.1 Participation in 3x30 minutes of sport per week based on age. (Active People Survey, Sport England, 2011)

Age group	October 2008	January 2011
16-34	26.7%	26.0%
35-54	15.9%	16.3%
55+	7.8%	7.3%

Table 2.2 Participation in 3x30 minutes of sport per week based on socio-economic group. (Active People Survey, Sport England, 2011)

Socio-economic group (based on occupation)	October 2008	January 2011
Managerial and professional	18.4%	18.8%
Intermediate	14.4%	13.8%
Small employer	14.3%	14.7%
Lower skilled and routine; unemployed	12.6%	12.2%

Table 2.3 Participation in 3x30 minutes of sport per week based on geographic region. (Active People Survey, Sport England, 2011)

Region	October 2008	January 2011
East	16.2%	15.9%
East Midlands	16.8%	14.9%
London	16.5%	16.3%
North East	16.3%	16.7%
North West	17.0%	17.4%
South East	17.1%	16.1%
South West	16.0%	16.4%
West Midlands	14.5%	15.1%
Yorkshire	17.2%	16.8%

Tables 2.1 to 2.3 provide a useful snapshot of participation rates in England, but a more valuable indicator is the data from the APS that charts any increase in participation levels (see Figure 2.4). Clearly, participation levels have remained fairly stagnant, which suggests that current initiatives aiming to raise participation in sport may not be having the desired impact. Moreover, such data may indicate that there remain a number of barriers to participation which need to be addressed through sports development programmes.

Figure 2.4 Active People Survey rate of participation in 3x30 minutes of sport per week 2005-2011. (Sport England, 2011)

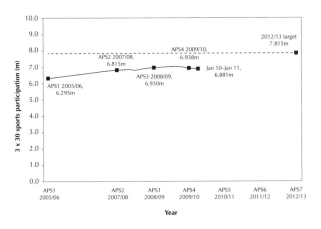

Participation in coaching

Recent research by sports coach UK (2009) indicates that over 1.1 million people are involved in the provision of sports coaching in the UK, with over 600,000 of these coaches holding a recognised governing body qualification. The same research found coaching to be largely voluntary (76%), with 21% of coaches receiving part-time payment for their coaching, and only 3% working full time in coaching. The study also identifies that the majority of coaches were male (69%), 8% of coaches had a disability and 3% were of an ethnic minority.

Barriers to participation

Chapter 6 addresses some of the key sociological aspects of sport and coaching. These aspects, such as gender, social class and ethnicity, can act as significant barriers to participation.

Gender

In many cultures, sports that are traditionally played by males take priority over those that involve predominantly female participation. Consequently, funding, media coverage and the standards for play tend to be focused around male participation, which can relay a message that only certain sports are appropriate for female participants. This message is not lost on a number of key agencies which have implemented many initiatives that are directly aimed at addressing the gender barrier.

Social class

As can be seen from Table 2.2, occupation or social class can have an important bearing on opportunities to access sport. Moreover, the sport choices that people from different social backgrounds have can be influenced by such factors as the cost of equipment and membership fees, or access to transport to travel to sport facilities. Much of the work undertaken by Home Country Sports Councils attempts to remove this barrier to participation by subsidising the cost of sport involvement or developing a wider network of facilities to make sport participation more accessible.

Ethnicity

In some sports there is a virtual absence of people of certain ethnicities, while other sports have an over-representation of a particular ethnicity. For those people who are considering entering sport, the proportion of ethnic participants who currently play that sport may influence which sports a new participant feels are accessible. For instance, there are very few Asian professional footballers in the UK, in comparison with Asian professional cricketers, which may influence sport choices for people in this ethnic group.

> ### Stop and think
>
> Conduct a search of sport organisation websites and identify a programme or initiative that is aimed to address gender, social class and ethnicity barriers to participation.

Other barriers

In addition to these major barriers to participation, other barriers may include the following.

- Changes to lifestyle. There are many time pressures in modern life that significantly impact on how people conduct their lives and the time they can spend on sport participation. For example, people often work longer hours, or on more days of the week, including at weekends when many sporting opportunities are scheduled. Also, in many families both parents work full time, which can impact on the opportunities that children have to participate in sport.

- Access to facilities. Despite an increase in the number of facilities that have been built for sport, there still remains a shortage of facilities to meet demand, particularly in rural areas of the country. Ironically, the increased urbanisation of many areas also has an impact with many sports fields being reclaimed for building development.

- Economic disadvantages. Evidence from the APS suggests that people from wealthier backgrounds have higher rates of participation in sport. For many sporting activities the user has to pay to participate, which means that opportunities to participate in sport can be reduced for those with less disposable income.

- Growth of other leisure options. Sport is very much in competition with the increased number of leisure forms that exist, in particular in the media and technology sectors. For example, people may choose to visit a gym or engage with virtual activities (such as the Wii) to keep fit, rather than playing sport. In addition, there are changes in the way people engage with leisure – choosing to participate in sport in a more casual and spontaneous manner, rather than through commitment to a club for an entire season, for example.

- Motivation. Many people are simply not motivated to engage in sport, or will require significant extrinsic rewards to get them to participate. Sometimes even those who start to be involved in sport may lack the intrinsic motivation to continue their participation.

Implications and opportunities for coaches

Many of the issues that have been discussed in this chapter relate more to increasing and sustaining participation in recreational sport than they do with improving the performance of participants. Therefore, coaches should be aware of the opportunities to contribute to the attainment of specific objectives in sports development work that go beyond merely improving the performance of

those who already participate and have the goal of high achievement in sport. Instead, coaches need to identify how their work could further increase participation and, more importantly, retain people in sport. Bolton and Smith (2008) propose that the role of the coach in the wider, sports development context could include the following.

- **Welcoming children and adults into sport.** For many people sport can be an intimidating environment as they may lack the skills to play effectively or they may not like competition. Coaches have an important role to play in making sport an inclusive environment.

- **Making sport fun.** Most participants play for intrinsic reasons like fun, rather than for extrinsic rewards; however, coaching is often seen as necessary only for those who want to win. Coaches need to consider how they can contribute to making sport fun.

- **Developing fundamental skills in participants.** Many sports share a range of fundamental sports skills, such as striking a ball with an implement. Improving an individual's fundamental skills may permit them to access a wider range of sporting opportunities.

- **Improving sport-specific skills to make participation more enjoyable.** A common reason for people dropping out of sport is that they lack the skills to participate effectively. Developing a participant's skills in a sport may allow them to get greater enjoyment from their sport involvement.

- **Developing fair play and respect.** Drop out from sport is likely if participants feel they are being cheated by other players. Coaches, as role models, have an important responsibility in ensuring fair play is upheld and that fellow participants demonstrate respect for each other.

- **Enhancing physical fitness and healthy lifestyles.** Coaches can reinforce the importance of sport participation in maintaining a healthy lifestyle. Coaching, in this sense, can become educational rather than about performance enhancement.

- **Keeping participants safe in sport.** To sustain participation in sport, participants need to feel safe and that their involvement in sport is not going to damage their health unnecessarily. By controlling the sporting environment, coaches can ensure that all participants engage in sport safely.

Stop and think

Which of these barriers do you believe has the biggest impact on sport participation? How could this barrier be addressed to increase participation opportunities?

Stop and think

You have been appointed as a sports development manager tasked with recruiting coaches to work on an initiative that aims to raise participation in sport among young people. What experience, qualification and personal attributes would you require from the coaches that you recruit?

Time to reflect

1. Consider your position on where sports development work should be aimed and relate this to the aims and objectives of your national Home Country Sports Council. How and where might you need to compromise your position in order to access funding?

2. Given your understanding of the key funding agencies for sports development, map your relationship with these agencies to identify the steps you could take to

   access funding for your coaching.

3. Research the participation rates in sport participation in your local region (see Table 2.3) and specify potential reasons for this participation rate in comparison to other regions.

4. Consider your coaching environment and identify the specific barriers that impact on participation in your coaching context.

Case study (for recommended answers, see www.pearsonfe.co.uk/foundationsinsport)

Rhianna is the coaching and development manager of a tennis club on the outskirts of a large city. The club has recently upgraded its facilities, which now consist of six hard courts, that are floodlit, and a clubhouse. Current use of these facilities tends to peak on Saturday and Sunday afternoons throughout the year and Friday evening use is popular with adult members during the summer months. In order to raise club membership, the tennis club committee have tasked Rhianna with identifying ways to increase the number of young players (under 16) participating at the club. A significant issue for Rhianna is that a new leisure centre offering a variety of sporting activities has recently opened in the city centre.

Questions

1. What activities should Rhianna adopt to recruit new players?

2. Which key agencies should Rhianna approach to support her programme?

3. What type and number of resources will Rhianna need to support the programme? (Think about facilities, equipment, coaches, transport, etc.)

4. What aspects of good practice should Rhianna implement?

5. What should the coaching programme entail to ensure that the newly recruited members sustain their participation in tennis?

Check your understanding (for answers, see www.pearsonfe.co.uk/foundationsinsport)

1. Define the terms 'development of sport' and 'development through sport'.

2. Summarise the influence of government on sport during the following eras:
   i   Pre-1960
   ii 1960–1990
   iii 1990–1997
   iv 1997–2010

3. Name three key agencies involved in the provision of sport in the UK and briefly outline their remit.

4. Clarify the differences between 'top-down' and 'bottom-up' approaches to sports development.

5. List the seven recommendations for good practice in community sports development projects.

6. Identify three barriers to participation in sport outlining the impact these have on sports development work.

Useful resources

To obtain a secure link to the websites below, see the Websites section on page ii or visit the companion website at www.pearsonfe.co.uk/foundationsinsport.

- International Journal of Sport Policy
- Department of Culture, Media and Sport
- Sport England
- Sport England – Recognised Sports
- Sport Scotland
- Sport Wales
- Sport Northern Ireland
- Youth Sport Trust
- UK Sport
- SportsCoach UK
- Sport and Recreation Alliance
- Sport England list of Regional Sports
- Wolfenden Report

Further reading

Beamish, R. & Ritchie, I. (2006). *Fastest, highest, strongest: a critique of high-performance sport.* London: Routledge.

Bolton, N. & Smith, B. (2008). Sports development for coaches. In R.L. Jones, M. Hughes & K. Kingston, *An introduction to sports coaching: from science and theory to practice.* London: Routledge, pp. 73–84.

Bloyce, D. & Smith, A. (2010). *Sport policy and development: an introduction.* London: Routledge.

Coalter, F. (2002). *Sport and community development: a manual.* Edinburgh: Sportscotland.

Department of Culture, Media and Sport and Strategy Unit, Cabinet Office (2002). *Game Plan: a strategy for delivering Government's sport and physical activity objectives.* London: HMSO

Department of Culture, Media and Sport (2008). *Playing to win: a new era for sport.* London: DCMS.

Department of National Heritage (1995) *Sport: Raising the Game.* London: Department of National Heritage

Hylton, K., & Bramham, P. eds. (2008). *Sports development: Policy, process and practice.* London: Routledge.

Sport England (2011). *Active People Survey.* London: Sport England.

sports coach UK (2009). *The coaching workforce 2009-2016.* Leeds: The National Coaching Foundation.

Wolfenden Report (1960) [online] See 'Useful resources' for source.

Chapter 3

Coaching knowledge and learning to coach

Introduction

In the profession of sports coaching there is a strong link between knowledge and competence. It is assumed that the more knowledgeable the coach, the more effective they will be at meeting the participants' needs. The process of becoming an effective coach evolves over time. Typically, you will acquire your knowledge on sports specific coach education programmes offered by the National Governing Bodies (NGBs) of sport or on context-free programmes run by organisations such as sports coach UK or 1st4sport. Additionally, knowledge is acquired through sports-related 14–19 qualifications, foundation and honours level degree studies, higher degrees and a range of teacher training qualifications (for example the Post Graduate Certificate in Education). However, sports coaching is a complex, relational activity. A coach must establish and maintain facilitative relationships within a positive coaching environment that is conducive to meeting the participants' goals for taking part in physical activity. Whatever the proficiency level of the participants with whom a coach is working, the journey of a coach towards expert practitioner necessitates supplementary learning. This chapter covers the wide ranging, multidisciplinary knowledge base that underpins the practice of sports coaching and explains the mechanisms through which you, as a coach, can acquire this essential knowledge.

Learning outcomes

After you have read this chapter you should be able to:

- understand the evolution of a coach from novice to expert practitioner
- understand what is sports coaching knowledge
- appreciate the areas of sports science knowledge impacting on coaching
- articulate the domains of knowledge important in sports coaching
- understand that sports coaching knowledge is constructed
- explain the formal, non-formal and informal contexts in which sports coaches construct knowledge.

Evolution of a coach

Not all coaches are motivated to complete the journey to becoming an expert practitioner or, because of their volunteering capacity, may feel no need to contemplate progression in their coaching practice. About 80% of the 1.2 million people involved in the practice of sports coaching are volunteers (Skills Active, 2011), but being a volunteer should not stereotype or restrict you progressing your coaching proficiency. Similarly, if you are lucky enough to be paid for coaching, this does not necessarily mean that you will be striving to become an expert practitioner. For most coaches, coaching is a vocation and not a career option, and so the development towards becoming an expert practitioner is unlikely to be a priority, not planned, can take a long time and will require direction and support from a range of individuals and organisations. **Career coaches** are paid on a full-time basis for their services. For these professionals, the completion of the journey to expert practitioner is essential for ensuring credibility with participants and employability in the coaching market place.

Stages of development

There are four progressive stages aligned with the development of coaching expertise.

1. Novice
2. Competent
3. Proficient
4. Expert

At the first stage, a novice (new) coach is not a blank canvas. They bring with them a range of sporting and life experiences that will influence their coaching practice. The emphasis on developing a *novice* coach is to focus on **participant management**, planning and organisation and immersion in real-life coaching situations.

A *competent* coach is comfortable with managing participants in the coaching environment and focuses on developing interpersonal relationships with their participants. The organisational and planning aspects of coaching a session are second nature. A competent coach focuses on the outcomes of their coaching sessions and is comfortable in adapting a coaching plan if things go wrong.

Proficient coaches anticipate problems and issues before they arise. They appreciate the contextual nature of the coaching environment and the individual needs of their participants and are able to adapt to situations as required.

Expert coaches are critical, **self-reflexive** practitioners. They have developed, over a long period of time, an extensive, multidisciplinary knowledge base and range of experiences that allow them to intuitively select and apply the appropriate action at the right time for each of their participants. Expert coaches continually look to increase their extensive knowledge base and have a voracious appetite for learning.

Experience

Emphasising the time commitment for developing into an expert coach, Ericsson et al. (1993) argue that it takes at least 10,000 hours of deliberate practice to develop the level of professional expertise that is associated with being an expert coach. This time commitment is reinforced by Côté (2006), who suggests that expert coaches should demonstrate a career winning record over a minimum of five years and possess a minimum threshold of athletic 'pre-coaching' experiences of around 3,000 hours. Gilbert et al. (2006) propose that expert coaches have accumulated at least 13 years of athletic experience in a range of sports and consider themselves to be better than average athletes in relation to their peers.

This 'pre-coaching' experience as a participant highlights that the journey towards developing into an expert coaching practitioner is initiated through participation in a range of sports from a young age. The journey does not have to begin from a standing start at the termination of an athletic career, and the experiences gained through participation can be drawn upon in some way to 'fast track' the transition from novice to expert practitioner.

The subconscious journey towards becoming a coach can start through participation in sport from a young age. Can you think of experiences you have had in sport that would help you become a coach?

The four stages indicate that a coach needs to invest time, effort and money in their development towards expert practitioner and that the development of coaching expertise cannot be left to accident or chance. Underpinning each stage of the development process is the need for coaches to acquire the required knowledge and skills associated with each of these stages.

Stop and think

Think about sportsmen and sportswomen who have made the transition from player to coach (for example, Martin Johnson, Roy Keane, Miles Maclagan, Hope Powell and Jess Garland). Discuss with a partner the advantages and disadvantages that could be associated with accessing coaching with or without a proven track record as an athlete.

What is sports coaching knowledge?

The Oxford Dictionary (2011) defines knowledge as 'facts, information, and skills acquired through experience or education; the theoretical or practical understanding of a subject', or put simply, 'the sum of what is known'.

There is some debate in sports coaching literature about whether the profession of sports coaching is a **science** or an art. Perceiving coaching as science suggests that coaches' **knowledge** can be systematically applied in a logical manner in order to bring about incremental performance improvements. Thinking of coaching as an art results in performance improvement by a more intangible application of the knowledge. The difference between these two positions is the way in which the knowledge that a coach possesses is applied in a coaching context.

The idea that sports coaching is divided into two parts (or subsets) that are jointly exhaustive (all aspects of coaching must be categorised as science or art) and mutually exclusive (coaching must be a science or an art) is problematic. Woodman (1993) highlights that coaching sport is neither one nor the other; in other words, presenting the practice of sports coaching as a **dichotomy** made up of science and art is not appropriate. Woodman (1993) suggests that the practice of sports coaching is a blending of the science and art traditions (see Figure 3.1). In order to be fully effective a coach must learn the science that directly relates to their participants and their performances.

Key terms

Science – knowledge gained from the systematic study of the physical world, especially through observation and experimentation, and the development of theories to describe the results

Knowledge – the sum of what is known

Dichotomy – the division of sports coaching into two non-overlapping theoretical traditions (science and art). Debate has existed about sports coaching comprising these two subsets that are mutually exclusive of one another

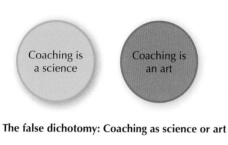

The false dichotomy: Coaching as science or art

Figure 3.1 The false dichotomy of science and art in sports coaching literature and their true relationship.

Areas of sports science knowledge impacting on coaching

Sub-disciplines

The academic **discipline** of **sports science** comprises many **sub-disciplines**. Many of these sub-disciplines of sports science have a direct impact on the practice of sports coaching. They include the following:

- anatomy
- physiology
- biomechanics
- growth and development
- statistics
- tests and measurements
- motor learning and skill acquisition

Remember

In the UK, the term Sport(s) Science(s) is used as an umbrella term for academic programmes that focus on the application of scientific principles and techniques with the aim of improving sporting performance. In the United States, the term Kinesiology is used and in Australia, Human Movement Studies.

- psychology
- sports medicine
- nutrition and hydration
- sociology
- pedagogy.

Key terms

Discipline – a branch of learning or scholarly activity that is taught and researched at university level

Sport(s) science(s) – umbrella term for academic programmes that focus on the application of scientific principles and techniques with the aim of improving sporting performance

Sub-discipline – a field of specialised study within the discipline of sports sciences

Even within the same sport, different coaching situations require a sports coach to draw upon different sub-discipline areas of sports science knowledge. For example, an athletics coach working with a group of adolescent high jump athletes will need to draw extensively on the sub-discipline areas of growth and development, motor learning and biomechanics; whereas an athletics coach working with elite female distance runners would need to be proficient in the science areas of physiology, tests and measurements and nutrition.

Stop and think

Working in pairs and using this list of sub-disciplines as a guide, rank in order of importance the top five sub-discipline areas of scientific knowledge that impact on the following different coaching situations:

- a badminton coach working with a junior player to develop their explosive power
- a fitness instructor working with a group of participants who want to lose weight
- a swimming coach working with an athlete who has repetitive shoulder injuries
- a lifestyle adviser working with a group of elderly participants to introduce a walking programme
- a football coach working with a team that consistently concedes goals in the last ten minutes of a match.

Although primarily working within a specific sport, other factors, such as the age and gender of participants and the focus of the coaching session, will require the sports coach to draw upon different sub-discipline areas of sports science knowledge. The body of knowledge from which sports coaches select information must be comprehensive in order to ensure that the appropriate knowledge can be drawn upon in a given **context**. The sub-disciplinary areas of scientific knowledge required by practising sports coaches are fluid and constantly evolving in order to meet the demands of each coaching situation that is presented.

The sub-disciplinary areas of scientific knowledge are not the only knowledge needed by sports coaches (if it were, then all graduates from sports sciences programmes would be equipped with the knowledge base for becoming an expert practitioner). In addition to sub-disciplinary knowledge, there are other knowledge '**domains**'.

Key terms

Context – the situation within which something exists

Contextual – relating to, dependent on, or using context

Domains – the term given to an area of knowledge

Remember

Coaching sport is highly **contextual**. The sub-discipline areas of scientific knowledge that you as a coach need to draw upon will be influenced by a range of external factors (such as the age, gender and expertise of participants). Therefore you must be knowledgeable in a wide range of scientific areas in order to be fully effective in different contexts.

Knowledge domains in sports coaching

A coach's knowledge must incorporate information about what is being coached (sports specific knowledge) and how to coach (**generic coaching knowledge**). This generic coaching knowledge incorporates coaching strategies, knowledge about learners and learning environments, planning,

organising, managing groups and communication. This domain of knowledge is referred to as **pedagogical** knowledge (see Chapter 5 for a detailed examination of coaching pedagogy). Pedagogical knowledge is non-sports specific (as is sub-disciplinary science knowledge), meaning that this knowledge is transferable between different sporting contexts.

As sports coaching is a relational activity, another important non-sports specific coaching domain is that of inter/intra personal knowledge. This domain is concerned with establishing and maintaining **facilitative** coach–participant relationships, self-awareness, personal coaching philosophies, ethical codes, personal learning and self-reflection.

The final non-sports specific domain is contextual knowledge and includes knowledge relating to the micro and macro factors that influence the coaching context.

Sports specific knowledge

Sports specific knowledge, sometimes referred to as content knowledge, is the technical, tactical and strategic understanding of a specific sport. Sports specific knowledge for coaches can be divided into two domains of knowledge (Shulman, 1986).

- Subject-matter content knowledge (SMCK): the knowledge that a coach has of the activity being coached. Coaches should possess the knowledge to cover the range of activities encompassed in a coaching session (for example, skills, tactics, strategies, rules and regulations).

- 'Curriculum' content knowledge (CCK): viewing 'curriculum' to mean a set of materials. Coaches must possess the knowledge of resources available to them to ensure currency in their delivery.

Key terms

Generic coaching knowledge – principles that can be applied to any learning context

Pedagogical – strategies for teaching and learning

Facilitative – a relationship that allows for actions and processes to make things easy or easier

---

Progression

One final aspect influencing the domains of coaching knowledge is the progression or development of the form of knowledge from a basic level to a more complex understanding. You would expect a novice coach to have rudimentary grounding in all of the domains of coaching knowledge; then as coaches move through the competent and proficient stages towards expert practitioner, you would expect their knowledge to become more refined and sophisticated.

Categories of knowledge

The domains of coaching knowledge can be divided into three categories or forms of knowledge (Metzler, 2000).

- Declarative knowledge (DK): knowledge which a coach can express verbally and/or in a written form. Also referred to as 'knowledge about'.

- Procedural knowledge (PK): knowledge which a coach can apply before, during and after the coaching session. Also referred to as 'knowledge how to'.

- Conditional knowledge (CK): knowledge which informs a coach about when and why to do something at a particular moment or in a specific context. Also referred to as 'propositional knowledge' or 'what will happen if'.

In a coaching context, declarative knowledge (knowledge about something) is a prerequisite for procedural knowledge (knowledge of how to do something), which in turn is a prerequisite for conditional knowledge (what will happen if?). So, when you talk about an expert coach being knowledgeable, you are talking about the coach possessing a comprehensive range of domains of conditional knowledge. This is why expert practitioners intuitively or automatically use processes and procedures in their sessions and exhibit what is commonly referred to as 'professional know-how'.

Figure 3.2 summarises the knowledge domains in sports coaching, presenting the sports specific domains, non-sports specific domains, the knowledge form and the link between the form of knowledge and level of coaching expertise. The central part of the diagram where all domains intersect represents the sports coaching knowledge (SCK) required by practising sports coaches.

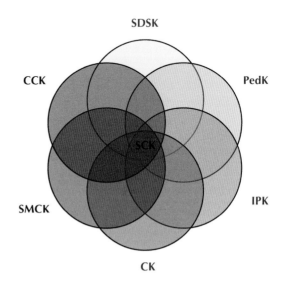

Key to acronyms

Non-sports specific:

SDSK: Sub-discipline sports science knowledge

PedK: Pedagogical knowledge

IPK: Inter/intra personal knowledge

CK: Contextual knowledge

Sports specific:

SMCK: Subject-matter content knowledge

CCK: 'Curriculum' content knowledge

Figure 3.2 Sports coaching knowledge (SCK) domains

Figure 3.3 represents how the form that the sports coaching knowledge takes will change with the level of expertise of the coach.

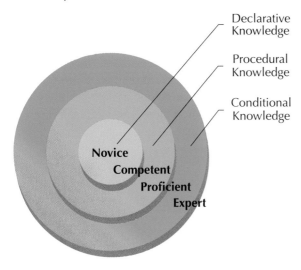

Figure 3.3 The different forms of sports coaching knowledge in relation to level of coaching expertise.

Constructing sports coaching knowledge

The domains of knowledge form the mass of knowledge from which a coach selects and applies the appropriate information in a given context. What is unclear, as you set out on your journey to 'becoming a coach', is just how you acquire, or **construct** this knowledge.

Key terms

Construct – it is thought that you cannot simply receive knowledge from a book or a teacher; in fact we take little bits from a wide variety of sources and create knowledge that is individual to us

Compartmentalise – divide into separate and distinct sections or categories

Stop and think

Think about your own classroom environment for a moment; how does your tutor or lecturer transfer knowledge on to you? Discuss the effectiveness of each method with a partner.

Constructing coaching knowledge is portrayed as straightforward as it is assumed – incorrectly – that knowledge can simply be passed from one person to another. This is typically seen in teaching and coaching environments.

Different people prefer to receive information in different ways. However, receiving information does not constitute learning and it is difficult to tell if you have constructed knowledge in this way. This is also true in coaching as the coaches and participants learn in different ways, depending on a range of factors (see Chapter 5 (Coaching pedagogy) for a full examination of maximising 'learning' in the coaching environment).

Coach education programmes

Coach education programmes (for example, National Governing Bodies, sports coach UK, and 1st4sport) are built on the idea that you can acquire sufficient knowledge to be an effective coach from a series of courses or workshops. These programmes have tended to **compartmentalise** a coach's knowledge into units drawn from a multidisciplinary base (for example physiology, biomechanics, nutrition, ethics, health and safety). This approach to the construction of coaching knowledge has led to the coach education structure in the UK being rather fragmented, making it difficult for coaches to effectively plan their journey. When knowledge is constructed in this manner, a coach needs help to put all of these areas together and make meaning of them in a coaching context as they have been taught in isolation from each other.

Jones (2000) suggests that this compartmentalised approach de-skills a coach. It assumes that knowledge is something that is sequential and given; whilst perhaps a coach actively constructs their knowledge on an individual basis. If you accept that coaching is relational, then you must examine the issues surrounding the construction of knowledge in coaching and the role of coach education in facilitating this.

A number of sporting bodies have recognised coach education as important. For example, sports coach UK, the leading body for coach education and coach development in the UK.

Knowledge is constructed by a coach on an individual basis. The different domains of knowledge cannot be simply passed on from one person to another. You need to make sense of knowledge and how it relates to you and your own coaching context. This making sense of knowledge emphasises the need for coaches to be **self-reflexive** practitioners.

Key term

Self-reflexive – the act of using individual experiences to guide future practice

Similarly, recent developments in terms of National Occupational Standards (NOS) for coaches working within the high performance environment and the development of a United Kingdom Coaching Certificate (UKCC), which intends to provide an agreed coach education framework for sport specific qualifications, should contribute positively to the development of the profession of coaching. So various bodies *are* trying to address some of the issues that are emerging in terms of how coaches and their learning should be developed.

Observations and experiences

However, because coaching is both an individual and a social process, and is based on our interactions (with participants and other coaches) and experiences, then it is not possible to address all the issues of constructing knowledge for coaching by improving coach education courses. In fact, observation and experience are a significant and often overlooked element in a coach's development. This is problematic for developing coach education programmes, given that not every coach's experience is the same.

Observations and experiences help a coach reflect on their work and the work of others in order to test their views on coaching (self-reflexivity). There is a clear understanding gained from interactions with other coaches in terms of what might be right or wrong in terms of coaching.

Receiving coaching as a performer and experiencing coaching as an assistant or co-coach are two distinct parts or phases of the **experiential learning** of a coach. Cushion et al. (2003) argue that when novice coaches are exposed to observing the behaviour of more experienced coaches during practices and games, there is an informal learning process that takes place. These interactions may reconfirm experiences gained as a player, therefore these **formative experiences** are essential to the development of coaches.

Key terms

Experiential learning – learning from direct experience

Formative experiences – help you to develop or make sense of the things you see and experience. These formative experiences, such as playing sport or being an assistant coach, provide you with various contexts in which you can construct knowledge

Contexts of knowledge construction

Nelson et al. (2006) provide a useful framework with which to consider the different contexts in which coaches can learn the appropriate domains of coaching knowledge. This framework provides three broad contexts that are useful for coaches to learn: formal, non-formal and informal learning.

Formal learning

Formal learning takes place in an institutionalised and structured educational system. The learning is designed around a core curriculum with certification on demonstration of the compulsory knowledge. Werthner and Trudel (2006) refer to this as **mediated learning**. Coach education is based around the UK Coaching Certificate (UKCC) and is focused on formal learning environments. Other formal learning environments would be academic and vocational courses (for example degrees, foundation degrees, BTECs and NVQs).

Typically, this learning is decontextualised and 'classroom' based and reduces the complexity of the role of a coach. Formal learning situations rarely deal with pedagogical and socio-cultural factors; something that Jones et al. (2004) clearly identify as integral to the construction of coaches' knowledge.

Additional difficulties with coach education programmes lie in the consistency of delivery and with issues surrounding intra-sport and inter-sport consistency. Also, each coach on any given course will bring with them unique experiences, values, behaviours and competencies that will influence their learning. Nelson et al. (2006) warn against coach educators prescribing a right way to coaching. The emphasis should be on the ability to adapt to the diversity inherent in the coaching process and highlighting the possible outcomes of a variety of different approaches.

Formal learning programmes are hierarchical and linear courses. That is to say you do a first year (or module) and then you are assessed, and you progress onto the subsequent years (additional modules) in this manner. The implication is that you are more skilled or knowledgeable in the final year (final modules) than you are in the first year. You are then certified as having met the curriculum requirements. This does not take into account individual **subjectivities** or the capacity of the learners to contextualise their knowledge and apply it appropriately beyond the classroom in real world coaching situations. Therefore, it is necessary to identify other learning opportunities for coaches to acquire the necessary domains of coaching knowledge.

Key terms

Mediated learning – learning directed by knowledgeable other

Subjectivities – individual differences (for example learning preferences, personality, experiences, values, morals, coaching philosophy)

Non-formal learning

Non-formal learning involves activities that take place outside the formal (coach) education system.

Such activities tend to be conferences, workshops and seminars that have a specific focus and which attract a particular group of coaches to attend. For example, high performance coaches, coaches working with participants with a disability, coaches who work with children or coaches wanting to develop nutritional or training strategies.

While similar to the formal structure, there is rarely an obligation to 'pass' or 'graduate' from these learning opportunities so the impact of this non-formal learning activity is difficult to gauge. These non-formal learning situations provide useful opportunities to contribute to learning, but they tend to be ad-hoc. As with formal learning situations, these learning situations still do not provide coaches with the context-based learning that is critical in constructing coaching knowledge.

Stop and think

In groups of four, discuss the formal and non-formal learning experiences or situations you have experienced. Once you have done this, create a list of formal and non-formal learning activities that you might pursue to help you develop as a coach.

Informal learning

Informal learning is the ongoing or lifelong process that is experienced by everyone – including coaches. Through interaction in the environment this process helps you to construct knowledge and develop skills, behaviours and attitudes that inform your coaching practice. This unmediated area is arguably the most important in the contribution to the development of an expert coach. You only need to consider the explanation of expert performance (Ericsson, 1993) to understand that the process of becoming expert requires considerable experience of being a practitioner. This is not to say that there is no engagement with academic, or other, texts (journals, books on coaching etc.) but that this is an exploration of an area, through a self-directed process. It is through this self-directed learning that Schon (1987) offers useful terminology when providing a framework for reflection. The practitioner does not learn simply by experiencing, but through reflecting (*in, on* and *anticipatory*) on experiences.

Reflection

By reflection during an experience, session, or game (*in*), reflecting after such episodes (*on*), or by using past experiences to predict an occurrence (*anticipatory*), you can facilitate deeper learning and development of coaching knowledge. Through developing **communities of practice** there is an opportunity to learn informally and so you might feel that mentoring, or working in and around a group of other coaches, is important for coach development.

> ### Key term
>
> **Communities of practice** – a group of people who share a common interest or profession. The group can evolve naturally over time or can be established specifically with the goal of developing knowledge or sharing good practice

Informal experiences

Given the development of a UK Coaching model, identified in the paper 'UK Action Plan for Coaching' (sports coach UK, 2006), there exists a model for coach education that allows both the formal and non-formal elements of coach learning, but also the informal element that is specific and unique to the practitioner. Informal experiences could be explored through the following:

- previous playing experience
- being coached by others
- being an assistant or volunteer coach
- being mentored by a senior coach
- observing other coaches
- reflection on coaching
- talking with others about coaching
- being a part of a community of coaching practice.

These different informal experiences allow you to reflect on what coaching is, refine your coaching philosophy and highlight the different domains of coaching knowledge that you need to build up. These informal experiences are essential in combination with the formal and non-formal learning experiences in developing the knowledge and skills of an expert coach.

If the coaching environment is a place where coaches' professional learning and development takes place, then this must be considered in coach education programmes. The knowledge gained through practice is as important as the knowledge gained through more formal routes of education. Therefore, coach education should not be based just on one form of learning. A coach's journey from novice to expert practitioner should incorporate ideas from formal, non-formal and informal learning.

Case study (for recommended answers, see www.pearsonfe.co.uk/foundationsinsport)

Tanya retired from a highly successful professional tennis career that lasted for 15 years. As well as playing in a number of tournaments in the United Kingdom and around the world, she also represented Great Britain in the Fed Cup and also at the Olympics. Tanya was a very talented athlete who trained hard, worked under a number of elite coaches and liaised with medical and sports science support staff in order to make the best of her abilities. Her playing career included playing singles, doubles and mixed doubles.

Tanya is passionate about going into coaching as she has loved her time involved in tennis but she would like to stay involved with international, elite level players. Her ambition is to work with the very top British players. Tanya has no coaching experience or National Governing Body coaching awards. Tanya does possess a sports science degree from her time at university.

Questions:

1. Does Tanya have the right skills to be a coach?

2. Identify some of the ways in which Tanya has already constructed knowledge that might help her develop as a coach.

3. Map out formal, non-formal and informal learning situations that Tanya will need to experience in order to develop all of the six knowledge domains comprising a sports coach's knowledge.

4. Do you think that all coaches should be ex-international players?

5. Is it possible to construct the knowledge domains you need to be an effective coach if you have not played a particular sport at the highest level? If so, how?

6. Do you think that Tanya will be able to construct the knowledge and acquire the skills to coach elite, male tennis players?

Tanya's ambition is to coach the very best British players. Do you think that constructing all six knowledge domains will be the only issue she has in fulfilling her dream?

Time to reflect

1. How can you use your sporting experiences to help you develop as a coach?

2. Identify sub-discipline areas of scientific knowledge that you would like to improve and investigate ways in which you can enhance your knowledge in these areas.

3. Drawing on the different methods of transferring knowledge that you have experienced, work out ways of implementing the most effective strategies in your coaching sessions.

4. Create a list of formal and non-formal learning activities that you might pursue to help you develop as a coach.

Check your understanding (for answers, see www.pearsonfe.co.uk/foundationsinsport)

1. What are the four progressive stages aligned with the development of coaching expertise?

2. Give a definition of knowledge.

3. List five sub-disciplines of sports science that have a direct impact on the practice of sports coaching

4. What are the six domains of sports coaching knowledge?

5. What do the letters DK, PK and CK stand for?

6. What is the difference between DK, PK, and CK?

7. What is meant by the use of the word 'construct' in relation to acquiring coaching knowledge?

8. What are the three contexts in which a coach constructs the domains of coaching knowledge?

9. What are the three ways that a coach can reflect on their experiences?

Useful resources

To obtain a secure link to the websites below, see the Websites section on page ii or visit the companion website at www.pearsonfe.co.uk/foundationsinsport.

- Coachwise
- Oxford Dictionary
- Skills Active
- sports coach UK
- Sport England
- Sports Leaders UK
- The British Olympic Association

Further reading

Armour, K. (ed.). (2011). *Sport pedagogy: an introduction for teaching and coaching.* London: Prentice Hall.

Côté, J. (2006). The development of coaching knowledge. *International Journal of Sports Science and Coaching,* 1 (3), 217-222.

Cushion, C., Armour, K.M., & Jones, R.L. (2003). Coach education and continuing professional development: Experience and learning to coach. *Quest,* 55, 215-230.

Ericsson, K.A., Krampe, R.T. and Tesch-Romer, C. (1993). The role of deliberate practice in the acquisition of expert performance. *Psychological Review,* 100, 363-406.

Gilbert, W., Côté, J. & Mallett, C. (2006). Developmental paths and activities of successful sport coaches. *International Journal of Sports Science and* Coaching, 1 (1), 69-76.

Jones, R.L. (2000). Toward a sociology of coaching. In R. Jones & K. Armour (Eds.), *Sociology of sport: Theory and practice* (pp. 33-43). London: Longman.

Jones, R.L., Armour, K.M. and Potrac, P. (2004). *Sports coaching cultures: from practice to theory.* London: Routledge.

Lyle, J. (2002). *Sports coaching concepts: a framework for coaches' behaviour.* London: Routledge.

Metzler, M. (2000). Instructional models for physical education. Needham Heights, MA: Allyn & Bacon.

Nelson, L.J., Cushion, C.J. and Potrac, P. (2006) Formal, nonformal and informal coach learning: A holistic conceptualisation. *International Journal of Sports Science & Coaching* 1(3), 247 – 259.

Oxford Dictionary. (2011). Knowledge [online]. See 'Useful resources' for source.

Schön, D. A. (1987). *Educating the reflective practitioner.* San Francisco: Jossey-Bass.

Shulman, L. (1986). Those who understand: knowledge and growth in teaching. *Educational Researcher,* 15 (2), 4-14.

Skills Active. (2011). Sport and recreation [online]. See 'Useful resources' for source. [Accessed 23 March 2011].

sports coach UK (2002). National standards for higher-level coaches. *Project Information Bulletin,* 1, April.

sports coach UK (2006) *UK Action Plan for Coaching.* sports coach UK, Leeds.

Werthner, P. and Trudel, P. (2006). A new theoretical perspective for understanding how coaches learn to coach. *The Sport Psychologist,* 20, 196-210.

Woodman, L. (1993). Coaching: a science, an art, an emerging profession, Sport Science Review, 2 (2), 1-13.

Chapter 4

The coaching process

Introduction

The coaching process encompasses all stages a coach goes through to bring about improvements in a player, athlete or team (Borrie and Knowles, 2003). Coaching is not restricted to delivering a coaching session or a series of sessions. An effective coach has to understand and deal with a wide range of variables beyond the coaching session (Cross and Lyle, 1999). In this chapter we consider the key stages of the coaching process – *plan*, *deliver* and *evaluate* – and the variables that can affect these stages. The roles, responsibilities and skills of a sports coach will also be examined. It is essential to understand these in order to continually improve and manage the coaching process.

Learning outcomes

After you have read this chapter you should be able to:

- define the coaching process
- understand how to plan, deliver and evaluate a coaching session
- understand the roles, responsibilities and skills of a sports coach
- understand coaching styles
- understand a coaching philosophy
- understand coaching techniques and key issues that affect the coaching process, including linear and non-linear approaches to coaching
- understand the importance of evaluation and assessment.

Defining the coaching process

Coaching is a cyclical process: **plan**, **deliver** and **evaluate**.

Figure 4.1 The coaching process

All coaches, no matter how experienced they are, should follow these basic principles so that they are constantly evaluating their own coaching in order to improve their planning and delivery of coaching sessions. Throughout this chapter we will look at each of these stages in turn.

Plan coaching

The first stage of the coaching process is to plan. Planning for any session or season must be carried out in advance so that you are prepared for every eventuality. You could ask a number of questions to assist in your planning.

- Who is being coached? (Team/individual?)
- What is being coached? (Technique, skill, progressions?)

- What are the aims and objectives for the session/season?
- What are the details of the participants? (Age, gender, ability?)
- What are the participants' motivations and expectations?
- How many sessions will there be?
- What resources (kit and equipment) will you need?
- What facilities and equipment do you have access to?
- Have you considered health and safety issues? (Medical kit, nearest first-aider?)
- Do you have a clear understanding of the rights, relationships and responsibilities of coaching?
- What are your own goals for the session/season?

You should always allow for some flexibility and include a contingency plan to allow you to deal with things that could go wrong, or that are unforeseen.

Aims and objectives

Before starting a coaching session, it is important to identify *what* you are setting out to achieve – the **aims** – and *how* you are hoping to achieve each one – the **objectives**. These should be written down once agreed so that you can later evaluate whether or not you are meeting these aims and objectives in your coaching session.

After setting the aims and objectives for each session or season, you should agree targets for each of the participants around their individual strengths and areas for improvement. Any targets you set could use the SMART model (Cox, 2007; Crisfield et al., 2003), as follows.

Specific – set detailed and precise targets for your athlete.

Measurable – be clear about how you will measure the success of the individual in meeting their target e.g. time/height/weight and when this will be met.

Achievable or **A**ction Oriented – be sure that the target is relevant for the athlete and can be achieved, and is actionable through changed behaviour.

Realistic – the target should be challenging but appropriate.

Time bound – include milestones for achievement and agree an overall timescale.

Often goals will take longer to achieve, or may be achieved quicker than planned, and part of the coaching process is the constant review and adaptation of these targets. Having clearly defined goals and planning effectively will allow a coach to keep an athlete motivated and have a clear picture about how they are going to develop. This makes the athlete more likely to engage in the coaching process, which allows the coach in turn to be more effective.

Planning the session

Once you have agreed aims and objectives with athletes and other coaches, you should be ready to devise your coaching session. All sessions should be planned carefully. You should produce an outline of the activities that will be followed, and adopt a structure for these – typically *warm up*, *main body* and *cool down* – as well as accounting for other considerations, as outlined in the table below.

> **Key term**
>
> **Key factors** – coaching points that are drawn from your sports specific knowledge that will make up the key points of your coaching session. For example, if your session was designed for defending in football you might want to plan your sessions to allow you to coach some of these key factors

Table 4.1 Components of a coaching session plan

Participants	Your participants are the key to your session. Have you considered their aims and objectives, the number of participants and any differences in age, ability, gender, special needs? These factors may determine the type of activities, and also the coaching styles and methods you adopt. A competent coach will ensure that equal opportunities are given to all participants regardless of age, ability, race, ethnicity, sexuality, religion or socio-economic status. (See Chapter 6 (Sociology for coaches.))
Facilities/ equipment	What equipment will you need and what facilities do you have access to? How will these be used? You need a clear understanding of the environment you are coaching in and must be aware of the location of changing rooms, toilets, showers, first aid box or treatment room, and other staff if appropriate.
Warm up	All coaching sessions should include a warm up that lasts for at least 10 minutes in order to prepare the participants for the session ahead. This should: • increase heart rate and blood flow • address stretching of muscles and mobilisation of the joints • include some practice and rehearsal of activities that are required for the sport.
Main body	The main body of the session will be aligned to the aims and objectives that have been set out. Ensure that your drills and practices are designed to meet these. The main body also often includes a competitive element to test or develop a skill or fitness component covered earlier in the session. You should consider **key factors** in your coaching session that you want to address.
Cool down	Allow participants to cool down and stretch to bring the body gradually back to a resting state. Participants will often want to get away quickly after a session so plan to have a cool down and use it effectively.
Contingencies	Despite planning your session carefully, you may find it does not always go as planned. It is important to plan for unexpected events. Perhaps you have planned to be outside but the weather is not appropriate for this. Perhaps the equipment or facilities you have planned to use are suddenly unavailable. Often, you will plan a session and the participants you need to make the session work do not turn up. You should have a number of ideas or plans to deal with a number of 'what if' scenarios.

Look at the example below of a completed plan for a coaching session. A blank version of this document is available at www.pearsonfe.co.uk/foundationsinsport

Coach(es)	Steve Owen	Date/time	23/08/11, 5pm
Number of participants	16 at training	**Age (s)**	15–17 years
Sport	Football	**Location**	Local school
Session aim	Improve defending. Prevent the ball from being played forwards. Notes: Mixed group of boys and girls and mixed ability tonight, need to ensure there are different practices to account for all of this. NB-Session is only 45 minutes tonight.		
Objectives/key factors	1. Prevent ball being played forwards. 2. Provide pressure on opponent, restrict space, intercept wherever possible. 3. Support play and team work when pressing. 4. Force and predict the play.		
Resources	Half a football pitch. No moveable goals. Need to plan for this. 16 balls, 16 bibs, stack of cones, whistle and stop watch		
Health and safety	Tanya is still injured slightly so don't include her in the main session. Ask to help with coaching after she has done her rehabilitation with the physiotherapist. All equipment is checked and safe.		
Warm up	• Dynamic movements • Include stretching • Rabbit tails game for defending practice • Introduce some 1 v 1 defending as part of the warm up.		
Main content	• 2 v 2 defending (go over principles of pressing, cover, support) • 4 v 4 v 4 game. The (x1) players keep the ball and have to try and pass through the (o) players to the (x2) players without it being intercepted. Keep swapping players in and work with the (o) players on their defending and support play. 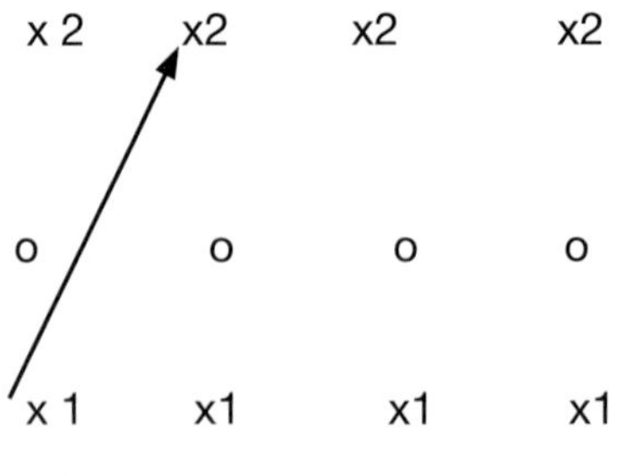 x 2 x2 x2 x2 o o o o x 1 x1 x1 x1 • Play an 8 v 8 game at the end and emphasis principles/key factors		
Cool down	• Jogging, walking, gentle stretching		
Reflection and aims for next session	• Session was ok but organisation could be better • Too many players stood around not involved • Team did well with the principles of defending, work next week on individuals as well as 11 v 11 if more are at training		

Figure 4.2 Coaching session plan

Health and safety

A key aspect of your planning is the consideration of health and safety. As a coach you must exercise your **duty of care** by providing a safe environment during your coaching sessions for all participants. If you are working with children under the age of 18, this is a legal obligation. Sport is an inherently hazardous activity and, although it may be impossible to eliminate all injuries or **risk** of injury, it is essential that you plan to reduce the risk of injury as much as you can in your sessions. A sports coach should be able to:

- assess risk

- protect athletes from injury and reduce the likelihood of risk

- know how to deal with any accidents or injuries if they occur.

Key terms

Hazard – something with potential to cause harm

Risk – the likelihood of a hazard occurring

Duty of care – a legal obligation imposed on an individual, requiring that they adhere to a standard of reasonable care while performing any acts that could possibly harm others (such as the hazard of sport)

Risk assessment

Your job as a coach is to assess the nature of **hazard** and risk and decide what is acceptable and what is not. For example, if you are a javelin coach and you and your athlete are practising on grass then there are some obvious hazards (the javelin, the grass may be wet, the skill of the performer) and you would need to assess the likelihood of these hazards actually causing harm. Risks can be classified as:

- low – no or minimal risk of injury

- medium – some risk of injury

- high – high risk of injury.

With an elite athlete, on a good surface, the risk of harm is low and so you might decide that it is acceptable to carry out the session. With a beginner, on wet grass, the risk of harm is high and so you might assess this risk and decide that it is not acceptable to carry out the session.

Activity

It is important to be able to assess risk as a coach. Approach a local coach in your area and ask them if it would be possible to carry out a risk assessment for a session they are coaching. Carry out a risk assessment of a coaching session using the table on the next page and report back to your classmates with any action points for your own coaching.

If the risk is deemed to be medium or high then you should put procedures and precautions in place to reduce the risk to low, or delay the activity until such time that you can reduce the risk to low. For example, you can carry out practical steps such as making sure balls are pumped up to the correct pressure, equipment is not worn and torn, there are no obstacles in the way of your session or that the participants are skilled enough to carry out what is being asked of them.

Safe practices

When considering safe practices in coaching and evaluating hazard and risk it is useful to categorise the issues you face into:

- participants (athletes and coaches, spectators)

- context (facilities, equipment, procedures)

- organisation (preparation, coaching style).

When carrying out a risk assessment ahead of a coaching session, you should record the following: each possible *hazard* (categorised by participants, context, organisation), the associated *risk*, likelihood of that risk happening (low/medium/high) and the *actions* you are taking to eliminate or minimise that risk. A simple table can be constructed with these as headings.

Table 4.2 below provides some considerations for you as a coach to review and implement in your own practice of risk assessment.

Table 4.2 Safe practices in coaching

Participants	Athletes	• Are the athletes thinking about safe practice? • Are athletes skilled and confident to perform without harm? • Are all athletes educated to perform safely and understand the hazards and risks of their sport?
	Coaches	• Do you understand that you have a duty of care? • Are you experienced and competent to teach each skill/practice? • Is there a code of conduct that ensures appropriate behaviour at all times, therefore minimising potential risk? • Are you planning for your coaching, and using approved practices for your sport/activity?
	Spectators (likely to be parents and guardians)	• Are spectators safe from harm? • Do they know the safety rules and will abide by them?
Context	Facilities	• Is the facility appropriate for the activity? • Is the facility hazard free? (Playing surface, goals, climbing equipment) • Are you using the facility/equipment for its intended use?
	Equipment	• Is equipment maintained for regular use? • Is equipment checked by you or someone else before use? • Is equipment stored safely?
	Procedures	• Do you have a code of conduct or code of practice that lists behaviours and actions that are acceptable? • Do all staff, parents, guardians, athletes know and accept these procedures? • Do you log accidents and injuries to note the types and frequency?
Organisation	Preparation	• Do you have a risk assessment for your session (up to date and accurate)? • Can you have an individualised session if you have mixed ability/confidence so that the risk is assessed differently for each participant? • Are you familiar with the code of conduct for your club/school/facility?
	Coaching	• Are you demanding an appropriate level of performance from athletes? (Do not push them beyond their capability to a point that is unsafe.) • Is your coaching practice appropriate for the activity? • Do your practices build skill and confidence progressively?

Emergency procedures

When planning a coaching session, you will need to be aware of the emergency procedures in case something unexpected occurs:

- fire and evacuation procedures at the facility

- first aid procedure

- location of all qualified first aid/medical staff

- location of mobile phone or facility phone in case of emergency

- risk assessment procedure of the facility in case there are specialist issues (e.g. setting up of a trampoline).

There are sports specific and facility specific issues that may impact on the emergency procedures and, as a coach, you should be informed of all issues and qualified where appropriate in specialist skills.

> ### Activity
>
> In pairs, design a coaching session for a sport of your choice to last approximately one hour using a coaching session plan. Alongside this, carry out a risk assessment by listing (under headings of participants, context, organisation) all of the hazards and risks for that session and how you would eliminate all risk wherever possible.

Roles and responsibilities of a coach

In addition to health and safety, a coach has a number of legal, personal and professional **roles** and **responsibilities** which you should be aware of throughout the coaching process. These extend to:

- the participants or athletes you are coaching

- the parents or guardians of those participants

- other coaches involved with the delivery of sessions or in competitive fixtures

- officials of the sport helping to ensure games and competitions can take place

- the sport that you are representing: your National Governing Body (NGB) will have specific rules on the responsibilities of a coach.

> ### Key terms
>
> **Roles** – a role often refers to the part played by an actor. A coach can be considered to 'play' a number of different roles and this will impact on the coaching process and how you plan for coaching
>
> **Responsibilities** – you have legal, personal and professional standards to maintain in coaching so that those in your care are given the best opportunity to enjoy and progress in their chosen sport

Legal obligations

In your work as a coach it is likely that you will often be coaching children. To work with this group you will be expected to have a Criminal Records Bureau (CRB) check. This gives potential employers the opportunity to consider any convictions you may have and your appropriateness to work with children. This is a safeguarding measure and is not intended to stop coaches from working but to ensure the safe protection of those in sport, especially given the powerful position coaches often undertake. Brackenridge (2001) notes that, despite certain types of abuse being prevalent in sport, the British sporting community was only really made aware of the potential issues of abuse in sport following the conviction of British Olympic swimming coach, Paul Hickson, in 1993.

Safeguarding participants

Children may look to a coaching environment as a safe environment, so it is your responsibility to be aware of the signs and symptoms of abuse as set out by the **Children Act (2004)**. This act is intended to provide a framework for those working with children and young people to improve the health, development and well-being of those in their care. As a coach you must be able to recognise the four main forms of child abuse (NSPCC, 2000) and ensure that you record any issues and report them appropriately. In order to develop your understanding, it may be useful to attend a sports coach UK or NGB specific safeguarding workshop.

Table 4.3 Different types of abuse that children may suffer from adults, other coaches and sometimes even other children in the form of abuse, bullying and harassment. (Adapted from National Society for the Prevention of Cruelty to Children (2000) *Child Maltreatment in the United Kingdom*)

Type of abuse	Description
Physical abuse	Physical hurt or injury caused to a child, sometimes displayed by bruising, cuts or burns.
Sexual abuse	Adults, both male and female, using children to meet their own sexual needs. This could be displayed when children are displaying over-sexualised behaviour themselves.
Emotional abuse	A persistent lack of love and/or affection can affect a child. They may become withdrawn from the rest of the group or from social contact with others.
Neglect	Failure to meet a child's basic needs such as food and warm clothing. Being aware of changes in a child's appearance and/or behaviour might help you to assess if there are any issues.

It is important to remember that a child may display some of the signs of abuse or even confront you directly with a concern. If you are a coach receiving this information you should:

- react calmly so as to not frighten the child
- tell the child they are not to blame and that they are right to inform someone
- take the allegation seriously
- keep questions to a minimum
- reassure the child
- make a full record of what has been said
- not promise that no one else will be informed as you will have to report the issue.

As soon as the conversation has ended, you (as the person receiving the information) should report the conversation to the designated child protection officer at the school, club or sports facility, or directly inform the police.

Personal responsibilities

As a coach you are expected to display a number of personal standards, as summarised here from the sports coach UK (2005) code of practice.

- Be fair, honest and considerate to performers and others in their sport.
- Project an image of health and cleanliness.
- Operate within the rules and the spirit of your sport.
- Educate performers on issues relating to the use of performance-enhancing drugs in sport and cooperate fully with UK Sport and governing bodies of sport policies.
- Maintain the same level of interest and support when a performer is sick or injured.
- Display high standards in the use of language, manner, punctuality, preparation and presentation.
- Encourage performers to display the same qualities.
- Do not smoke, drink alcohol or use recreational drugs before or while coaching. This reflects a negative image and could compromise the safety of your performers.
- Display control, respect, dignity and professionalism to all involved in your sport.

Professional responsibilities

As a professional coach, you should try to continually develop your knowledge of coaching by engaging in ongoing training and gaining coaching qualifications and further education. The sports coach UK (2005) code of practice suggests the following as key considerations of professional responsibility.

- Ensure the environment is as safe as possible, taking into account and minimising possible risk.
- Be professional and accept responsibility for your actions.
- Actively promote the positive benefits to society of participation in sport, including the positive contribution sport can make to achieving improved outcomes for children and young people.

- Contribute to the development of coaching as a profession by exchanging knowledge and ideas with others, and by working in partnership with other agencies and professionals.

- Plan all sessions so they meet the needs of the performers and are progressive and appropriate.

- Maintain appropriate records of your performers.

- Recognise and accept when it is appropriate to refer a performer to another coach or specialist.

- Seek to achieve the highest level of qualification available.

- Demonstrate commitment to Continuing Professional Development (CPD) by undertaking/attending learning opportunities to maintain up-to-date knowledge of technical developments in your sport.

- Undertake/attend CPD opportunities to maintain up-to-date knowledge and understanding of other issues that might impact on both you and your performers.

- Engage in self-analysis and reflection to identify your professional needs.

- Do not assume responsibility for any role for which you are not qualified or prepared.

(Personal and Professional Responsibility in Coaching as adapted from the sports coach UK Code of Practice for Coaches – 2005)

Your responsibilities as a coach will also need to be aligned with a *code of conduct* in coaching for your particular sport – your National Governing Body (NGB) will have specific rules around the rights, **relationships** and responsibilities of coaches. Their code of conduct outlines how you should behave as well as your responsibilities towards players, parents and the officials and organisers of the sport. You should be familiar with these responsibilities in order to be able to perform to the highest standard.

Key term

Relationships – the connections and bonds that are formed between you as a coach and the participants in your care

Activity

Go to www.pearsonfe.co.uk/foundationsinsport and visit the sports coach UK website. Register as a student member. Find the sports coach UK resource for the code of practice that covers rights, relationships and responsibilities of a coach and list some of the key messages you find in this document.

Table 4.4 Some examples of the different roles a coach may have to play as they engage in the coaching process (adapted from Miles, A. 2004)

Role	Description
Innovator	Coaching requires new, exciting and original ways of approaching sessions. An innovator will be original in their coaching and provide new thoughts to the group or individuals they are coaching.
Friend	When spending a considerable amount of time together a participant and coach may form a strong bond and a friendship. It is important to be aware of the boundaries of this friendship as well as understanding the positive and negative experiences that might be faced when you have both a professional and personal relationship.
Role model	It is important to be a positive role model for the participants you are coaching. Remember that a coach often has the respect of the group they are working with and so the clothing, language and behaviour of a coach need to be of the highest standard.
Educator	As a coach you will educate those in your care. When working with children or beginners, it is important to not only introduce them to the basic skills and principles of the sport but also help them to develop personally. As an educator, a coach needs to understand that each participant in their care will learn and develop differently.

Different roles as a coach

As a coach, your role exceeds that of planning and delivering training sessions and trying to improve athletes. You will at times in your coaching career also be called upon to play any number of roles such as strength and conditioning expert, sports scientist, psychologist, motivator, disciplinarian, innovator, teacher, social worker, friend, mentor, administrator, role model, taxi driver, manager and accountant, as well as many others (see Chapter 1 for a comprehensive discussion of coaching roles). This is in addition to having at your fingertips all the knowledge you will need as a coach (see Chapter 3 (Coaching knowledge and learning to coach)).

You will experience many of these roles over time and develop the skills required to be effective, but one of your roles is to know when you need to get expert help. For example, you may coach a child who is experiencing a difficult home life or who suffers bereavement in their family and it would be unwise to think you can deal with every situation yourself. Often a sports coach will be the person who children may approach with their problems, having developed a positive and enjoyable relationship with them; you need to know when to deal with the situation yourself and when to refer to others for support.

Activity

As part of your development, reflect on the roles you may assume as a coach.
- How confident are you that you can fulfil each of these roles?
- What areas of your coaching do you need to develop in order to be able to carry out these roles?
- Create an action plan for your own professional development over the next 12 months.
- Visit the sports coach UK website (or www.pearsonfe. co.uk/foundationsinsport) and consider the type of developmental activities and workshops you might engage with as you plan for coaching.

Deliver coaching

The second stage of the coaching process is to deliver coaching. Delivering the coaching session may be the smallest part of the whole coaching process but it is the point where all your hard work comes to fruition. You should include all the things identified in your planning as you take the individual or team through a warm up, the main content of the session and cool down. This is your chance to help the participant(s) reach their goals by instructing, demonstrating, setting problems, practising and providing feedback. In delivering a session you will be considering the following questions.

- When and where will you be coaching?
- What will you be coaching?
- What are the learning styles of your participants?
- What coaching style and philosophy will you employ?
- How will you communicate?
- How will you analyse performance?
- When and how will you give feedback?
- Will the session be safe?
- How will you adapt your coaching if your plans have to change?

Stages of learning

Athletes learn in different ways and at different stages and as a coach you should consider how they will take all the information on that is presented to them during the delivery of a coaching session. You should pay attention to the stage of learning your athletes are at and adapt your coaching style and practice to fit this accordingly.

For more information on learning styles, see Chapter 5 (Coaching pedagogy).

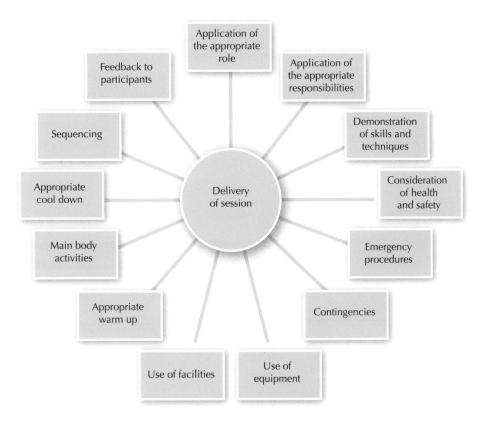

Figure 4.3 Vital factors to consider when planning and delivering a coaching session

Table 4.5 Matching instructions to the appropriate stage of learning

The stages of learning		
Cognitive	**Associative**	**Autonomous**
Participants are trying to grasp the basics of the skills/tasks set; they often have few experiences to relate to in the sport being coached. They will demonstrate a lot of errors and technical inefficiences.	Participants try to develop skills and techniques. They do this through practice. As they develop, they make fewer errors, although there will still be errors in the application of skills.	Participants can produce skills with little effort and almost 100% accuracy and success. At this stage they should be able to apply skills successfully in competitive situations.
Coach should: • use simple technical explanations and demonstrations • use simple basic drills and practices to develop skills • create fun and enjoyable sessions • encourage performers to practise unopposed.	Coach should: • use instructions and demonstrations to give athletes more information on the correct application of the skills • simulate training sessions and activities to develop specific skills • provide constructive feedback and promote peer- and self-analysis to assess performance.	Coach should: • use video demonstrations to demonstrate perfect application of skill • use complex technical instructions to fine-tune skills • discuss tactical application of the skills mastered.

Coaching styles

'Coaching style' describes an individual's coaching behaviour. We often refer to four key coaching styles: **autocratic**, **co-operative**, **democratic** and **laissez-faire**. Many factors can impact on coaching style, such as type of sport and the gender, age and ambition of the participants you are coaching (see Chapter 9 for coaching special populations).

It is likely that coaching style will also be affected by the knowledge a coach has (see Chapter 3 on coaching knowledge), their own coaching philosophy (see page 51) or the organisation they work for. For example, an organisation may have a selection policy that dictates every player has to have some playing time or that players are not allowed to be late and get fined a percentage of their wage at a professional club. Some key points are laid out in Table 4.6.

Table 4.6 Coaching styles and which participants they are best suited to. (Adapted from Cross and Lyle, 1999)

Coaching Style	Orientation	Characteristics	Advantages	Disadvantages
Autocratic	Coach centred	Instructional and authoritarian. Command-style coaching	Good for beginners when explaining basic skills and techniques. Good way of controlling large groups in a safe manner.	The coach controls the session so may only work on single skills or drills. Difficult to allow participants to express themselves and be innovative. Difficult to assess prior knowledge and understanding of participants.
Co-operative	Player centred	Offers leadership and negotiates with participant. Reciprocal coaching.	Good for developed participants, and allows a strong relationship to be formed as participants are involved with decision-making process. Develops communication and confidence, as well as understanding.	Can be time consuming and takes longer for success to take place. Differing opinions in a team setting can cause issues.
Democratic	Player centred	Problem-based learning. Guided discovery. Participants can be in control of sessions.	Good when working with expert/professional participants. Can increase understanding, decision-making skills and motivation. Participants become problem solvers.	Can seem chaotic and lack structure in sessions. Will take longer for success to take place (goals to be met).
Laissez-faire	Player focused	Problem-based learning but little or no intervention.	For expert performers this may be acceptable as they are more aware of what they need to do. Will increase responsibility, understanding and decision making.	Can be de-motivating if the participant feels the coach is uninterested. Bad practice can be developed without coach's intervention.

Key terms

Autocratic – an instructional and coach-centred style of coaching

Democratic – a problem-based and athlete-centred style of coaching

Co-operative – offering leadership and involving athletes in decision making

Laissez-faire – often provides little direction and allows performers to learn from themselves and their sport

Stop and think

Reflecting on these coaching styles, consider the following.

- Which style best describes how you coach?
- Why do you think you currently utilise this coaching style?
- What can you do in the future to ensure your coaching style is flexible and best responds to the needs of your participants?

Chapter 1 offers a useful introduction to different coaching approaches and this needs to be considered when carrying out your coaching. Adopting a problem-based approach to coaching where the responsibility to solve problems is given to the athlete demonstrates a very democratic approach to coaching. This puts much of the expectation upon the athlete to take responsibility for their learning and development and is an accepted approach for some sports (Bunker and Thorpe, 1982). At the same time, the coach could be very autocratic when it comes to issues of discipline such as timekeeping or wearing appropriate kit. These decisions are often made by the coach depending upon the context they are in or the constraints placed upon them (youth development, winning, saving money). They may also make decisions about their coaching style based upon the needs of the athlete, or the satisfaction of the athlete as they build up an understanding of and a relationship with the individuals they are coaching. Coaching style is placed on a continuum because you may have to adapt your coaching style depending on the

situation you are in. A coach's philosophy will help to determine their coaching style.

Coaching philosophy

It is widely accepted that the beliefs and values of a coach will shape their behaviours and provide direction and focus to their coaching practice (Cassidy, Jones and Potrac, 2009). It is good practice to reflect on your own coaching philosophy and to let others know what your philosophy for coaching is. A **coaching philosophy** should allow a coach to provide their coaching practice with a framework within which to deal with emerging issues. It ought to be the building block that allows you to deal with the 'everyday lived experiences' that are faced by you as a coach; for example, who to select, whether to emphasise winning or participation, and how to approach the coaching process. Wilcox and Trudel, (1998, page 41) suggest that 'a coaching philosophy is a set of values and behaviours that serve to guide the actions of a coach'. This makes a coaching philosophy an integral part of the coaching process because it allows us to understand what guides our actions. If you consider Arsene Wenger (Head Coach of Arsenal Football Club at the time of writing) it is notable that as a coach he has a clear philosophy, underpinned by technical development, the development of young players and attacking flair.

Key term

Coaching philosophy – a set of values and behaviours that serve to guide the actions of a coach

The knowledge you have as a coach (see Chapter 3), ethical issues (see Chapter 14), as well as your experiences and the context in which you work, will all impact on your coaching philosophy and so the philosophy of each coach will be unique. Creating a consistent and clear philosophy is likely to make you more effective as a coach because the athletes you work with will receive a more consistent message, thus making improvement more likely. A coaching philosophy also gives direction to each coach and so you are more likely to understand your motives and thus develop your career more effectively.

A coaching philosophy can offer stability to the coaching environment and to the coach-athlete relationship, which also improves the coaching process. Kidman and Hanrahan (1997) suggest that the power that exists between coach and athlete can often be harmful. For example, if a coach has the power to select or deselect an athlete then the relationship may be affected. However, if a coaching philosophy is developed and transmitted to an athlete then it is thought that the athlete will be more aware of the reasons behind their selection/deselection and, as such, interaction between coach and athlete will still lead to effectiveness in coaching.

A coaching philosophy will need to be flexible and developed over time. Of prime importance is the need to be reflective and to develop a coaching philosophy over time that deals with a number of key questions.

Activity

Answer the questions below in order to start reflecting on your own coaching philosophy.

- What is coaching to me?
- Why am I a coach?
- What style of coaching do I use?
- How will I coach in the most effective way?
- How do I ensure I have enough knowledge to coach?
- How will I make sure I know my athletes well enough to respond to their individual needs?
- How could I improve my coaching?

Coaching techniques

When delivering the session you must employ the appropriate techniques and practices to improve the performance of the athletes you are working with.

Observation analysis

As a coach it is important to be able to assess the development of your athlete. Your analysis will be both objective and subjective. *Objective* analysis involves the measurement of performance data and the observation of technique, allowing you to improve this data against results you record in

other sessions and/or by other athletes. You might compare the number of successful passes from different matches, or the development of speed over pre-season through effective testing.

Subjective analysis involves making use of your own opinions and philosophies as a coach when analysing performance and development. It is important that this analysis is not subject to bias based around whether you have a good relationship or a poor relationship with an athlete. Expert coaches who have developed years of experience and knowledge can often provide excellent subjective analysis because they have built up a profile of what an expert athlete looks like.

Fitness assessment

In order to provide some objective data for training, a coach and a team of sports scientists or strength and conditioning coaches might provide some form of fitness assessment or screening. This allows the coaching team to develop effective training programmes. (See Chapter 13 for a comprehensive review of training programmes and testing for athletes.)

Goal setting

Goal setting is an integral part of enhancing the motivation and confidence of athletes (Cox, 2007). Alongside the SMART goal setting outlined previously (see page 41), it is important to set goals over the short, medium and long term. This will enable the athlete to stay focused and motivated, while constantly being challenged. Despite the fact that these goals might change, it is still a useful part of the coaching process. All goals should be discussed and agreed with the athlete(s) you are working with.

- Short term – one session, day, week or even a month. There may be small performance gains or tactical and technical improvements that have a short-term focus.

- Medium term – these goals may be specific points in a season or year that mark progress towards long-term goals.

- Long term – goals are often set for a season or even as far ahead as an Olympic cycle (four years). Often they are performance-related targets and they provide a focus for short and medium-term goals.

Simulation

Simulation involves the introduction of more game-like situations or competition-like situations for the athlete to experience. Simulated coaching environments are a move away from drills and guide the performer as they seek to develop greater understanding of 'when' and 'where' to use the skills they have developed. Equally, it could be the simulation of training in the rain to prepare a performer for that, or at a particular time of day. If you consider the globalisation of sport today, athletes are increasingly being asked to race, or play at differing times to meet the demands of television audiences. Coaches can simulate situations such as this to better prepare their athletes. This practice is related to concepts of non-linear coaching (see page 54).

Modelling

Modelling is a useful coaching technique to provide the athlete with a picture of the technique or skill being learnt. This could be in the form of a demonstration from the coach or another competent performer, or it could be from something like a video of a performer. One problem with demonstrations is that there is an assumption that there is one perfect or correct way to achieve a successful outcome – which is not true. As a coach, you have to be careful when demonstrating as you need to take account of the fact that a demonstration provides a powerful visual cue for athletes – one they will often try to copy. Depending on the learning stage of the athlete, this could be positive or detrimental to learning. Remember, that if you are providing a model for athletes, to help them understand a complex skill, you must allow them the individuality to adapt that to their own stage of physical, technical and psychological ability.

Demonstration

When providing a demonstration, while we may debate the notion of correct or perfect, there are obviously issues of safety and development that should be addressed. If an athlete is attempting a rugby tackle, it may be wise to demonstrate, as well as help guide them through it, as it would be unsafe to let them explore such a skill on their own. There is some debate as to the effectiveness of demonstrations and this is related to the current skill of the performer, the type of skill or task being performed and the appropriateness of the demonstration provided. You need to consider the ability and stage of development of your athlete, but a good and appropriate demonstration can help an athlete to model complex movements and build the motor skill necessary (Hodges and Franks, 2002).

Technical instruction

Communication is a key factor in technical instruction and is underpinned by the knowledge of a coach. Coaches may use feedback, demonstration and observational skills to help provide technical instruction during a performance. As a coach, you must consider a number of issues when providing technical instruction. Demonstrations tend to take place before a performance or skill execution while technical instruction will take place during and after such a performance. Therefore, a coach needs to consider issues such as the athlete's focus and attention, what they are going to say and how much instruction they are going to give, as well as the amount and accuracy of the instruction. It is important as a coach to keep instructions simple and to check understanding from the athletes.

Linear and non-linear approaches to coaching

There are several theories which explain how athletes learn from both a psychological and sociological perspective (Cassidy et al., 2009). This section deals with two different approaches to coaching that can bring about learning in athletes. These are often thought of as traditional/linear or non-traditional/non-linear approaches to coaching and utilise different theoretical approaches for the coaching environment.

Linear coaching approach

Linear coaching approaches are typically autocratic, technique-based, skill-acquisition approaches to coaching and are often considered to be drill-based (Kidman and Hanrahan, 2011). As a coach, you may have heard that practice and repetition is important for skill development. This is based on a traditional/linear perspective and learning is seen to take place more quickly using this approach, although retention of information and enjoyment are lower in relation to a non-linear approach to coaching. Learning is considered sequential and takes place in order. A coach might feel that their athlete needs the 'basic technique or skill' before being able to do more complex activities. If this is an idea that you can relate to, then this approach may suit you. Rather like an autocratic coaching style, this approach is centred on the coach and is less concerned with the athlete's satisfaction. This may be suitable for a beginner coach, or for dangerous activities such as a gymnastics vault with a young athlete.

Non-linear coaching approach

Kidman & Hanrahan (2011) support a more dynamic, non-sequential approach to coaching often referred to as non-linear coaching or dynamic systems. This approach suggests that athletes are self-organising and that manipulating the coaching environment will ensure that athletes self-organise and problem solve in order to develop solutions technically, tactically or through movement in a realistic sporting context.

This constraints-led approach (Chow, 2009) was originally presented as Teaching Games for Understanding (TgfU) by Bunker and Thorpe (1982) but has been re-presented as 'game sense' and the constraints led-approach. Although there are small differences between each approach, they all have game play and problem solving at their core. If athletes are involved in problem solving they are likely to be more intrinsically motivated. As a coach, you might consider games as a site for learning and manipulate different games to make sure they are realistic and relevant to the sport you are coaching. Here, the game itself provides a question or problem for the athlete that they have to answer physically. It is suggested that, while learning may take longer initially with these non-linear approaches, the complex nature of sport and this approach can mean that retention of knowledge is more effective and may meet individual requirements more effectively.

Communication skills

It is obviously important to have all the knowledge required to be a coach and to plan good sessions. However, the most effective coaches are those with good communication skills who are able to get their message across to participants. You need to ensure that you are engaging with your participants in a constructive and positive way, gaining their trust and respect while also listening to them and trying to get your coaching points across to individuals and the group you are with. Effective communication will draw on a number of things, such as your knowledge, good planning, coaching philosophy and coaching style; but you should also try and consider some of the following issues in order to be an effective communicator.

- Ask questions: what do your athletes enjoy, what motivates them, what are their goals?

- Listen to players, other coaches, parents and officials.

- Plan in advance what you are going to say.

- Avoid technical jargon.

- Do not talk just to fill the gaps: this can communicate the wrong message.

- Talk with participants – they may also have important points to share.

- Be constructive in your comments. It is not enough just to say 'well done' or 'good' all the time, and equally it is not effective to be overly critical. Think carefully about the words you use.

- Consider the pitch, tone and speed of your voice.

Communicating effectively involves both **verbal** and **non-verbal** communication and the power of both of these should not be overlooked. (See also Chapter 5, page 71 on the process of communication.)

Verbal communication

Good verbal communication does not mean you must have the loudest, most powerful voice. It simply means that each athlete should be able to take the key factors on board. You will be required to use your voice effectively so that athletes can hear and understand what you as the coach are saying. You may have to change the tone, pitch or speed of your voice and equally it may be worth going to talk to individuals if you have a particular message that you want to get across to one person. You must think about what that communicates to the others in the group if you are always talking to individuals and not sharing the message. Talking in a quiet and patient manner can often help you as a coach and planning your sessions will also be useful as you will have a number of key factors you know you want to discuss.

Non-verbal communication

Much of our communication actually happens non-verbally through our body language and facial expressions, being professional and punctual, being well organised, even through the clothes we wear, as well as many other factors. Without saying anything, you are already conveying messages to your participants – so you need to think about that. This can be positive in terms of demonstrations in coaching that will be part of your sessions.

When you are coaching, reflect on your body language as well. How many times do you clap, laugh, point, gesture, cross your arms and so on? The eye contact you make is also important.

These points are all worth thinking about. If a player accidentally misses a shot and you throw a water bottle to the floor in frustration or anger – is this communicating an appropriate message to your player?

Feedback

Coaching can often involve the analysis and detection of error to allow further improvement in an athlete's performance (at whatever level). In order for that analysis from a coaching perspective to be given to the athlete, you need to consider the role of feedback. Feedback can provide motivation to your participants as well as providing them with relevant information upon which to improve. Remember that both the verbal and non-verbal communication you provide will impact on the participant and this feedback is essential to the participant when trying to bring about change in their performance.

Martens (2004) suggests there are two types of feedback: *intrinsic* and *extrinsic*.

Intrinsic feedback

Intrinsic feedback involves kinaesthetic, tactile, visual or auditory sensory systems. For example, when you hit a golf shot and it goes off to the left in the trees, then you can see it is off line (visual), you have probably felt the vibration of a bad shot in your hands (tactile), you have heard that the sound it makes does not sound like a good connection (auditory) and you can sense in your muscles and feelings that your head was slightly raised and you went too quickly through your shot (kinaesthetic). This feedback for athletes is essential and as discussed above (linear and non-linear coaching) you may be able to control the environment and training practice in order to manipulate the type of intrinsic feedback that occurs with athletes. As a coach you can ask key questions here such as 'how did that shot feel?' or 'did that sound right to you?' so that athletes develop their own self-awareness which is key in a coaching setting (Cassidy et al., 2009).

Extrinsic feedback

Extrinsic feedback tends to be the first option for coaches who are uncomfortable with non-linear approaches to coaching and 'letting the game be the teacher' in approaches such as TgfU (Bunker and Thorpe, 1982). You may find yourself talking all the way through sessions, giving what you think is good feedback, saying things like 'well done', 'good', 'great shot', when it may not be appropriate or accurate to give such feedback. You have to judge the appropriate moments to give extrinsic feedback, and the method by which you do so.

If you decide to give feedback, consider if this should be *immediate* or *delayed*. Immediate feedback tends to be given at the moment when you see something that is 'coach-able'. Do not wait five minutes and then go back and say, 'When you were in this position you should have done this instead of that'. The athlete is unlikely to remember the exact context and will have a different picture in their head so you will not be able to affect or improve their performance. You may want to give delayed feedback after a performance by using video analysis or other forms of performance analysis (see Chapter 12) but this is not the same as delayed feedback as it focuses on other coaching factors.

When providing extrinsic feedback, try to make sure that you focus on the specific part of the session as otherwise you may overload athletes with information. If the session is focusing on shooting in netball, it may be distracting for athletes if you give them feedback about movement or defending as well (incongruent feedback). You need to ensure that you know your athletes and how much information they can process – depending upon their ability – but it is often better to be specific about the feedback and relate it to the focus of the session (congruent feedback).

Being adaptive

Another skill you will need to employ during the delivery of a coaching session is the ability to respond to the needs of those you are coaching by considering some of the following points.

• Is the session too slow or fast?

• Do your coaching styles and practices need to be adapted in some way?

• Are you making full use of the facilities, resources and other coaches at your disposal?

Often you will need to make changes on the spot. You should consider keeping detailed records of what is successful and what needs improving in your coaching so that you are better prepared for these situations in the long term. You should consider keeping a reflective diary of a number of issues such as your feelings and thoughts, your successes as a coach, as well as a log of all of the sessions you deliver in order to improve your practice. Being adaptive in coaching is essential to your success as a coach. For a more detailed review of adaptive coaching see Chapter 9 (Coaching special populations). It may be useful to consider the STEPS model for inclusive coaching (sports coach UK Quick Guide for Inclusive Coaching).

Evaluate coaching

The evaluation stage is an integral part of the coaching process. Evaluation should allow you to assess the effectiveness of your coaching as well as helping you to plan for future sessions.
The coaching process is a cycle that is continual and, although the evaluation stage comes last in this chapter, it is actually the start point of our next cycle. If you can imagine that you have planned and delivered a session, and you are evaluating that session, this now becomes the start point of your next coaching episode.

You should consider a number of factors.

• How did you meet your aims and objectives?

• How did you meet the SMART targets that were set for the participants?

• List what went well.

• Describe what went worse than expected.

• How can you assess what the participants have learnt?

• In what way was your interaction with the participant(s) effective?

- What have you learnt as a coach and what might you do differently?
- How did you ensure that you used an appropriate coaching style for the participants?
- In what way did you compromise your coaching philosophy?
- How have you judged the success of the session? (Improvement/success)
- How did you get feedback from participants/ other coaches?
- Have you had a coaching observation from a senior coach/mentor?

You might consider some of the following tools to help you reflect and evaluate:

- a reflective diary
- an interview with another coach
- flip cameras or other video devices to allow you to watch your own coaching later
- a dictaphone to comment throughout your coaching
- talking to your participants to get them to feed back to you
- asking coaches and participants to fill out a feedback form for you to note down areas of strength and weakness
- filling out a performance profile.

You could ask your participants to give you some simple formative feedback to help you devise a development plan as part of the coaching process.

> **Remember**
>
> Coaching is a complex activity. Evaluating your own ability/development as a coach is an ongoing part of the coaching process.

Performer Feedback Sheet

Please circle your answers.

Did you enjoy the session?

Did you enjoy the warm-up?

Did you enjoy the drills in the session e.g. the dribbling between the cones, the shooting into the hockey net?

Did the sports leader communicate clearly?

Did the sports leader demonstrate clearly what you had to do in the session?

Did you feel that your performance improved in the session?

What extra activities would you like to have done in the session?

- -

- -

Figure 4.4 An example of a questionnaire on a coach's performance (available to print out at www.pearsonfe. co.uk/foundationsinsport

Assessment

Session Plan

Did the learner produce a lesson plan (prior to the start of the session/event?)   YES/NO
Was the session planned appropriately for the needs of the participants?   YES/NO
Will the session/event meet the aims and objectives of the session?   YES/NO

Targets

Did the learner set targets for participants?   YES/NO
Were these targets met during the session/event?   YES/NO
Before the session:
did the learner carry out a safety check of the participants and of the venue
and equipment prior to the session/event?   YES/NO
did the learner produce a risk assessment for the event/session?   YES/NO

Delivery

Did the learner communicate effectively throughout the session/event?   YES/NO
Did the learner use the facility and equipment effectively throughout the session?   YES/NO
Did the learner organise the session effectively?   YES/NO
Did the learner demonstrate effective application of the roles and
responsibilities of a sports coach?   YES/NO
Did the learner demonstrate appropriate knowledge and language of the
sport and the techniques and skills covered in the session?   YES/NO
Which techniques did the learner use to develop the performers within the session?   YES/NO

Did the learner wear appropriate clothing for the session?   YES/NO
Did the learner motivate the performers throughout the session?   YES/NO
Were the components of the session delivered effectively and appropriately?   YES/NO
Did the learner conclude the session with a summary and provide
opportunities for feedback to all performers?   YES/NO

Which areas could be improved?

Signed _ (assessor)   Date _ _ _ _ _ _ _ _ _ _ _ _ _

Figure 4.5 An example of an observation record that an assessor may use when assessing
your coaching session (available to print out at www.pearsonfe.co.uk/foundationsinsport)

If you can reflect on the type of things an assessor will look for when providing a summative or formative assessment of your coaching it might help you to plan for all eventualities.

You may often find yourself as a coach working on your own and completing the coaching process on an individual basis; you will often be required to reflect on your own practice. Developing some reflective and evaluative skill will allow you to develop your coaching performance from beginner to expert. Be sure to consider 'how' you might improve and 'why' things went well in order to improve your coaching. Reflection is a complex process and is more than just looking back at your session. Writing or recording some notes immediately and then returning once you have had time to reflect objectively is important. Reflection is not merely an isolated practice and it is essential that you use reflection in order to respond and change as necessary. This may take place before, during or after a session. Schon (1987) states that a practitioner cannot learn simply by experiencing, but only through reflecting (**in**, **on** and **anticipatory**) on experiences. As a coach you need to apply your reflections and utilise them at the earliest opportunity to practise your coaching. You would not want a particular episode, such as a particularly bad day at work or college, to cloud your judgement.

Types of assessment

You should try and continually review your performance as a coach at different points in your development. **Formative** types of **assessment** help to construct or form ideas of how we might improve. This might be another coach giving you development feedback, or your performers providing you with a **development plan** over the short and medium term.

Summative assessment is the sum of something, and occurs at an end point. This could be a qualification or an external assessor giving feedback on your coaching. It is also an essential part of your development as a coach; even if it is negative or constructive feedback it should help direct your development.

Key terms

Formative assessment – takes place informally and will support the development of a coach

Summative assessment – takes place formally and is normally an assessment of your competence or performance as a coach

Development plan – using the feedback and assessment you receive as a coach can help create a development plan for future improvement

Being an effective coach

Over a period of time, many people such as athletes, parents, supporters, owners, committee members, sponsors or the media will judge whether or not a coach has been successful. They may all have a different opinion but judgements are often made based on issues such as enjoyment, safety, winning or cost (Cassidy, Jones & Potrac, 2009).

Our own experiences can help us to form ideas of what a good coach is and this can determine how you yourself approach coaching. For example, if your coach was strict or good fun and you enjoyed that experience, then you might think that you need these attributes to be a good coach.

Stop and think

How would you judge whether a coach has been effective?

What do you think makes you effective as a coach?

Effectiveness in coaching can be assessed through observations of the coaching process to determine what is effective in improving the athlete's performance. Cross and Lyle (1999) suggest that effective coaching should be related to how the coaching process is managed and that a reflective coach will try to improve different areas of their coaching. Some of these improvements might be related to the attributes that make a good coach, although they might equally be related to the potential of an individual or group that the coach is working with. There are many different ways to classify effective coaches but it is clear that the ability to be flexible and modify coaching behaviour is important in order to be effective in different situations. One coach may be effective by being instructional while another may be more effective by letting the athlete take more control.

Some elements of effective coaching include:

- leadership style
- provision of feedback
- personalised coaching
- planning
- reflection
- improvement.

You are working with a local athletics club where there is a mix of participation and performance athletes. There is also a wide range of social factors, such as background, age, ethnicity, disability and gender. You have been promoted to Head Coach of the club and so you are working with other coaches as well. You have been asked to produce a coaching pamphlet for the club to include the following.

1. A coaching philosophy for the whole club
2. An example session plan to include warm up and cool down for other coaches to utilise
3. A list of the areas you might wish to evaluate and how you will do so

Case study (for recommended answers, see www.pearsonfe.co.uk/foundationsinsport)

Case Study: engaging in the coaching process

Jody is a Level 2 qualified football coach and has played at an amateur level in rugby, hockey and football. Jody is interested in working with developing players rather than elite players. Jody has been to college and studied Sports Coaching. She is organised and feels really comfortable writing a session plan and is also very reflective in her coaching. Jody keeps a reflective diary that helps her to keep notes on all her best sessions and even some of the worst ones that have gone really badly. Jody has been working with the group of players she has for two years now and feels that she knows them really well. She has a clear coaching philosophy as well as a coach mentor that she speaks to on a regular basis to try and improve her understanding of coaching. The players are all 14 years old and are enjoying playing for the team and for Jody as a coach. Jody feels she is starting to be really effective as a coach as her team have gone unbeaten for ten games now. The players are responding well to her autocratic style of coaching and they are carrying out all of her plans well in games. Jody has always used a very linear approach to coaching as

she felt that drills were good for young footballers and it was important that they knew the basics before trying out some more difficult sessions. However, Jody has recently been reading some academic texts on coaching and really likes the idea of a 'constraints-led approach' or 'Teaching Games For Understanding'. She wants to try out this game-related approach in order to make her coaching more realistic and to try and get her young participants to make more decisions for themselves and become problem solvers.

Questions

1. Which approach do you think is most effective for this group of players?
2. Should Jody be changing her coaching approach after two years?
3. How do you think this will impact on the players' learning?
4. Could Jody use both approaches in a session?
5. Does Jody's coaching style link well to her coaching philosophy?
6. Is it important that a beginner coach continues to plan-do-review?
7. Is Jody judging her effectiveness as a coach in an appropriate way?

Time to reflect

1. How can you use goals to help plan your coaching?
2. Identify the key stages of the coaching process.
3. Create a list of the components of a coaching session.
4. Drawing on the different issues in health and safety, consider how you will manage the risks involved in an upcoming coaching session.
5. What are the roles and responsibilities involved in your own coaching?
6. Drawing on the different coaching techniques that you have experienced, work out how you are going to approach coaching in your next session.
7. Create a list of ways in which you can evaluate your own coaching.

Check your understanding (for answers, see www.pearsonfe.co.uk/foundationsinsport)

1. Describe the coaching process.
2. List some important factors in each section of the coaching process.
3. Name two coaching styles.
4. What is a coaching philosophy?
5. What is the difference between linear and non-linear approaches to coaching?
6. List five factors that you would include in a session plan.
7. Describe and list the goal-setting process.
8. What types of communication are important?
9. What types of feedback can take place to help both athletes and coaches develop?
10. List the ways in which you would evaluate your own performance.

Useful resources

To obtain a secure link to the websites below, see the Websites section on page ii or visit the companion website at www.pearsonfe.co.uk/foundationsinsport.

- sports coach UK

- Sport England

- UK Sport

- Quest

- International Journal of Sports Science and Coaching

Further reading

Armour, K. (ed.). (2011). *Sport pedagogy: an introduction for teaching and coaching.* London: Prentice Hall.

Borrie, A. and Knowles, Z. (2003). Coaching Science and Soccer. In T. Reilley and M. Williams (eds.) *Science and soccer.* (2nd edition) London: E & FN Spon (181–197).

Brackenridge, C.H. (2001) *Spoilsports: Understanding and preventing sexual exploitation in sport.* London: Routledge.

Brackenridge, C., Bringer, J.D. and Bishop, D. (2005). Managing cases of abuse in sport. *Child Abuse Review,* 14, 259–274.

Bunker, D. and Thorpe, R. (1982) A model for teaching games in secondary schools. *Bulletin of Physical Education,* 18 (1), 5–8.

Butler, R. (1996) *Performance profiling.* Leeds: National Coaching Foundation.

Cassidy, T., Jones, R. and Potrac, P. (2009) *Understanding sports coaching: The social, cultural and pedagogical foundations of coaching practice.* (2nd edition). London: Routledge.

Children Act (2004). London: HMSO.

Chow, J., Davids, K., Button, C., Renshaw, I. and Uehara, L. (2009). Nonlinear pedagogy: Implications for Teaching Games for Understanding (TGfU). In T. Hopper, J. Butler, and B. Storey (eds.), *TGfU…Simply good pedagogy: Understanding a complex challenge* (pp.131–144). Ottowa: Ottowa Physical Health Education Association.

Cox, R. H. (2007) *Sport psychology: Concepts and applications.* London: McGraw-Hill.

Crisfield, P., Cabral, P. and Carpenter, F. (eds.) (2003). *The successful coach: Guidelines for successful coaching practice.* Leeds: The National Coaching Foundation.

Cross, N. and Lyle, J. (eds) (1999). *The coaching process: Principles and practice for sport.* Oxford: Butterworth-Heinemann.

Gilbert, W., Côté, J. & Mallett, C. (2006). Developmental paths and activities of successful sport coaches. *International Journal of Sports Science and Coaching,* 1 (1), 69–76.

Hodges, N.J. and Franks, I.M. (2002). Modelling coaching practice: The role of instruction and demonstration. *Journal of Sports Science,* 20, 793–811.

Jones, R.L., Armour, K.M. and Potrac, P. (2004). *Sports coaching cultures: from practice to theory.* London: Routledge.

Kidman, L. and Hanrahan, S. (1997) *The coaching process: A practical guide to improving your effectiveness.* Palmerston North, NZ: Dunmore Press.

Kidman, L. and Hanrahan, S.J. (2011). *The coaching process: A practical guide to becoming an effective sports coach.* London: Routledge.

Lyle, J. (2002). *Sports coaching concepts: a framework for coaches' behaviour.* London: Routledge.

Martens, R. (2004) *Successful coaching. (*3rd edition*)* Leeds: Human Kinetics.

Miles, A. (2004) *Coaching practice.* Leeds: sports coach UK.

National Society for the Prevention of Cruelty to Children. (2000). *Child maltreatment in the United Kingdom.* London: NSPCC.

Schön, D. A. (1987). *Educating the reflective practitioner.* San Francisco: Jossey-Bass.

sports coach UK. (2005). *Code of practice for sports coaches: Rights/Relationships/Responsibilities.* Leeds: The National Coaching Foundation.

Wilcox, S. and Trudel, P. (1998). Constructing the coaching principles and beliefs of a youth ice hockey coach. *Avante,* 4, 39–66.

Chapter 5

Coaching pedagogy

Introduction

In the practice of sports coaching, it is not enough to be a knowledgeable coach. A coach must be able to transfer information to participants in the coaching environment, and to do this effectively requires an intimate understanding of pedagogy. At a basic level, pedagogy is viewed as 'how to' coach and as such something that is relatively straightforward. However, this chapter explains in detail the complexity of how you can coach more effectively through a more sophisticated appreciation of the multiple dimensions and multiple layers of pedagogy. This added complexity comes through understanding the interplay between how your participants learn, how you coach, what you are coaching and the context in which your coaching is taking place. Possessing a detailed understanding of coaching pedagogy and being able to apply it in the coaching environment often makes the difference between good coaches and great coaches.

Learning outcomes

After you have read this chapter you should be able to:

- explain what is meant by 'coach as teacher'
- understand the pedagogy of coaching
- explain the main theories of learning in relation to coaching
- understand learning styles and multiple intelligences
- discuss the difference between coaching style, coaching method and coaching strategy
- understand the different coaching styles
- understand the process of communication and the communication channels used by coaches.

Drawing on your own experiences in sport, think about the times when you have had difficulty in understanding what your coach has wanted you to do and similarly the times when your understanding of the coach has been second to none. Share these with other members of your group and look for similarities and differences in your experiences.

The coach as teacher

Coaching sport is a social activity, with all the complexities of a coach–participant relationship at its core. For this reason the process of how to coach is a crucial and often overlooked element of being an effective practitioner. For many years the professions of teaching and coaching were presented as being different; however, sports coaches have become more aware of the need to totally develop the individuals who they are working with in line with established practice in a school setting. This is referred to as **holistic** coaching practice, and has blurred the distinction made between the professions of teaching and coaching.

Contemporary thinking among academics and leading coaching figures suggests that good coaches act like good teachers. This position is reinforced by Sir Clive Woodward (England Rugby Union 2003 World Cup winning coach) who argues that 'the best coaches are good teachers' (Cain, 2004, p.19). Similarly, Graham Taylor (former coach of the England Football team) considered himself as possessing the qualities to become a teacher or a coach, and if he had known in advance that his professional football playing career would be relatively short lived, he says that he would have remained in school to become a teacher. Graham Taylor affirms this by saying that 'coaching really is a form of teaching, so I guess, in a way, I've ended up in the same place!' (Jones et al., 2004, p.21).

Therefore coaching sport is about much more than improving the mechanistic performance of participants through training and skill development and, as such, you should consider establishing an environment conducive to participant learning wherever and whenever you coach. To establish and maintain an effective **learning** environment, **pedagogy** becomes central in coaching sport effectively.

Remember

Coaching sport is about much more than simply improving the performance of an individual or team. As a social activity it is important that you maintain a positive relationship with the participants with whom you are working and create a positive coaching climate. A positive coaching climate creates an atmosphere that is favourable to you creating an effective learning environment. This atmosphere, in a sports coaching context, is referred to as the motivational climate.

Key terms

Holistic – dealing with the whole and not just a part

Pedagogy – the principles and practices designed to enhance learning in an individual

Learning – the activity of obtaining knowledge

Motivational climate – situationally induced psychological environment that influences achievement strategies of participants

The pedagogy of coaching

The simple term that is used to define how to coach is the 'science of coaching'. However, the most appropriate term to describe what this is in reality is the 'pedagogy of coaching'. In Chapter 3 (Coaching knowledge and learning to coach) the pedagogy of coaching is presented in Figure 3.2 as Pedagogical Knowledge (PedK). If participants are to get the best out of the physical activity that they are engaged in, then someone has to be responsible for bringing together the multiple sub-discipline areas of sports science in meaningful and helpful ways for the participants (Armour, 2011). This complex undertaking is the task faced by coaches in creating positive learning experiences for participants in the coaching environment. Each of these learning experiences can be termed a **pedagogical encounter**.

Even the best athletes need help learning from a coach. How important do you think it is for elite athletes to be helped by a coach?

Three dimensions of coaching pedagogy

Each learning experience will be influenced by a number of factors. These complex factors grouped together can be presented as being three dimensions underpinning the pedagogy of coaching (see Figure 5.1). The three dimensions are as follows.

- **Context**: the selection of what knowledge to be coached is always contextual. The coaching might be taking place in a school setting, professional club, private club or community centre, but the reasons for participation will influence what knowledge is appropriate to be coached.

- **Learners and learning**: participants will have different needs and ways in which they prefer to learn. An appreciation of learning theories is central to this dimension. In addition to how participants learn, learners will be impacted by multiple factors that will impact upon learning (for example, disaffection, health levels, disability, gender, sexuality, age, class, ethnicity, interest).

- **Coaches and coaching**: coaches will draw upon a range of pedagogical tools in order to maximise learning in each pedagogical encounter in the coaching environment. Coaches will tend to default to their own learning preferences unless they have the awareness, relevant skills and ability to operate outside this.

The pedagogy of coaching, in articulating the interchange between context, learners and coaches in a pedagogical encounter, can therefore be described as multidimensional and multilayered (Kirk et al., 2006). In order to be effective, coaches must be proficient at establishing a coaching environment that is conducive to enhancing participant learning through arranging high quality pedagogical encounters. This chapter focuses on the dimensions of the learners and also that of the coaches.

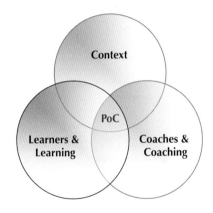

Figure 5.1 The three dimensions of the pedagogy of coaching (PoC)

Main theories of learning

Learning is a complex concept and can be defined as the act, activity or process of acquiring knowledge or skill. Understanding a range of learning theories helps you to understand how your participants receive and make sense of the information that you are giving to them. There are four main theories of learning that have evolved over the last century: behaviourism, cognitivism, constructivism and social theories of learning. Table 5.1 summarises four main theories of learning.

Table 5.1: Theories of learning (adapted from Chambers, 2011)

Theory	Behaviourism	Cognitivism	Constructivism	Social theories of learning
Main theorists	Pavlov Skinner Thorndike Watson	Ausubel Bruner Gagne Koffka Lewin	Dewey Piaget Rogoff Vygotsky	Bandura Engestrom Eraut Lave and Wenger
How does learning happen?	Behaviour changed due to external stimulus	Internal mental processes	Constructing meaning from what we already know	Observation and interaction with others
Purpose of learning	Produce behaviour change in a desired direction	Develop reason, intuition and perception	Construct new knowledge linked to existing knowledge	Model new roles and behaviour
Implications for coaches	Coach is viewed as transmitter of knowledge Participant viewed as a passive recipient of coach's knowledge Coach controls coaching environment	Coach prepares information and transmits it to learners Participant viewed as information processor Coach controls the information-input process Participants receive, store and act on information	Coach builds upon participants' prior learning Participant actively constructs new understandings Coach facilitates learner agency	Participants develop shared practice with all learners Learning takes place between all members of the group Coach orchestrates social interaction
Coaching strategies	Rote learning Learning drills Clear objectives Learning by doing Repetition Positive reinforcement Activity important	Empower internal mental processes Tasks broken down into steps Start with most simple steps Work towards more complex steps	Task oriented Hands-on Self-directed Activities oriented towards design and discovery Coaching environment is active, energetic and noisy	Individual and group work Use mentors to guide newcomers Establish a community of practice

Learning styles and multiple intelligences

There are many theories that attempt to explain how participants learn. For practising coaches, theory is often perceived as being detached from reality. For this reason, it is necessary to outline how these theoretical positions manifest in the learning styles of participants.

Learning style is the term given to describe a person's preferred way of learning. It highlights the manner and conditions in which a person receives, deals with and gains understanding of the things they are trying to learn. At a basic level, the learning preferences of participants have been presented as hear learners, see learners or do learners. Fleming and Bonwell (2001) developed a questionnaire based on how our senses influence learning preferences. Focusing on three senses (seeing – visual, hearing – aural, and touching – kinaesthetic), they named their tool a VARK:

- Visual
- Aural
- Read/write
- Kinaesthetic

A coach who understands these different preferences for receiving and processing information can therefore try to present information in different ways to their participants. A coach can ensure that by using premeditated *cue* words (in italics below), an activity (such as questioning a participant to extend knowledge) can be explicitly designed to engage learners with different preferences.

For example, if coaching a high serve in badminton, the following is an illustration of the use of cue words in questioning.

- Visual: *Watch* my demonstration of the high serve. Tell me what are the three most important things in relation to generating power in the shot?
- Aural: *Listen* to the sound of the impact on the shuttle on your strings as you strike it. Why does the sound differ when you slice the shuttlecock to the right of your target?

- Read/write: *Read* this article on serving with accuracy. How can you incorporate some of these things into your service action?
- Kinaesthetic: *Feel* the transfer of weight from your back foot through to your front foot during the service action. What can you do differently to increase the transfer of weight?

However, defining a participant's learning style only by these perceptual strengths has limited effectiveness. The work of Howard Gardner (1993), who outlined the concept of a participant possessing multiple intelligences, is a more suitable starting point for coaches to begin to think about the way in which their participants can receive information in the most effective way. Gardner (1993) identified eight intelligences (see Table 5.2) that are independent of each other but which are also interrelated. Development or progress in one of the intelligences often leads to the whole constellation of intelligences being improved.

Table 5.2 Multiple intelligences (adapted from Gardner, 1993)

Intelligence	Learner characteristics: what does it involve?
Verbal/Linguistic	Reading, writing, and speaking
Logical/Mathematical	Number and computing skills
Visual/Spatial	Visual perception, mental images and orientation of body
Bodily/Kinaesthetic	Physical co-ordination and dexterity
Musical/Rhythmic	Understanding and expressing through music and rhythmic movements
Interpersonal	Communication, understanding and working collaboratively with others
Intrapersonal	Controlling one's inner world of emotions and thoughts
Naturalistic	Understanding the natural world of plants and animals

Possessing an awareness of the existence of multiple intelligences, a coach should ensure that opportunity for practice is given for bodily/kinaesthetic learners, opportunity for discussion for verbal/linguistic learners, setting movement practices to music for musical/rhythmic learners, or creating opportunity for independent work for intrapersonal learners. Coaches working on a one-to-one basis with a participant or with a small group of participants could utilise one of the multiple intelligence questionnaires (for example, Gardner (1993) or the Birmingham Grid for Learning) to provide background information about their participants' intelligence profile. It is not feasible in a large group situation for a coach to match all activities to all participants' intelligences; however, coaches should be encouraged to be creative and develop a range of activities that stimulate as many of the multiple intelligences as possible.

Other factors

In addition to perceptual strengths and intelligences, there are a number of other factors that will influence a person's learning preferences:

- biological rhythms (time of day)
- sociological (whole group or individual)
- psychological (attention span; concentration; confidence; motivation)
- environment (noise level; temperature; weather)
- physical (fitness levels).

When working with your participants in the coaching environment you will need to remember that some will not learn very well in the morning, but perform very well in the afternoon. Some work well in groups or bright, noisy environments; others do their best work on their own in quiet places with subdued lighting. Some participants need short, precise information; others need time to ask questions and reflect. Some participants need and want to be told what to do and excel with highly structured, coach directed instructional methods; others do far better when working on their own initiative in informal, unstructured coaching environments.

Using Honey and Mumford's (2001) four-factor framework for learning styles provides a very useful scaffold for coaches to build a working understanding of the complex issue of how their participants learn. Honey and Mumford (2001) use the terms activist, pragmatist, reflector and theorist to classify the different learning styles (see Table 5.3). The table presents, for each learning style, how the participant prefers to learn, their dislikes, behaviour clues to look for, relevant skills that they possess and coaching strategies to fully engage learners of this type.

Table 5.3 Learning styles and coaching (adapted from Robinson, 2010)

Style	Activist	Pragmatist	Reflector	Theorist
Prefers to learn	By doing Variety teamwork Role play	By trying Demonstrations Experimenting	By discussion Time to consider response	Facts Structured presentations Mental stimulation
Dislikes	Lengthy presentations Working alone Following instructions	Abstract theories Irrelevant discussions	Facts without meanings Tight deadlines	Irrelevant facts Emotional decisions
Behaviour clues	Competitive First of group to answer Attention wanders	Energetic Impatient Ideas into action	Watches from sidelines Thinks before speaking	Organised Deep thinker Challenges ideas
Skills	Evaluating Chairing	Predicting Exploring Problem solving	Questions Visualises Draws conclusions	Analytical Organised Prioritises
Coaching strategies	Demonstrations Visual aids Feedback Discussion	Demonstrations Repeated practice Feedback	Requires verbal articulation of skill Opportunities to talk Use video	Provide information to analyse Set problems Ask questions

Stop and think

Using Table 5.3 as a guide, for a sport and skill of your choice explain how you would as a coach engage an activist, pragmatist, reflector and theorist fully in your session.

Coaching style, method or strategy?

There is often a debate over the use of the terms coaching style, coaching method or coaching strategy in the coaching literature. Academics tend to use the terms loosely and interchangeably but this leads to confusion when wishing to articulate the use of a particular **style**, **method** or **strategy**.

For the purpose of this chapter, a coaching style is independent of the personal characteristics of

Key terms

Style – the way in which the coaching is performed

Method – the style of coaching adopted by the coach

Strategy – the actions taken by the coach in response to identified priorities for coaching

Table 5.4 The Spectrum from a coaching perspective

Letter	Name	Key characteristics	When to use it
A	Command	Coach takes decisions Participants follow instructions	Conformity Activity Safe learning
B	Practice	Coach takes most decisions Participants make some decisions Participants work at own pace	Sustained practice to refine skills Development of new skills
C	Reciprocal	Participants work in pairs Pupils receive feedback from partner	Develop co-operative behaviour Develop observational and analytical skills Practising and refining skills
D	Self-check	Participants assess own learning against given criteria Tasks set conducive to assessment	Evaluate own performance Sustained independent practice Adapting and refining skills
E	Inclusion	Allows for individual practice at appropriate level Assumes self-motivation of participants Awareness by participants of limitations needed	When working with a wide ability range Progression at own pace Responsibility for own learning Adapting and refining skills
F	Guided discovery	Coach leads participants to discover predetermined learning target Questioning used by coach	Understanding of work undertaken (e.g. tactics, game plays etc.) Participant involvement in learning wanted
G	Problem-solving	Coach presents problem Participants find many alternate solutions	Development of planning and evaluation skills Compositional skills Developing creativity
H	Individual programme	Coach decides general area to work on Participant takes decisions about what and how to do it Coach as facilitator	Develop decision-making capability
I	Learner initiated	Participant takes initiative about content and learning process Coach acts as advisor when approached by participant	Develop reflective capabilities
J	Self teach	Participant takes full responsibility for learning	Develop independence from coach (personal autonomy)

the coach and as such can be described as an instructional method. A coaching strategy identifies the priorities for coaching and is therefore directly related to the participants, the coach, and the coaching environment. As part of a coaching strategy, a coach will use a range of coaching styles or instructional methods.

What is a coaching style?

As important as *what* you are coaching is deciding on *how* you are going to coach in a particular session. Coaching styles should not be viewed as something simply implemented by a coach, but more as a component of a strategy aimed at maximising learning.

The work of Mosston and Ashworth (2008) in the field of education provides an invaluable framework for classifying the variety of styles available to a coach to maximise learning. Referred to as Mosston and Ashworth's Spectrum of Teaching Styles (The Spectrum), it presents a decision making **continuum** that gradually shifts specific clusters of decisions from the teacher to the learner to produce significantly different learning opportunities. Table 5.4 presents the ten teaching styles (A-J), documenting the name of the style, its key characteristics, and when to use it in the coaching environment.

The Spectrum can be categorised into two distinct clusters of styles: one associated with reproduction (reproduce, repeat or recall motor skills and known information – styles A to E) and the other with production (discover new information, solve problems and foster independence – styles F to J). These two clusters are divided by what is termed the discovery threshold. Figure 5.2 presents the Spectrum in diagrammatic form. **Practice** coaching

behaviour is synonymous with the 'practice styles' to the left of the discovery threshold and **discovery** coaching behaviour is associated with the 'discovery styles' located to the right.

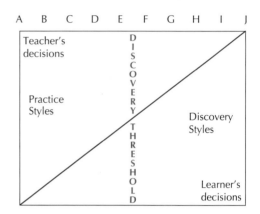

Figure 5.2 The Spectrum

Observation of coaching styles

It is a useful skill for coaches to be able to observe another coach in action and identify the range of styles that are deployed and to understand why that style was used. The following proforma is a useful tool for recording such observations.

Style	Task(s)	Why was this style used?
Command		
Practice		
Reciprocal		
Self check		
Inclusion		
Guided discovery		
Problem solving		
Individual programme		
Learner initiated		
Self teach		

Figure 5.3 Proforma for recording observations of coaching styles (available to print out at www.pearsonfe.co.uk/foundationsinsport)

Different coaching styles

The full spectrum of teaching styles developed by Mosston and Ashworth (2008) can sometimes be a cumbersome and intimidating framework for some coaches to engage with. Therefore, the simplified framework for coaching styles by Kirk et al. (1996) is a valuable summary of the most frequently used styles in the coaching environment. Kirk et al. (1996) adapted a number of Mosston and Ashworth's styles as follows.

- Direct: as Mosston and Ashworth's (2008) command style (Style A)
- Task: as Mosston and Ashworth's (2008) practice style (Style B)
- Reciprocal: as Mosston and Ashworth's (2008) reciprocal style (Style C)
- Guided discovery: as Mosston and Ashworth's (2008) guided discovery style (Style F)
- Problem solving: as Mosston and Ashworth's (2008) convergent discovery style (Style G)

Remember

The styles are positioned on a continuum. Therefore it is likely that the characteristics associated with a particular style are not necessarily exclusive to that style. Those styles positioned next to each other will share a number of the same characteristics.

The selection of a particular coaching style depends on a range of factors: the coach's own preference, intended learning outcomes, the coaching context and environment, and a range of learner characteristics such as ability, reasons for participation and learning preferences. Coaching lessons requires the use of episodes representing both sides of the Spectrum in order to accomplish the skills and thinking necessary for competent performance. Ultimately, the most effective coaches are able to switch, adapt and blend a range of styles seamlessly to match the range of factors influencing the learning experience.

Stop and think

For the following learning experiences, which of the coaching styles would be the most appropriate? Discuss your responses with a partner.

- Coaching a group of novice track and field participants in the javelin
- Developing tactical awareness in a team sport
- Coaching a group of mixed ability footballers in passing and receiving skills
- Developing personal autonomy in your participants
- Fostering co-operative behaviour between your participants

The process of communication

Once a coach decides on a particular approach or strategy to adopt in the coaching environment, information must be communicated as effectively as possible to the participants. Effective communication is dependent upon a number of different processes or stages:

- selection: selecting the information to communicate
- coding: putting the information into an agreeable form
- transmission: sending it
- reception: another person receiving the information
- decoding: recognition of the information
- interpretation: making meaning of the information.

Traditionally the process of communication has been presented as a one-way transmission of information from the coach to the participant. Usually however, a learning experience will involve the transmission of information both ways, from coach to participant and from participant to coach. Effective communication occurs when this complicated series of stages flows without any **ambiguity**, misinterpretations or mistakes. It places an emphasis on the coach and participant using multiple codes (verbal and visual) that are appropriate to the learning experience. For example, this could mean ensuring that the form of language (for verbal codes) is appropriate for the participants in the coaching environment. So when coaching children, the form of language will need to be very different from the language used when working with elite athletes. The codes selected by the coach/participant are commonly referred to as the communication channels.

> ### Key term
>
> **Ambiguity** – inexactness or being open to more than one interpretation

Communication channels

How many words do you need to coach effectively?

Fabio Capello (current England Football Manager) claims that a grasp of only '100 words' was sufficient to communicate with England's players (Daily Telegraph, 2011). Being able to communicate effectively is a crucial component of coaching practice, and this statement highlights that verbal communication is only one component of many communication channels available.

These communication channels can be roughly divided into two types:

- verbal (spoken)
- non-verbal (body language, facial expressions, gaze, posture and gestures).

The verbal channel can be further subdivided into the following:

- what is spoken
- how it is spoken (paraverbal).

The paraverbal communication channel is composed of how we modify what we say by patterns of speech (pauses, pace, intonation, volume, speed, pitch and hesitations). Put simply, the paraverbal communication channel consists of elements of speech that go beyond vocabulary and grammar. Importantly for coaching, it is crucial to consider the impact on your participants of how you say something and to take care that what you are saying is not misinterpreted. For example, is what you are saying a question, statement or a command to do something? Are you talking with irony, sarcasm or cynicism? Do you want to emphasise a particular point or draw a contrast between two things? Are you talking in a monotone voice that is demotivating for your participants?

Generally, communication channels are not used independently of one another. In coaching, a demonstration (by either the coach or a skilled participant) is seen as a crucial element of coaching effectively. Combining a visual model of a skill or technique in combination with precise verbal information is a powerful tool for engaging most learners. Following this up with opportunities to practise provides the optimum opportunity for maximising learning in the pedagogic setting. Finally, if maximising learning is the objective of coaching science, then the following quote attributed to William Glasser could help coaches in developing the most appropriate coaching strategy.

We learn:

- 10% of what we read
- 20% of what we hear
- 30% of what we see
- 50% of what we see and hear
- 70% of what we discuss
- 80% of what we experience
- 95% of what we teach others.

> ### Stop and think
>
> Drawing on the bullet point list relating to how we learn, discuss the implications of this for your coaching and identify at least two meaningful action points for your own coaching practice.

Time to reflect

- How will you ensure that you take account of the learning preferences of your participants in your coaching sessions?
- What coaching strategies would you use in order to fully engage a theorist in your coaching sessions?
- Ask a friend to observe you coaching in a variety of settings and to complete Figure 5.3 each time. Review

the coaching styles that you use and look to use as wide a range of styles as possible in your future sessions.

- Experiment in your coaching sessions with coaching styles that you are less comfortable using. Reflect on the effectiveness of these styles in different coaching situations.

Case study (for recommended answers, see www.pearsonfe.co.uk/foundationsinsport)

John is a coach working with a group of mixed ability participants. The participants all partake in weekly sessions; however, John notices that the group are not progressing at the pace which they should. John favours autocratic coaching styles and maximising participant activity in his sessions because this is what he feels more comfortable with.

Questions

1. Should John coach in a style that he feels comfortable with?

2. What coaching styles can John use that will be more democratic?

3. Tactically the participants are very naïve. What can John do to encourage tactical development?

4. Decision making in competitive situations is a real problem for his participants. What activities can John include in his sessions that would develop their decision-making capabilities?

5. What coaching styles are conducive to developing the skills of John's participants?

Check your understanding (for answers, see www.pearsonfe.co.uk/foundationsinsport)

1. Explain what is meant by 'coaching is like teaching'.
2. What is the pedagogy of coaching?
3. What are the four main theories of learning?
4. What does the acronym VARK stand for?
5. What are the four main learning styles?
6. List five multiple intelligences that a coach needs to be aware of in their participants.

7. Explain the difference between coaching style and coaching strategy.
8. List Kirk et al.'s (1996) five coaching styles.
9. List the three communication channels in ascending order of the percentage contribution of information in a message.

Useful resources

To obtain a secure link to the websites below, see the Websites section on page ii or visit the companion website at www.pearsonfe.co.uk/ foundationsinsport.

- Birmingham Grid for Learning (Multiple Intelligences Questionnaire)

- Daily Telegraph

- VARK Questionnaire

- Discover Your Preferred Learning Style

- Learning Style

- Skills Active

Further reading

Armour, K. (ed.). (2011). *Sport pedagogy: an introduction for teaching and coaching*. London: Prentice Hall.

Cain, N. (2004). 'Question time for the coaches: the six men plotting their countries' fortunes on the best and worst of their jobs'. *The Sunday Times*, Sport section, p.9.

Cassidy, T., Jones, R.L. and Potrac, P. (2009). *Understanding sports coaching: the social, cultural and pedagogical foundations of coaching practice* (2nd edition). London: Routledge.

Chambers, F. (2011). Learning theory for effective learning in practice. In: K. Armour (ed.). *Sport pedagogy: an introduction for teaching and coaching*. London: Prentice Hall, pp.39-52.

Denison, J. (ed.). (1997). *Coaching knowledges: understanding the dynamics of sport performance*. London: A&C Black.

Department for Culture, Media and Sport (DCMS). (2002). *The coaching task force: final report*. London: DCMS.

Dunn, R. & Griggs, S.A. (1988). *Learning styles: quiet revolution in American secondary schools*. Reston, VA: National Association of Secondary School Principals.

Fleming, N. and Bonwell, C. (2001). *How do I learn best? A student's guide to improved learning*. Christchurch, NZ: Fleming and Bonwell.

Gardner, H. (1993). *Multiple intelligences*. New York: Basic Books.

Honey, P. and Mumford, A. (2001). *The learning styles helpers guide*. Maidenhead, UK: Peter Honey Publications Ltd.

Jones, R.L., Armour, K.M. and Potrac, P. (2004). *Sports coaching cultures: from practice to theory*. London: Routledge.

Kirk, D., Macdonald, D. and O'Sullivan, M. (eds.). (2006). *The handbook of physical education*. London: Sage.

Kirk, D., Nauright, J., Hanrahan, S., Macdonald, D. and Jobling, I. (1996). *The sociocultural foundations of human movement*. Melbourne: Macmillan.

Kidman, L. and Hanrahan, S. (2011). *The coaching process: a practical guide to improving your effectiveness* (3rd edition). Palmerston North: Dunmore.

Lombardo, B.J. (1987). *The humanistic coach: from theory to practice*. Springfield, Ill: C.C. Thomas.

Lyle, J. (2002). *Sports coaching concepts: a framework for coaches' behaviour*. London: Routledge.

Martens, R. (2004). *Successful coaching* (3rd edition). Champaign, Ill: Human Kinetics.

Mehrabian, A. (1968). Communication without words. *Psychology Today*. 2 (9), 52-55.

Mosston, M. & Ashworth, S. (2008). *Teaching physical education*. First online edition http://www. spectrumofteachingstyles.org/ebook

Robinson, P.E. (2010). *Foundations of sports coaching*. London: Routledge.

Skills Active. (2011). Sport and recreation [online]. See 'useful resources' for source. [Accessed 23 March 2011].

Daily Telegraph. (2011). England v Ghana: all I need is 100 words of English, claims Fabio Capello [online]. See 'useful resources' for source. [Accessed 06 April 2011].

Chapter 6

Sociology for coaches

Introduction

An interpretation of physiology, psychology and biomechanics gives you a greater understanding of athletes and their performances. An understanding of how the body functions in relation to sport, or how the mind copes with the pressures of athletic performance, can inform a coach of the best practices. However, a coach also needs to understand how best to manage their athletes. Coaches and athletes interact with one another on a routine and perhaps daily basis. The way in which coaches manage this interaction and their relationship with athletes is vital and helps to ensure that optimal performances are achieved.

Research has highlighted the importance of approaching coaching from a sociological perspective (Jones, 2000). Issues such as gender, race and ethnicity, class and religion are prominent social forces that impact upon the coaching process. Coaches must be aware of the social role they play within the coaching process as how they interact with their athletes, on an individual and group basis, plays a large part in achieving excellence. Sociology helps us to explore everyday interactions between coach and athlete – providing an understanding of behaviour displayed within the coaching process. A sociological perspective allows you to gain a deeper insight into the wider social forces that shape the interactions which occur between the coach and athletes.

Learning outcomes:

After you have read this chapter you should be able to:

- define the concept of sociology
- understand the terms 'culture' and 'society'
- understand and apply the term 'macro-sociology' to sport
- identify how race, ethnicity, gender and class impact upon the coaching process
- understand and apply the term 'micro-sociology' to sport
- identify how a coach's behaviour, role and position of power can impact upon the coaching process.

As part of a community coaching project you have been asked to coach a group of young recreational footballers (9–11 years old). The group includes boys and girls who come from varying ethnic backgrounds.

- Consider how you would gather the relevant 'need to know' information that would help to build an effective coach–athlete relationship.

- Consider the differences you may encounter when coaching both male and female athletes.

- In this instance, what is the most important role to adopt as coach and why?

- How may your behaviour and use of language as a coach differ between this age group and adult players?

The concept of sociology

Giddens (1989, p. 7) states that, 'sociology is the study of human social life, groups and societies. It is a dazzling and compelling enterprise, having as its subject-matter our own behaviour as social beings'. As Giddens (1989) indicates, **sociology** is primarily concerned with the study of human life, social groups and wider social issues. The study of sociology aims to understand how individuals within society interact within their cultural settings. Studying these interactions offers a greater understanding of a person or group's behaviour and actions. In addition, sociology can provide the knowledge and understanding of how broader social issues, such as politics, economics and law, may influence our behaviour on a daily basis. Sociological investigation can range from analysing everyday interactions between individuals in a classroom or on a training ground up to the investigation of global social processes that impact upon how you make sense of the world.

Key term

Sociology – the study of human life; observing how individuals interact and examining the cultural settings in which people live

Much of what we learn about our immediate surroundings and, to a certain extent, the wider social sphere, can be determined through common sense. However, as Mills (1959) suggests, society is constantly evolving, producing increasingly more complex problems that require more than common sense to understand and address. A sociological perspective helps us to understand the consequences of our actions and how they impact upon the immediate and wider social settings of our varied cultures. The study of sociology also provides the tools to describe what can be understood as rather complex social relations, such as the impact of government policy on sport and sports development. Additionally it may help us to understand the quite simple social relations and interactions that occur within our lives, such as behaviour at work or in leisure time.

Social structure

An important concept that explores the link between individual behaviour and the wider social setting is the concept of 'social structure'. Giddens (1989, p. 19) notes that 'the social environments in which we exist do not just consist of random assortments of events or actions. There are **underlying regularities**, or **patternings**, in how people behave and in the relationships in which they stand with one another'. The social environments that Giddens (1989) refers to are made up of human actions and relationships. Within a given social environment, regularities of behaviour occur over a period of time to give these social structures a pattern. How we interact as human beings among our peers is greatly affected by the structural characteristics of the cultural settings and societies in which we are raised and live. At the same time we can recreate and perhaps even modify those **structural characteristics** that help to form and shape our actions. Sociology helps

Key terms

Underlying regularities or **patternings** – patterns of social behaviour and relationships that occur regularly within a particular social environment. These patternings or regularities help to build social structure

Structural characteristics – social structures are comprised of the human interactions and relationships that are present within a society to explain how human cultures and societies are built, and re-built, by the very actions of individuals who exist within them.

Culture and society

The terms **culture** and **society** are frequently used within the study of sociology; therefore, it is important to have a good understanding of these.

> ### Key terms
>
> **Culture** – consists of the shared values of a group of people that guide specific behaviour
>
> **Society** – a distinct collection of people who are bound together through the same political system and sense of self-identity

Culture

Brislin (1993, page 4) suggests that culture 'consists of ideals, values, and assumptions about life that are widely shared among people and that guide specific behaviours'. Culture, therefore, comprises the key elements that shape our way of living. Culture is shaped by the interaction you experience between groups of people and can have a huge influence upon your lifestyle choices. It could be said that culture is created by people.

The concept of culture can relate to a number of different aspects within a certain society and can be analysed from an ethical, artistic, political and **socio-economic perspective**. An understanding of culture helps to explain the customs, values and attitudes that occur within a particular society.

> ### Key term
>
> **Socio-economic perspective** – highlights the importance of using economics in the study of society

Sport as a cultural practice

A number of specific activities that are human creations exist within the fabric of cultures, such as music, dance and art, all of which help to express the thoughts, feelings and core values of a given culture. These particular activities may be referred to as cultural practices and can differ from place to place and over time. Sport may also be considered a cultural practice.

According to Coakley (1998), sport is composed of human interaction, varying in its structure and meaning from place to place and constantly changing over time. The perception of certain sports can vary from place to place, reflecting the key values of a particular culture. For example, netball in the UK is still perceived as a 'girls' sport with relatively little male participation, whereas in Australia it is viewed as a mixed gender sport with an increasing number of male netball players. Australia has even established an 'All Australian Men's and Mixed Netball Association'.

Sport may also alter over time; for example, how you view, appreciate and understand soccer within the UK has changed dramatically since the unruly days of 'mob football'.

Cultural values

Cultural values within any society can change over time, but certain values, usually those central to a particular culture, remain relatively stable and can be quite difficult to change. For example, it was not until 1990 that Augusta National Golf Club, a prestigious golf club located in Georgia, United States of America (USA), accepted its first black member. Moreover, it was not until September 1998 that a woman was allowed membership to the exclusive Marylebone Cricket Club (MCC), thus ending 212 years of male exclusivity.

Culture may be viewed as having both static and dynamic components. Certain values that are associated with a specific culture may remain stable for long periods of time, whereas other values can be changed or introduced to a particular culture. These changes can be affected by outside influences, such as the colonial influences of introducing cricket to the West Indies or hockey to India, or through the introduction of technological and industrial advancements within a certain society. That said, the concept of culture is of great importance as it allows you to explain the way a given society functions and how those participants within the society interact with one another.

Society

The term society relates to the structural make-up of a given community of people. As Coakley (1998, page 3) suggests, society can refer to 'a collection of people living in a defined geographical territory and united through a political system and a shared sense of self-identification that distinguishes them from other collections of people'. In this instance you may refer to society as a national identity, where a large number of individuals belong to a group that is distinctive from others.

It is evident that China's political system and the Chinese population's sense of identity will be very different from that of individuals living in the UK. China and the UK present different societies that incorporate a different way of living and uphold different cultural values. There are certain sports or games in China, such as Tai Chi or Mahzhong, that convey specific meanings that can only be understood in relation to Chinese culture, society and history. Therefore, societies and the cultural practices within them may be unique and should be understood within a specific context. To gain a comprehensive view of society it is necessary to understand this concept from a theoretical position. A useful theory that helps to explain the structure and functioning of a society is **functionalism**.

Key term

Functionalism – a social theory used to understand society. Functionalism suggests that society contains many interrelated social systems that aim to promote balance in order to continue to operate efficiently

Theory and society

A functionalist perspective provides a useful analysis of the concept of society and provides a holistic approach to the topic area. Herbert Spencer, an influential figure in the modern version of functionalism, provided a useful understanding of the structure and functioning of societies. Spencer's interpretation of the structure and functioning of society include the following key findings.

- Society represents a structure that is able to grow and develop.

- An increase in the size of a given society tends to lead to an increase in the complexity and separation of that society.

- A progressive separation within the structure of a given society is accompanied by a separation in its function.

- Parts of a society are interdependent with a change in one part having an effect on other parts.

- Society is comprised of many **micro-societies** that are interlinked to form the whole.

Key term

Micro-societies – smaller social groupings that are interrelated help to make up the wider picture of society

A functionalist approach indicates that society is best understood as containing many social systems that are interrelated to help maintain balance and form the structure of the wider society. Functionalism suggests that the social systems of society are bound by a shared group of norms or values that promote acceptance and conformity.

If we take sport as an example of one such social system we can see how specific norms and values related to social cohesion, leadership, fair play and team work are adopted by athletes within sport and contribute to the preservation of social order through promoting such values within a team. However, social systems can become dysfunctional; Loy and Booth (2000) note that structural imbalances occur within a society when individuals adopt different cultural goals or different means to achieving these particular goals.

In order to gain a greater understanding of a particular society, it is necessary to view the individual social systems, such as family, the economy, religion, politics and sport, and how they interact or relate with one another to ensure that they contribute towards a balanced society. Although this is not the only social theory that explains the notion of society (more examples are provided in Table 6.1) it does provide a good basis for exploring the structural components that make up a given society. From this perspective an analysis of smaller social systems can provide a broader picture of how certain societies are structured and function. Therefore, as the functionalist perspective suggests, making sense of the whole requires you to look at the individual parts of society to see how they function and interact and, eventually, impact upon the wider social structure.

Table 6.1 Social theories used to understand sport in society

Social theories	Application to sport
Interactionist perspective	Seeks to discover how athletes and coaches make sense of their identity. Explores the key values associated with sports subcultures identifying how they are created and sustained through the process of interaction.
Feminist perspective	Explores the notion that sports may reproduce or contest gender stereotypes in society. Suggests that the sports world can also reinforce or challenge common ideas concerning masculinity and femininity.
Critical perspective	Indicates that sports are socially constructed and can be understood by adopting a historical context. Highlights the importance that sports can reflect society but simultaneously challenge, transform and resist the way in which social life is organised
Conflict perspective	Suggests that sport promotes the interest of people with economic power, coercing and controlling athletes. Sport can also be seen to perpetuate the unequal distribution of power witnessed within society.

Stop and think

Review the relevant social theories identified within Table 6.1. How can they be applied to specific examples within the modern world of sport?

Coaching and a macro-sociological approach

Society is composed of many different social systems. One way in which you can gain a useful interpretation of how such social systems function is through the use of a macro analysis. **Macro-sociology** is concerned with how the broader social systems, such as work, education, religion, the media or the economic order, impact upon the way in which people interact or live their lives. A macro-sociologist will attempt to understand the institutional nature of society, analysing the framework in which you live and explore it in relation to the social interactions that occur. Macro-sociology also looks at how certain institutions in society develop over time, such as the growth of industrialism and the rise of **urbanism**. A macro analysis can help you to understand how the broader institutional framework of sport impacts upon the social experiences of those involved at all levels.

Key terms

Macro-sociology – the study of large-scale social phenomena, especially the comparison of whole societies with each other (Douglas, 1973)

Urbanism – an analysis of the geographical, political, economical and social factors that impact upon and arise within urban areas

Social perspectives of sport

The coach–athlete relationship witnessed in sport can be explained as a social phenomenon as it is not only the small scale interaction that comes to influence this dynamic relationship. A consideration of the wider social processes including politics, class, gender and ethnicity is important when exploring the coaching process from a sociological perspective. Such large-scale social factors play an influential part in shaping the coaching process. The impact of these wider social processes informs your understanding of the nature of sport and the social experiences of a range of athletes who participate. Jones (2000, page 36) notes that 'if coaches are to truly maximise the potential of their athletes, an understanding of the social context which could influence behaviour seems obvious'.

By adopting a broader social perspective of sport, a coach can begin to gain a greater understanding of the social framework in which their athletes exist and thus help them to reach their full potential.

Four useful examples that will help you draw upon the wider social forces that impact upon your interpretation and understanding of sport are race, ethnicity, gender and class. By analysing these factors from a macro perspective you can see how they shape or form your perspective of sport at the level of coach–athlete interaction.

How race and ethnicity, gender and class impact upon the coaching process

Race and ethnicity

Issues surrounding race and ethnicity have impacted greatly upon the world of sport and have come to form many perceptions regarding athlete participation over the years. A macro analysis of race and ethnicity has unearthed and exposed patterns of participation that reflect wider social beliefs regarding such concepts.

The concept of 'race' was developed in the 1700s to explain the differences among populations. This concept was closely linked with specific biological categorisations of different races. Championed by the white European colonial powers of the time this notion of race ideology suggested that white-skinned people were intellectually superior to people of other colours. Such beliefs were reflected in sports participation as achievements of white athletes were supposedly related to their character, culture and organisation. Conversely, the achievements of black athletes were believed to be based upon biological prowess and natural physical abilities.

Effects of racial stereotypes

This particular 'race logic' witnessed within society and the effects of racism have been reflected in sports participation as many athletes face common **stereotypes** concerning sports participation; for example, that black athletes are naturally quick and strong and white athletes are calm under pressure and good tactical thinkers. This has led to players being placed in specific sporting positions within a team simply because of racial stereotypes. This particular phenomenon can be described by the social process of '**stacking**', i.e. 'Where members of particular minority ethnic groups are

disproportionately represented in certain positions in team sports' (Fleming and Jones, 2008, pp. 47).

Obvious examples of 'stacking' in sport could be seen in soccer (Maguire, 1988). Positions that require speed, strength and power, such as the wide players or attacking players, were traditionally reserved for black footballers. Positions that required more cognitive ability and tactical skill, such as central midfield positions, were notably occupied by white players. This concept has been closely linked to the notion of '**centrality**' (Loy and McElvogue, 1970). Central positions within team sports often require frequent and wide-ranging interaction between teammates. Black athletes are excluded from central positions as athletic stereotypes suggest that they do not possess interaction and decision-making skills.

This way of thinking also impacts upon the career transition of athletes into coaching and management when head coaches or previous managers look to select former players with a proven record in decision making. Preconceived views regarding race and athletic ability in sports dictate wider patterns of participation as people may start to play certain sports based on the stereotypical views that determine race logic.

Race and ethnicity continue to present contested issues in the wider social sphere. How we perceive race and ethnicity within society can be reflected or amplified in sport and sports participation. However, sport is becoming increasingly more culturally diverse; therefore you as a coach must be aware of the varying cultural backgrounds of the athletes.

Ethnic and cultural issues enter into the interaction between coach and athlete and coaches must be aware of the cultural sensitivities that are common to many different ethnic groups. It is clear that certain stereotypes related to race and ethnicity continue to exist within society and continue to infiltrate their way into sport. Coaches must be adept at recognising such stereotypes and act to ensure that participation does not reflect or perpetuate the particular values that are associated with the traditional construction of race logic often witnessed on the playing field.

Key terms

Stereotypes – a popular belief about a particular type of individual or specific social group based on prior assumption. Often stereotypes can be misleading and give an unfair or inaccurate representation of a particular individual, social group or culture

Stacking – the disproportionate representation of particular ethnic minority groups in specific positions in team sports

Centrality – the exclusion of ethnic minorities from central positions of power and decision making in team sports and organisations

Stop and think

Think of a coaching session you have been involved with. Did players from certain ethnicities favour specific positions? If so, why may this have been the case? If not, what does this say about the theory of 'stacking' in sports?

Gender

The dominant ideology associated with femininity in modern society suggests that the female form should be 'firm but shapely, fit but sexy, strong but thin' (Markula, 1995, p. 424). These particular values that are demonstrated throughout society can be reflected, and often perpetuated, within sport. Women who show interest or participate in certain sports that are viewed as reserved typically for men, such as football or rugby, risk facing judgements regarding their sexuality. To challenge the **dominant norms** associated with femininity in both sport and society leads to the labelling of female athletes as 'abnormal' or 'unnatural'.

Gender stereotypes in sport

Research investigating gender relations in sport (Koivula, 1999; Lenskyj, 1998, and Stevenson, 2002) has suggested that the print and televised media contribute towards the construction of gender differences in sport. An over-emphasis on the sexualisation of female athletes or women's sport in general helps to perpetuate the stereotypical values and images that are often associated with women in sport.

Key terms

Dominant norms – the key values usually associated with a concept or identity. Values or ideas that inform your opinion relating to common issues in society such as gender, ethnicity and class

Sexualisation – presenting a person, group or thing as sexual in nature. In sport this is usually conducted by the print and televised media focusing on the body image of female athletes to attract increased audiences and readers

Women's tennis provides a useful example when issues of sexuality and gender differentiation are discussed, including the case of Anna Kournikova. Much of the media attention throughout Kournikova's career focused on her body shape and sexuality rather than her performance. The media's focus and portrayal of Kournikova reinforced the dominant ideology surrounding the female form in sport. However, Amelie Mauresmo, another successful tennis player, appeared to contradict the dominant discourses of femininity and sexuality displaying a muscular frame. Consequently Mauresmo was labelled as overtly masculine by the print media and immediately faced issues concerning her sexuality.

Although many different types of body shape can be associated with female tennis, it would appear that social systems, such as the media, influence society's perception of body image and understanding of gender in sport. The view of society and the media's portrayal of what is seen as desirable within women's sport takes the focus away from the achievements and performance of the athletes. Coaches must be aware of the gender stereotypes within society and commonly witnessed throughout sport. In order to achieve greater gender equity in sport, coaches must change the way in which they organise and promote participation with greater integration between male and female athletes.

Structural changes to the world of sport will help to achieve greater equity. This should include a greater number of women situated in positions of power and authority within the realm of 'men's sport' both on and off the field of play. However, before such change can be instigated, society's view of gender relations also needs changing and the stereotypical notions and values that form our understanding of men and women both in sport and the wider society must be abolished.

A typical media image reinforcing the gender stereotypes associated with women in sport. How can this image be both beneficial and detrimental to women's sport?

Stop and think

When considering the notion of equity in sports coaching, discuss with a partner whether female coaches should coach male sports teams. What barriers would female coaches face when having to coach an all-male sports team? What barriers might a male coach have when faced with coaching an all-female team? How do they differ?

Class

Throughout society, class issues have come to shape the type and level of participation that is witnessed within sport. Sport reflects the inequality of social classes throughout society. The link between class, power and economic wealth has meant that those who control and organise sport come from an elitist background. Those in positions of power and wealth are able to organise and control certain resources that are necessary to establish sports events and organisations.

Economic and social inequalities

The economic inequalities witnessed within society have contributed towards certain sports participation patterns. Coakley (1998, page 299) suggests that 'the long-term impact of economic inequality in people's lives has led to connections between certain sports and the lifestyle of people with differing amounts of wealth and power'. Bourdieu (1994) closely associated the notion of lifestyle with a social group's class, suggesting that economic capital and cultural values may determine the patterns of sports participation among the social classes. Cultural values that impact upon your lifestyle can relate to the clothes you wear, the food you eat, the books you read or the music you listen to. Sports such as polo, golf, rowing and sailing are associated with an upper-class lifestyle as access to these sports often requires wealth and high social status. These particular sports can promote social exclusivity as those who do not posses wealth or hold cultural values associated with the upper-classes are often denied access.

Despite the implications of social class, sports may provide avenues to success for some; however, it is clear that for many individuals sports participation is connected to patterns of social inequality that are present in society. The sports you play and the sports you watch or follow are largely associated with the values you hold in relation to the lifestyle you lead. Certain values are therefore associated with specific sports; for example, boxing is perceived as a working-class sport where values relating to hard-work, desire, self-sacrifice and 'hunger' are prominent. Those who do not fit the required 'social profile' may be excluded from excelling within the sport or may not even compete.

Implications for coaching

Sports coaches must therefore be aware of the diverse social backgrounds of the participants who shape certain sports teams or groups. An understanding of the variety of interests and differences in athletes' experiences will allow coaches to gain a greater consideration for their athletes' personal backgrounds and views on participation. An improved knowledge of the wider concepts relating to class and social status will allow coaches to reflect upon the ways in which they may contest – or perpetuate – certain inequalities related to social class (Armour, 2000).

Class is an important issue for you as an aspiring coach and should be understood as part of the wider coaching process, as the way in which coaches view class relations in sport will determine their opinions concerning participation. Like gender, race and ethnicity, class is an integral feature of sport that can promote and reflect dominant ideologies associated with the wider social view.

Soccer is still perceived as very much a working-class sport

This opinion, however, is slowly changing. However, soccer is still played and watched by people from some of the poorest countries in the world. Why do you think soccer is accessible to such a large audience? Consider your answer in relation to the cultural values of the sport and the cost needed to participate.

Stop and think

Reflect upon a recent coaching session. Can you identify the class of your athletes? Were they a mixed group in terms of class? What criteria did you use to identify their class status?

In pairs, discuss the perceived barriers to participation that stem from issues of class inequality. Refer to Chapter 2 (Sports development: coaching in context) to help inform your answer.

Remember

Both your social and economic class status has a huge impact upon the sports you play and enjoy. Sport provides a platform for reflecting inequalities in class and can also help to perpetuate such inequalities. As coaches you must be aware of how class can dictate patterns of participation to ensure that you provide a more inclusive approach towards player selection and promotion.

Coaching and a micro-sociological approach

In recent years very little importance has been placed upon the social forces that help to shape coaching practices. Jones et al. (2002, page 34) indicate that 'despite the recent increase of research into coaching, the essential social and cultural nature of the process has received little attention'. An increased scientific approach towards coaching has steered attention away from the fact that coaching occurs within a social context. This particular social context is shaped and defined by the interaction and power relations that occur between the coach and athlete.

In order to gain a greater understanding of the coach-athlete relationship a micro analysis is required. Giddens (1989, page 113) defines **micro-sociology** as 'the study of everyday behaviour in situations of face-to-face interaction'. Rather than focusing on the larger social systems that shape the coach–athlete dynamic, a focus on the face-to-face interaction between the coach and athlete helps you to understand the role which both play. This understanding can include an investigation into the construction of a coach's identity and the power relations that exist between both a coach and his or her athlete.

Coaching behaviour and identity

A micro-sociological analysis helps you to understand and explain how coaches may sustain and perpetuate their identity in relation to their social surroundings. Such an approach exposes the dominant values that are often associated with the practice of coaching itself. An **interactionist**

perspective, one that looks at face-to-face interaction, can help to explore the complexities of the coach–athlete relationship.

The interactionist perspective

An interactionist approach suggests that when you adopt a particular position within a social setting certain values are predetermined and, as social actors, you must adhere to them as best you can in order to live out that particular role or position successfully. This theory suggests that these values or meanings associated with an identity or role are constructed through forms of social interaction. When you walk into a social setting you know how to act as you become aware of the social norms and values that surround you; once they are adopted and displayed successfully you become accepted as part of that particular social environment. An interactionist perspective explores what it means to *be* a coach, how coaches come to construct their own identity and the key values associated with a sporting subculture.

In order to sustain the identity of a coach you must go through what Goffman (1959) termed 'impression management'. Goffman (1961, page 87) suggested that 'in performing a role the individual must see to it that the impressions of him conveyed in the situation are compatible with role-appropriate personal qualities effectively imputed to him'. Therefore, a coach must possess the required knowledge and ensure that they display the desired role – upholding the appearance of a well-informed and effective coach.

A coach takes on a varying number of roles (see Figure 6.1) such as a paternal or maternal role, a motivator, disciplinarian, manager and even friend. How they display the desired role that they wish to convey may be demonstrated through their use of language, behaviour or interaction among the athletes. For example, it is quite common to witness an authoritarian style of coaching within youth football where abusive language, threats of physical exercise as punishment and personal criticism are commonplace (Cushion and Jones, 2006). This is perceived as normative behaviour and reinforces the role of the coach as disciplinarian and an **autocratic leader**.

Coaches may also tailor their behaviour to fit the requirements of the players and the coaching environment that surrounds them, in order to ensure that respect is generated from the athletes they coach (Potrac et al. 2002). In this instance the coaching process may be viewed as a performance, where the importance lies in how they are viewed amongst the athletes they coach. Here coaches are striving to portray an idealised view of what they perceive a coach *should* be – through the eyes of their athletes. The coach must continuously use a role to ensure that they get the best out of their athletes. However, they are simultaneously fulfilling the expectations of their athletes as they will also have a firm understanding of what a coach *is* and how they should behave. The coaching process can be viewed here as a social interaction where meaning and identity are attached to the role of the coach because of the way that the athletes and the coach each fulfil their expectations.

A key part of the coach–athlete interaction is the position of power that coaches hold over their athlete. The concept of power may also be viewed from a position of interaction and may explain certain behaviours that are displayed by both the coach and athlete.

Figure 6.1 (below) demonstrates the different roles a coach can adopt. Can these roles overlap? Are some more important than others? Does the age of the athletes have an impact upon your role as a coach?

Key terms

Micro-sociology – the study of everyday behaviour and the face-to-face interaction of individuals within a particular social setting

Interactionist perspective – a sociological perspective that examines how roles are established through interaction between individuals and adherence to predetermined social values

Autocratic leader – in sport a leader who takes control of the athlete, dictating their actions and decisions. Autocratic leaders rarely consider the perspective of the athlete and their opinion of athletes is heavily influenced by successful or unsuccessful performances

Coaching behaviour, role and power

Coaches are often in positions of power and the way in which they use this particular position may also dictate their interaction with the athletes around them. Power is an essential element of the coaching process and, as Jones et al. (2002) suggest, it is integral to use the position of power if coaches want athletes to fulfil their respective potential. Athletes are also reliant on their coaches, in terms of supplying knowledge, and in terms of measuring performances, organising training activities, guiding their lifestyles and ultimately constructing their identities as elite or professional athletes.

Hierarchy and deviancy

The hierarchical relationship established between the coach and athlete illustrates the amount of power that a coach can hold over an athlete and the dependency an athlete may have on a coach. Often athletes will carry out a number of tasks requested by the coach without resistance or hesitation. These tasks may be detrimental to the athletes' performance and health, such as training while injured or ill, adhering to a strict and limited diet or even using performance enhancing drugs – all in an attempt to achieve excellence. In this instance it is quite common to hear of a gymnast who lives by eating an apple a day and nothing else, a footballer who plays with a badly sprained ankle or a cyclist involved with blood doping.

Coaches, in some instances, may form a detached view of their athletes and treat them in mechanistic ways – focusing upon the regimented shaping and training of their bodies. Due to this established hierarchy, and the convincing role that coaches portray, athletes may buy into this particular social relationship and become subject to power regimes that are established by the coaches. It is through this social construction that athletes may engage in deviant behaviour that is enforced through pressures applied by coaching staff.

Although this power is effective in ensuring that athletes follow the required instructions, not all coaches adopt this style of coaching. As Jones et al. (2002) suggest, power does not simply rest in the hands of the coach; the athlete must consent to power being used upon them before it can be effective. Therefore, an autocratic or authoritarian approach may be ineffective as athletes can resist it. That said, it is still important for a coach to realise the vulnerability of athletes and the potential power and control they hold over the individuals they train.

The way in which coaches interact with athletes, including the language they use, the behaviour they adopt and the relationship they sustain, requires attention. A sociological perspective highlights the common behavioural traits witnessed within the coaching process. Adopting a sociological perspective helps coaches to understand and become more aware of the athletes they coach. By considering their actions, and position of power, coaches can ensure that a wholesome and productive relationship is established and sustained with their athletes.

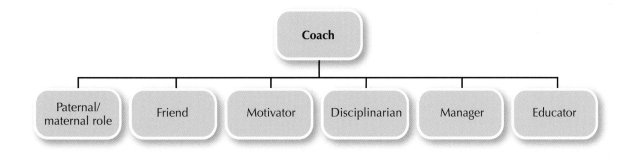

Figure 6.1 Different coaching roles

Stop and think

How may a coach's behaviour impact negatively upon the individuals they train?

When coaching different age groups, how does the role of coach differ?

Discuss with a partner as to whether the coaching style should differ between elite and recreational athletes – provide reasons for your answer.

Remember

A coach's position of power will influence an athlete's level of performance significantly. The level of power you hold over an athlete, if managed incorrectly, can lead to de-motivation and a decrease in performance. As an effective coach you must consider the amount of power and decision making that is given to an athlete.

Time to reflect

- Have you ever witnessed 'stacking' in sport? Think of the sports you play and watch on TV: are the positions in team sports related to race and ethnicity?

- What about specific sports? Are some dominated by one particular ethnic group? Discuss why this might be the case.

- How does media coverage impact upon our understanding of women in sport? In pairs, consider the print media in sport: how much is devoted to female coverage?

- How are women portrayed by the media? What do they focus on: performance or body image? Think of the language they use.

- In groups of three, consider a variety of sports that you either play or would like to play: how has the issue of class impacted upon patterns of participation?

- Are some sports reserved for the upper-classes? Can class, from a social and economic perspective, explain how and why people participate in these sports?

- In pairs, discuss how a coach's position of power can impact upon the athletes they coach. What sort of roles does a coach have to adopt?

- What sort of behaviour may an athlete engage in under the influence of their coach?

Case study (for recommended answers, see www.pearsonfe.co.uk/foundationsinsport)

Ali is the head coach of a top ten ranked female tennis player and she takes pride in her disciplined approach to training. She ensures that her star athlete adheres to a strict diet to maintain the correct body weight and shape in order to excel in her sport. Ali also emphasises the importance of maintaining a feminine physique to ensure that her star athlete continues to please her commercial sponsors. Ali continues to reinforce the importance of training hard, a disciplined lifestyle and suggests that playing with pain and injury is a necessary part of the game. As a coach with a history of success within the game, Ali feels that a distanced approach towards her athlete is the best possible coaching role to adopt in order to create success. Ali also feels that an autocratic approach to coaching fulfils the requirements of an effective coaching role and should not be altered.

Halfway through the season Ali witnesses a noticeable decline in the performance of her athlete and her ATP ranking begins to fall. Due to increasing pressure from her sponsors, Ali's star athlete begins to focus on her body image rather than her performance and it has become apparent that she has developed an eating disorder. In addition she appears to have been playing and training the second half of her season with a stress fracture in her left foot. Ali continues to adopt an authoritarian role in relation to training to see if she can improve her athlete's performance but motivation to play continues to decline and her performance slips even further.

Questions

1. How does the coach's role impact upon the performance of the athlete?

2. How does the coach's position of power influence the athlete's behaviour towards training?

3. What can be done to alter the coach's perception of a good coaching practitioner?

4. How can an awareness of gender relations in sport help the coach to understand the athlete's obsession with body image?

Check your understanding (for answers, see www.pearsonfe.co.uk/foundationsinsport)

1. Define the concept of sociology.

2. Provide an example of how sports may differ from culture to culture.

3. How does a functionalist approach attempt to explain the notion of society?

4. What is the difference between macro-sociology and micro-sociology?

5. Define the term 'stacking' and provide a relevant sporting example of this particular social phenomenon.

6. What is the traditional perception of women's body shape in sport?

7. How are those women who play traditional 'male sports' viewed in the public eye?

8. Explain how class impacts upon patterns of participation in sport.

9. How does a coach construct and maintain their identity among the athletes they train?

10. Why is the concept of power important and how can it impact negatively upon the coach–athlete relationship?

Useful resources

To obtain a secure link to the websites below, see the Websites section on page ii or visit the companion website at www.pearsonfe.co.uk/foundationsinsport.

- International Review for the Sociology of Sport
- Sociology of Sport Journal
- Journal of Sport and Social Issues
- Sport, Education and Society Journal
- All Australian Men's and Mixed Netball Association

Further reading

Armour, K. M. (2000). 'We're all middle class now'. Sport and social class in contemporary Britain. In Jones, R. L. and Armour, K. M. (eds) *Sociology of sport: theory and practice*, Harlow, Pearson Education

Brislin, R. (1993). *Understanding culture's influence on behaviour.* New York: Harcourt Brace College Publishers.

Bourdieu, P. (1994). *Distinction: a social critique of the judgement of taste.* London: Routledge.

Coakley, J. (1998). Sport in society: issues and controversies. (6th edition) Boston, Massachusetts: McGraw-Hill.

Cushion, C., and Jones, R. L. (2006). Power, discourse, and symbolic violence in professional youth soccer: the case of albion football club. *Sociology of Sport Journal,* 23, 142-161.

Douglas, J. R. (1973). *Introduction to sociology situations and structure.* New York: The Free Press.

Fleming, S., and Jones, R. L. (2008). Sociology for coaches. In Jones, R. L., Hughes, M., & Kingston K. (eds). *An Introduction to Sports Coaching from Science and Theory to Practice.* London: Routledge, pp. 43-51.

Goffman, E. (1959). *The Presentation of Self in Everyday Life.* London: Pelican Books.

Goffman, E. (1961). *Encounters.* Indianapolis: The Bobbs-Merrill Company.

Giddens, A. (1989). *Sociology.* Oxford: Polity Press.

Jones, R. L. (2000). Toward a sociology of coaching. In Jones, R. L. and Amour, K. M. (eds). *Sociology of Sport Theory and Practice.* Harlow: Longman, pp. 33-43.

Jones, R. L., Armour, K. M., and Potrac, P. (2002). Understanding the coaching process: a framework for social analysis. *Quest,* 54, 34-48.

Koivula, N. (1999). Gender stereotyping in televised media sport coverage. In *Sex Roles,* 41, 8, 589-604.

Lenskyj, H. J. (1998). 'Inside sport' or 'on the margins'?: Australian women and the sport media. *International Review for the Sociology of Sport,* 33, 19-32.

Loy, J. W., & Booth, D. (2000) Functionalism, sport and society. In Coackley, J., & Dunning, E. (ed). *Handbook of sport studies.* London: Sage. (pp. 8-27).

Loy, J. W., and McElvogue, J. F. (1970). Racial segregation in American Sport. *International Review for the Sociology of Sport,* 5, 5-21.

Mills, C. W. (1959). *The sociological imagination.* Oxford University Press: London.

Maguire, J. (1988). Race and position assignment in English soccer: a preliminary analysis of ethnicity and sport in Britain. *Sociology of Sport Journal,* 5, 3, 257-269.

Markula, P. (1995). Firm but shapely, fit but sexy, strong but thin: the postmodern aerobicising female bodies. *Sociology of Sport Journal,* 12, 424-453.

Potrac, P., Jones, R., and Armour, K. (2002). 'It's all about getting respect': the coaching behaviour of an expert English soccer coach. *Sport, Education and Society,* 7, 2, 183-202.

Stevenson, D. (2002). Women, sport, and globalisation: competing discourses of sexuality and nation. *Journal of Sport and Social Issues,* 26, 209-225.

Woodman, L. (1993). 'Coaching: a science, an art, an emerging profession.' *Sport Science Review,* 2, 1-13.

Chapter 7

Anatomy and physiology for coaches

Introduction

A comprehensive understanding of anatomy and physiology is essential for any good sports coach. It can make the difference between you passing or failing your foundation degree, or excelling within the industry. Understanding and learning human anatomy and physiology is particularly important to the sports coach. If an individual is to work with an athlete, it is important to have a stable understanding of the human body and how it functions. This is important, for example, to ensure safe and effective practice, optimise sporting performance and be able to communicate effectively within a multidisciplinary team, such as sports therapists, sports scientists, sports psychologists, physiotherapists and medical personnel. In order to analyse sports performance, the coach must be able to understand and apply anatomy knowledge such as understanding the structure of joints and movements permitted, how a muscle contracts to provide movement, muscle actions and the type of contraction taking place. Anatomy and physiology can be learned through books and the internet, but there is no substitute for first-hand learning and application.

The body is a complex machine which needs to be fully understood in order to ensure that sporting movements are executed optimally, and performance is improved with specific goal planning and effective performance analysis. Knowledge of anatomy will address the structure of the skeletal system, skeletal functions, types of bone, movements possible at each joint and common postural disorders; while information on the muscular system will address topics such as function and types of muscular tissue, gross and micro structure as well as muscular contraction. Physiology will address structure and function of the cardiovascular and respiratory system.

Learning outcomes

After you have read this chapter you should be able to:

- understand anatomical terminology
- describe the structure and function of the skeletal system
- describe key structures of the muscular system
- describe the structure and function of the cardiovascular system
- describe the structure and function of the respiratory system.

Get into pairs and take it in turns to be the model for the activities below.

- Using sticky notes, write down as many names of bones and muscles as possible. Can you place the names of the bones and the muscles on the correct location on your model?

- Using sticky notes, write down as many joint names and their classification as possible (do not forget joints such as sternoclavicular). Place them correctly on your model.

- Using an eyeliner, draw as many muscles as you can onto the anterior and posterior surfaces of your model (ask for consent).

If you do not have a model, use a body outline on paper, borrow a doll or use an art model.

Anatomical terminology

Anatomical text is commonly used within the sporting world, within the medical profession in treatment notes and in communication between professionals. It is therefore important that you are able to understand the most common terms used. The anatomical position is the position your athlete assumes when you are documenting your anatomical terms (or the position your model assumes when demonstrating anatomical terms).

Three common anatomical terms used are sagittal, transverse and coronal planes (see Figure 7.1).

- **Sagittal plane** – vertical plane (from head to toe) passing through the navel dividing the body into left and right.

- **Transverse plane** – also known as the horizontal plane, divides the body into superior and inferior body segments.

- **Coronal plane** – also known as the frontal plane, divides the body into dorsal and ventral segments (front and back).

Key term

Supinated – when the forearm is supinated the palm of the hand is facing forward when in the anatomical position

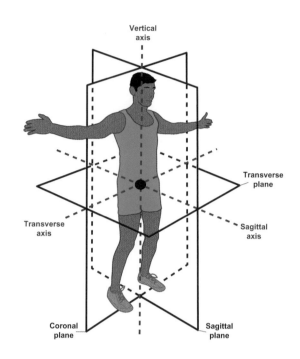

Figure 7.1 Planes

The anatomical position of an athlete is anteriorly viewed with arms by the side with forearms **supinated**. This is the position used for all anatomical references (see Figure 7.1). Table 7.1 describes common anatomical terminology used within sports coaching.

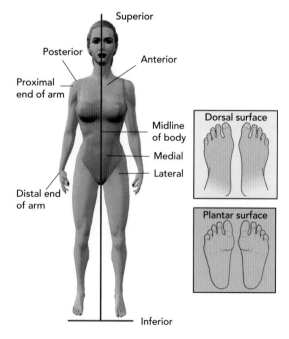

Figure 7.2 Anatomical positions

Table 7.1 Anatomical terminology

Terminology	Description
Anterior	Front view, in front or towards the front of the body
Posterior	Rear view, behind or towards the rear of the body
Medial	Towards or at the midline of the body
Lateral	Away from or at the midline of the body
Proximal	Near to or closer to the centre of the body
Distal	Away from or further from the centre of the body
Superior	Above or towards the head of the body
Inferior	Below or away from the head of the body
Superficial	Nearer to the surface
Deep	Away from the surface
Ipsilateral	Same side as the body
Contralateral	Opposite side of the body
Prone	Lying face down
Supine	Lying face up

As a sports coach you need to understand the movements available at each joint. Table 7.2 describes common movement terminology used in sports coaching. (Movements available at joints are addressed later in the chapter on page 101.)

Table 7.2 Movement terminology

Movement	Description	Picture
Flexion	Reduction of the joint angle	
Extension	Increasing the joint angle	

Table 7.2 Movement terminology (contd)

Movement	Description	Picture
Abduction	Taking away from the midline	
Adduction	Taking towards the midline	
Pronation	Palm turning downwards	
Supination	Palm turning upwards	
Plantar flexion	Pointing the toes away, pushing the sole of the foot away	
Dorsiflexion	Moving the top of the foot towards the body, showing the sole of the foot	
Hyperextension	Increased extension beyond the norm	
Rotation	Movement of a bone (or the trunk) around its own longitudinal axis	
Medial rotation	Turning towards the midline	
Lateral rotation	Turning away from the midline	

Structure and function of the skeletal system

The average adult skeleton consists of 206 bones. The precise number varies and with age some bones may become fused. The skeleton can be divided into two components: the **axial skeleton** contains 80 bones and the **appendicular skeleton** contains 126 bones.

The number of bones can vary in the human body due to anatomical variation such as an extra lumbar vertebrae, cervical rib, lumbar rib or **sutural bones** in the skull. The appendicular skeleton is not fused, allowing for a much greater range of motion.

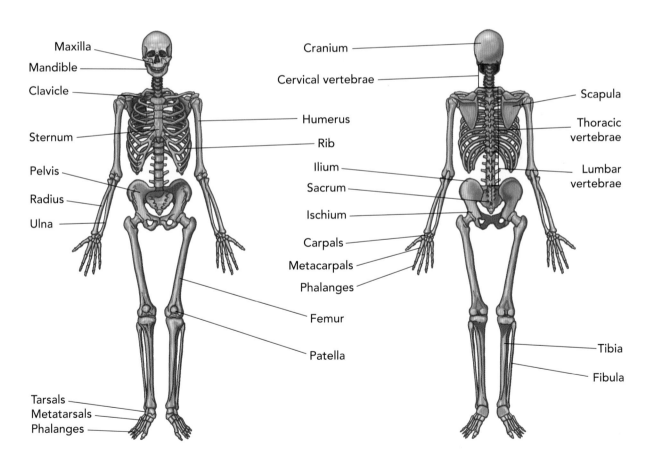

Figure 7.3 Bones of the skeleton

Axial skeleton

The axial skeleton (see Figure 7.4 a to c) forms the upright axis of the body and consists of the:

- cranium – which consists of the parietal, temporal, frontal, occipital, ethmoid and sphenoid bones

- facial bones – consisting of maxilla, zygomatic, mandible, nasal, palatine, inferior nasal concha, lacrimal and vomer bones

- hyoid bone – which is a u-shaped bone located in the neck

- vertebral column – consisting of the cervical, thoracic and lumbar vertebrae, as well as the sacrum and coccyx

- thoracic cage – consisting of the sternum and ribs

- auditory ossicles – consisting of the malleus, incus and stapes found in the inner ear.

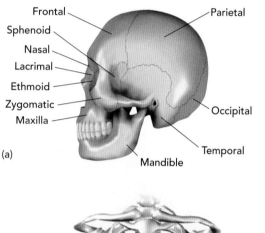

(a)

Frontal · Parietal · Sphenoid · Nasal · Lacrimal · Ethmoid · Zygomatic · Maxilla · Occipital · Temporal · Mandible

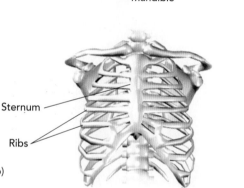

(b)

Sternum · Ribs

Cervical vertebrae (seven)

Thoracic vertebrae (twelve)

Intervertebral discs

Lumbar vertebrae (five fused)

Sacral vertebrae (five)

Coccygeal vertebrae (four fused)

(c)

Figure 7.4 Bones of the axial skeleton: a) the cranium, b) the thorax, c) the vertebral column

Appendicular skeleton

The appendicular skeleton (see Figure 7.5 a to d) consists of all the bones which attach to the axial skeleton, and can be divided into six regions.

- Each arm and forearm consists of the humerus, ulna and radius.

- Each hand consists of eight carpals, five metacarpals, five proximal phalanges, four middle phalanges, five distal phalanges and two sesamoid.

- Each pectoral girdle consists of two clavicles and two scapula.

- The pelvis consists of the left and right os coxae, which are formed by the fusion of the illium, ischium and pubis.

- Each leg consists of a femur, tibia, patella and fibula.

- Each foot contains seven tarsals, five metatarsals, five proximal phalanges, four middle phalanges, five distal phalanges and two sesamoid bones.

Functions of the skeletal system

The skeletal system has a number of physiological and mechanical functions.

- **Protection** – the skeletal framework protects the vital tissues and organs in your body. The cranium protects the brain, the thorax protects the heart and lungs, the vertebral column protects the spinal cord and the pelvis protects the abdominal and reproductive organs.

- **Attachment for skeletal muscles** – the skeleton provides a framework for attachment of the skeletal muscles via tendons as well as the attachment of ligaments. The skeletal system provides a lever system in order to create joint motion and movement.

- **Support** – the skeletal frame provides a structural framework, giving the body a supportive framework for soft tissue, and shape.

- **Source of red blood cell production** – red bone marrow found within the bone produces red blood cells, white blood cells and platelets.

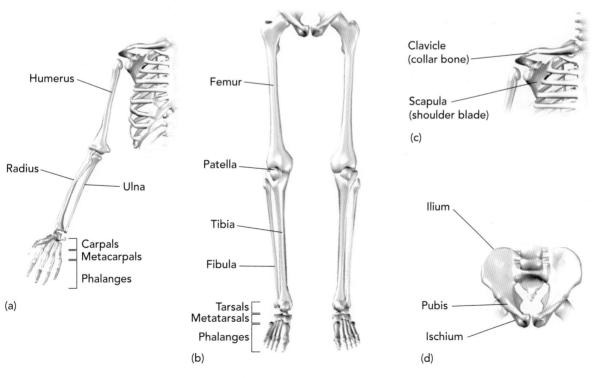

Figure 7.5 Bones of the appendicular skeleton: a) the upper limbs, b) the lower limbs, c) the shoulder girdle and d) the pelvis

- **Store of minerals** – bone stores minerals such as calcium, phosphate (a stored form of phosphorus) and magnesium, which are essential for growth and bone health. Minerals are released into the bloodstream as the body requires them. The yellow bone marrow stores fat.

Remember

Functions of the skeleton can be remembered with the acronym PASSS.

Protection

Attachment

Support

Storage

Source

The male and female skeletal systems differ. A female pelvis is wider and flatter to assist childbirth, with associated widening of the sacrum. The cartilage found at the pubic symphysis in a female is broader – allowing a greater spreading of the pelvis during childbirth. The female rib cage is more rounded and smaller than a male rib cage, with the lumbar curve greater and pelvis anteriorly tilted. The greater hip width results in an increased femur angle from the hip to the knee (increased Q angle). Males generally are taller and have heavier bones. Males have greater muscle bulk with tendon attachments being more prominent and easier to palpate.

Stop and think

The function of calcium is to promote healthy bone mass. Calcium also plays a vital role within exercise; an additional supply of calcium is required to ensure levels of calcium ions are adequate for working muscle to elicit the relaxatory response. Ninety nine per cent of calcium is found in bones and one per cent in the body's fluids and cells. A diet deficient in calcium can lead to osteopenia in later life. What kind of foods do you think contain calcium?

Types of bone

Bones are a specific shape and size for a reason.

- **Long bones** (see Figure 7.6) such as the tibia, fibula, humerus and ulna are found in the limbs. They have a long shaft known as the **diaphysis**. Each end of the bone is known as the epiphysis.

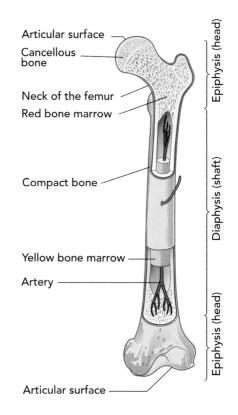

Articular surface
Cancellous bone
Neck of the femur
Red bone marrow
Compact bone
Yellow bone marrow
Artery
Articular surface
Epiphysis (head)
Diaphysis (shaft)
Epiphysis (head)

Figure 7.6 Structure of a long bone

- **Short bones** such as the carpals and tarsals (see Figure 7.5a and 7.5b, page 95) are found in the wrists and ankles. These are strong, small, light and cube shaped, consisting of cancellous bone encased by compact bone.

- **Flat bones** include the scapulae, sternum and bones of the cranium (see Figure 7.5c, 7.4a and 7.4b). They are thin, flat, have a large surface area and aspects curved in shape to allow for a strong attachment site. Flat bones are particularly strong and their function is to provide protection.

- **Sesamoid bones** such as the patella (see Figure 7.5b) are small bones located within a tendon.
- **Irregular bones** such as the vertebrae (see Figure 7.7) have irregular shapes and do not fit into any of the above categories.

The vertebral column

This is a segmented flexible pillar made up of five regions: the cervical, thoracic, lumbar, sacral and coccyx. Before the developmental years, the vertebral column consists of 33 single vertebrae. The cervical, thoracic and lumbar regions comprise a total of 24 single vertebrae. During the developmental years, five vertebrae fuse to form the sacrum and between two and four fuse to form the coccyx.

The second cervical vertebra (C2) to the sacrum (S1) consists of individual **articulations**, held firmly in position by intervertebral discs (made up of **fibrocartilage**) and ligaments. Due to the natural **lordosis** in the cervical and lumbar areas, the disc tends to be thicker **anteriorly**. Each vertebra consists of various processes, an arch and a body which supports the weight. The vertebral foramen is a hole through which the spinal cord passes (see Figure 7.7).

> ### Key terms
>
> **Diaphysis** – main shaft of the bone
>
> **Articulation** – the contact of two or more bones at a specific location
>
> **Fibrocartilage** – this cartilage is very rich in type 1 collagen and is strong and durable. It can be found, for example, in the menisci of the knee and intervertebral disc
>
> **Lordosis** – exaggerated curvature of the lumbar spine
>
> **Anteriorly** – towards the front

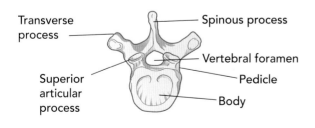

Figure 7.7 A vertebra

The movements available within each section of the vertebral column differ widely due to the complex anatomical structure. The vertebrae increase in size from the top down and are held together by strong ligaments, allowing minimal movement between individual vertebrae, but allowing the vertebral column a considerable amount of flexibility. Generally, the degree of movement permitted reduces from top down. Gross movements of the vertebral column include flexion, extension, lateral flexion and rotation (see Table 7.2, pages 91–92). The vertebral column is approximately 72–75cm in length, with the intervertebral discs responsible for 25% of this length. 40% of a human's height is due to the length of their vertebral column. As we age, height may decline due to the thinning of the discs.

Regions of the vertebral column

The five regions of the vertebral column are as follows.

- **Cervical section of the vertebrae** – this is the upper seven vertebrae (C1–C7) which form the cervical curve of the vertebral column in a convex shape. In functional anatomy the **occipital condyles** play an important function in transferring the weight of the head to C1. The first cervical vertebrae (C1) is known as the **atlas**, and the second vertebrae (C2) is known as the **axis** (its function is to rotate the head). The atlanto-occipital joint and atlanto-axial joint do not contain **intervertebral discs**. The joint type formed is a pivot joint, allowing movement of the cranium. The cervical vertebrae directly support the weight of the head, and therefore have the most available movement, although stability is compromised. The cervical spine is further more vulnerable due to the vertebrae rising above the shoulders.

- **Thoracic section of the vertebrae** – the next 12 vertebrae (T1–T12) form the thoracic curve of the vertebral column in a concave shape. The peak of the thoracic curve is around T6–T8. The true ribs (first seven ribs) articulate directly with the sternum originating from the thoracic vertebrae to form the rib cage. Ribs eight to ten either 'float' or attach to the **costal cartilage**.

- **Lumbar section of the vertebrae** – these are the next five vertebrae (L1–L5). The lumbar region bears the largest portion of the body's weight, therefore the vertebrae are larger. L1–L5 are an important site for muscle attachment, in particular for the hip flexor (illiacus and psoas). L1–L5 form the lumbar curve of the vertebrae in a convex shape.

- **Sacral** – the sacrum is triangular in shape and articulates with the pelvis. It plays a significant role in absorbing the ground forces from the lower limb and weight of the body above. The sacrum is formed from five fused vertebrae. The articulation between L5/S1 is known as the lumbosacral disc, while the articulation between the sacrum and coccyx forms the sacrococcygeal joint.

- **Coccyx** – the second fused section of the vertebrae consisting of approximately two to four vertebrae forms the remnants of the tail.

Key terms

Occipital condyles – kidney-shaped with convex surfaces. There are two occipital condyles located either side of the foramen magnum. They articulate with the atlas bone

Intervertebral disc – a fibrocartilage disc which lies between each adjacent vertebrae of the spine

Costal cartilage – hyaline cartilage which connects the sternum to the ribs

Functions of the vertebral column

The main functions of the vertebral column are to:

- encase and protect the spinal cord from injury
- distribute and absorb impact (the unique curvature and intervertebral discs act as a shock absorber)
- provide a surface for the attachment of the muscles which are responsible for moving the vertebrae, in turn maintaining balance and erectness of the trunk
- provide a surface for the attachment of the muscles of the pelvic girdle and pectoral area
- support the rib cage.

Vertebral abnormalities

Lordosis, kyphosis and scoliosis are acquired and congenital vertebral abnormalities. A coach should be aware that over-exaggeration of the vertebral curves can hinder movement, affect muscular alignment, cause nerve compression, protruding or ruptured discs and possibly affect sporting performance.

Activity

Using a model, practise executing the range of movements possible at a joint. Draw up a table which has three columns labelled: Joint name; Joint type; Movements permitted. Complete the table for every joint.

Remember

If you should observe an athlete with kyphosis, lordosis or scoliosis you may need to refer your athlete to a sports therapist for further examination. The sports therapist will ascertain whether referral to a medical practitioner is required if they suspect medical problems such as **ankylosing spondylitis**.

Key term

Ankylosing spondylitis – an inflammatory arthritis affecting mainly the joints in the spine and the sacroilium in the pelvis. However, other joints of the body may also be affected as well as tissues including the heart, eyes, lungs and kidneys.

Lordosis

This is caused through an exaggeration of the lumbar curve, resulting in an increased anterior tilt of the pelvis. Hamstrings and abdominal muscles present as lengthened and weak, while the opposing muscles – the quadriceps and muscle found in the lower back – present as shortened and strong.

Kyphosis

This is caused through an exaggerated curve in the thoracic vertebrae. The scapulae are protracted, putting the scapulae and clavicles (shoulder girdle) under constant pull of gravity. Muscles responsible for scapular retraction and on the posterior aspect of the thoracic region, such as the trapezius and rhomboids, present as lengthened and weak. The opposing muscles – those of the anterior muscles of the thoracic region, such as the pectoralis major and minor – present as shortened and strong.

Scoliosis

This can sometimes be observed or, on palpation of the vertebrae, an S or C shape can be felt deviating to the right or left.

- On observation of the spine, if the curve deviates to the left, muscles on the left aspect of the spine have shortened creating tension on the vertebrae to the left; the muscles on the right adapt by lengthening.

- If the curve deviates to the right, then muscles on the right aspect of the spine have shortened creating tension on the vertebrae to the right; the muscles to the left adapt by lengthening.

To maintain correct posture the vertebrae should sit in neutral alignment. Many factors affect the *neutral* position of the vertebrae; for example, poor posture, injury, the sport played, incorrect exercise techniques, pregnancy, excess body composition

(obesity), injury and disease. All of these can predispose the athlete to injury. It is important when performing exercise to consider safety at all times by ensuring a 'neutral spine alignment'.

Joint classifications

A joint is a junction where two or more bones articulate (meet). It plays a vital role in allowing movement to occur. Joints act as levers, allow movement and transmit and absorb forces. As a sports coach you need a good understanding of joints and their movement. The **force transmission** as a result of sports participation can be excessive causing damage and requiring therapeutic intervention. Chapter 12 (Analysis of sports performance) will allow you to further explore force transmission and biomechanics. Joints can be classified into three groups and each category can be further subdivided.

> **Key term**
>
> **Force transmission** – impact forces transmitted through the body

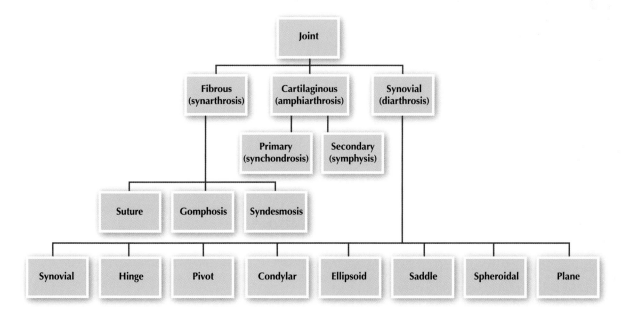

Figure 7.8 Types of joint

Synarthrosis/fibrous/fixed joints

The bones which articulate at fibrous joints are connected via fibrous connective tissue. They allow very limited movement. The three sub categories are:

- **suture**(s) – example = found between the cranial bones
- **gomphosis** (-es) – example = tooth in its socket
- **syndesmosis** (-es) – example = inferior tibiofibular joint.

Amphiarthrosis/cartilaginous/slightly moveable joints

The bones which articulate at cartilaginous joints are connected by either **articular (hyaline) cartilage** forming a primary joint, such as first sternoclavicular joint, or fibrocartilage forming a secondary joint, such as intervertebral disc, which may contain an internal cavity or nucleus. Movement permitted is greater than at fibrous joints.

Diarthrosis/synovial/freely moveable joints

Synovial joints allow a greater degree of movement than fibrous and cartilaginous. See Figure 7.9 for the structure of a synovial joint. Articular cartilage encases the end of bones that articulate at the joint, allowing freedom of movement and reduction of friction. The joint is surrounded by a strong fibrous capsule, which is lined with a synovial membrane (synovium) providing lubrication and nourishment to the articular cartilage. The **ligaments** attach bone to bone and further strengthen the fibrous capsule. Ligaments are located internal and external to the capsule, and further supported by the surrounding muscle attachments and strong **tendons**. The function of ligaments is to provide joint stability, thus preventing dislocation. If excessive movement occurs ligaments may become damaged.

Bursae are common features. They are fluid-filled sacs preventing friction between the sliding surfaces of structures such as ligaments, tendons and the capsule. Bursae are vulnerable to injury, resulting in a condition known as bursitis. The suffix 'itis' identifies inflammation is present. Bursitis is therefore inflammation of the bursa. Another common inflammatory condition is synovitis; inflammation of the synovial fluid or capsule.

Key terms

Articular cartilage – (also known as hyaline cartilage) is smooth and covers the surface of bones

Ligament – a band of tough fibrous tissue connecting bone to bone

Tendon – a band of inelastic tissue connecting a muscle to bone

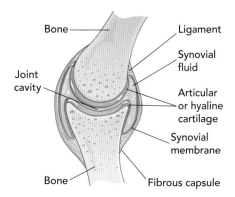

Figure 7.9 Structure of a synovial joint - transverse section of knee joint

Synovial joints can be subdivided into six categories as shown in Table 7.3.

Activity

Choose a sporting movement relevant to your sport, such as the arm movement when throwing the javelin. Devise a table identifying the joints involved, and for each joint the movements which comprise the techniques.

Table 7.3 Sub categories of synovial joints

Joint name	Example	Movement	Figure
Hinge	Humero-ulnar joint	Flexion and extension	Humerus, Trochea, Ulna, Trochlear joint
Pivot	Proximal radio ulnar joints	Rotation	Atlas, Axis
Ellipsoid (condyloid)	Metacarpophalangeal	Flexion and extension Abduction and adduction	Scaphoid, Radius, Ulna, Lunate
Saddle (sellar)	First carpometacarpal joint	Some rotation	Trapezium, Metacarpal of thumb, Radius, Ulna
Spheroidal (ball and socket)	Coxal joint	Flexion and extension Abduction and adduction Rotation	Acetabulum of hipbone, Head of femur
Plane (gliding)	Intercarpal joint	Sliding movements	Navicular, Second cuneiform, Third cuneiform

Key structures of the muscular system

The human body contains three types of muscle tissue:

- **skeletal** such as gastrocnemius
- **smooth** which is found in the intestines
- **cardiac** which comprises the heart.

Skeletal tissue constitutes approximately 30–40 per cent of total human body mass, and is of great interest to sports coaches. It is vital you understand the function of skeletal muscle in relation to complex sporting movements.

Muscle tissue has two main functions: movement and posture.

- Production of movement: muscles are attached to the skeleton via a tendon or broad **aponeurosis**. When a muscle contracts, it exerts a force on the bone and produces movement. Muscles can pull but cannot push, and are positioned across joints in order to produce movement.

- Stabilisation of body positions: body positions are the result of skeletal contraction. Postural muscles contract continually to maintain body positions. The abdominal muscles help to stabilise the spine when standing or sitting, while the erector spinae works to keep the spine erect.

Other functions of the muscular system include:

- assisting the movement of substances within the body such as blood, food, faeces, urine, gases and lymph
- **thermogenesis** – muscle contraction produces a by-product, heat, which helps maintain the normal body temperature of 37°C. Shivering, which is an involuntary contraction, can increase the rate of heat production considerably
- regulation of organ volume such as the stomach and bladder.

The muscular system contains over 640 named muscles. The main muscles relevant to a sports coach can be seen in Figure 7.10.

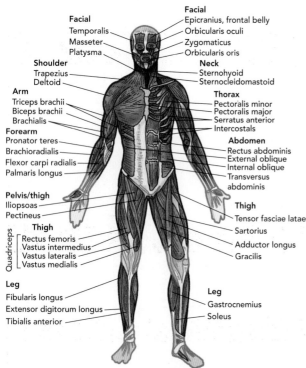
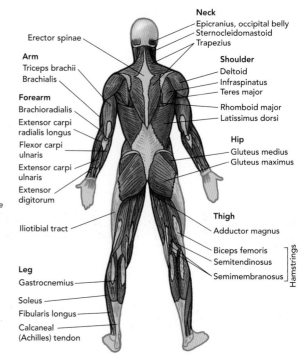

Figure 7.10 Anterior and posterior muscular system

As a sports coach it is not enough just to learn the name and location of the muscles. You need to understand the action of each muscle. Muscle **origin** and **insertion** knowledge will assist the therapist in assessment, diagnosis, treatment and clinical justification. There are many resources which you can use to learn your origin and insertions, and in time progress to nerve innervations.

Properties of muscle

Muscle tissue has four main properties that enable the tissue to function optimally:

> ### Key terms
>
> **Aponeurosis** – a flat, broad tendon
>
> **Thermogenesis** – the process of heat production
>
> **Origin** – the attachment site of a muscle to bone (in a few exceptions, muscle). The origin is a fixed location
>
> **Insertion** – the attachment of a muscle usually via a tendon to bone. The insertion on the bone is moveable as a result of muscle contraction

> ### Stop and think
>
> The functional part of the muscle name generally represents its function, with the exception of the ankle. For example, a flexor decreases the angle at a joint bringing the anterior surfaces closer together (flexor carpi radialis main function is wrist flexion). Think about the following terms: extensor, adductor, supinator, pronator, levator and sphincter. Can you name a muscle and state its function for each term? Think of sports movement you coach – which muscles are responsible for which movements?

- **excitability**: it responds to stimuli (excitability is the property of the neuromuscular junction to respond to a stimuli)
- **contractibility**: it can contract forcefully when stimulated, resulting in isometric or isotonic contraction
- **extensibility**: it can stretch without tearing, and can contract forcefully after being stretched
- **elasticity**: after stretching or contracting it can return to its original length.

Gross muscle structure

A skeletal muscle consists of thousands of individual muscle fibres, encased by connective tissue called the **endomysium**. Individual muscle fibres are made up of muscle cells. Muscle fibres are bundled together into fascicles, around ten to 100 in any bundle, further encased by connective tissue called the **perimysium**. All the fascicles are collated together and encased by connective tissue called the **epimysium**, which surrounds the whole muscle. The endomysium, perimysium and epimysium all extend from the deep **fascia**.

The endomysium, perimysium and epimysium are continuous connective tissue that may extend

> ### Key terms
>
> **Endomysium** – connective tissue encasing individual muscle fibres
>
> **Perimysium** – connective tissue encasing fascicles
>
> **Epimysium** – connective tissue which encases all the fascicles surrounding the whole muscle
>
> **Fascia** – fibrous tissue binding together or separating muscle

> ### Activity
>
> Using a resource such as the *Muscle Atlas* from the University of Washington's Department of Radiology (see *Useful resources*, page 116) draw up a table like the one below. Complete the table for each muscle. An example has been completed for you. This will provide a valuable resource for the rest of your sports therapy career.
>
> | Muscle | Action | Origin | Insertion | Nerve innervation |
> | --- | --- | --- | --- | --- |
> | Biceps brachii | Supinates forearm, when supine flexes forearm | Short head: tip of coracoid process of scapula
Long head: supraglenoid tubercle of scapula | Tuberosity of radius and fascia of forearm via bicipital aponeurosis | Musculocutaneous nerve (C5 and C6) |

beyond the muscle tissue and form the tendon. The tendon is therefore a dense regular connective tissue. The Achilles tendon is a cord of dense connective tissue which is extended from the gastrocnemius and attaches to the calcaneous. Extension of connective tissue from some muscles can be as a broad, flat layer known as an aponeurosis. The structure of the skeletal muscle is shown in Figure 7.11.

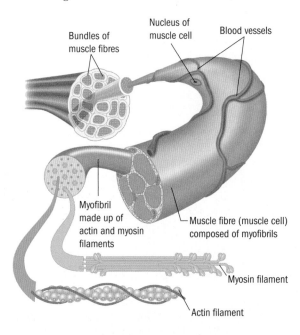

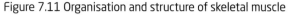

Figure 7.11 Organisation and structure of skeletal muscle

Superficial fascia separates muscle from the skin, provides protection, reduces heat loss and is storage for fat and water. Deep fascia holds similar functioned muscles together, facilitates free movement of muscles, carries blood vessels, lymphatic vessels, nerves and fills any gaps between muscles. Deep fascia also divides muscles into compartments. For example, the lower leg is divided into four compartments by the deep fascia, anterior, lateral, posterior and deep posterior compartments.

The anterior compartment consists of the tibialis anterior, the extensor digitorum longus, and the extensor hallucus longus. Their function is to **dorsiflex** at the ankle. The tibialis anterior also **inverts** the foot.

The lateral compartment comprises the peroneus longus, peroneus brevis and peroneus tertius. The function of the peroneus longus and brevis is to **plantarflex** and **evert** the foot, while the peroneus tertius dorsiflexes and everts the foot.

Key terms

Dorsiflex – move the top of the foot towards the body, showing the sole of the foot

Invert – move the sole of the foot towards the midline of the body

Evert – move the sole of the foot away from the midline of the body

Plantarflex – point the toes away, pushing the sole of the foot away

The posterior compartment comprises the gastrocnemius, soleus and plantaris. Their function is to plantarflex at the ankle. The gastrocnemius is the most superficial of the muscles and has two heads – lateral and medial. The soleus lies under the gastrocnemius and above the plantaris. All three insert into the Achilles tendon onto the calcaneous.

The deep posterior compartment comprises the tibialis posterior, flexor digitorum longus and flexor hallucus longus. Their combined function is to aid plantarflexion. However, flexor hallucis longus also flexes the big toe, flexor digitorium longus flexes the rest of the toes and tibialis posterior inverts the foot. Remember that the posterior and deep posterior compartments all plantarflex at the ankle.

Micro muscle structure

In order to understand muscle contraction, you must understand the micro-structure of a muscle fibre. The cell membrane of the muscle fibre is known as the **sarcolemma**. A muscle fibre consists of long myofibrils (the length of the fibre) between which organelles such as mitochondria, glycogen granules and myoglobin are suspended in the sarcoplasm.

Myofibrils are the contractile elements, consisting of thin and thick myofilaments known respectively as actin and myosin (see Figure 7.11). The myofilaments do not run the length of the myofibril

Key term

Sarcolemma – cell membrane of the muscle fibre

– they are organised into units called sarcomeres. Sarcomere units are repeated along the length of the myofibril, where actin and myosin are present in an overlapping formation.

Sliding filament theory

The sliding filament model of muscle contraction is a complex process. When a muscle receives a nerve impulse (stimulus) the lengths of actin and myosin (myofilaments) do not change, but are drawn closer together by sliding across each other forming cross bridges. The result is that the sarcomeres shorten due to the contraction of the myofibril. The myofibril becomes shorter and thicker, resulting in muscle contraction.

The relaxation phase is a passive process, where the cross bridges relax, actin and myosin return to their original position, thus the sarcomere and myofilament lengthen to their original position. The muscle relaxes.

The nerve impulse is based on the 'all or nothing law'. Each fibre is capable of either contracting or not contracting – there is no in-between stage. As the athlete begins to fatigue, it is the strength of the contraction which may decrease.

Characteristics of muscle

The **fascicular arrangement** of a muscle affects the power and range of motion. The cross-sectional area of a muscle is the dependant factor for power output; a short fibre can contract as powerfully as a long fibre. A muscle fibre can shorten up to 70 per cent of its resting length upon contraction. Therefore, the greater the length of the fibres, the larger the range of motion produced.

The arrangement of fascicles is dependent on the muscle function and is generally structured to provide a compromise between power and range of motion. There are five fascicle arrangements of a

muscle: parallel, fusiform, circular, triangular and pennate (Figure 7.12a).

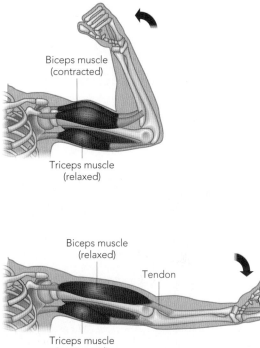

Figure 7.12 Muscle shortening on contraction

1. **Parallel** – the fascicles are arranged parallel to the longitudinal axis of the muscle. The fascicles form a flat tendon at each end.

2. **Fusiform** – similar in structure to the parallel arrangement. However, the fascicles taper towards the tendons, resulting in the muscle belly greater in diameter than the tendon attachments, e. g. biceps brachii. These muscles are limited in power.

3. **Circular** – the fascicles are in a circular arrangement. Sphincter muscles are circular and enclose an orifice (opening).

4. **Triangular** – the fascicles are spread over a broad area and taper into a thick tendon, which is central to the muscle belly. The appearance is that of a triangle, e. g. pectoralis major. Triangular arrangement often occurs where restrictive leverage is required.

5. **Pennate** – the tendon extends nearly the entire length of the muscle, with short fascicles. There are three types of pennate structure: unipennate, bipennate and multipennate:

Key term

Fascicular arrangement – the arrangement of fascicles, which ultimately affects power output and range of movement

- unipennate – the fascicles are arranged on one side, e.g. extensor digitorium longus
- bipennate – the tendon is located centrally, with fascicles on each side, e. g rectus femoris muscle
- multipennate – there are several tendons, with fascicles attached obliquely, e.g. deltoid muscle.

Due to the short arrangement of fascicles and the increased number of fibres in a smaller space, these muscles are very powerful.

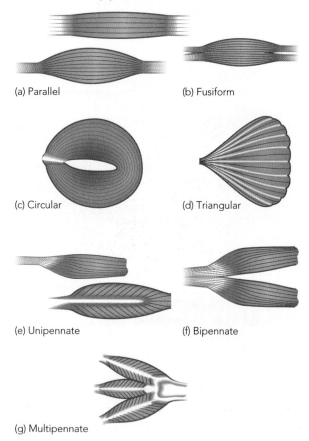

(a) Parallel

(b) Fusiform

(c) Circular

(d) Triangular

(e) Unipennate

(f) Bipennate

(g) Multipennate

Figure 7.12a Fascicle arrangement

Muscle attachments

Several muscles are used to produce effective movement. A high proportion of muscles have two attachments – an origin and insertion. However, there are also some muscles which have more than one origin and/or insertion. When the muscle receives a stimulus it contracts, attempting to bring the origin and insertion closer together. The contraction does not always result in muscle shortening. To achieve a wide variety of movements, muscles either work together or in opposition. To enable movement to occur, additional muscles are required to provide support and stabilisation. Skeletal muscles are referred to as **agonists**, **antagonists** and **synergists**.

Agonists are the prime movers producing the main movement, for example during knee extension the prime mover would be the quadriceps group. The hamstring group relax and lengthen allowing the knee to extend, referred to as the antagonist. However, when the hamstrings contract to produce knee flexion they become the agonist, while the antagonist (the quadricep group) relaxes to allow the movement to occur. Movements are rarely isolated, particularly during sport, therefore synergists and fixators play a major role.

Synergists are particularly important if the agonist muscles cross two joints to prevent any unwanted movement at the intermediate joint. For example, the biceps brachii crosses both the shoulder and elbow joint. Its primary action is on the forearm to provide flexion at the elbow. Synergists contracting at the shoulder prevent any unwanted movement. Synergist muscles may assist the agonist muscle in producing movement by altering the direction of pull to allow the most effective movement. During knee flexion the gastrocnemius and poplitues act as the main synergist.

Key terms

Agonist – the muscle producing the action (movement)

Antagonist – the muscle opposing the action (movement)

Synergist – synergist muscles assist the agonist muscles and provide stabilisation to prevent any unwanted movement

Fixator – provides stabilisation at the proximal end of the limb

Fixators are muscles which stabilise the origin of the agonist muscle, to allow the agonist to act more efficiently. The origin of the muscle is usually found at the proximal end of the limb which is stabilised by the fixators, while the movement occurs at the distal end where the muscle inserts.

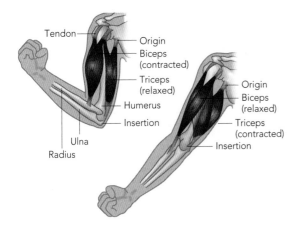

Fig. 7.13 Agonist and antagonist muscles

Muscles are capable of performing contractile work in a variety of ways. Isotonic contractions result in the muscle creating movement such as concentric and eccentric contractions. Isometric contraction results in no movement.

- **Concentric contraction** – the muscle shortens as the tension in the muscle increases to overcome the opposing muscle (resistance), resulting in the muscle attachments moving closer together causing movement. The agonist muscle performs concentrically. During the elbow flexion phase of a bicep curl, the biceps and brachialis are the agonist muscle contracting concentrically.

Fig. 7.13a Concentric muscle contraction

- **Eccentric contraction** – the tension remains the same in the muscle. As the opposing force is greater the muscle lengthens. The antagonist muscle performs eccentrically. During elbow flexion the triceps contract eccentrically. Eccentric contraction is important in slowing down and controlling movement, which would otherwise be rapid due to gravity.

- **Isometric contraction** – the tension within the muscle increases, although the length of the muscle does not alter, thus no movement is created. If the bicep curl is held in mid range the muscles perform isometrically. The muscles do not change in their length, but support the weight.

Fig 7.13b Isometric contraction

Key terms

Concentric contraction – muscle contraction generates force which causes muscle shortening

Eccentric contraction – the muscle lengthens due to the opposing force being greater than the force generated by the muscle

Isometric contraction – force is generated by the muscle without changing length

Fibre types

Skeletal muscles differ in their composition of fibre type and function, with individuals varying in their specific makeup. Muscle fibre types are categorised as slow twitch (red muscle fibres) named type 1, fast twitch (white muscle fibres) named type 2a (fast oxidative glycolytic fibres (FOG)) and 2b (fast glycolytic fibres (FG)). Training influences the efficiency of the fibres and to some extent the percentage of fibre types the muscle contains.

Type 1 muscle fibres, as their name 'slow twitch' denotes, contract slowly. Muscle fibres are smallest in diameter, therefore producing a low level of force, fatigue resistance and are able to produce contractions for long periods of time. The fibres appear as dark red due to large amounts of blood capillaries and myoglobin, accompanied with many mitochondria required to sustain **aerobic** cellular respiration. The fibres are therefore recruited for aerobic endurance activities, such as long-distance running, cycling and swimming; as these activities are lower in the intensity needed to be sustained over a longer period of time.

Type 2a (FOG) muscle fibres are intermediate in size. They also appear as dark red due to the large content of blood capillaries and myoglobin, are fairly resistant to fatigue and are therefore recruited for aerobic exercise. These fibres differ from slow twitch as they also contain a high level of intracellular glycogen, allowing generation of energy and force via **anaerobic respiration**. They result in faster contractions than slow twitch fibres, with peak contraction reached earlier, although for a shorter duration. These fibres are suited to events such as middle distance running, e.g. 800m or 1500m, and walking activities.

Type 2b (FG) muscle fibres are largest in size and produce the most powerful contractions due to the high number of myofibrils. The fibres appear white in character due to low levels of blood capillaries, myoglobin and mitochondria. They have the capacity to contain large amounts of glycogen, and contract quickly and strongly; however they will fatigue quickly. They are completely dependent on anaerobic respiration. These fibres are suitable for high intensity, short duration activities such as sprinting, weight lifting, jumping, e.g. high jump or long jump, and throwing events such as javelin or shot putt.

Key terms

Aerobic – cellular respiration requiring oxygen

Anaerobic respiration – cellular respiration not requiring oxygen

Stop and think

Which muscle fibres (type 1, type 2a or type 2b) will be dominant in the following sporting events: 100m, sprint, 800m, marathon running? You should consider whether the event relies on aerobic or anaerobic respiration.

Structure and function of the cardiovascular system

Function

The cardiovascular system is made up of the heart (cardio), blood vessels and blood (vascular system). The heart has several functions.

The heart is the body's pump and its function is to pump blood through the network of blood vessels including the arteries, arterioles, capillaries, venules and veins.

The function of the blood is to carry oxygen, nutrients and other essential components to the tissue cells, while products such as carbon dioxide and waste products are carried away from the cells of the tissues by the blood and delivered for removal to the kidneys and liver (waste products) and lungs (carbon dioxide).

The function of the right side of the heart is to receive de-oxygenated blood via the superior vena cava and the inferior vena cava into the right atrium. The deoxygenated blood passes through the tricuspid valve into the right ventricle. The deoxygenated blood is pumped under pressure from the right ventricle via the pulmonary artery to the lungs.

The functions of the left side of the heart is to receive oxygenated blood via the pulmonary veins from the lungs into the left atrium. The oxygenated blood passes through the bicuspid valve into the left ventricle. The oxygenated blood is pumped via the aorta under considerable pressure to the rest of the body.

- Thermoregulation. In order to maintain thermal (heat) regulation of the body, particularly during exercise, the cardiovascular system needs to function by altering the blood flow to tissues to maintain a constant thermal balance.

During exercise, energy expenditure is increased, requiring alterations in blood flow to facilitate oxygen delivery to working tissues and removal of the by-products, such as waste and carbon dioxide. The cardiovascular system uses vasodilation and vasoconstriction to alter blood flow.

- Vasodilation: is the dilation of blood vessels to allow an increased flow of blood; for example, to working muscles during exercise. This occurs due to the increase in the diameter of the blood vessel and decrease in resistance to blood flow.

- Vasoconstriction: is the constriction of blood vessels to allow a decreased flow of blood to an area. This occurs due to the narrowing of the diameter of the blood vessels and increased resistance to blood flow.

Structure of the heart

The heart is situated at the midline of the thoracic cavity, lying within the **mediastinum**, resting on the diaphragm. The heart weighs approximately 250g for a female and 300g in a male and is approximately the same size as a fist – 12cm long, 9cm wide at the broadest point and 6cm thick (Tortora and Grabowski, 2003). The heart is commonly described as positioned on the left; this is because approximately two thirds of the heart's mass lies left of the midline of the body.

> ### Key term
>
> **Mediastinum** – a mass of tissue between the lungs, extending from the sternum to the vertebral column

The **pericardium** is the membrane which protects and surrounds the heart, allowing freedom for contraction and also securing the heart to the mediastinum. The pericardium consists of two main structures – the fibrous pericardium and the serous pericardium. The serous pericardium can be further divided into two layers – the outer (**parietal layer**) and inner (**visceral layer**); between these two layers the **pericardial fluid** can be located. The fluid provides lubrication, reducing the friction between the layers as the heart moves during contraction. The inner layer is also referred to as the epicardium. The epicardium is important as it surrounds the surface of the heart tightly, also forming the outer layer of the heart wall. There are two further layers to the heart wall – the middle and inner layer. The middle layer, named as the myocardium, forms most of the heart wall, is strong and its main function is the heart's pumping action. The inner layer, called the endocardium, provides a continuous layer of smooth lining to the heart chambers, valves and attached large blood vessels.

> ### Key terms
>
> **Pericardium** – membrane surrounding the heart, containing two layers – fibrous and serous layer
>
> **Parietal layer** – outer layer of the serous pericardium
>
> **Visceral layer** – inner layer of serous pericardium, also known as the epicardium, surrounding the heart tightly
>
> **Pericardial (serous) fluid** – fluid found between the parietal and visceral layer

The heart is divided into the left and right chambers divided by a solid wall known as the interventricular septum. The main function of the septum is to prevent blood from either the right or left side coming into contact. The right and left side of the heart can be viewed as two separate pumps with distinct functions (see Figure 7.14).

Key
← = oxygenated blood
← = deoxygenated blood

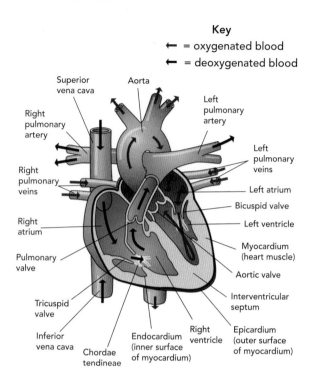

Figure 7.14 Diagram of the heart

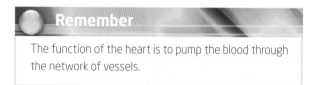

Remember

The function of the heart is to pump the blood through the network of vessels.

Pulmonary and systemic circulation

The right side of the heart works under low pressure. The pulmonary artery, arterioles and capillaries deliver deoxygenated blood to the lungs, allowing gaseous exchange to take place. Carbon dioxide diffuses from the capillaries to the alveoli in the lungs (moving from an area of high pressure to an area of low pressure, known as a pressure gradient), while oxygen diffuses from the alveoli to the capillaries (again from an area of high pressure to low pressure). Oxygenated blood is returned to the left side of the heart via capillaries, venules and veins (right and left pulmonary vein). This is known as pulmonary circulation (see Figure 7.15).

The left side of the heart is surrounded by a thicker heart wall, allowing for a stronger contraction and therefore creating a high pressure in the left side of

the heart. This is because the left side of the heart pumps oxygenated blood via the aorta, arteries, arterioles and capillaries to all the tissue cells. In the cells, gaseous exchange occurs in the same way it does at the lungs. Oxygen diffuses from the high pressure in the capillary to the low pressure in the cells, while carbon dioxide diffuses from high pressure in the cells to low pressure in the capillaries. The deoxygenated blood returns to the heart via the capillaries, venules and veins (superior and inferior vena cava) to the right side of the heart. This is known as systemic circulation (see Figure 7.15).

The left and right atria contract simultaneously once full, pumping blood into the respective ventricles via one-way valves – preventing the back flow of blood on ventricular contraction. The valve between the right atrium and ventricle are called the tricuspid valve, and on the left the bicuspid (mitral) valve. The ventricles contract simultaneously, pumping blood through another set of valves. The valve on the right is known as the pulmonary valve, situated between the ventricle and pulmonary artery; the valve on the left is known as the aortic valve, situated between the left ventricle and the aorta.

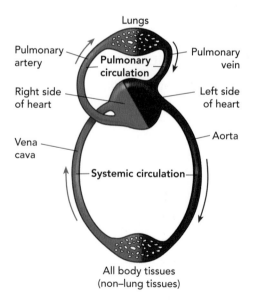

Figure 7.15 Double circulation of the blood through the heart

Key information about the heart

- Atria – the upper chambers of the heart. The right atrium receives deoxygenated blood via the superior and inferior vena cava, while the left atrium receives oxygenated blood from the pulmonary veins (left and right).

- Ventricles – the lower chambers of the heart, responsible for the pumping action. The walls of the ventricles are thicker than atria, with the left wall being the thickest. The right ventricle pumps blood to begin the pulmonary circulation, with the left ventricle pumping blood to begin the systemic circulation.

- Bicuspid, tricuspid, aortic and pulmonary valves – on contraction they prevent the backflow of blood.

Arteries and veins

Arteries transport blood away from the heart, while **veins** always transport blood to the heart. Generally arteries transport oxygenated blood away from the heart; however, you should remember that the pulmonary artery carries deoxygenated blood away from the heart to the lungs. Arteries carry blood under high pressure at high speed. When blood leaves the heart via the aorta it is under most pressure and at the highest speed, therefore expansion is at its maximum. Arteries have two properties – elasticity and contractility – they do not contain valves due to the high pressure, although there is a valve at the point where blood leaves the heart through the pulmonary artery. The walls of the artery are thick to cope with the high pressure and are comprised of three layers (coats or tunicae) the tunica interna, media and externa. Arteries deliver blood to arterioles (see Figure 7.16).

Arterioles are small arteries delivering blood to **capillaries**. The arteriole at its junction to the artery is made up of the same structure; as the arteriole progresses towards the capillary its structure changes to represent that of the capillary. Its main function is to regulate blood flow to the capillaries in response to the body's demands. During exercise the arterioles vasodilate to increase blood flow to the working muscles and vasoconstrict to other areas, such as the intestines, to compensate for the change in blood flow requirements.

Capillaries are microscopic vessels forming a complex network connecting arterioles to venules. This is known as microcirculation. They are found in almost every cell of the body, varying in density. Tissues such as tendons and ligaments contain fewer capillaries and thus have a poor blood supply. Their main function is to allow for gaseous exchange (see below), therefore they have a small diameter and a very thin wall. The wall is made of only one endothelial cell, thick enough to facilitate gaseous exchange (see Figure 7.17).

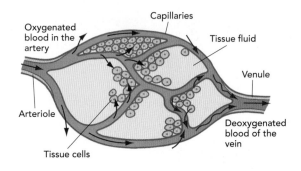

Figure 7.17 The capillary system

Venules connect capillaries to veins. They are formed when several capillaries unite to form venules and represent the structure of capillaries. As venules move towards their vein connection, they change to represent the structure of the vein. Their main function is to collect blood from the capillaries and drain in to the veins to facilitate venous return.

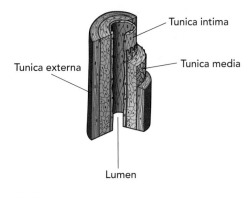

Figure 7.16 Structure of an artery

Veins always carry blood – usually deoxygenated – to the heart; however, the pulmonary vein carries blood to the heart which is oxygenated. The main function of veins is to facilitate venous return. When the blood reaches the veins the pressure is low and the flow has reduced considerably. The walls are thinner than arteries although the diameter is relatively large. The wall is less elastic and contractile, and therefore requires the musculoskeletal system to support venous return. When the muscles contract the veins are compressed, which facilitates pushing the blood towards the heart. An important function of veins is the way their valves work, preventing the backflow of blood when the vein is not compressed (see Figure 7.18).

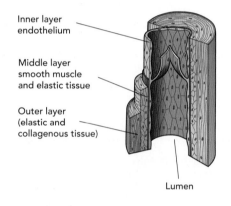

Figure 7.18 Structure of a vein

Inner layer endothelium

Middle layer smooth muscle and elastic tissue

Outer layer (elastic and collagenous tissue)

Lumen

> ### Key terms
>
> **Arteries** – carry blood away from the heart, usually oxygenated
>
> **Arterioles** – connect arteries to capillaries
>
> **Capillaries** – allow for gaseous exchange at the tissue cells and connect arterioles to venules
>
> **Venules** – connect capillaries to veins
>
> **Veins** – carry blood to the heart, usually deoxygenated

Structure and function of the respiratory system

The respiratory system can be described in terms of structure and function. Structurally it is referred to as the upper and lower respiratory systems. The upper system includes the nose and pharynx, while the lower system includes the larynx, trachea, bronchi, bronchioles and lungs (see Figure 7.20). With reference to function, the system is divided into the conducting and respiratory section. The conducting section comprises the nose, pharynx, larynx, trachea, bronchi and bronchioles. Its function is to filter, warm and moisten the air and conduct it into the lungs. The function of the respiratory section is to allow gaseous exchange to occur, and it comprises the bronchioles, alveolar ducts, sacs and alveoli.

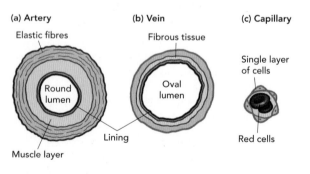

(a) Artery
Elastic fibres
Round lumen
Muscle layer
Lining

(b) Vein
Fibrous tissue
Oval lumen

(c) Capillary
Single layer of cells
Red cells

Figure 7.19 Major blood vessels

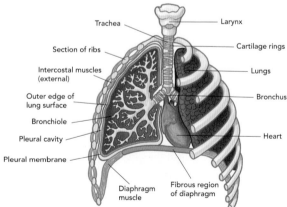

Trachea
Larynx
Section of ribs
Cartilage rings
Intercostal muscles (external)
Lungs
Outer edge of lung surface
Bronchus
Bronchiole
Pleural cavity
Heart
Pleural membrane
Diaphragm muscle
Fibrous region of diaphragm

Figure 7.20 Cross-section through the thorax to show the respiratory organs

Key structures of the respiratory system

See Figure 7.20.

- Nasal cavity – divided into the internal cavity and external cavity. The external cavity comprises a supporting bone framework, such as the frontal, nasal and maxillae bone, and hyaline cartilage, such as the septal cartilage which is lined with a mucous membrane. The internal cavity is large in size also, including structures such as muscles and mucous membranes. During inhalation, air enters the nasal cavity – passing through the nostrils where the air is filtered of, for example, pollen and dust by nasal hairs. Air passes through the left and right nasal passages, is warmed and moistened, and passes into the nasopharynx.

- Epiglottis – a small thin leaf-shaped flap comprised of cartilage and mucous membrane. It is located behind the tongue and covers the entrance to the larynx. When swallowing food or drink, the epiglottis closes at the larynx, so preventing food and drink from passing down the trachea. The epiglottis provides an important function in transporting food and air to the correct structure.

- Pharynx – this is commonly called the throat and its function is a passage for the transport of food and air. The nasal cavity and larynx are connected to transport air, and the nasal cavity and oesophagus to transport food. It is a muscular (skeletal) tube lined with a mucous membrane.

- Larynx – responsible for the production of vocal sounds; commonly known as the voice box, it also serves as an air passage to the lungs. It is made up of nine areas of cartilage held together by ligaments and muscles and lined with mucous membrane.

- Trachea – commonly known as the windpipe, it is comprised of rings of cartilage to prevent the structure from collapsing, although it is very flexible and branches into the left and right bronchi.

- Right and left bronchus – formed from the division of the trachea; comprised of cartilage and contains mucous glands in its wall. The right bronchus is shorter although wider than the left bronchus. The bronchus further subdivide into five lobar bronchi (three on the right and two on the left), branching into 20 segmental bronchi, and subsequently smaller and smaller structures. The structure denotes the nature of a tree, and thus may be referred to as the bronchial tree.

- Bronchioles – subdivisions from the bronchus, they do not contain cartilage or mucous glands. Bronchioles further subdivide before reaching the terminal bronchioles from which the alveoli open.

- Alveoli – the resultant factor of the bronchioles, these appear in clusters which represent the appearance of grapes. There are around 300 million tiny sacs with thin walls (per lung), providing a vast area for gaseous exchange to occur. A dense network of capillaries surrounds the alveoli to facilitate gaseous exchange (external respiration).

- Lungs – one of the pair of organs of respiration which occupy the majority of the thoracic cavity. The right and left lungs are situated in the chest cavity, either side of the heart, enclosed by a membrane called the pleural membranes – known as the pleura. The membranes contain a cavity which is filled with fluid, providing lubrication between the surfaces, allowing the lungs to glide easily over the thoracic wall and reducing friction on expansion and compression. The lungs are elastic in nature, allowing for expansion and compression during inhalation and exhalation. The lungs are divided into lobes; the right lung contains three lobes, the left lung contains two lobes and is smaller than the right (see Figure 7.21).

- Diaphragm – a thin musculo-membranous dome-shaped muscle separating the thoracic and abdominal cavities. It is attached to the ribs at each side and to the sternum. On contraction the volume increases – drawing air into the lungs – on relaxation the volume reduces – pushing air into the atmosphere.

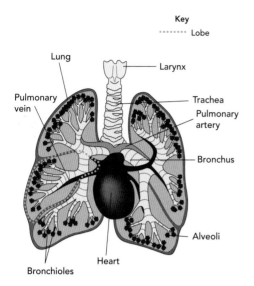

Figure 7.21 The lobes and pleural membranes of the lungs

Gaseous exchange

The function of the respiratory system is to allow for gaseous exchange (see Figure 7.22). This involves providing the intake of oxygen for delivery to the tissue cells and removing carbon dioxide as a waste product of the tissue cells. All tissue cells are living and require this process in order to function. Gaseous exchange is made up of three stages.

1. Pulmonary ventilation
2. External respiration
3. Internal respiration.

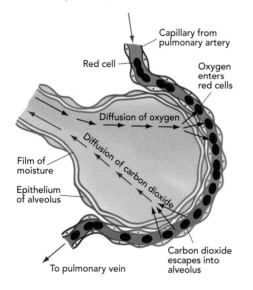

Figure 7.22 Gaseous exchange in the alveoli

Pulmonary ventilation

Also known as breathing, pulmonary ventilation is the mechanical process of air flowing from the atmosphere into the lungs – more specifically the alveoli. This is possible due to the alternating pressure differences created by contraction and relaxation of the respiratory muscles, such as the intercostal muscles.

External respiration

External respiration is the exchange of gases between the alveoli and the capillaries. Oxygen diffuses from the alveoli, which is at higher pressure, moving to lower pressure in the capillaries; while carbon dioxide diffuses from high pressure in the capillary to lower pressure in the alveoli.

Internal respiration

Internal respiration is the exchange of gases during systemic circulation – the exchange of gases from the capillaries to the tissue cells and vice versa.

Inhalation and exhalation

Pressure changes during pulmonary ventilation are caused by inhalation (also known as inspiration – breathing in) and exhalation (also known as expiration – breathing out). Air moves into the lungs when the pressure inside the lungs is less than the pressure outside the lungs; this pressure is created during inhalation. Air moves out of the lungs when the pressure inside the lungs is greater than the pressure in the atmosphere created during exhalation.

During inhalation the intercostal muscles contract, lifting the ribs up and outwards, and the diaphragm is forced downwards with the sternum pushed forwards – increasing the volume of the chest cavity. The pressure inside the lungs is lower than that of the atmosphere, drawing air into the lungs. Consequently, oxygen diffuses into the capillaries and carbon dioxide into the alveoli.

During exhalation the intercostal muscles relax, the ribs are drawn in and downwards, the sternum moves inwards and the diaphragm is drawn upwards – decreasing the volume of the chest cavity. The pressure inside the lungs is higher than that of the atmosphere, expelling air into the atmosphere.

Remember

The function of the respiratory system is to allow for gaseous exchange.

Time to reflect

- Do you know and understand all relevant anatomical terminology?
- Can you name each bone, discuss which type of bone it is and which bones it articulates with at the joint?
- For all joints, can you identify the type of joint, describe its structure and demonstrate which movements occur at the joint?
- Can you identify the action, origin and insertion of all the muscles?

- Are you able to watch a sporting movement and explain the movements occurring at the joints, identify the muscle responsible for the movement and explain the type of contraction taking place?
- Can you describe the structure and function of the cardio system?
- Can you describe the structure and function of the vascular system?
- Can you describe the structure and function of the respiratory system?

Case study (for recommended answers, see www.pearsonfe.co.uk/foundationsinsport)

Jo Lee is a triathlete and has recently had her most successful triathlon yet. The sprint triathlon consisted of a 400 m swim, 20 km on the bike followed by a 5 km run. Jo achieved an overall time of 1 hour 11 minutes 21 seconds, finishing second in the 25–29 years age group, with an overall ranking of thirteenth female. Jo's swim split was impressive – fastest woman with 6 minutes 4 seconds positioning her seventh fastest overall of all male and female competitors and age groups, with a modest ride on the bike with a split of 41 minutes 12 seconds and a 5 km run in 21 minutes 30 seconds.

Questions

1. Discuss the joint movements involved in front crawl swimming.
2. Discuss the muscles responsible for the movements identified in front crawl swimming.
3. Describe the muscle fibre types required during cycling and spinning.
4. Describe the process of internal and external respiration.

Check your understanding (for answers, see www.pearsonfe.co.uk/foundationsinsport)

1. Describe the axial and appendicular skeleton, making reference to the names, types of bones and their function.
2. Briefly describe the three classifications of joints.
3. Describe the gross and micro structure of a muscle.
4. Differentiate between the functions of a ligament and a tendon.
5. Describe lordosis and its effect on the muscular system.
6. Describe kyphosis and its effect on the muscular system.

7. Observe a rugby player performing a squat and complete the following table for the up and down phase.

Agonist muscle	Action

8. Describe the structure of the cardiovascular system.
9. Describe the function of the cardiovascular system.
10. Describe the structure and function of the respiratory system.

Useful resources:

To obtain a secure link to the websites below, see the Websites section on page ii or visit the companion website at www.pearsonfe.co.uk/foundationsinsport.

- Musculoskeletal Radiology, Department of Radiology, University of Washington

- Instant Anatomy

- Visible body

- BBC Science: Human Body and Mind

- Get Body Smart

- IMAIOS: E-Anatomy

- MEDtropolis

- Gray's Anatomy for Students Flash Cards

- Netter's Anatomy Flash Cards

Further reading

Agur, A. and Dalley, A. (2009). *Grants Atlas of Anatomy* (12th edition). Philadelphia: Lippincott, Williams & Wilkins.

Behnke, R. (2001). *Kinetic Anatomy*. Champaign: Human Kinetics.

Field, D. and Hutchinson, J. (2006). *Anatomy Palpation and Surface Marking*. London: Elsevier.

Harris, P. and Ranson, C. (2008). Atlas of Living and Surface Anatomy for Sports Medicine. China: Churchill Livingstone

Jarmey, C. (2008). *The Concise Book of Muscles*. Chichester: Lotus.

Kingston, B. (2005). *Understanding Muscles. A Practical Guide to Muscle Function* (2nd edition). Cheltenham: Nelson Thornes.

Kingston, B. (2001). *Understanding Joints. A Practical Guide to Their Structure and Function*. Cheltenham: Nelson Thornes.

Manocchia, P. (2007). *Anatomy of Exercise*. London: A & C Black.

Palastanga, N., Field, D. and Soames, R. (2006). *Anatomy and Human Movement* 5th edition. London: Elsevier.

Seeley, R., Stephens, T. and Tate, P. (2000). *Anatomy and Physiology*. Maidenhead: McGraw-Hill.

Standring, S. (2008). *Gray's Anatomy: The Anatomical Basis of Clinical Practice, Expert Consult* (online and print). Spain: Churchill Livingstone.

Tortora, J.T. and Grabowski, S.R. (2003). *Principles of Anatomy and Physiology* (9th edition) New York: John Wiley & Sons.

Wirhed, R. (2006). *Athletic Ability and the Anatomy of Motion* (3rd edition). China: Mosby.

Chapter 8

Psychology for coaches

Introduction

Whether you are coaching young performers or elite level athletes, their psychological state has a significant bearing on their sporting performance and well-being. Issues such as anxiety, concentration, enjoyment and motivation, are all related to whether athletes perform to the best of their ability, persist when times are tough and draw positive experiences from their involvement in sport. Therefore, you need an understanding of the factors that are likely to influence an athlete's mental state. These diverse factors include relationships with parents, peers and teammates, personality characteristics and properties of the situation itself, such as audience or opponent characteristics. As a coach, you have a key role to play in positively developing the psychological well-being of your athletes. This chapter focuses upon the role of the coach in relation to athlete psychology and you will learn how factors, such as the coaching environment you create and the relationships you form with your athletes, are useful tools in helping them achieve their potential.

Learning outcomes

After you have read this chapter you should be able to:

- define motivation – both *intrinsic* and *extrinsic* motivation

- explain why motivation matters in the context of sport

- understand achievement goal theory

- explain why achievement goals matter

- identify the ways in which coaches can affect motivation in their athletes

- understand key features of the coach–athlete relationship and how to positively develop it

- understand about the psychological impact of sports injuries and the role of the coach

- explain the importance of *task* and *social group cohesion* and the role of the coach

- understand about anxiety and arousal in sport and the role of the coach.

Starting block

You are coaching a group of 9-year-old children. The children have enrolled on a summer sports camp and you have been assigned to coach them every afternoon for a week in a sport of your choice. The children are of mixed ability – some have experience of the sport while others are novices.

- How would you structure your coaching sessions in order to maximise the opportunity for all children to enjoy them and feel a sense of pride and competence in relation to the activity?
- What kind of problems might you encounter in relation to the above objectives?

Motivation

Motivation can be thought of as the *intensity* and *direction* of your efforts (Weinberg and Gould, 2010). Intensity of effort refers to the *amount* of effort you devote to a particular objective or task. It is common for coaches and athletes to speak about motivation in this way, suggesting that one individual has lots of motivation whereas another appears to have none. However, you can also think about motivation in terms of quality. From this perspective you would be less concerned with intensity of effort than with direction. For example, while two runners may both be putting in effort, they may be *directing* their efforts towards different goals; so one runner may be concerned about winning the race, whereas the other may want to beat her personal best.

Intrinsic and extrinsic motivation

Motivation is often thought of in terms of **intrinsic** and **extrinsic motivation** (Deci and Ryan 1985), i.e. the different reasons that explain why individuals are engaged in an activity. When you are intrinsically motivated the activity is 'an end in itself'. Factors related to doing the activity (such as the feelings, emotions or pleasure you get while doing it) are the motivating force that attracts you to engage in it. In contrast, when you are extrinsically motivated the activity is a 'means to an end'. In this case, it is not inherently rewarding in any way but is viewed as something you have to do in order to obtain an external reward (such as, money, trophies, praise or glory) or to avoid external punishment.

Key terms

Motivation – the intensity and direction of effort

Intrinsic motivation – doing an activity because the activity is an end in itself

Extrinsic motivation – doing an activity because the activity is a means to an end

Why motivation matters in sport

These different types of motivation matter because they influence the manner in which we undertake specific activities. Imagine reading a book or watching a film that you find particularly engaging and interesting. This is an intrinsically motivating activity because the driving force behind your engagement is the pleasure, intrigue and excitement of the activity. It is difficult for others to distract you from such activities (because you *want* to focus upon them and are *absorbed* in them); it is a shame that such activities have to end (because they are so inherently pleasurable). Your general attitude towards them is positive (you cannot wait to pick the book up again next time).

Contrast your experience of such activities with your engagement in the lesson you found least enjoyable at school (an extrinsically motivated activity that you probably only attended because you *had* to – to avoid punishment from parents or teachers, for example). You probably found it was easier for others to distract you in the course of such lessons (because doing *anything*, other than the activity, was more enjoyable to you), that you could not wait for the end of the lesson (to escape the activity) and that you dreaded the next timetabled session. These sorts of differences in the way we go about intrinsically and extrinsically motivated activities make it more likely that we will experience pleasure, satisfaction, concentration and a positive attitude when we are intrinsically motivated.

Where do intrinsic and extrinsic motivation come from?

As a coach, it is useful to know whether there are factors that make it more likely that individuals will be intrinsically or extrinsically motivated towards a particular activity. This enables you to structure your activities so they foster intrinsic motivation.

Interestingly, it is not the case that athletes are always intrinsically motivated towards their sports. In his autobiography, tennis legend Andre Agassi, wrote of his hatred for tennis and suggested that he simply played tennis for a living – even though he hated it with a passion and always had.

Research (Deci and Ryan, 2008) suggests that individuals are more likely to develop an intrinsic motivation towards an activity if it allows them to feel three important feelings: **competence** (e.g. they feel they are good at the activity), **autonomy** (e.g. they feel the activity is something that has arisen out of their personal choice and not out of external pressure) and **relatedness** (e.g. they feel like they are valued by and connected to others during the activity).

These feelings are psychological *needs* that all humans have and activities that allow us to satisfy these needs are more likely to be attractive (and therefore intrinsically motivating). In contrast, activities that starve us of these needs will be unappealing (and if we engage in them it will not be out of pleasure). If coaches are able to develop an environment that fosters these feelings of competence, autonomy and relatedness then they will maximise the chances of intrinsic motivation developing in their athletes.

Achievement goal theory

Achievement goal theory focuses on the idea that individuals' feelings of competence are closely related to their motivation. For example, in the starter activity above (page 118), suppose you were

able to help the children to experience a sense of pride and to feel competent in their ability to do the activity. If this is the case they are more likely to: (a) feel a sense of enjoyment, pride and relaxation while doing the activity, and (b) *want* to do the activity again. Imagine how it would feel to take part in a coaching session where you spent most of the time feeling ashamed and incompetent about your abilities. It would be unlikely that you would find the experience enjoyable and you may spend a lot of the time worried and anxious. Ultimately, you would not want to repeat the experience. Figure 8.1 illustrates the simple role that feelings of competence play in the motivation process.

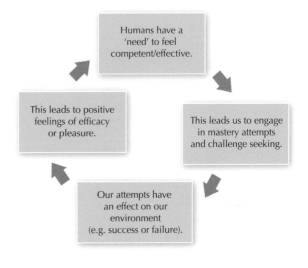

Figure 8.1. The role of feeling competent in the motivation process

Mastery and performance goals

Feeling competent seems to be a central issue in motivation and most psychologically healthy individuals have an implicit desire to feel good (and not to feel bad) about themselves in the context of sport (or any achievement context). However, what if different athletes had different ideas about what it *takes* to be competent? Achievement goal theory suggests that athletes can have different *achievement goals* that essentially reflect the manner in which they tend to *define* competence in sport. When athletes adopt **mastery goals** it is suggested that they are able to feel a sense of pride, success or competence when they demonstrate that their personal ability is improving, that they are learning something new and that they have tried as hard as they can (regardless of how their ability compares to other athletes).

However, these achievements would not be enough to make an athlete with **performance goals** feel competent about themselves. When performance goals prevail, athletes think of themselves as competent when they are able to demonstrate that they have superior ability to other athletes (simply improving or learning is not viewed as an achievement in its own right). Figure 8.2 demonstrates the fundamental differences in relation to how mastery- and performance-oriented athletes ultimately view competence.

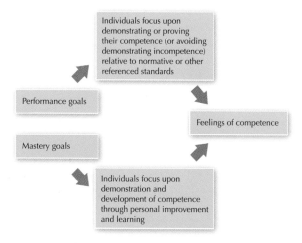

Figure 8.2 How do individuals with mastery and performance goals tend to obtain feelings of competence?

Table 8.1 Key differences in the thinking of individuals with mastery versus performance goals

Key terms

Achievement goals – personal definitions of the meaning of success

Mastery goals – success is synonymous with learning, improvement and effort

Performance goals – success is synonymous with ability compared to others

Stop and think

Think about the two types of achievement goals discussed (mastery and performance goals). Consider two athletes – one with strong performance goals and the other with strong mastery goals. How might the following issues be thought about or experienced differently for the two athletes?

- When they fail at a task or make mistakes – what does it mean?
- How might they view particularly challenging tasks that offer a moderate to low chance of success?
- In terms of difficulty, what sort of tasks would best enable them to satisfy their achievement goals?
- Is cheating likely to be helpful to them?

Why do achievement goals matter?

Achievement goals matter because they mean that individuals think, feel and behave differently. Table 8.1 illustrates the typical ways that mastery- and performance-oriented athletes have been shown to think in relation to the questions posed in the above stop and think activity.

	Athlete with **mastery goals**	Athlete with **performance goals**
(1) What does it mean to fail at a task or make mistakes?	Your aim is to improve and learn. Failure and mistakes can provide valuable information that helps you satisfy this aim. For this reason, they are viewed positively.	Your aim is to show that you have superior ability to others. Failure and mistakes do not help you achieve this aim. For this reason, you view them negatively.
(2) How do you view particularly challenging tasks?	In light of your aim, a challenging task is the sort of task where you will learn most about your strengths and weaknesses. This is the best type of task for you to learn from and improve.	In light of your aim, a challenging task carries with it a higher risk that you will not appear superior. It is not the best task for you to achieve your aim.
(3) What sort of task difficulty is best suited to your goals?	A relatively difficult task. An easy task will not help you to learn about your abilities and develop them.	An easy task. This is because this type of task carries maximum certainty that you will look like you have high ability.
(4) Is cheating likely to be of use to you?	No. Your objective is to learn and if you cheat you will ultimately be cheating yourself by denying yourself the opportunity to benefit from the task.	It could be. If your ultimate aim is to win and nothing else matters then perhaps it is worth doing *anything* to win?

The motivational climate

The two quotes below are from interviews with high-level athletes. They demonstrate different ideas in relation to the athletes' definition of success in sport. For Layla, success seems to be about demonstrating her superiority over others (despite the fact that she believes success *should* be about improvement and personal progression); this would appear to reflect a performance goal orientation.

> It should be about personal improvement but I think for me it's in my nature…it's human nature…that if you beat someone, if you're the clear winner, that's the *definite* sign of success. If you work hard and you personally improve but you don't beat someone then you sit down and there's a kind of dissonance because you actually think 'Well, have I *really* achieved?' 'Was I *really* successful or wasn't I? 'I've improved…but I've not won – that's not success to me.'
>
> (Layla, 22 years old, elite volleyball player)

For Alice, success is viewed as related to the personal progression and developments that she makes in her sport (suggesting a stronger mastery orientation).

> Success is when you know about your strengths and weaknesses and your limitations and where you can push yourself. It all makes you wiser…and I always think a better athlete is someone who's wiser…who knows about themselves…who knows what they *can* do. In terms of being 'clearly superior' or 'the best', whilst it would make me feel good, of course, to be the best person…it's not for the reasons you might think. I feel like it makes me feel good in the sense that I can help others if you know what I mean. I've got something that none of these people have and so I can educate them and teach them about what I know about the game that they don't necessarily know.
>
> (Alice, 22 years old, elite netball player)

Stop and think

Discuss what you believe are likely to be the main factors responsible for athletes adopting stronger mastery or performance goals.

Why do some athletes adopt stronger mastery goals (like Alice) whereas others seem more concerned with performance goals (like Layla)?

The answer to this question is complex and depends upon an interaction of factors ranging from athletes' deeper personality traits, their early socialisation experiences with parents and family, and the characteristics of the sporting environment in which they function. It is encouraging for those involved in coaching to know that research (for example Carr, 2006) strongly suggests that athletes are more or less likely to adopt performance or mastery goals in sport as a response to the **motivational climate** that is constructed by their coach. Through the way that they coach, coaches are responsible for sending athletes signals that implicitly suggest that either performance or mastery goals are more or less important. Athletes' personal achievement goals are often shaped in response to the motivational climate created by the coach.

When a **mastery climate** is created, the signals from the coach suggest that success is synonymous with improvement and learning, regardless of **normative ability**. When a **performance climate** is created, coaches are suggesting that success is about the level of ability you show compared to others and little to do with your personal progression. Athletes can pick up on these cues and their thinking may be partially shaped by them.

Key terms

Motivational climate – the way in which coaches structure the sporting environment in order to send signals to athletes about the meaning of success

Mastery climate – the environment sends signals suggesting success is synonymous with improvement and learning

Performance climate – the environment sends signals suggesting success is synonymous with demonstration of ability

Normative ability – Your ability compared to another – referenced norm

How coaches can affect motivation

How do coaches tend to create a motivational climate that reflects either a mastery- or performance-oriented environment? It can be helpful to think of this in terms of the acronym 'TARGET' (Epstein, 1989):

- **T**ask
- **A**uthority
- **R**ecognition
- **G**rouping
- **E**valuation
- **T**iming

Each letter here represents a structural feature of the sporting environment that coaches can control in order to convey mastery or performance-oriented coaching climates.

Task

Coaches are often responsible for assigning athletes *tasks* as part of training and competition. A coach who predominantly presents athletes with tasks that require them to demonstrate their superiority (e.g. training is nothing but a series of races or competitions) is creating a performance climate. A mastery climate is more about constructing tasks so that an athlete's objective is to develop their personal ability and learn.

Authority

In a performance climate an athlete's developmental progress is solely in the hands of the coach. That is, athletes tend to be told what skills they will practise, for how long and in what order, and are not involved in the decision-making process. Such an environment is less sensitive to different athletes' personal progression as it is predetermined that everybody needs to work on the same skills for the same amount of time. In reality, if learning is the ultimate goal then the environment should be sensitive to the fact that certain individuals need more or less time to work on different activities. A mastery climate therefore places more authority in the hands of athletes, enabling them to have a say in how and what they develop. Giving authority to athletes means they are also more likely to learn about themselves and their sport.

Recognition

A coach who consistently recognises individuals (through use of praise or material rewards) simply for demonstrating their superiority and punishes (through lack of praise, verbal or physical punishments) those who demonstrate weaker ability is creating a performance climate. Conversely, a coach who allocates rewards to those who are making personal progressions, learning or improving (regardless of their normative ability) is creating a mastery climate.

Grouping

In a mastery climate the coach's objective is that all individuals learn as much as they can. With this sort of ethos, the formation of groups with mixed abilities, where those with stronger abilities at certain tasks are actively involved in helping those with weaker abilities to develop and improve, helps to obtain this objective. However, in a performance climate, individuals are consistently grouped according to their normative ability.

Evaluation

How do coaches ultimately judge their athletes as having succeeded or failed? When this evaluation judgement is solely based upon outcomes or winning, then a performance climate prevails. When it is based upon personal improvement, learning and effort, a mastery climate prevails.

Timing

If your overall goal is the learning and development of your athletes, then an environment that is insensitive to the fact that some individuals need to devote more time to developing certain aspects of themselves than others is unhelpful. A performance climate tends to involve coaches dictating the timing required for athletes to develop their skills and abilities, whereas a mastery climate is sensitive to the time various athletes require in order to learn and develop fully.

Mastery climate and motivation

When athletes are exposed to a mastery climate from their coaches (in accordance with the features of the TARGET acronym identified above) they are more likely to adopt mastery goals in the context of sport, to enjoy sport, to be less anxious and more focused, and to remain involved in sport for longer. A mastery climate has been linked to the development of higher levels of intrinsic motivation and this may be because a mastery climate is more likely to support feelings of competence, autonomy, and relatedness in individuals (which are the fundamental psychological needs hypothesised to underpin intrinsic motivation).

Stop and think

In practice, it is not easy for coaches to create a mastery climate. For a typical coaching session in a sport of your choice, outline how you might structure each of the features of the TARGET acronym in order to create a mastery-oriented climate.

Key features of coach–athlete relationships

Athletes often suggest that their sporting achievements are to a large extent attributable to the quality of the relationship they are able to form with their coach. For example, Kalinowski's (1985) interviews with Olympic swimmers prompted him to suggest that no one can get to the level of an Olympic swimmer without the support and direction they receive from individuals such as coaches.

Former Olympic runner, Steve Cram, described his relationship with his coach as something more than an athlete–coach relationship and even went so far as to suggest his coach was something of a second father figure to him. In his autobiography, Sir Alex Ferguson suggested that forming a relationship, characterised by key features such as loyalty and commitment, with footballers is one of the most important parts of his role as a coach.

The 3Cs of coach–athlete relationships

What might be some key ingredients of a positive coach–athlete relationship? The 3Cs model is a theoretical framework that suggests that coach–athlete bonds are most likely to be experienced positively by both athletes and coaches when they are characterised by **closeness**, **commitment** and **complementarity** (Jowett and Cockerill, 2003).

Stop and think

Are there key features necessary for an effective coach–athlete relationship? If so, what might they be and how might you foster them?

Think about your own experiences with coaches in the past or present and discuss the following issues.

- Have you ever experienced what you would describe as a positive or a negative coach–athlete relationship?

- Related to your answer above, what made these coach–athlete relationships particularly positive or negative for you?

- Do you believe coaches can learn skills that would help develop more positive relationships with their athletes?

Closeness

The notion of 'closeness' seems like an obvious ingredient to recommend in any successful human relationship. In the context of the **3Cs** model, closeness refers to the general **emotional tone** of the relationship. When closeness is a characteristic of a given coach–athlete bond, the relationship tends to be underpinned by central features of human relationships such as a general 'liking' for one another, trust and respect. Conversely, when closeness is lacking we might expect to see dislike of one another, a lack of trust and disrespect.

Commitment

Commitment, in the context of the coach–athlete relationship, might be defined as the sense that there is a long-term orientation towards the relationship from both parties. Both parties seem committed to the relationship for the long haul (or at least committed to achieving the goals they have set out to accomplish). In reality, this is likely to mean making personal sacrifices in order to help the relationship achieve its goals, appreciating the sacrifices that your partner has made and communicating and working with the other person in order to achieve the goals that have been set. The harmony of the relationship is likely to be negatively affected if such commitment is unevenly distributed.

Complementarity

In essence, complementarity reflects a relationship where both coaches and athletes occupy roles that complement the role of the other party and both partners cooperate effectively. For example, complementarity is present in a relationship where both parties **accept** that the coach is responsible for instruction of the athlete during training sessions and the athlete's task is to follow these instructions. Both parties are ready, at ease and accepting of the roles they have assigned each other during training. Conflict may arise when relationship partners do not occupy complementary roles (e.g. perhaps both parties wish to see themselves in the role of the 'instructor' during training sessions, causing a conflict of desired roles).

The 3Cs play a significant role in regulating important psychological factors that ultimately impact performance and well-being (Jowett and Cockerill, 2003). For example, when athletes and coaches perceive that the 3Cs are **positively** experienced in the context of their relationship then they are more likely to feel satisfied, to feel passionate about their involvement in sport and/or coaching and to be motivated. They are also less likely to fear failure and experience burn-out linked to sport involvement.

Key terms

Closeness – the emotional tone of the relationship

Commitment – the degree of commitment to the relationship

Complementarity – the manner in which the roles of each party complement each other

Fostering a positive relationship

The 3Cs seem to underpin coach–athlete relationships that are most likely to provide an environment in which athletes can experience success and enhanced psychological well-being.

It is also useful to know what effective coaches actually *do* that serves to enhance the likelihood that the 3Cs will characterise the relationships they form with their athletes. Interviews with successful coaches have suggested that the COMPASS model (Rhind and Jowett, 2010) is an effective list of the ways in which coaches facilitate and maintain these relationship features. The COMPASS model is an acronym that reflects key features linked to facilitation of the 3Cs.

- **C**onflict management – successful coaches care about identifying, understanding, resolving and managing any sources of conflict that arise in their relationships with athletes. As a result of this, athletes probably feel that their coach cares about their feelings and is committed to making the relationship work.

- **O**penness – successful coaches promote open lines of communication and athletes feel that they can always approach their coach with regard to their feelings and suggestions.

- **M**otivation – successful coaches are good at making the relationship *itself* a source of athletes' motivation. Athletes want to be part of their *sport* and want to be part of the *relationship*.

- **P**reventative – successful coaches are concerned about discussing what would happen if expectations about the relationship were not met. In this way, they are helping to foresee and prevent any difficulties that may arise.

- **A**ssurance – successful coaches implicitly assure athletes that they are committed to the partnership by acting in ways that show the athlete that they too are making personal sacrifices.

- **S**upport – successful coaches are concerned with helping their athlete through emotionally difficult times both on and off the sports field, signifying to the athlete that they are cared about as a human being.

- **S**ocial networks – successful coaches will often socialise with their athletes in order to reinforce to the athletes their commitment to the relationship and that they simply 'like' the company of the other partner.

Stop and think

For each of the elements of the COMPASS acronym above, outline what you think you could do to develop this aspect of your relationship with athletes you are coaching.

Psychological impact of sports injuries

Stop and think

Can you identify a time when either you or somebody you knew suffered a serious injury that meant they could not participate in sport for a prolonged period of time? In what ways do you think this affected you/them psychologically and socially? Make a list of the different factors you identify.

Injury is an integral part of the sporting experiences of most elite and recreational athletes. Table 8.2 highlights how prevalent injury can be at various levels of participation. It is therefore useful for coaches to understand the psychological impact that injury can have on athletes and the potential role of the coach in the process of psychological recovery.

Table 8.2 Injury prevalence statistics

Injury statistics
11–22% of children are injured each year while taking part in a form of organised sport. (Backx, Beijer and Bol 1991)
Research identified an injury rate of 97 injuries per 1000 athletes in the 2007 World Athletics Championships. 56% of these injuries were serious enough to prevent athletes from training and competing. (Alonso et al., 2009)
From 1991 to 2005 there were 45 instances of serious injuries to British jockeys that resulted in direct career termination. (Balendra, Turner and McCrory, 2007)

Emotional and behavioural responses

Sporting literature has examined athletes' emotional and behavioural responses to sport injury. Injury can be a demoralising experience for most athletes. From an emotional perspective, research has associated athletic injury with significant changes in mood and emotional responses ranging from anger, frustration and boredom to depression. For some athletes the sense of loss associated with injury is particularly strong, with some experiencing extreme negative responses including depression that often surpasses the levels required for clinical intervention.

On the positive side, there have been suggestions that if athletes can learn to cope with the emotions and hardships associated with injury then they may ultimately experience significant post-traumatic growth.

In terms of behavioural responses to athletic injury, research suggests that those athletes who use psychological skills, adhere to programmes of rehabilitation, use social support and invest significant effort in the rehabilitation process, are more likely to recover effectively from athletic injury and to experience the process more positively (Walker et al. 2007).

Coaches and rehabilitation

Coaches can help to ensure that athletes adhere to rehabilitation programmes and are motivated to invest effort into what is often a long and challenging process. Much of the literature on motivation and coach–athlete relationships is also applicable in the context of injury. For example, athletes are more likely to invest in the process of rehabilitation when they are intrinsically motivated to do so. This requires careful consideration of how the basic psychological needs of athletes (competence, autonomy and relatedness) can be supported during the process of recovery. Athletes often report issues such as feeling that they have lost their ability or a sense of disconnectedness to the team and the coach during rehabilitation. Coaches need to work hard to create a motivational climate for injured athletes which ensures that they are able to maintain their psychological needs.

Stop and think

As a coach, what might you do to ensure that an injured athlete maintains a feeling of competence/achievement and a sense of connection to the team during the process of rehabilitation?

Cognitive appraisal approach

Cognitive appraisal perspectives on athletic injury propose that it is the athletes' interpretation of the injury that can dictate how they respond. It is likely that individual differences (such as personality) and situational factors (e.g. family dynamics, social support provision) will underpin these interpretations. For example, it might be suggested that an injured athlete who has a strong social support network beyond sport might find it easier to adapt to the sense of isolation experienced when they are disconnected from their team (due to injury) as opposed to an athlete who has no social support outside sport. Encouraging athletes to form an identity beyond their sporting life may be helpful when they encounter issues such as injury.

Task and social group cohesion

As sport often has a very 'social' context (particularly team sports), it is likely that the relationships between group members will have a significant impact on factors such as performance and well-being. Researchers (Carron et al. 1998) have defined **cohesion** as the tendency for a group to stick together and remain united: (a) in its attempts to reach its goals, and (b) in its desire for all members to remain satisfied with their group involvement.

There are many examples of scenarios where seemingly less talented sport teams have overcome overwhelming odds and succeeded, attributing their successes to factors such as a 'team bond,' 'teamwork,' or 'group chemistry' (Carron et al. 2007). For example, the 1988 FA Cup winning squad, Wimbledon FC, were victorious despite facing opponents (they overcame Liverpool FC in the final) with significantly more talented individuals. They attributed their success to a collective mentality (they called themselves the Crazy gang). There are also examples of situations

Key term

Cognitive appraisal – a mental evaluation that leads to an interpretation of a specific event (such as a sport injury)

where exceptionally talented teams of individuals have failed to succeed in sport due to an apparent absence of the ability to work together as a team, to respect each other and to form a coherent unit. Carron et al. (2007) refer to the 2004 US Olympic men's basketball team ('the dream team') who, despite possessing by far the most talented group of individuals, were defeated in the opening round of the competition by Puerto Rico – with the lack of success attributed to an absence of group chemistry in the US team.

Sport groups and teams can demonstrate cohesion in two senses. **Task cohesion** refers to cohesion in relation to group objectives and goals (e.g. everyone is united in their attempts to pursue group aims – but they need not 'like' each other) and **social cohesion** refers to a unity in relation to socialising with each other (e.g. members are socially close and seem to 'like' each other on a level that goes beyond simple pursuit of group goals). When individuals belong to groups that are characterised by these elements of cohesion in sport they show higher levels of satisfaction, greater levels of effort, a stronger desire to sacrifice themselves for the sake of the team, higher self-esteem and a propensity to share responsibility for their failures collectively (Hardy et al. 2005).

Key terms

Task cohesion – a group is united in its attempts to achieve group goals and objectives

Social cohesion – a group is united in the sense that it is 'socially close'

Fostering group cohesion

How can coaches help to foster a cohesive group? The following factors relate to the likelihood of a sports team or group developing cohesion.

- Role clarity and acceptance: you can increase the likelihood of a team working together effectively by ensuring that all members *know*, *understand* and *accept* their roles.

- Proximity: individuals are unlikely to form bonds with each other if they are not given the opportunity to develop relationships. This is only likely to occur if they are in close proximity. Close proximity in the form of team social events, outings and road trips does not guarantee cohesion but provides an essential ingredient to help it.

- Group identity: when a group has a distinct identity it gives it a sense of uniqueness. This uniqueness (shown in specific team logos, clothing, habits, or mottoes) can help the group to develop a sense of identity.

- Fairness: for athletes to feel that they are a valued member of the group all members must be treated fairly. Athletes need to develop a sense of trust that their efforts and contributions to the team are valued, judged and accepted equally when compared with other individuals.

- Social support: creating a climate where athletes feel that they are supported by their teammates facilitates cohesion. For example, when athletes are faced with difficulties or injury, how does the coach utilise relationships with other team members to help the injured athlete remain supported and valued?

Arousal and anxiety

The psychological terms arousal and anxiety are often used interchangeably by those involved in sport and coaching. However, in the literature, arousal has been thought of as a general *activation* of our physiological and energy systems (Weinberg and Gould, 2010). A highly aroused individual is therefore neurologically and physiologically *ready for action* and their bodily systems tend to reflect this (e.g. they are likely to have increased heart rate, increased respiratory rate and 'butterflies' in their stomach). Increases in arousal tend to reflect the fact that our brain perceives that we need to be 'ready' for something and this might be something good (e.g. we are excited and ready to go on a date with a new boyfriend or girlfriend) or bad (e.g. we

are ready to flee from an angry dog that looks as if it is about to attack us).

Anxiety has been described as a negative emotional state that is characterised by worry and apprehension in relation to perceived psychological threat or harm (Weinberg and Gould, 2010). *Cognitive anxiety* is the mental component of anxiety and reflects worry and apprehension about a perceived threat. *Somatic anxiety* is the physical component that seems to accompany these worries and consists of classic physical symptoms such as butterflies, sweaty palms and increased heart rate (it may be that somatic anxiety is simply arousal that is a specific product of cognitive anxiety).

Key terms

Arousal – a general activation of our physiological and energy systems

Anxiety - a negative emotional state that is characterised by worry and apprehension in relation to perceived psychological threat or harm

How do arousal and anxiety influence athletes?

Stop and think

Can you identify any famous sporting moments where athletes appear to have 'collapsed' or 'choked' due to them apparently experiencing overly high levels of arousal or anxiety? Why do you think they developed such high levels of arousal or anxiety in the moments you identified? Furthermore, how might such arousal or anxiety have contributed to their apparent 'collapse' in performance?

Would you suggest that being in a state of high *arousal* would be beneficial for athletic performance? If so, is it simply a case of the more arousal the better? Or would different levels of arousal be required for different moments within a specific sporting event (e.g. taking a penalty in football versus going in for a hard tackle)?

These sorts of questions have been addressed by researchers. For example, inverted-U theory (Landers and Arent, 2001) has predicted that increases in arousal are likely to benefit performance – but only up to a point (see Figure 8.3).

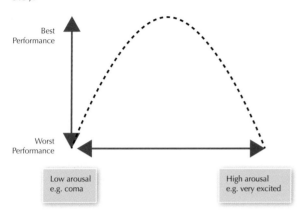

Figure 8.3 Inverted-U theory

Obviously, an absence of arousal would be unlikely to benefit athletic performance (because 'zero' arousal is akin to being in a coma) so increased arousal will bring physiological activation that probably assists performance. However, if arousal becomes too strong it may produce physiological activation that makes focus, concentration and coordination more difficult, which is detrimental to performance. It might also be the case that there would be different inverted-Us for different sporting events or for different skills within the same sporting event (see Figure 8.4).

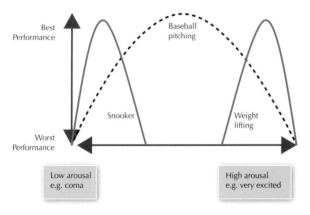

Figure 8.4 Different inverted-Us for different events?

High levels of anxiety – both **cognitive anxiety** and **somatic anxiety** – have been linked to a number of negative outcomes including:

- medical and psychological symptoms (such as gastrointestinal complaints and sleep disturbance)
- lower levels of satisfaction and enjoyment of sport
- avoidance behaviours (people attempt to avoid the specific factor that they perceive as a trigger for their high anxiety)
- impaired cognitive functioning (such as alterations in concentration ability).

Key terms

Cognitive anxiety – the mental component of anxiety (e.g. worries and apprehension)

Somatic anxiety – the physical accompaniment to cognitive anxiety (such as sweaty palms, butterflies in stomach or increased heart rate)

However, the relationship between anxiety and performance has been thought of by Hanin (1997) in terms of *individual zones of optimal functioning*. This theory suggests that every individual has a specific optimal 'zone' of anxiety within which they tend to produce their best performances. Therefore, one athlete may perform better under relatively low levels of anxiety but another athlete may perform better when they experience a moderate level of anxiety. Figure 8.5 illustrates this idea more clearly.

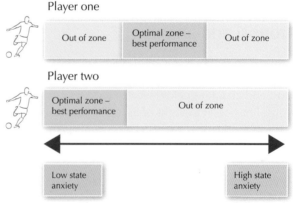

Figure 8.5 Individual zones of optimal functioning

How can coaches facilitate optimal arousal and anxiety?

These issues in relation to arousal and anxiety suggest that it would be useful for coaches to develop an awareness of how to help athletes develop optimal levels of either arousal or anxiety.

The levels of arousal and anxiety that athletes experience are likely to depend on a complex array of factors that stem from the specific *personality* of an individual athlete (e.g. individuals with high **trait anxiety** have a natural tendency to be more anxious at any given moment) to the characteristics of the coaching climate (a *performance climate* has been linked to higher anxiety as athletes tend to feel more threatened). However, there are also other factors for helping athletes to either cope better with higher levels of arousal and anxiety or to regulate their levels to a comfortable or optimal point. Here are some of these strategies.

- The use of music has a potent influence on anxiety and arousal levels (either to 'psych-up' or to relax) and is particularly useful prior to competition.

- Teaching athletes mental skills in order to cope with and regulate their arousal and anxiety is a popular and effective strategy. These mental skills might include techniques such as mental imagery (learning to create images in your mind), self-talk (paying attention to your internal dialogue), relaxation and goal setting.

- The creation of supportive motivational climates and coach–athlete relationships has been shown to help with experiences of anxiety.

Key term

Trait anxiety – a personality disposition that predisposes individuals to higher levels of anxiety at a given moment

Time to reflect

How can you create a mastery climate for your athletes by manipulating the features of the TARGET acronym?

How can you ensure you maintain a positive relationship with your athletes by utilising the constructs of the COMPASS acronym?

How might you ensure your teams or groups of athletes are likely to develop a cohesive bond?

In what ways can you help athletes who are going through difficult times with injury?

What might you do as a coach in order to help athletes deal with anxiety and arousal that they experience during competitive situations?

Sally is a pole vaulter. She is standing at the end of the runway ready to vault. She has never cleared a bar this high before and this is her final attempt of three. The whole athletics team is surrounding the runway clapping and the team's ultimate success is hinging on the outcome of Sally's pole vault. She is filled with adrenaline. She takes her run up, digs in her pole and years of training take over. Her body begins to clear the bar. The crowd is roaring and the outcome is uncertain.

In life, we will all find ourselves in such situations. Whether you are taking a crucial exam, raising children or clearing a bar, you may have put in the hard work but the outcome is still uncertain. Success can be defined by extremely slim margins. On some days Sally may barely touch the bar and it falls down – on others she may barely clear it and it stays up. Either way, the effort and preparation she put in were the same – enormous.

Sally clips the bar slightly. The crowd gasps. The bar wobbles and falls off. Sally's devastated. So is everybody else.

Questions

1. How do you believe athletes should (a) judge themselves and (b) be judged by others as successes or failures? Should it be based upon such *outcomes* (as opposed, for example, to the *efforts* they exerted in preparing for them)?

2. Think about your answer to the previous question. Do you believe the same is true in life outside sport (e.g. should we be judged as failures at maths if we just miss out on a grade 'A' – despite the fact we revised extremely hard and learned an awful lot)?

3. Do you think this moment was characterised by high levels of anxiety and arousal? If so, what was behind such elevations in anxiety and arousal? What could Sally have done to help her deal with this?

4. What type of reaction might her coach have at this moment that would ultimately serve to create a performance-oriented motivational climate?

5. What type of reaction might her coach have that would ultimately serve to create a mastery-oriented motivational climate?

6. What could the coach do (in response to her experience of failing to clear the bar) that might serve to greatly enhance Sally's perceptions of the 3Cs in their relationship? Why would this enhance the 3Cs?

7. What could the coach do that might serve to impede the 3Cs in their relationship? Why would this impede the 3Cs?

1. What do athletes' personal achievement goals reflect about them?

2. What are the differences between mastery and performance goals?

3. Describe what the motivational climate is and why it is important for coaches.

4. What are the features of the TARGET acronym and how can they reflect a mastery or performance motivational climate?

5. What are the 3Cs in the context of the coach–athlete relationship?

6. How does the COMPASS acronym suggest coaches can foster and maintain the 3Cs in the context of the coach–athlete relationship?

7. What is the difference between intrinsic and extrinsic motivation?

8. In fostering intrinsic motivation what key feelings should coaches focus upon?

9. How can coaches develop cohesion in sport groups?

10. What is the difference between arousal and anxiety?

11. What strategies might coaches use to facilitate optimal arousal and anxiety levels in athletes?

Useful resources

To obtain a secure link to the websites below, see the Websites section on page ii or visit the companion website at www.pearsonfe.co.uk/foundationsinsport.

• Journal of Sport and Exercise Psychology

• Psychology of Sport and Exercise

• The Coach

Further reading

Agassi, A. (2009). *Open: An autobiography*. New York: AKA.

Alonso, J. M., Junge, A., Renstrom, P., Engebretson, L., Mountjoy, M. & Dvorak, J. (2009). Sport injuries surveillance during the 2007 IAAF World Athletics Championships. *Clinical Journal of Sports Medicine*, 19, 26–32.

Backx, F. J. G., Beijer, H. J. M. and Bol, E. E. (1991). Injuries in high risk persons and high risk sports: A longitudinal study of 1818 school children. *American Journal of Sports Medicine*, 19, 124–130.

Balendra, G., Turner, M. and McCrory, P. (2007). Career-ending injuries to professional jockeys in British horse racing. *British Journal of Sports Medicine*, 42, 22–24.

Carr, S. (2006). An examination of multiple goals in children's physical education: Motivational effects of goal profiles and the role of perceived climate in multiple goal development. *Journal of Sports Sciences*, 24, 281–297.

Carron, A.V., Brawley, L. R. and Widmeyer, W. N. (1998). The measurement of cohesiveness in sport groups. In J. L. Duda (Ed.), *Advances in sport and exercise psychology measurement* (pp. 213-226). Morgantown, WV: Fitness Information Technology.

Carron, A. V., Shapcott, K. M. and Burke, S. M. (2007). Group cohesion in sport and exercise: Past, present and future. In M. Beauchamp and M. Eys (eds.), *Group Dynamics in Exercise and Sport Psychology: Contemporary Themes* (pp. 117–135). New York: Routledge.

Deci, E.L. and Ryan, R.M. (1985). *Intrinsic motivation and self-determination in human behavior*. New York: Plenum.

Deci, E.L. and Ryan, R.M. (2008). Self-determination theory: A macrotheory of human motivation, development, and health. *Canadian Psychology*, 49, 182–185.

Duda, J. (1992). Motivation in sport settings: A goal perspective approach. In G. Roberts (Ed.), *Motivation in sport and exercise*. Champaign, IL: Human Kinetics.

Duda, J. L. (1993). Goals: A social cognitive approach to the study of achievement motivation sport. In R. N. Singer, M. Murphy and L. K. Tennant (Eds.), *Handbook on research in sport psychology* (pp. 421–436). New York: Macmillan.

Epstein, J. (1989). Family structures and student motivation: A developmental perspective. In C. Ames and R. Ames (Eds.), *Research on motivation in education* (Vol.3, pp. 259–295). New York: Academic Press.

Ferguson, A. (2000). *Managing my life: My autobiography*. London: Hodder & Stoughton.

Hanin, Y.L. (1997). Emotions and athletic performance: Individual zones of optimal functioning. *European Yearbook of Sport Psychology*, 1, 29–72.

Hardy, J., Eys, M. E. and Carron, A. V. (2005). Exploring the potential disadvantages of high cohesion in sports teams. *Small Group Research*, 36, 166–187.

Jowett, S. and Cockerill, I. M. (2002). Incompatibility in the coach–athlete relationship. In I. M. Cockerill (Ed.), *Solutions in sport psychology* (pp. 16–31). London: Thomson Learning.

Jowett, S., and Cockerill, I.M. (2003). Olympic Medallists' perspective of the athlete-coach relationship. *Psychology of Sport and Exercise*, 4, 313–331.

Kalinowski, A. G. (1985). The development of Olympic swimmers. In B. S. Bloom (Ed.), *Developing talent in young people* (pp. 139–192). New York: Balantine Books.

Landers, D.M. and Arent, S.M. (2001). Physical activity and mental health. In R. Singer, H. Hausenblas and C. Janelle (Eds.), *Handbook of Sport Psychology* (2nd edition, pp. 740–765). New York: Wiley.

Ntoumanis, N. and Biddle, S.J.H. (1999). A review of motivational climate in physical activity. *Journal of Sports Sciences*, 17, 643–665.

Rhind, D.J.A., and Jowett, S. (2010). Relationship maintenance strategies in the coach-athlete relationship: The development of the COMPASS model. *Journal of Applied Sport Psychology*, 22, 106–121.

Treasure, D. (2001) Enhancing young people's motivation in youth sport: An achievement goal approach. In G. Roberts (Ed.), *Advances in motivation in sport and exercise*. Champaign, IL: Human Kinetics.

Walker, N., Thatcher, J., and Lavallee, D. (2007). Psychological responses to injury in competitive sport: A critical review. *The Journal of the Royal Society for the Promotion of Health*, 127, 174-180.

Weinberg, R. and Gould, D. (2010). *Foundations of Sport and Exercise Psychology* (5th edition). Champaign, IL: Human Kinetics.

Chapter 9

Coaching special populations

Introduction

In the UK, sport and physical activity are a key part of the government agenda for creating a healthier, happier nation. It means that more people are being encouraged to participate in sport, so understanding special populations in sports coaching is integral to being an effective and employable coach. Sports coaches will often work with children and will be expected to understand best practice for this, including the different stages of development for boys and girls. However, a coach should also consider that the individual who they are working with might have an illness, physical or mental impairment, be pregnant or require specific medical treatment that is being supplemented by sporting activity. This chapter aims to explore some of the special populations that you might work with as a sports coach and explains some of the key issues related to working with individuals in a sports setting.

Learning outcomes

After you have read this chapter you should be able to:

- understand that coaching ought to be athlete-centred
- understand what a special population in coaching is
- appreciate the different special populations you may encounter as a coach
- explain some of the characteristics of some special populations
- apply this knowledge to a practical sports coaching setting to be inclusive in coaching.

Athlete-centred coaching

It is easy to say 'coach everyone as an individual' but in reality this can be hard because as you start your journey in coaching you very rarely have the skills or the time to consider each individual. Part of this involves thinking about the practices you engage in during the coaching process (see Chapter 4). You may wish to be very **linear** (traditional) in your approach to coaching, which can often mean being sequential and autocratic. This may be deemed necessary in certain situations; for example, when coaching a dangerous activity (such as coaching a rugby tackle, or gymnastics vault) that requires the control of a more linear environment; but generally this approach does not allow the freedom, exuberance, independence and individuality that sport can and should offer. In contrast, by using **non-linear,** humanistic approaches to coaching you will put the athlete at the centre of the process (Kidman, 2005). As Workman (2001, page 85) highlights, this 'humanism in sport accentuates joy in movement, personal meaning in participation, and positive interactions with all other participants, including the so-called opponents'. Renshaw et al. (2009) note that the human being is a dynamical system that learns in a multitude of ways, and certainly not in a sequential and linear fashion. Because of this, coaching ought to be non-sequential and non-linear.

If we take an example: learning to pass a football in a linear fashion often involves two participants passing the ball to each other in a non-contested practice and learning each of the phases of the pass (head position, foot position, body position). This does not replicate the decision-making processes involved in the pass (e.g. relating to an opposition

defender) or the dynamic environment in which the pass occurs (the area of the pitch, the time of the game, the conditions, how the ball arrives to them and where the ball needs to be played).

For these reasons we might say that coaching someone to pass a football is better done in a non-linear fashion involving a more realistic game or conditioned setting so that the athlete can learn how to make those decisions. That is not to say you cannot coach the principles of the pass (head position, foot position, body position), but doing so in a non-linear practice will be more realistic for the learner.

In order to retain the focus on the individual, it is important to understand each individual participant or athlete as they strive for enjoyment and participation. It may be that some wish to become elite athletes, but the vast majority will want to be sports participants – and centring their learning and enjoyment at the heart of what you do as a coach is essential.

It is important to understand each individual

Coaching special populations

The term '**special population**' is used to describe a group of people with something in common that is worth paying special attention to. In medicine, for example, special populations might be the young (paediatrics) or the elderly (geriatrics) because these different groups have particular, special needs that are different from other populations. The elderly are perhaps more frail and have suffered from the ageing process and so require special treatment or care. That is not to say that everyone in that population requires the same care and treatment but they will share similarities with others from the same population or group.

The same is true in sports coaching, and recent attention has been directed towards understanding special populations in coaching in order to deal with individual needs and requirements so that all individuals might benefit from sport and physical activity. When we consider what a 'special population' might be, it is useful to consider any group that may share some physical, psychological, medical or genetic similarities. These may be young children, the elderly, boys, girls or those with a disability. It is unlikely as a sports coach that you will have to deal with every population at once, as often in sports coaching these groups will be differentiated so that you can coach those with similar needs together. However, it is worthwhile developing your coaching knowledge to have an appreciation of a number of special populations so that you can deal with each scenario you face as a coach. For this chapter, while acknowledging that there are many more populations that could be

addressed, the following special populations will be considered in detail:

- men
- women
- children
- pregnant women
- people with disabilities
- differing illnesses
- disaffected groups (such as black and minority ethnic groups and youth groups, as well as those who are underprivileged or under-represented).

Coaching men and women

Key term

Special population – a population or group that shares particular needs, wants and similarities (physical, psychological, medical or genetic)

As a coach, it is important to recognise key differences between men and women that could affect your practice. Vilhjalmsson and Kristjansdottir (2003) argue that competitive sports settings, socialisation into sport and physical activity patterns are different between males and females. To echo this, Hargreaves (1997) states there are differences between men and women in terms of physiology, psychology and sociological factors. These differences are not restrictive in any way for men and women, they simply mean that as a coach you need to address these differences and design your training appropriately. We will consider each in turn.

Physical differences

Dick (2002) suggests that differences in males and females exist physiologically regarding pelvis width (creating a greater angle between the femur and tibia in females as their pelvis is generally wider) which leads to a higher injury potential in the knee, hip and lower back. He also states that the shoulders of female athletes are narrower than in males, which potentially impacts upon the force application in pulling and pushing exercise or practice. Willmore et al. (2008) state that while there are further differences in hormone levels, body size and composition (muscle, fat) as well as socialisation into sport, there are in fact fewer differences between males and females than many believe. As a coach, it is important to understand and research the differences between males and females so that you can adapt training and coaching accordingly. It is important to avoid making the assumptions that men are always better, bigger or faster in sport as this is not evidenced in research.

Socialisation into sport

Women and men can also be considered as special populations because their roles in society can be perceived to be different. Cashmore (2010, p206) offers a startling view of sport and **gender** when he argues that, historically, '(1) women were not regarded as capable either intellectually or physically as men; (2) their natural predisposition was thought to be passive and not active; (3) their relationship to men was one of dependence'. For example, women were not allowed to run any race further than 800 metres until the 1960s. Despite increases in participation and excellence in women's sport, Theberge (1993) states that 'sport remains a setting in which ideas about gender and gender differences are powerfully constituted and expressed' (page 301).

You may have heard people say that men are stronger and quicker than women or that women are more emotional and cannot take criticism like men can. These types of myths are extremely damaging in a sporting context as they create stereotypes that are often acted out, as people believe these ideas without challenging or testing them.

These views are also **socially constructed**. This means that society has a shared view of gender and, while it is not true for all people, there is often a stereotype of how we see men and women which can impact on their experience in sports.

Added to this, is the under-representation of girls and women in sport in a number of areas. There are also fewer female coaches, managers and administrators working in sport which creates barriers that continue to make sure that stereotypes stay in place and that there are fewer role models to inspire more girls and women to take part in sport. Equality Standards (to obtain a secure link to this website, visit the companion website at www.pearsonfe.co.uk/foundationsinsport) are being used to encourage sports to address issues around under-representation and to embed equality and it is useful to consider such issues as you develop your coaching practice. The table below outlines some of the key barriers faced by women in sports participation.

Table 9.1 Some barriers faced by women in sport

Barrier	Description
Body image	Magazines and media today portray a view of the male and female body that is often unobtainable by most people. For women, in particular, these feminine body images are often slender whereas the body type required for sport is often more muscular and athletic which creates a negative stereotype of the athletic female.
Media coverage	There is a distinct lack of sporting coverage of females in sport, and even when there is coverage the focus is often on the sexuality of women in sport. This leads to the creation of poor role models for the sporting female.
Negative attitude	There is a negative attitude to women in sport. Often this attitude is based on socially constructed notions of the role of men and women in society, which is reflected in sport.
Stereotyping	Stereotypes exist around the physical and psychological prowess of women in sport that is often misguided and generalised. There are ideas that men are quicker than women, more powerful and 'better' at sport. These stereotypes are not constructive and are damaging to women in sport.

Stop and think

Consider men and women in sport, and the stereotypes you may have of them. In pairs, create a list of your views of men and women.

A number of the barriers faced by women and girls in sport are cultural and social barriers, that can be overcome if you as a coach can treat each athlete as an individual. If, for example, you consider the individual differences of the girl or woman you are coaching; such as age, class, background, religion, physical characteristics, sporting ability; then you are likely to act in such a way that engages the participant, and helps to create opportunities for them to be successful in sport. As a coach, your job is to look beyond the gender of the individual and actually coach them as a person. Each individual will be able to do different things and be successful in different ways and that is not determined by gender.

Stop and think

Consider the types of barriers that might exist when coaching men or women. Discuss the ways in which your coaching can be adapted and developed in order to address these barriers.

Competitive sports settings

Competition is often seen as a masculine trait (Hargreaves, 1997) and this is manifested in the way in which competitive sports are often seen as male or masculine. This leads to certain issues when considering the nature of sport for males and females. For example, males who participate in sports that are seen as feminine or females who participate in sport that are seen as masculine, often suffer from stereotypes or face barriers to participation. As a coach, it is your job to see beyond these barriers and attempt to include people irrespective of gender and ensure that you deal with the differences in individuals.

Research suggests that young people who participate in sport and physical activity have higher levels of self-esteem, more positive moods, attain more in school, have higher educational aspirations and a greater sense of positive body image (Dishman et al, 2006; Findlay and Bowker, 2009; Marsh and Kleitman, 2003). It is further suggested that the positive effects may be more exaggerated in females. But it is clear that as a coach it is important to use a competitive sporting environment in a positive way, focusing on the development of skill, physical competency and levels of enjoyment, and helping athletes to deal with winning and losing in a mature and responsible way.

Paula Radcliffe

Paula Radcliffe is a successful athlete irrespective of her gender. Most men could not compete with her yet we assume men are stronger than women. This highlights the importance of dealing with every athlete and participant as an individual. See Table 9.2 for some important considerations when coaching girls and women.

Table 9.2 Coaching checklists. Some key questions you might ask yourself as a coach when working with girls and women.

Key question	Issues to consider
How can you ensure that your coaching environment is appropriate?	You may be coaching women who have certain religious beliefs or who are self-conscious about their body – the coaching space you select could impact on participation.
How do you make your practices appropriate?	Because of participation and stereotypes, girls may have been exposed to less sport than boys. You may have to pace your practices differently to begin with and not assume that everyone has had the same background in physical activity.
How will you be flexible in the requirements for your coaching?	There are often rules in sports clubs about clothing and behaviour. Can you be flexible with issues such as female-only sessions, clothing requirements (some religious beliefs may not allow certain clothing for females) and participation and entry to clubs?
How do your sessions create social interactions?	Girls may sometimes lack the confidence that boys exhibit in a sporting environment to begin with. Are you creating social interactions and building people's self-perception and confidence?
How are you challenging stereotypes?	Think about the language you use as a coach. Are you demeaning girls and women or being patronising at all? They are participants and athletes just as men are, and will be able to achieve the same things. Do not pre-judge based on gender.

Coaching children

Coaching children carries a very different responsibility from anything else you may face as a coach. Some of the benefits of sports participation at an early age can include development of confidence and interpersonal skills such as communication, organisation, leadership and decision making as well as the forming of social friendships. It is therefore clear to see the positive – or potentially negative – impact that coaching can have on children in sport.

Novice coaches are often employed to work with children and adult beginners who are in the most formative phases of their learning and so it is essential as a coach in this stage of your development that you consider the types of knowledge you may need to develop (see Chapter 3).

A novice can often be very autocratic in their style, often with lots of cones set out to ensure that there is a great deal of organisation and control of the session. This can be a good thing, but equally it can stifle a child's creativity, autonomy and flair in sport. A games-based approach to coaching, such as Teaching Games for Understanding (Bunker and Thorpe, 1982 – see Chapter 1 and Chapter 4 for a review) can often encourage discovery learning in a structured setting. Experienced coaches who understand the developmental needs of children and the complex nature of development (see Chapter 10) will be better placed to develop participants in such a way that they can remain participating in sport or, equally, continue to master a sport if they are hoping to become an elite athlete one day.

Stop and think

Arrange to watch a coaching session with young people. Ensure you gain permission to watch the session. You should critique the session looking for strengths and areas for development and note these down for discussion with a classmate.

This does not mean that a coach should approach their sessions with children with no structure in place. In fact, it often requires more planning and structure to create the appropriate types of activity for learning.

Factors to consider

When coaching children, it is important to consider their stage of development with regard to a number of issues:

- age
- biological growth
- psychological development
- sociological factors
- physiological factors
- motor skill development
- technical development.

Baechle and Earle (2000) highlight some of the issues when training young people as they note that a child's **chronological age** (years and months) may be different from their **biological age** (bone and muscle development). Given that children are often grouped chronologically, there are clear issues in terms of designing appropriate training practices that meet the biological and psychological maturation of a child (see Chapter 10 for a comprehensive review of maturation and the effects on skill development in children).

As a coach you should pay attention to all of these and ensure that the coaching environment you create allows each of those to be enhanced and rewarded. If the focus lies in winning then there is a tendency to select children who are bigger, and seem stronger and perhaps physically more developed, as the focus is on 'right now' rather than a longer-term strategy.

Remember

Long-term development is important. The child's development should be the focus of your coaching – looking beyond the 'here and now' in order to allow the growth of the individual at their different pace.

Key terms

Biological age – this will often be different from the actual age of a child as young people develop at different rates for lots of different reasons

Chronological age – the age of the child in years and months. This is important to note as it may help you to assess how psychologically mature a child is and ready for intensity of coaching

Stop and think

Think about your own coaching. How are you going to develop your coaching skills to consider the long-term development of young people you are coaching? Discuss this with a partner.

With the current focus on sport in the government and the media, being successful at local, regional, national and international level is becoming ever more important. Add to this, the vast sums of money now available in professional sport and the ever-growing trend to identify and train athletes at a younger age rather than focusing on a developmental philosophy (Ford et al. 2009).

Remember

Not every individual is going to become an elite athlete and so sports coaching should consider the developmental needs of all participants.

This trend in identifying talent does yield success and can be witnessed in a range of sports, as young performers become world-renowned stars at an early age. Think of individuals such as Wayne Rooney in football, Amir Kahn in boxing and Lewis Hamilton in motor racing. However, for the majority, if the coaching environment in sport is inadequate or inappropriate for their development, then there is the likelihood that drop-out from sport will occur; this is particularly prevalent in young people once they reach the school-leaving age of 16. This can then lead to issues in later life.

Coaching pregnant women

Pregnancy brings about a number of physiological changes in a woman's body that need to be considered by a coach when placing the individual at the centre of their coaching philosophy. It may be that you are coaching an athlete who becomes pregnant and wishes to continue training and competing, or that you are a fitness coach or strength and conditioning coach who has to understand the physiology of coaching a woman when pregnant; or you might simply be coaching someone who wants to keep playing recreationally for fitness.

Brown (2002) notes that a woman's social circumstances during pregnancy can be a barrier to participation in sport, as well as the obvious health concerns, and so it is vital for sporting and health organisations to address this issue. Whilst there is an ever increasing understanding that some forms of physical activity are safe and, in fact, are good for the health of mother and baby, there is obviously some risk involved in continuing to be physically active during pregnancy, that you as a coach must consider.

Pre-natal women

The pregnancy of a woman is divided into three trimesters (0–3 months; 4–6 months; 7–9 months). There are physiological changes occurring all the time as the embryo (first trimester) develops into a foetus (second and third trimesters). The embryo/foetus is protected in the womb in a fluid-filled sac containing amniotic fluid which allows the embryo/foetus to maintain stability and maintain temperature, while also being protected from disease and being able to access nutrients and oxygen through the placenta attached to the wall of the uterus. This is a complex environment that can

be enhanced through physical activity of the mother but there are also obvious concerns you may have as a coach:

- risk of miscarriage
- physical damage to the embryo/foetus
- joint problems, ligament damage, back pains
- overheating of the mother and foetus/embryo
- loss of oxygen to the foetus/embryo.

Post-natal women

A woman will often hope to return to physical activity for a number of reasons after giving birth to their baby. As a coach, you may want to consider how your sports club or centre can accommodate women and their babies. You may have encountered mother and baby swimming sessions or a crèche at a sports club to allow women to return to physical activity as soon as possible. Because of the major changes and possible damage to the body endured during pregnancy, there may be issues with damage and instability in the joints, pelvic and abdominal muscles.

Exercise can benefit a woman who has given birth by:

- promoting weight loss
- improving self-image
- returning tone to abdominal muscles
- returning strength to the muscles
- returning flexibility to muscles
- improving posture.

Part of the **post-natal** process is handled by the GP in terms of recommending activities for the mother to engage with. Often, it will be six to ten weeks before a woman returns to normal activities and exercise after giving birth and it is at this point that you may be engaged with the mother in physical activity and coaching. Artal and O'Toole (2003) note that pregnancy should not lead to lack of activity and that women with uncomplicated pregnancies should be encouraged to continue and engage in physical activity. A number of the ACOG guidelines are useful at this point again and it is advisable to use low impact, developmental activities as you look to design coaching and training sessions specific to this special population.

Coaching disability

Coaching should be inclusive and, in fact, an effective and good coach will often design their practices to focus on the individual needs of athletes. Consider all of the special populations we have focused on so far, and you will note that the attention has been on an athlete-centred, individualised approach to coaching. There seems to be an emphasis on inclusive coaching when working with athletes with a disability because it is a slightly more politicised issue than many others and this can create as many issues as not being mindful of disability.

Oscar Pistorius

Oscar Pistorius is a South African Paralympic sprinter who has tried to argue that he should be allowed to compete in the 'able-bodied' events despite having a double leg amputation. He has a great deal of physical and sporting ability and in fact there have been claims that his prosthetic limbs give him an unfair advantage over able-bodied athletes. Could society change the way it views disability?

Brittain (2004) argues that there are two accepted models of disability: the social model and the medical model. The medical model focuses on the 'physical and/or mental impairments' (Brittain, 2004; p.430) that are faced by those with a disability. This model contends that the issues faced by someone with a disability are the physical and mental manifestations of that disability which places the focus on a biological or physical discussion. It is difficult for society, and therefore coaches, to see the individual at the centre of coaching and in fact to see the very clear 'ability' the individual has and we seem to classify the individual based on their disability. The social model of disability contends that our views and perceptions are socially constructed and, as such, we should change the way we look at those with a perceived disability. Brittain (2004) summarises much of the recent research regarding the social model of disability, suggesting that changes in policy regarding disability (which lead to reduction of barriers to participation and inclusion) could be addressed if 'underlying attitudes and levels of understanding were to change in a positive manner' (page 431). This suggests that if society could shift its attitude towards disability then in fact we would see a change in the barriers that are currently faced by people classified with a disability.

Key terms

Pre-natal – the period during the pregnancy before the birth of the baby when there are major physiological changes experienced by the mother

Post-natal – the period directly after the birth, usually extending for approximately six weeks

Athletes with a disability will require a coach to consider their needs, just like any other athlete, but often a coach will be more cautious and careful. This can often be more harmful to the coach–athlete relationship. When you are coaching, you should try to work with an athlete to find out what works for them and what does not work; but do not assume that a disability means that an athlete is incapable. Disabled athletes are inspiring and may have overcome many obstacles in order to become an athlete or sports participant, and you as a coach need to concentrate on the athlete's abilities and the areas they need to develop in order to improve as an athlete rather than focusing on any perceived disability. As a coach, you need to focus on the person and their needs and not make any judgements based on your own assumptions.

Inclusive coaching

The inclusion spectrum offers a practical insight into the ways in which you can approach coaching athletes with a disability and non-disabled athletes in an inclusive way, focusing on the ability of individuals.

Table 9.3 presents the five types of activity that can be utilised, according to Stevenson and Black (2007), when attempting to make your coaching inclusive for all.

When coaching athletes with a disability it is important to treat them like any other athlete but be conscious that there may be individual issues that need to be addressed for that athlete. It may be that you need to adapt your coaching to be **inclusive**.

> ### Key term
>
> **Inclusive coaching** – changing your coaching practice to meet the needs of all the individuals in the group

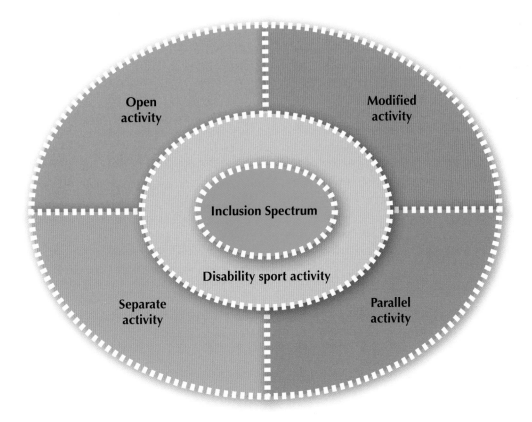

Figure 9.1 The inclusion spectrum (cited from Stevenson and Black, 2007)

Table 9.3 The inclusion spectrum: Practical steps to inclusive coaching (adapted from Stevenson and Black, 2007)

Activity	Description
Open activity	Irrespective of the disability you may be working within a group of athletes, an open activity is one which may be accessible to all and will require little or no modification to a session. (You may be working with a swimming group who can do the same pool session even if some athletes are amputees.)
Modified activity	You may be able to modify the activity you are doing but still in essence have all participants taking part in the same session. This will be able to provide different challenges based on the ability of each individual. (You may have individuals who are more mobile than others in a football session, so restrict the touches allowed for those who are more mobile.)
Parallel activity	The focus of the coaching session is the same for a parallel activity but you may decide to split the groups up. The challenge is the same and the focus of coaching is the same, but participants can develop at a suitable pace for them. (You may have a group of 12 and split them into three groups of four – for example you may be teaching ground work in judo, and want to split the groups so that the challenge can suit the strengths of each smaller group.)
Separate activity	The focus here is on separate sessions. If you have a large group and some athletes are non-disabled and some are disabled then you might need to separate the two groups for some special requirements. (You may have competitions coming up for both groups and the rules are different in one/both of the competitions so you need to have specific preparations where combining the groups is detrimental to development.)
Disability sport activity	Here, you are 'reverse-integrating' the non-disabled athletes to include them in a disability sport activity where the rules are adaptive for disabled athletes. (So you may get your able-bodied athletes and disability athletes to take part in a sport such as sitting volleyball which is adapted to meet the needs of the disabled athletes in the group.)
When applying the Spectrum model to practical situations, there will always be some individuals who will require an individualised approach.	

GP referral schemes: populations with different illnesses

The aim of **exercise referral schemes** is to provide an alternative method to treating a patient with medication. Gidlow et al. (2005) note that the incidence of **GP** exercise referral schemes has been growing; although the effectiveness of such schemes is still an issue of contention.

Nevertheless, it is widely understood that sport and physical activity can help to promote and manage health. You may have been exposed to health promotion initiatives which emphasise the importance of being active for 30 minutes a day, five times a week. This is further emphasised by the Chief Medical Officer's report (Department of Health, 2009) which highlights the fact that physical activity is a major factor in guarding against disease and promoting health. In fact, the Chief Medical Officer's reports of 2004 and 2009 have noted such issues as physically active adults having:

- 20–30 per cent reduced risk of premature death
- up to 50 per cent reduced risk of developing diseases such as coronary heart disease or diabetes
- reduced risk of back pain
- increased independence (elderly)
- increased bone density and reduced risk of associated bone disease
- improved psychological well-being
- reduced risk of stress and anxiety
- improved weight loss and weight management.

The GP referral scheme is a structured referral system that includes a comprehensive client assessment by the patient's doctor (GP) in order to assess the best treatment for the individual. Once the GP has declared that exercise is the most effective treatment for an individual, the client or patient will be referred to a local sports centre or fitness specialist. The referral programme will usually last 10 to 12 weeks and may be on an individual or group basis. As a coach, you may be involved in working with clients who have been referred to your sports centre. For example, you may be asked to work with a middle-aged male who is overweight or an elderly lady with a heart condition. You would have to work with the GP to design the most appropriate exercise programme to address the individual needs of the client.

There will be differences in each scheme across the country but there is a set of guidelines called the National Quality Assurance Framework (NQAF), developed by the Department of Health in 2001, that allow each local authority to deliver schemes based on common criteria. The scheme is based on the following stages.

1. Selection of the patient by the GP

2. Physical assessment of the patient and appropriate intervention applied

3. Long-term support to help the patient stay physically active

4. Evaluation of the patient experience and health outcome

5. Return to the community.

When working within a GP referral scheme it is important to be aware of your role and responsibilities as a coach. You will have to carry out an assessment of the client in order to determine what type of exercise is suitable for them, as well as being responsible for the safe management and delivery of their exercise programme. You will also be expected to manage a relationship with the client and the GP, maintaining confidentiality with the client while also being sensitive to the need to refer back to the GP if you think that is most appropriate.

Unfortunately there are different barriers that can stand in the way of those being referred to an exercise scheme, such as available facilities, inappropriate exercise programmes and intimidating fitness environments, as well as various socio-economic issues that have led to the individual being referred in the first place. These barriers are important to consider as the goal of the GP exercise referral scheme is to try to ensure that adults with a range of illnesses, diseases and conditions can enjoy the benefits of being physically active. Williams, Hendry and France (2007) state that GP referral schemes can have a significant impact – to bring about changes in the lives of individuals so they can manage and reduce the risk of illness.

Activity

Working in pairs create a list of the benefits associated with a GP referral scheme for:

- a middle-aged woman suffering from being four stone overweight

- an elderly gentleman who struggles to get up and down the stairs at home due to arthritis

- a young woman suffering from severe stress and anxiety due to a high-pressured job

- a young man, who hasn't been physically active for 12 months, reporting back pain.

Key terms

General Practitioner (GP) – often thought of as the family doctor, providing primary health care for patients in the community

Exercise referral scheme – the scheme that refers those who are sedentary (inactive) in order to help improve and manage health and activity

Coaching disaffected youths

The power of sport to address wider needs in society is currently at the heart of sport initiatives. Whether it is through the improvement of health and activity or attainment in the classroom, sport and physical activity is seen as a powerful and empowering tool. When we consider the impact of sport on **disaffected** people in society, there is often inconclusive evidence of the statistical outcome of sporting intervention (Smith and Waddington, 2004). However, it is clear that since the 1960s, when sport became an integral part of public sector policy, there has been a move to try and include disaffected elements of society, particularly young people, when trying to reduce boredom and frustration – using sport in order to combat issues of crime and delinquency (for example the government policy on sport for all – see DCMS, 2002).

The debate about the impact of sport focuses on two issues (Coalter, 2007), which relate to the rehabilitation of those who have committed crimes or the prevention of delinquent behaviour by engaging and giving opportunity to those who are disaffected.

If we consider the potential positive benefits of sport and physical activity that have already been discussed, such as improved self-esteem, confidence, interpersonal and leadership skills; then it is apparent that sport can help and support such behaviour – both in terms of rehabilitation and prevention. However, it is not clear whether this is a long-term solution to the problem of disaffected young people or simply a practical, short-term response to a perceived social problem (Hartmann, 2001).

A survey carried out for the Office for National Statistics (ONS, 2011) notes that it is young people who have historically experienced the highest rates of unemployment when compared with other age groups. For example, in the period between January and March 2009, the unemployment rate stood at 7.1% of the population. However, examining the figures for those aged 16 and 17 years, the unemployment rate was 29.3% of that age group. Clearly, this is often an age when people choose to go to college, but it offers an insight into the likelihood of becoming disaffected through lack of opportunities and expendable income.

Added to this is a reduction in green areas in inner cities in particular and this heightens the issues regarding disaffected youths. If there is no space to be active, no jobs, and limited opportunity, it is clear that young people will become bored and frustrated, leading to disaffection.

Anti-social behaviour tends to occur when young people are disaffected (Coalter, 2007) and this can simply be young people seeking fulfilment, excitement and adventure – which sport can also provide. However, Smith and Waddington (2004) suggest that the simple participation in sport is not the antidote to being disaffected; there needs to be direction in sport and therefore coaching that allows

Stop and think

In pairs, discuss why you think a young person might be disaffected in their community. Who should be providing support? Also, consider how you might support the re-engagement of the disaffected youngster as a coach. Develop an action plan that you could implement when working with disaffected youths in the community.

Key term

Disaffected – implies that an individual or group is alienated from the rest of society, and may be resentful or rebellious as a result

those who are disaffected to be empowered and integrated into the community.

Government initiatives

In practical terms, there have been many attempts by different governments (for example, *Game Plan*, DCMS, 2002) and sporting organisations (for example, Sport England, 2002) to combat disaffection among young people using sport as a tool. Sport England (2002) attempted to 'reduce anti-social behaviour, crime and drug use among 10–16 year olds' (page 1) by introducing the Positive Futures programme. The aim was to combat issues relating to disaffected youths; for example, by providing midnight basketball leagues (Hartmann, 2001) – taking place when young people would be bored and perhaps when they might turn to other activities. Evidence suggests, however, that while there is some success with these types of interventions, there also needs to be a focus on outcomes such as leadership, communication, empowerment and community involvement. It would also seem that it is necessary to meet various developmental needs in young people, such as those for adventure and excitement as well as interpersonal development.

In Table 9.4 (below) there are some key questions you could reflect on as a coach to consider whether or not your coaching can impact on disaffected young people and include them – fostering a positive experience of sport and physical activity.

Conclusion

When considering the coaching environment, it is important to remember that you will be faced with a myriad of individual differences relating to race, religion, ability, disability, gender, age and background. As a coach, it is important that each of these different contexts brings a set of 'special' circumstances that should be considered when working with each individual. Coaching should be 'athlete-centred' – taking into account all of the hopes, desires, needs and requirements of those you work with and, while you should treat each person equally and fairly, you should also be aware of their differences in order to create a positive coaching environment.

> ### Activity
>
> Working in groups of four, design a coaching programme to help engage young disaffected youths in sport.

Table 9.4 Practical steps to including disaffected youths in coaching

Key question	Issues to consider
Is your coaching environment accessible?	Often young people who are disaffected are from poorer backgrounds and may not be able to afford to participate in sport. Can your coaching be accessible to all?
Are your practices appropriate?	It may be more important to concentrate on the personal development of the individual rather than to develop their sporting ability. Can your practices meet individual needs to develop the person (communication, self-esteem, discipline) as well as the athlete?
Are you focusing on the correct outcomes for the sport you coach?	Sport often has winning as a focus. If this is the focus of your coaching then disaffected groups may become more excluded by experiencing losing. You do not have to take competition out of the coaching environment but remember to be balanced and inclusive.
Can you be flexible in the requirements for your coaching?	Disaffected youths may be put off by the formal nature of a sporting environment, such as behaviour, clothing and language. How can you adapt your coaching to include those who are disaffected and work towards your goals?
Are your sessions creating social interactions?	Can you include others in the community? Simply segregating those who are disaffected only serves to further alienate the group. If the community they live in can be involved it may help to foster a positive community spirit.
Are you challenging stereotypes?	Often, we will have stereotypical views of those who are disaffected. Do not make assumptions based on clothing, language or background. Many elite athletes are from poorer backgrounds, as sport can be a powerful tool for change. Treat everyone as an individual.
How will you monitor success?	A key problem with schemes that aim to address excluded young people is that there is often a lack of effective and consistent evaluation of such programmes. Consider how you will monitor the effectiveness of your coaching.

Case study (for recommended answers, see www.pearsonfe.co.uk/foundationsinsport)

You are employed as a coach to work with a group of mixed ability athletes from a range of backgrounds. The group is an all-female netball group, ranging in age from 16 to 37 years old, and with differing ability as netball players. They are entered in a Saturday league and are keen to keep up the success of the club, having won the local club competition three times in the last seven years. You are employed as their coach as a result of a Sport England grant and, while you are expected to be successful by the club members, you also have a duty to work with the local community to ensure that participation and physical activity are increased and improved.

Questions

1. How important do you think it is to win with this group of players?
2. What considerations will you need to make for this group – given the wide range of members?
3. Do you think it is your job to increase participation and physical activity, given that the players want to be successful?
4. How would you increase participation and physical activity in the community?

Time to reflect

How can you ensure your coaching is athlete-centred?

Given the different populations you may encompass in your coaching, how will you adapt your coaching to ensure you are sensitive to all participants you work with?

Create a list of differences and similarities in coaching men and women.

What are some of the social barriers that exist when coaching different populations (think about coaching children, men and women or individuals who are considered to have a disability).

Create a list of physical or medical issues you need to consider when coaching certain populations.

Drawing upon information about inclusive coaching, consider how you will adapt your coaching in the future to ensure that you respond to the needs of the individuals you are working with.

Check your understanding (for answers, see www.pearsonfe.co.uk/foundationsinsport)

1. What is athlete-centred coaching?
2. List five special populations that may impact on the way you coach.
3. List and explain the five domains of inclusive coaching.
4. List some key issues when coaching disaffected youths.
5. Describe the GP exercise referral scheme.
6. List some differences to consider when coaching men and women.

Useful resources

To obtain a secure link to the websites below, see the Websites section on page ii or visit the companion website at www.pearsonfe.co.uk/foundationsinsport.

- sports coach UK

- Office for National Statistics

- Sport England

- Sports Leaders UK

- The British Olympic Association

- English Federation of Disability Sport

- Skills Active

Further reading

Allender, S., Cowburn, G. and Foster, C. (2006) Understanding participation in sport and physical activity among children and adolescents: *A review of qualitative studies*, 21 (6), 826 - 835.

Artal, R., and O'Toole, M. (2003). Guidelines of the American College of Obstetricians and Gynecologists for exercise during pregnancy and the postpartum period. *British Journal of Sports Medicine*, 37 (1), 6 - 12.

Baechle, T. and Earle, R. (2000) *Essentials of strength training and conditioning*. Leeds: Human Kinetics.

Brittain, I. (2004) Perceptions of disability and their impact upon involvement in sport for people with disabilities at all levels. *Journal of Sport & Social Issues*, 28 (4), 429 - 552.

Brown, W. (2002) The benefits of physical activity during pregnancy. *Journal of Science and Medicine in Sport*, 5 (1), 37 – 45.

Bunker, D. and Thorpe, R. (1982) A model for teaching games in secondary schools. *Bulletin of Physical Education*, 18 (1), 5–8.

Cashmore, E. (2010) *Making sense of sports*. London: Routledge.

Coalter, F. (2007) *A wider social role for sport: who's keeping the score?* London: Routledge.

Department of Culture, Media and Sport/Strategy Unit (2002) *Game Plan: A strategy for delivering government's sport and physical activity objectives*. London: DCMS/Strategy Unit.

Department of Health (2004) *Annual Report of the Chief Medical Officer*.

Dick, F.W. (2002) *Sports training principles*. London: A & C Black.

Dishman, R.K. Hales, D.P., Pfeifer, K.A.., Felton, G., Saunders, R. and Ward, S. (2006). Physical self-concept and self-esteem mediate cross sectional relations of physical activity and sport [participation with depression symptoms among adolescent girls]. *Health Psychology*, 25, 396 - 407.

Ericsson, K.A., Krampe, R.T. and Tesch-Romer, C. (1993). The role of deliberate practice in the acquisition of expert performance. *Psychological Review*, 100, 363-406.

Findlay, L.C. and Bowker, A. (2009). The link between competitive sport participation and self-concept in early adolescence: A consideration of gender and sport orientation. *Journal of Youth Adolescence*, 38, 29 – 40.

Ford, P.R., Ward, P., Hodges, N.J. and William, A.M. (2009) The role of deliberate practice and play in career progression in sport: The early engagement hypothesis. *High Ability Studies*, 20 (1), 65 - 75.

Gidlow, C., Halley Johnston, L., Crone, D. and James, D. (2005) Attendance of exercise referral schemes in the UK: A systematic review. *Health Education Journal*, 64 (2), 168 – 186.

Hargreaves, J. (1997). *Sporting females: Critical issues in the history and sociology of women's sports*. London: Routledge.

Hartmann, D. (2001) Notes on midnight basketball and the cultural politics of recreation, race and at-risk urban youth. *Journal of Sport and Social Issues*, 25(4): 339 - 371.

Kidman, L. (2005) *Athlete-centred coaching: Developing and inspiring people.* Christchurch, NZ: Innovative Print Communications Ltd.

Marsh, H.W., and Kleitman, S. (2003). School athletic participation: Mostly gain with little pain. *Journal of Sport and Exercise Psychology,* 25, 205 – 228.

Office for National Statistics (ONS) (2011) Young People: Labour Market [online]. See 'Useful resources' for source. [Accessed 10 June 2011].

Renshaw, I., Davids, K.W., Shuttleworth, R. and Chow, J.Y. (2009) Insights from ecological psychology and dynamical systems theory can underpin a philosophy of coaching. *International Journal of Sport Psychology,* 40 (4), 540 - 602.

Rosenbloom, C.A., Louck, A.B. and Ekblom, B. (2006) Special populations: The female player and the youth player. *Journal of Sports Scientists,* 24 (7), 783 - 793.

Skills Active. (2011). Sport and recreation [online]. See 'Useful resources' for source.[Accessed 23 March 2011].

Smith, A. and Waddington, I. (2004) Using 'sport in the community schemes' to tackle crime and drug use among young people: Some policy issues. *European Physical Education Review,* 10 (3), 279 – 298.

Sport England (2002) *Positive Futures: A review of impact and good practice. London*: Sport England.

sports coach UK (2006) *UK Action Plan for Coaching*. Leeds: sports coach UK.

Stevenson, P. and Black, K. (2007) The Inclusion Spectrum in sports coach UK. *Quick Guide to Inclusion Coaching*. Leeds: sports coach UK.

Theberge, N. (1993) The construction of gender in sport: Women, coaching and the naturalization of difference. *Society for the Study of Social Problems,* 40 (3), 301–313.

Vilhjalmsson, R. and Kristjansdottir, G. (2003) Gender differences in physical activity in older children and adolescents: The central role of organized sport. *Social Science and Medicine,* 56, 363 – 374.

Williams, A.M. and Ford, P.R. (2008) Expertise and expert performance in sport. *International Review of Sport and Exercise Psychology,* 1 (1), 4–18.

Williams, N.H., Hendry, M., France, B., Lewis, R. and Williamson, C. (2007) Effectiveness of exercise referral schemes to promote physical activity in adults: Systematic review. *British Journal of General Practice,* 57, 979–986.

Willmore, J.H., Costill, D.L. and Kenney, W.L. (2008) *Physiology of sport and exercise,* Leeds: Human Kinetics.

Workman, G. J. (2001). Humanistic ideology in sport: Time for a change, In B.J. Lombardo, T.J. Carvella-Nadeau, K.S. Castagno, & V.H. Mancini (Eds.), *Sport in the Twenty-first Century: Alternatives for the new millennium* (pp. 84-87). Boston, MA: Pearson Custom.

Chapter 10

Coaching young performers

Introduction

Youth sport and activity is better supported, more highly developed and covers more diverse activities than ever before. Millions of children and young people take part in formally organised sport programmes in the evenings and at weekends, often in school and club play schemes, instructional courses and competitive fixtures. They participate for many reasons, including fun, affiliation and the health benefits associated with their chosen activity. They are supported in their quest for improvement and enjoyment by thousands of dedicated coaches, teachers, parents and officials. Young performers can expect to be given fair and equitable opportunities to learn, be effectively coached, be selected to play and generally have a satisfying time growing up through sport. They have certain developmental requirements and individualised lifestyle, personal and training needs, which those responsible for their care must recognise. This chapter considers how you, as an aspiring coach, can develop and inform your practice in preparation for arguably the most challenging and rewarding coaching experience possible – being an effective supporter and developer of young people in sport.

Learning outcomes

After you have read this chapter you should be able to:

- understand how children and adults differ physically, mentally and emotionally
- understand child growth patterns and physical changes
- know about stages of motor development and movement co-ordination
- understand how children acquire fundamental movement and sports skills
- understand psychosocial development and the psychological demands of competition for children
- understand professionalism in coaching and the role of the coach as mentor, motivator and guardian
- know the basis of making training fun, challenging and related to competition.

Starting block

Each week you take your younger sister to her midweek tennis training session and stay to watch her progress. An official of the club asks if you – as a former player who has recently qualified as a coach – would be interested in hitting with some of the under-16 team members and helping them prepare for upcoming competitions. Their coach has a shoulder injury and can no longer provide the consistency they need for competitive play and is keen to act as your mentor.

- What information would you need to know at the end of talking to the coach about your support role?

- How might you effectively observe and analyse the group to best prepare for your coaching with the team?

- How could you provide player feedback to positively impact future practice design?

Physical changes, growth and coaching

The most obvious and visual indicator of change during childhood is physical growth as children become bigger and stronger. Pre-adolescent changes in stature or linearity precede increases in muscularity. Overall, changes in body size occur in a set pattern with increases in upper body length occurring before the development of longer legs, wider hips or broader shoulders. The unequal nature of this physical change in limb proportions is mirrored in boys and girls, even if the rate of growth differs. While girls appear to be developmentally ahead of boys, which accounts for their earlier entry into puberty, the later but more sustained growth spurt of boys leads to boys emerging as taller and more muscular, particularly in the upper body, than girls.

Despite this, important research by Drabik (1996) seems to imply that it is girls who are better suited to attempting more adult forms of physical training at an earlier age than boys, in terms of strength, speed and endurance development. For example, post-pubescent girls can be introduced to plyometric training, which involves the cross training of speed and strength, before boys and are also more able to increase the duration and intensity of their workouts more progressively than boys of a similar age. Similarly, as girls' hips tend to widen more than boys post-puberty, their stride length will shorten which can affect both their running style and movement speed (Earle, 2003). Running drills, dynamic flexibility and postural awareness components can help to maximise technique following accelerated growth. Clearly, you should regularly revisit fundamental movement skills during your sessions to ensure technical correctness as the limbs of young performers develop. You can also help with this aspect of development by making a DVD for your young performers so they can see for themselves how they look and become motivated to work harder on these elements in training.

Development of boys and girls

Boys will develop broader shoulders, providing them with greater power to throw, hit or lift objects or opponents, compared with girls of a similar age. What they gain in power, however, is often lost in balance and flexibility, which become worse post-puberty unless developed in training (Gervis et al., 1999). You should encourage boys to develop muscle strength in tandem with flexibility, or range of movement, to ensure that they can control movements when required.

Both boys and girls can be given the same amount of work to do in training, but the resistance applied and your expectations of the quality they will produce, may differ. Untrained girls may tire more easily than boys of a similar fitness level but you should not differentiate between them on that basis. In essence, try to make the work you plan for your athletes fit their physical abilities and gender needs, as well as the requirements of their sport. If you are interested in engaging in further learning, you may wish to consider attending a sports coach UK fundamentals workshop (see www.pearsonfe.co.uk/foundationsinsport for a link to the sports coach UK website

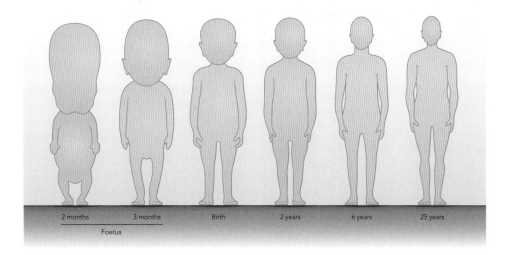

2 months   3 months   Birth   2 years   6 years   25 years

Foetus

Figure 10.1 Age-related proportional growth

Remember

With changes in limb length, expect that young performers' abilities will regress as well as improve. Try to keep things positive as they temporarily struggle to reproduce smooth and effortless sports skills during growth spurts.

An in-depth knowledge of the physical changes that young people go through can help you plan safer, more meaningful and enjoyably challenging sessions for your performers. You should focus on playing simple fun games, such as tag and shuttle races, to develop generalised movement skills such as running, jumping and balance when children are young (before the age of 8 to 9 years). In the skill-hungry years between 9 and 12 years, you should try to introduce as wide a range of sports skills as possible, so avoiding early specialisation to reduce associated outcomes of staleness, burn-out and over-use injuries. In early adolescence, you can introduce conditioning to supplement skills development, so that fitness elements such as endurance and strength are trained in an age-related manner as shown in Table 10.1. This is a good time to bring elements of competition into your training as preparation for facing opponents when you consider it beneficial. For those interested in learning more about the development of physical abilities, see the pioneering work of Istvan Balyi

on long term athlete development and how this has been integrated into player pathways in many sports.

Table 10.1 An overview of the development of physical abilities (adapted from Stafford, 2005)

Boys	Girls	Key characteristics
6–9 years	6–8 years	Fun and participation Agility, balance, coordination and speed Core running, jumping and throwing
9–12 years	8–11 years	Overall sports skill learning Development of movement literacy across a variety of activities Resistance work to control own bodyweight
12–16 years	11–15 years	Sport specific training Development of stamina and muscular endurance Introduction of free weight strength development
16–18 years	15–17+ years	Specialisation Special training for position or event specialisation Considerable increase in training loads/frequencies
19+ years	18+ years	Maintenance and further development of physical capacities High performance focus Methodical planning of training
From 20 years	From 20 years	Retaining and withdrawal

Proportional growth

Proportional change has implications for balance, agility and whole body control during mid-childhood (6 to 9 years of age). During this time, children are motivated to attempt and learn more challenging and complex skills just when neural movement centres are further away from the limbs they are trying to control. This makes previously acquired skills appear awkward and clumsy while they catch up by re-learning key actions and movements. Recapping and revision of skills such as starting, stopping and turning are useful in class or group settings where children will be at different stages of development. This is particularly important in maintaining self-esteem, personal confidence and perceptions of competency during this period.

Bone and muscle growth

The lengthening of limbs is caused by the hardening or **ossification** of long bones. Most of this growth occurs at the sites of **epiphyseal plates**, making these particularly sensitive to damage by **overtraining**. This process can take more than 20 years to fully complete, as bone reforms from cartilage at different rates dependent on body part and inherited rates of maturation. During this process, and while bones often appear resilient to loading caused by handling increased dynamic or power type activities (sprint starts, turns or jump landings), there is a need to carefully plan the amount and scheduling of this kind of sports training. **Musculotendinous junctures** can be damaged at times when young performers have more flexibility than strength. This can cause problems in knees, when increasingly strong tendons pull bony appositions or nodules away from the main shaft, causing disfigurements and pain associated with growing problems such as **Osgood Schlatter's Syndrome** and related 'growing pain' issues such as shin splints or **tendinitis**.

As a coach, you should make regular checks of wear sites on performers' footwear and assess whether playing surfaces to be used are appropriate for growing bodies. (Grass, redgra and woodtrail are preferable to concrete and asphalt surfaces when coaching in outdoor settings.) This is sometimes overlooked but ensures that young bodies can safely dissipate the forces which might be beyond

the control of muscular systems still undergoing development. Predominantly, the amount of **plyometric** and **ballistic** work of rebound, counter movement or directional change nature should be limited, until you observe that strength changes have kicked in during adolescence. You should keep a log of the number of repetitions children are asked to perform, in line with recommendations of paediatric physiologists, (for further information visit the BASES or Youth Sport Trust websites (at www. pearsonfe.co.uk/foundationsinsport)). Scheduling training breaks with muscular relaxation and stretching activities ensures a balance to the varying work types that the programme attempts. This will help to prevent 'over-use' injury and mean that children will enjoy your sessions more.

> ### Key terms
>
> **Ossification** – the developmental process by which cartilage hardens to form bone
>
> **Epiphyseal growth plates** – specific points at the end of long bones where the majority of physical growth occurs
>
> **Overtraining** – training too hard and too frequently to adapt and improve. Often causing mental staleness and over-use injuries
>
> **Musculotendinous junctures** – the point where muscles and tendons merge and a key site for over-use injury
>
> **Osgood Schlatter's Syndrome** – bony appositions which are pulled out from soft bone just below the knee by overtrained tendons before muscles fully develop
>
> **Tendinitis** – a type of over-use injury common in young performers when serious training is first undertaken. Normally found in the elbow, wrist, knee and ankle
>
> **Plyometric training** – powerful jump, sprint and resistance training designed to improve dynamic or explosive movements in sport
>
> **Ballistic training** – rapid and vigorous limb actions associated with the development of speed

Nutrition and monitoring

Physical growth is fuelled by balanced nutritional intake, moderated by appropriate exercise types and normalised by having a disproportionately strong

Remember

Young performers should combine generalised, special and competition-specific types of training every week. General training helps their movement skills, special training helps them cope with the demands of their sport and competition-specific training keeps them ready for the challenge of the upcoming game.

immune system as a child. Children need sufficient high quality sleep, predominantly taken at night, as this is crucial to channelling energy into growth and recovery (when more energy is required for growth than recovery). Giving young children healthy and well-balanced nutritional intake, with sufficient vitamin and mineral content, is also essential for healthy growth (see also Chapter 11).

Similarly, fluid rehydration will also provide preventative effects which are arguably more important than regular exercise for normalised development. Advice about diet, pre-training snacking, correct hydration and post-exercise recovery regimes can be implemented by you as coach, with supportive work by parents and teachers. (A visit to an accredited sports nutritionist or state-registered dietician would be a good starting point. Otherwise check nutritional information provided on the internet by sports coach UK or the Australian Institute of Sport.)

Postural checks by health professionals are important to check **spine curvature anomalies**. These checks go hand in hand with the prescription of **core stabilisation exercises** to ensure that the musculature of the **torso** – responsible for the architectural support and control of body stability – is maintained from preadolescence. Similarly, ensuring that those involved in early maturing sports (such as gymnastics, swimming and tennis) are not pushed too hard and that signs of physical over-use and psychological burn-out are monitored, helps to prevent injury and **mental staleness**. The maintenance of training diaries, with the recording of training loadings, recovery times and perceptions of difficulty, are key to ensuring that those with talent can continue to develop their abilities.

For some, involvement in sports such as tennis

and swimming may require **prehabilitation** to strengthen, stretch and develop training sustainability in muscles and joints which will be disproportionately tested. This is when young performers become better able to cope with the stresses of competition, which require physical skills to be over-learned or sufficiently resilient against increasingly better opposition. In such cases, water-based yoga and massage types of post-exercise sport therapies can have an increasingly important restorative role to play.

Key terms

Spine curvature anomalies – structural abnormalities in the back (normally mild in nature) such as scoliosis or rounded shoulders which may prevent young people from training and competing (as reported by Olympic champion, Usain Bolt)

Core stabilisation exercises – static exercises often using swiss balls, mats and medicine balls to strengthen abdominal muscles associated with postural control

Torso – the trunk or mid section of the body

Prehabilitation – joint- and muscle-specific exercises which strengthen limbs in preparation for certain sports; for example, to prevent shoulder injuries sustained from practising the service action in tennis

Mental staleness – a negative emotional state caused by undertaking too much or poorly balanced training of the same type

Stop and think

A young butterfly swimmer you coach has started to complain about his shoulders aching and his back being tight. He also seems less motivated at the start of training and is asking more frequently how many metres he is doing tonight. He has a big competition in three weeks' time but does not seem very enthusiastic about it.

- How might you rearrange training to help reduce muscle soreness?
- How could you include the young performer in competitive preparation?
- How might you persuade your swimmer that he still has a realistic expectation of doing well in the upcoming competition?

Training sensitivity

Researchers have made important discoveries about the benefits of training as it influences physical improvements in ability during periods of child development and growth. Balyi (2003) and Stafford (2005) have found that in preadolescent, early years boys (5–8 years of age), improvements in cardio-respiratory endurance are far more likely to emerge from growth coupled with normalised activity, than through adherence to strict training regimes. It appears that at this stage, children improve by play and activity alone and that time is better spent on skill acquisition than physical training.

> ### Key term
>
> **Training sensitivity** – the amount of stress tolerance a young performer inherits and develops which helps them cope with heavy training phases

As boys, and even more importantly girls, approach adolescence, weight gain and changes in limb mechanics reduce the chances that stamina will continue to develop as a by-product of simply playing and that specific training is the only means of maintaining, let alone improving, these abilities. As a coach, you are advised to provide age-related training which is specific to the needs of the youngsters being trained at the time, rather than just as preparation for the more adult forms of training to be encountered later in life. Providing young performers with coping strategies to build mental strength in order to tolerate increasingly more demanding training loads will help maintain progress (Gervis and Brierley 1999).

Motor development

Physical development is a natural extension of brain growth and neural control. Both combine to allow

> ### Remember
>
> Coaches always need to apply child-centred thinking to the abilities, efforts and expectations of young performers they coach. Childhood is an important developmental stage in its own right, not just a preparation for later life.

initial movement control in infancy, coinciding with the need to explore, gain finer body control and the later engagement in the process of acquiring movement literacy.

The development of muscular and limb control occurs in a predictable pattern – infants learn to gain co-ordinated control from nearby to far away.

> ### Key term
>
> **Motor development** – the normal pattern of movement progression throughout the early years and completed in adolescence involving growth, neural and mental changes in function

This enables them to develop eye tracking or perceptual control before they can reach and grasp, so providing motivation for later learning. Young learners need activities which match their current stages of **motor development** if they are to have successful early learning experiences which will be reinforced and repeated.

Order of development

Well-documented motor milestones (see Table 10.2) provide a progressive guide to inform expectations of the development of movement control. Generalised skills proceed in a logical order, in line with the control of vertebral strength (as a baby learns first to control their head and neck muscles) and the ability to sit upright, required before observation and exploration can begin. This is the precursor to four-limbed control used in crawling which in turn provides the basis for walking.

All other actions develop in stages at the appropriate time, with immature models of skills which evolve into the adult version. Once skills for normal daily activity have been mastered, then more generalised sport-related movement patterns can be attempted. As a generalisation, the parts of actions of young performers quickly represent those of adults, but often the internal timing and control of the whole movement, or sometimes one critical part of the action, is different or even missing.

Table 10.2 Recognised motor milestones (adapted from Gallahue and Ozmun, 2003)

Action or ability	Typical age
Pulling self up to standing position	8–9 months
Stands alone	11 months
Walks	9–17 months
Runs	13–18 months
Kicking	18 months onwards
Throwing and catching	2 years to 30 months
Jumping off the ground	2.5 years
Balance and ride a bike	From 3 years
Climbing	3.5 years
Swimming	4–5 years
Hit a ball	4–6 years
Play basketball	8 years and onwards

Walking and skipping sequences of movement are noted before running, which involves extended stepping with small flight phases often with extended arms anticipating a fall. This is the first activity in which children develop an appreciation and perception of the speed of their movements in relation to others and comparison of effort and ability becomes a factor in their enjoyment of sport from that point onwards.

The motor reflexes, which prevent movement and aid personal safety at a time before we can fully co-ordinate actions, and which we inherit as infants, are involuntary and deliberately restrictive. These failsafe systems, such as the swimming and startle reflexes, become controlled and in some cases unlearned to allow more challenging physical tasks to be accomplished. The head righting reflex and head–shoulder linkage of the **asymmetric tonic reflexes** need to be bypassed before diving, golfing and waterskiing can be fully embraced later in life. Once this has occurred, reflexes are combined, such as the **plantar reflex** and the kicking reflex as the basic movement pattern of supporting the body, extending forward and taking the ground again, which forms the basis of walking.

Key terms

Asymmetric tonic reflex – the unconscious (automatic) muscular reaction linking head movement with arm movements like an archer pose

Plantar reflex – reflex action naturally developed in infancy which controls the pointing of the toes

Children learn through this burgeoning physical exploration and often their manipulation and control of their environment is the catalyst for their cognitive development. They integrate the outcomes of previous experiences, both positive and negative, within their memory systems as their experiential bank from which to strategise how they will undertake new activities. After surprisingly few attempts, the link between practice and movement control becomes more evident and they start to perform with greater consistency, purpose and increased confidence of achieving success. In the case of ball throwing, information about the weight and composition of the ball would be integrated with the distance to target, technique to be used and environmental conditions which existed immediately before the throw. By evaluating the outcome in the light of these pre-throw factors, children start to appreciate why movements succeeded and how they can be better controlled in the future.

Activity

Imagine you are coaching individuals of different age groups in the same training group (e.g. figure skaters, high jumpers or divers). How would a knowledge of learning stages specifically improve the way you organise, deliver and evaluate the success of your coaching sessions? Consider how the capabilities of performers at different developmental ages will impact their expectations of their learning and progression, and yours.

In essence, the task for you as coach, therefore, is relatively simple, in that providing wide-ranging, randomised learning experiences, i.e. to learn by doing, will be the best basis for boosting motor memory, physical decision making and strategic planning. You also need to ensure that children are given plenty of opportunities to reflect upon and evaluate their performance, such that they might be even more successful in similarly novel situations in sport. In essence, a coach should seek to make him or herself increasingly redundant as the facilitator of evaluatory information – safe in the knowledge that young performers are developing independence of thought, which will be vital in competitive situations in sport and the wider world.

Acquiring skills

Increased child interest in learning typically coincides with a physical or mental trigger but at times it might also reflect a specific window of practice opportunity – this is known as a critical learning period. At these times, children are most responsive to engagement in the learning of specific types of skills. Coaches and instructors should try to capitalise by providing well-controlled, scheduled practice and making full use of stimulating equipment and interesting activities. It may also help coaches to account for the boredom threshold, indicating that it is best to move on to new activities in order to prevent performance plateaus and de-motivation.

Uninterrupted practice, with general encouragement and an interesting practice environment, will eventually provide sufficient stimulus for demonstrating increasingly mature skilled performance. Modifying equipment and playing areas (short tennis courts, HK balls and catching large balls for example) to better suit the dimensions, fitness and talents of the learner, allows for the all-important successful initial practice which provides the desire and satisfaction to

Activity

Consider your current view of working with young performers with novice, intermediate and advanced skill levels in a sport you know well. How would you expect them to compare in terms of the accuracy, smoothness and consistency of their performances in new skills, as well as those already mastered? Then make a list to contrast expected differences in relation to their attitude, persistence and concentration in learning situations.

undertake increased play and involvement.

The skill-hungry years

The process of acquiring skills can be difficult and frustrating for some, while enjoyable and providing drive for others. In spite of the oft-heard comment about some performers being naturals in sport, physical skills are typically unnatural in that they always require a learning phase and considerable practice. It is true that some performers get the idea of a skill much more quickly than others, but this may be for reasons of related experience, physical prowess or having a more positive initial learning experience. Whatever the reason, previous research from skill learning settings has established that young performers need to have developed an accurate and distinctive mental representation of themselves executing a skill correctly, before they are able to progress and become consistent, effortless and stylish. This is known as the cognitive stage of skill learning.

Cognitive stage of skill learning

This stage of learning is often reached when young people have learned visually through watching a performer demonstrate or model the skill successfully, have attended to critical cues which determine success and are better at deciding when and where to carry out the skill. Initially, young performers at this cognitive stage have a poor reference of correctness and make many errors in execution.

They need considerable practice with lots of generalised encouragement but often benefit from reduced technical input. At this point it may not be helpful to say too much about how to do something as uninterrupted repetition often prevails. The young performer's frustration at not being able to get an idea of how to be successful requires that a number of different strategies are used by the coach to retain interest and foster perseverance. Visualisation of successful images, the use of motivating trigger words and watching short moving images of themselves with a coach or informed parent are the best way of overcoming these initial obstacles to skill learning.

Associative skill learning

Once young performers start to associate what they need to do with their own actions, they are on the way to producing repeatable performances of the chosen skill. They now actively seek more challenging feedback and pre-activity instruction from coaches and teachers and often start to raise expectations of their own performance. They begin to reflect more realistically on why they were unsuccessful and expect you as coach to be more honest about their performances. At this point, the way that training sessions have been set up can be revisited.

Initially, you will need to organise the coaching environment to provide the best possibility of participant success but that may not reflect a realistic sense of how a performer will need to perform in a game or competitive setting. Hence, running with a ball, crossing a ball moving towards you and hitting a bouncing half volley, will provide more game relatedness in relation to dealing with and learning about how to control a ball under game conditions.

As young performers' memory systems develop, they start to reminisce or use unstructured daydreaming to cognitively organise the flow and rhythm of new movements in breaks between practice sessions. This can make for quicker learning progression and the possibility of making training more competitive in nature during the early post-pubertal years.

Autonomic stage of learning

After considerable practice, a level of skill execution which requires little or no conscious control starts to appear. This **automaticity** allows skilful young performers to more fully consider the context in which they will use the skill for their own or their team's advantage. The experience they have gained allows them to be more creative in deciding how to execute action as part of a more complicated sequence or in order to deceive an opponent.

They often attempt to speed up movements to reduce decision-making time for their opponent, combine skills at the same time and use physical and verbal distraction strategies as evidenced by a brilliant Cristiano Ronaldo running with the ball for Real Madrid or Chris Ashton's weave and try for the England Rugby team. Young performers in these situations often like to experiment with ways of using more flair and creativity as they become more confident on the ball.

For those interested in learning more about alternative views of learning in sport, look at the work of GTI (1969) on the four stages for learning any new skill as suggested by the Conscious Competence model.

Stop and think

A young female gymnast is coming to the end of her career and looking for a new sporting challenge. Think about the type of skills she has already **over-learned** from the vault, floor and uneven bars.
- What athletics event might she be best suited to and how would she need to modify her training?
- What difficulties might she face in switching from one sport to another?
- How might her coach help her come to terms with the new challenge?

Key terms

Over-learning – frequent and continued practice of key performance skills that have already been learned to prevent poor technique under the pressure of competition

Automaticity – expert performance of a learned skill where the action is executed with little conscious thought but in a mature and consistent manner

Remember

Try to appreciate how novices acquire a new skill rather than simply relying on your current expertise or how you were coached. Re-learn a skill on the non-dominant side (e.g. throw or hit a ball on your less practised side) or in a new environment (kick a ball against a corner of two walls and control the bounce back). Can you identify which stage of the leaning process applies to you? What coaching strategies might you use to coach improvement in someone at a similar level?

Quicker reactions and the ability to anticipate

During adolescence, well-rehearsed sports skills start to benefit from quicker **reaction times** and anticipation skills normally associated with greater experience and natural motor development. Quickest reactive times naturally peak in the twenties and are retained by appropriate and regular progressive practice for the next decade or so. What young performers naturally lack is the competitive experience with which to make decisions about what might happen in the future and so, while they have the physical abilities to react very quickly, their anticipation is less accurate than that of their older peers.

Anticipation training requires knowing what signs and signals to look for prior to action occurring and so involves the integration of recollections of previous outcomes with perceptual and decision-making mechanisms. Structuring their training, so that performers play against different opponents or train under varying environmental conditions, in addition to technological consideration of cause and effect through performance analysis, are the main ways of increasing sport-specific experience and can help athletes to anticipate new situations in the heat of competition. Good coaches plan to include decision-making situations into their practices so that their young performers can learn how to judge situations in the relative calm of training before they are faced with such eventualities in competition. For those interested in learning more about developmental influences on practice, see Daniel Coyle's 'The Talent Code' and 'Bounce' by Matthew Syed.

Key terms

Reaction time – the shortest time taken for the body to start to produce movements following one physical signal to do so

Anticipation – the learned ability to make advance judgements in sport based on past experience in similar situations

---

Psychosocial development

Sports involvement is hugely important to young performers. Many children, when asked, respond that they would rather do well in sports than in the classroom but, more tellingly, would rather have it reported that they had done badly in the classroom than on the sports field. Unfortunately, involvement does not always signify improvement or competitive success. Equally, there is no doubt that those who find they are more comfortable coping with the demands of competition are more likely to strive for continued performance involvement and be rewarded with having more satisfying experiences through sport.

Not everyone can win in sport in the strictest sense and not everyone copes equally well, especially when the game is not going to plan, but the mistake often made is in thinking that mental skills are any more 'natural' than physical ones. Children should be emotionally robust and ready for competition as well as physically ready. This means that children should only be put in for competition when there is more than a passing chance that they will be neither injured or out of their depth, which can lead to despondency and the desire to quit. Exposure to competition needs to be progressively increased so that the level of challenge is always, but only marginally, ahead of coach expectations and young performer abilities. This is best achieved by utilising a child-centred approach to coaching, where the developmental needs of the young performer are central to the learning opportunities and competitive experiences they are provided with or encounter.

Perceived competence and self-esteem

Essentially, young performers primarily develop their **self-esteem** or value of self-worth through their perceptions of competency, with motivation centred on their need to achieve and desire for recognition by those important to them. They want coaches to believe in them so that they can, more consistently, believe in themselves. Satisfying experiences in sport (**sport satisfaction**) boost self concept and make all of us feel we have greater self-worth when those experiences are noted and we get positive feedback from coaches, peers, teachers, parents and significant others, such as talent spotters or other family members with recent experience playing high level sport.

The role of the current coach, in particular, has been singled out recently by elite young performers as an important factor in the evaluation of success in sport – to the extent that many wish to stay with their current **mentors** for the rest of their careers. Coaches are also singled out for having important roles to play in developing the social skills of athletes in their charge and helping to raise worthwhile human beings – regardless of their ultimate achievements on the playing field.

Key terms

Self-esteem – the value a young performer places upon themselves

Sport satisfaction – the pride and rewarding feelings associated with being successful at something you enjoy

Mentor – an experienced and knowledgeable person who advises and guides a less experienced colleague early in their career

Activity

Young performers may be highly self confident in one situation but struggle to believe in their abilities in another. Imagine you are coaching young performers to be more consistent in an activity where target accuracy is important (e.g. basketball, archery or water polo). How might you modify practice to maximise scoring opportunities or passing success by manipulating certain practice variables? Consider distance and angle from target, technical instruction and performer feedback for reinforcement and increased motivation. How might teammates also be involved in this process of boosting the chances of individual, and team, performance success?

Ages and stages of development

Young people develop feelings, attitudes and emotions in a related process which sees them gain independence, develop views about others who they come into contact with and question their place in the world. Those changes start to

surface at common age bands and you should be aware of the influence that your words, actions and conduct will have upon impressionable young people in your training sessions. This will impact on the ways in which you attempt to motivate or convince them to do things in training that might be hard work, difficult to achieve or not valued by them. Knowing what to expect from young people at different ages can help to prevent communication difficulties which could detract from your abilities as a coach. Table 10.3 provides more detail of these developmental changes.

Table 10.3 A summary of mental and emotional development of young people

Age (in years)	Characteristic
0–1.5	Children are nurtured by their parents or trusted carers and develop a sense of security.
2	The 'terrible twos' where the fear of parental separation can create anxiety and tantrums.
3–5	Children become more secure as they develop independence, social interaction and cooperation through play and games.
6–10/11	Young people start to develop attitudes and feelings towards things and people. They become motivated to work hard to achieve adult-set goals and be rewarded by praise. Comparison can cause worry about ability in certain situations. They begin to understand their place in the community and their responsibilities to others.
12–15/16	The teenage years see some young people becoming more confident and socially adept as they seek to understand their identity. Others may be shy and fearful of standing out, or vocal in dealing with parents, from whom they wish to become more independent, or even aggressive when questioning those who lead or instruct them. They also demonstrate strong allegiances to their friends, teachers and coaches, often volunteering as their moral code and as their character develops.

Coach–athlete relationship

Coaching young performers successfully is often said to be based upon a good coach–athlete relationship, particularly in relation to participant motivations and the degree to which they desire success. Motives for involvement, as previously mentioned, include having fun, staying in shape and demonstrating **mastery**, with boys, additionally, having the need to achieve in competitive situations; this often goes counter to girls with their (generally) greater need to exercise, learn new skills and be with friends. This suggests a number of important considerations for those charged with coaching these age groups.

Key term

Mastery – knowledge, ability and control in relation to specific learned situations in sport

Girls primarily need encouragement and social support in non-competitive settings and want to be included in decisions made with the coach in relation to training loadings and work types – or at least the discussions as to why they are being undertaken. Boys, on the other hand, generally prefer the coach to take charge and be autocratic in directing what they do in training, without too much discussion apart from creative and offensive aspects of play, when they appreciate input and taking ownership of new team plays and moves (Sherman et al., 2000). Both girls and boys like well-organised, stimulating training practices and want the coach to have new ideas and activities ready as and when required. Generally though, there appear to be more similarities than differences between the genders in relation to preferred styles of behaviour used by their coaches (Weinburg & Gould, 2003).

Sports compliance

Younger performers choose to persist with sport as a function of the benefits of gaining greater competency (as measured by goal attainment and skill improvement). The general pattern is that sports participation is thought to peak as children start their secondary school experience, with the numbers involved gradually reducing over the rest of their time at school. This might appear to be a very negative conclusion given the time and effort that is invested in organised activity but simply reflects changing interests and a desire to attempt other and new activities.

Key term

Sport compliance – the degree to which a young performer persists with and continues training for their chosen sport

On occasions, however, it is also a sign of success in sport being made into too big an expectation by parents and others – leading to excessive pre-competition anxiety and lower perceived competence and self-worth by the athlete in question. This is largely a negatively oriented self-fulfilling prophecy causing reduced satisfaction, gradual withdrawal and eventual drop-out from activity in what is otherwise perceived to be an emotionally healthy and non-stressful pursuit for young performers. The need for the agreed sporting goals of the coach and athlete to be verbalised and communicated to parents is vital. This will help to ensure that undue and extremely unhelpful additional emotional pressure to achieve is not going to drive the young performer away from the sport they love.

Psychological skills in sport

Certain situations in sport will make getting this balance more difficult to achieve. In individual sports, particularly, there can be excessive worry following defeat (and not performing up to expectations). Where the level of sports competition is perceived to be important most of the time, situational stress and anxiety can predominate. In these situations, a well-planned educational programme, which focuses upon motivational management through effective goal setting and strategies for coping with adverse situations linked to the use of **imagery**, is the most effective way to plan for emotional stability in sport. The sense of knowing what to do ahead of things happening and not being upset by the process, is one best prepared for by informal talks with the coach and then leading to dedicated sessions enhanced by physical practice.

If we look at the examples of Tom Daley in Olympic diving, Laura Robson in tennis and, in the past, Boris Becker, we can see the importance that mental toughness, through a combination of self belief, positive affirmations and coping under pressure, can have in helping to create senior champions at a very early age. In principle, when athletes are old enough to understand and embrace the concept of training, they are old enough to start simple psychological skills training

Table 10.4 Overview of the development of psychological abilities (adapted from Gervis and Brierley, 1999; Smith and Smoll, 2002; Stafford, 2005)

Young performer age	Key psychological readiness factors
2–4 years	Ability based on skill mastery alone No direct comparisons with others Subjective assessment of personal success
4–6 years	Start to assess personal ability objectively against independent measures Make no distinction between effort and ability
6–7 years	Ability starts to become linked to the achievement of others Have basic drives and motivations to acquire new skills Improve through uninterrupted practice more than coach feedback
7–9 years	Young performer perceives effort as directly linked to success Believe in the notion that hard work produces successful outcomes Start to appreciate the difference between play and training
9–10 years	Begin to distinguish between effort and ability of themselves and others which impacts upon their self concept Can benefit from mental rehearsal
11–14 years	Have variable **self-confidence** and perceived competence due to unfavourable comparisons with others Can tolerate repetitive training due to changes in motivational strategy

Key terms

Self-confidence – the degree to which a person is confident about their ability to perform well in a given situation

Imagery (in sport) – the use of mental rehearsal to improve physical performance by means of motivating pictures, visions and words

At the very highest levels of sporting excellence, the work ethic undoubtedly separates those identified with talent from those who actually make it to the top. Those with sport expertise are defined by having done a lot of specialised practice at a very early age and less by the fact that they have special, identifiable traits or talents. These performers are self-starters, often undertaking many more hours of extra individualised practice than their rivals. It has been consistently suggested that to get to the top in a sport, young performers probably need to log up more than 10,000 hours of deliberate play and purposeful practice in their chosen sport (Ericsson 1991). They work on those aspects of performance which are most needed for competitive improvement and are constantly looking at ways of making their sessions more in line with what they want to happen on match day. Similarly, the difficulty level of training (particularly the number of times performers got it wrong or failed in training without giving up that they undertook as young performers) is also far higher for those who get to the top and seems to be related to higher levels of achievement motivation.

A word about working with young performers

The pleasure of introducing children to a sport that you derive great satisfaction from as a coach does not come without its accompanying regulations and responsibilities (see Chapter 14). Coaches have a duty of care to the young performers in their charge which should not be taken lightly.

Whether you are a volunteer coach in either an assistive or fully empowered leadership capacity in sport, the same principles apply. Having decided that you think you have the enthusiasm, patience and desire to work with young performers in their formative years, you should plan to develop your coaching abilities as outlined in Table 10.5 below.

Table 10.5 Professional development pathway for aspiring coaches

Pass the appropriate National Governing Body qualification as a coach
Register to be given CRB clearance to practise by that same governing body as soon as you qualify
Purchase Public Liability Insurance to top up to at least £2m insurance cover currently provided by your NGB
Join a club which has an established coaching structure
Gain a First Aid/CPR qualification as soon as possible
Attend workshops about Child Protection in coaching and safeguarding young performers as regularly hosted by sports coach UK/Youth Sport Trust/NSPCC/County Sports Partnership
Listen to/observe other practising (senior) coaches who can guide and mentor you as you begin your coaching career, particularly in relation to performer safety, training organisation and parent relationships
Attend county and regional coaching days and workshops
Maintain a detailed training diary noting individual differences in young performers' physical and mental response to training activity intensities
Attend competitive fixtures and coaching demonstrations. Consider joining coaching forums and internet roundtables
Consider gaining a refereeing or officiating course to keep current with rule changes
Assist more experienced coaches on away trips, training camps and overseas competitions to learn more about acclimatisation, preparation and specific types of competition

As you will probably coach at a club or sports centre, there will be several issues for you to consider that relate to safe practice, lines of communication and safeguarding young people in sport.

These elements come under the banner of risk assessment (for fuller detail, see Chapter 4) and will need to be addressed before you begin to plan the training sessions themselves. Sports coaching should always be conducted appropriately, safely and with the rights of the performers in your care being of primary importance. Generally, the organisation will take the lead by informing you of the risk assessments that they have undertaken to ensure that any significant hazards meet standards set by local and national authority legal requirements. However, you should ensure that you have scrutinised the environment in which you will be coaching to check:

- facility structure (flooring, lighting and temperature control)
- general security (fencing to keep equipment in and dogs and others out)
- equipment (state of repair of small items and movement and storage of apparatus too heavy for young people to attempt to move)
- cleanliness of showers, toilets and work areas
- warning instructions to users and others
- spectator safety if applicable
- safety for other user groups
- emergency and evacuation policies.

More and more coaches now work within schools, providing specialist sport provision to support the work of the Physical Education department. Assistance with compulsory after-school sport provision requires knowledge of a wider range of student interests, abilities and motivations than the traditional coaching setting. It also requires a shift of emphasis for some coaches who may have concentrated more on technical development to more educational styles of facilitation and learning. It is possible that many coaches who wish to take advantage of these opportunities will undertake postgraduate qualifications at university or apply for the Graduate Teacher Programme (GTP) vocationally within an accredited school. Regardless of the situation in which you wish to professionalise your career, you should be fully up to date with government-led initiatives to better protect and safeguard young people in sport.

Table 10.6 Key legislation which impacts upon coaching practice

The Children Act (1989, updated 2004 and 2006)	Moved away from the concept of parental rights towards the welfare of the child being paramount.
Care Standards Act (2000)	Local authorities were required by government to be regulated and meet the same minimal care standards as all other providers.
The Childcare Act (2006)	Delivery of childcare by voluntary bodies, such as sports clubs, became regulated and inspected by government agencies.
Protection of Children Act (2002)	Sought to ensure that adequate checks were made on the suitability of people working with children and young people.
Safeguarding Vulnerable Groups Act (2006)	Following the Soham Inquiry, this recommended that those who wish to work with children or vulnerable adults should be vetted, then registered or barred from doing so.
Every Child Matters (2003)	Looked at the problem of children at risk who may fall between the boundaries between a range of child protection providers.
PESSYP (2008)	Physical Education and Sport Strategy for Young People aims to give every young person (aged 5 to16 years) access to 3–5 hours of PE and sport per week.

An example of a coaching session plan is shown on page 164.

Your coaching role as mentor, motivator and guardian

In addition to planning sessions and organising training venues, you will also be aware of the wider role of the coach and the expectations that society will place upon you. Your view of yourself primarily as a coach, with a specialisation in a particular sport, is less important than your responsibilities for the young people in your care and the need to safeguard their health, security and well-being. Your experience and knowledge of working with other coaches, being in competitive situations and reflections upon dealing with winning and losing, make you the ideal person to advise young people in relation to their conduct, expectations and enjoyment through sport.

Giving pertinent and responsible advice is vital at a time when young people may be impressionable and vulnerable and you are often acting *in loco parentis* (i.e. as if you are their parent). Your young performers will expect you to demonstrate your good character, sense of fair play and work ethic in the way you behave, and you will encourage them by using appropriate language, setting realistic goals and listening to their views and concerns. In this way you will gain their trust and, with greater experience, their respect and shared belief for future success.

Making training fun, challenging and related to indicators of competitive success

Your performers will need to spend a lot of time honing their techniques and abilities if they are to be successful in competition. You will be a key figure in how much they can both work hard towards their targets and enjoy the experience at the time. Adding variety to your coaching programmes, for example, by changing location, using guest coaches and modifying the way you introduce and revisit training drills, will be crucial to their sustained interest and longevity within the sport. Their self belief as competitors will develop as a result of joint observation and honest analysis of their performances to inform your future planning, so that training mimics competition and they are successful in both.

Coach(es)	Helen Brown		Date	25.05.2011
Sport			Athletics (Field Events)	
Number of Participants	8		Age (s)	8–9 years

Health and Safety Issues
Special Requirements: Dry surfaces / sandpit dug and raked / rake & broom to be provided.
Risk Assessment attached: Yes (i.e. Check weather for under foot conditions / YP footwear / Jumping Pit conditions for glass and animal mess / sweep takeoff board).

Location and Resources
Local athletic club sandpits, grass infield and 2 lanes of the back straight on the track.
Tape measure, stopwatch, run up markers, coloured cones for distance markers.

Main Session:

Aims and Objectives	Aim/Objective: To introduce young athletes to the generic skills of jumping for distance (Long Jump and Triple Jump).
	Key Factors: Generating speed and converting it into controlled height at takeoff and implementing the principles of safe landing in sand.
Warm Up (10 minutes)	Hopping and Skipping Relays ('Follow my Leader' or 'Leap the island' style) along a 30m section of track. Emphasis safe head, back and foot positions on landings and takeoffs (3 mins).
	Dynamic Flexibility using the spectator rail (swinging, flexing and adduction work for the hips, and lower back. (5 mins).
	Simple running drills (quick feet, heels only, knee pick ups and giant steps) to develop good contact (2 mins).
Main Content (45 minutes)	(a) Skill Revision: Standing Long Jump for Distance into Sandpit – experiment with single and double leg take off. Use Questioning style to determine which is most effective.
	(b) Skill Development: 5 step run up Long Jump for Distance. Put athletes in pairs and give them two marker cones. Have them practice measuring a short run up with each other. Ask what happens as they run quicker (A: length of run up gets shorter / markers need to be adjusted).
	(c) Competition: Put two pairs together so you have two teams of four. Place a different colour cone alongside the pit every 30 cms from the board. Give each team 12 jumps (three each) and award point for each cone they jump past (120cms = 4 points, etc). Keep a team score to include all performers. Ask how they tried to improve their best jump.
	(d) Skill Introduction: Hopping (on one leg). In pairs get the group to try to hop through the sandpit, recording how few jumps, as a pair, they took to get to the other end. 2 attempts per team, one using left foot, second on the right.
	(e) Explain that they now know how to hop and jump. Add a step in between. Practice the Standing Triple Jump. Check for flat-footed landings, rhythmic movements and equal effort on all phases.
	(f) Finish with a Standing Triple Jump competition for distance. Aim for twice their best long jump plus a metre.
Cool Down (10 minutes)	Jog – Skip – Walk with limb swinging for half a lap of the track. Each 50m slower than the one before.
	Static Stretching – each young performer to lead a stretch that they can do well followed by one they find more difficult.
Reflection and Aims for Next Session	Refection: How well did they understand and demonstrate the differences between hopping, stepping and jumping? How much did they maintain their techniques as speed was introduced?
	Aims for next session: Develop the running triple jump. Introduce 4 jump competitions. Explain about No Jumps and Rules for Competition.

Figure 10.2 An example of a coaching session plan (available to print at www.pearsonfe.co.uk/foundationsinsport)

Case study (for recommended answers, see www.pearsonfe.co.uk/foundationsinsport)

Picture the scene: a mother watching her son playing competitive hockey – lots of energy and endeavour on display but few scoring opportunities so far. Losing a little interest, she glances at the match programme and notes an unexpected trend in the player detail section. Instead of seeing an even spread of birthdates throughout the year, it appears that the children are much more likely to be born in one particular part of the year, i.e. immediately after the competition cut-off date, which is normally either 1 January or more often 1 September, for sports played in the UK. She shows the discovery to her researcher friend who finds that the number of players born further away from that start of age group date reduces month by month. Some young players are still in the team but there are far fewer of them compared to those born immediately after this cut-off date.

Some other interesting facts that have emerged since the original research (Barnsley, 1985) include the following.

- Boys and, to a lesser extent, girls born with what is known as high relative age are more likely to get into youth age group teams and stay there until they have risen to some of the highest levels of representative performance including becoming a senior international.

- They practise with other older and often more physically mature players gaining greater match experience and developing better decision-making skills.

- They play against better opposition at an earlier stage than many late maturing young

performers and become more self-confident and have better self-esteem.

- This pattern is consistently found in many teams and some individual sports in this country and in all other continents of the world.

- While children who are behind with their academic abilities normally receive additional support and so catch up, the same situation does not occur in sport.

- Late-maturing young performers often have the greatest potential to achieve at senior levels in sport but frequently they drop out too early to achieve their sporting goals.

Questions

1. Why do coaches tend to select older and more mature-looking players in many team sports?

2. How does an athlete's date of birth advantage or disadvantage them in relation to selection for sporting teams?

3. How might a governing body of sport make competition selection or cut-off dates fairer?

4. How might this relative age effect influence the motivation of a late developer?

5. What problems might the performer with a high relative age effect have later in their sporting careers?

6. Why might this effect be reversed (i.e. with the youngest in a year group being more favoured by coaches) in sports such as gymnastics?

Check your understanding (for answers, see www.pearsonfe.co.uk/foundationsinsport)

1. How do children and adults differ physically in relation to their stage of growth?

2. How do boys and girls differ in relation to post-pubertal training abilities?

3. Why should you understand about bone growth before planning sprint type training?

4. What are the main differences between cognitive and autonomic learners?

5. What is a critical learning period and why is it important?

6. How would psychological skills training be useful to novices in sport?

7. Why should coaches praise effort over ability?

8. Explain the link between self-esteem, perceived competence and sports satisfaction.

9. How do boys and girls often differ in relation to their views on competition?

10. What sorts of instructional behaviours do girls generally prefer in their coaches?

Useful resources

To obtain a secure link to the websites below, see the Websites section on page ii or visit the companion website at www.pearsonfe.co.uk/foundationsinsport.

- Association for Physical Education

- Australian Institute of Sport

- British Association of Sport and Exercise Sciences

- County Sports Partnerships

- Gordon Training International

- sports coach UK

- Youth Sport Trust

Further reading

Barnsley, R. and Thompson, A. (1985) Hockey success and birth date: the relative age effect. *CAHPER* Journal, 51, 23–28.

Balyi, I. & Hamilton, A. (2003) Long term athlete development update – Trainability in childhood and adolescence. *FHS,* (20) 6–8.

Coyle, D. (2009). The Talent Code. London: Random House.

Cox, R. (2007) *Sport Psychology: Concepts and Applications*. New York: McGraw.

Crisfield, P. (2003) *Analysing Your Coaching*. Leeds: sports coach UK.

Cross, N. and Lyle, J. (1999) *The Coaching Process*. Oxford: Butterworth & Heinemann.

Drabik, J. (1996) *Children and Sports Training*. Island Pond VT: Stadion.

Earle, C. (ed.) (2003) *Coaching Young Performers*. Leeds: sports coach UK.

Gallahue, D. and Ozmun, J. (2003) *Understanding Motor Development*. Madison, WS: Brown & Benchmark.

Gervis, M. and Brierley, J. (1999) *Effective Coaching for Children*. Marlborough: Crowood.

Gordon Training International (1969) *Learning a new skill is easier said than done*. See 'Useful resources for source. [Accessed July 7th 2011].

Grisogono, V. (1996) *Children and Sport: Fitness, Injuries and Diet*. London: John Murray.

Jennett, S. (ed.) (2008) *Dictionary of Sport and Exercise and Medicine*. Philadelphia: Churchill Livingstone Elsevier.

Lara-Bercial, S. (2010) *Quick Guide: Child Development for Coaches*. Leeds: sports coach UK.

Lee, M. (2003) *Coaching Children in Sport*. London: E&F Spon.

Rowland, T. (2005) *Children's Exercise Physiology*. Champaign, IL: Human Kinetics.

Sherman, C., Fuller, R. & Speed, H. (2000) Gender comparisons of Preferred Coaching Behaviour in Australian Sports. *Journal of Sport Behaviour, 23, 4.*

Smoll, F. & Smith, R. (2002) *Children and Youth in Sport – A Bio-psychosocial perspective*. Dubuque, IW: Kendall-Hunt.

Stafford, I. (2005) *Coaching for Long-Term Athlete Development*. Leeds: sports coach UK.

Troop, B. (ed.) (2007) *Coaching Young Performers*. London: P2P.

Syed, M. (2010). Bounce – How champions are made. London: Fourth Estate.

Weinberg, R. & Gould, D. (2003) *Foundations of Sport and Exercise Psychology*. Champaign, IL: Human Kinetics.

Chapter 11

Nutrition, exercise and lifestyle

Introduction

The process of coaching successful athletes involves commitment and sacrifices by both parties so that the coach can help the athlete to achieve their potential. The role of the coach includes the nurturing and development of athletes, including aspects such as nutrition and lifestyle factors, which are important for the health and well-being of athletes, in order to fulfil their sports ambitions.

Lifestyle factors can have strong positive and negative influences on athletes. Pressures created upon the individual's lifestyle may affect participation and/or performance in training and competition. As a coach, you must have an understanding of the factors which may affect your athletes.

Nutrition plays an important role in the athlete's health, well-being, sports participation and performance. As a coach, you need knowledge and understanding of a balanced diet and key nutritional concepts, such as macronutrients and micronutrients and their function, in order to facilitate your athletes in making appropriate nutritional choices.

This chapter is not intended to equip you with the skills and knowledge to calculate energy requirements or plan an appropriate nutritional diet plan, but will broaden your knowledge of nutrition and lifestyle concepts in relation to those who participate in sport and exercise. Further advice may be needed, or referral to a medical practitioner, sports dietician or nutritionist.

Learning outcomes

After you have read this chapter you should be able to:

- understand how lifestyle factors may affect an athlete
- understand nutrition terminology
- describe what is included in a balanced diet
- describe macronutrients and their function
- describe micronutrients and their function
- understand the importance of hydration
- understand about food labelling.

Lifestyle factors affecting an athlete

The age of your athlete, and their level of competition, means that lifestyle factors are likely to impact on them in different ways. An athlete of 25 years old, competing at international level, will endure a multitude of factors including finding the time to train and compete at this level (the volume and intensity of training will be high), financial pressures (balancing training and working to earn money to fund training, accommodation and food, if they are not a paid professional sportsperson) and social pressures, as well as considering their behaviour on and off the pitch. A younger athlete of 12 years old, competing at club level, will have factors to consider such as peer pressure and inappropriate activities such as smoking and under-age drinking.

Current initiatives focus on supporting athletes and their lifestyles, particularly in relation to achieving performance goals for London 2012. The Sky Sports Living for Sport programme supports athletes and disaffected young people, while the Youth Sports Trust provides athlete mentors within schools. The English Institute of Sport employs performance lifestyle advisors who work closely with national governing bodies to ensure athletes reach their performance goals for London 2012.

'ChangingLIVES' is currently supported by Sky Sports Living for Sport. The scheme provides world-class athletes as mentors to schools. Schools that choose to partake are offered the opportunity of an athlete mentor to support the programme.

The mentors engage with learners to overcome challenges such as bullying, dyslexia, exclusion and living with a disability. They aim to instill the British Athletes Commission's 'Six Keys to Success' – belief, determination, hard work, belonging, people skills and time management.

Youth Sport Trust operate an initiative called 'Junior Athlete Education'. Below is the rationale for the initiative:

> Pupils performing to a high level in sport may be involved in intensive training and competitions outside of school time. The Junior Athlete Education framework includes a range of resources and training opportunities for young people which aims to support the individual needs of talented pupils and to achieve a manageable balance between schoolwork and out-of-school participation in elite sport.

> Source: http://gifted.youthsporttrust.org

The initiative aims to provide a mentor for each talented school athlete; however, where this proves difficult due to a limited number of mentors within schools, group mentoring may be offered as an alternative.

The English Institute of Sport employs performance lifestyle advisors. Performance lifestyle advisors would have many responsibilities including:

- delivering individual and group performance lifestyle sessions: this would involve supporting both current performance demands as well as their future personal and professional development
- working with national governing bodies
- providing lifestyle support, ensuring key areas of lifestyle are targeted and balanced with the sporting commitment
- ensuring identified athletes receive appropriate and timely support and information to adopt a performance-focused approach to planning and managing their non-athletic commitments and leading a performance-focused lifestyle
- developing relationships with education establishments, employers and other athlete

stakeholders to ensure that athletes have the flexibility and support they need to accommodate their training and performance requirements

- developing performance lifestyle programmes that reflect core discipline principles

- working and operating as a multidisciplinary team to deliver performance lifestyle support to elite athletes and coaches.

Source: www.eis2win.co.uk

Different lifestyle factors

As a coach you should be aware of a multitude of lifestyle factors which can have positive and/or negative effects upon an athlete. It is important that factors are identified and managed in order to facilitate the athletes' performance. These can include the following factors.

Peer pressure

Peer pressure can be described as a person who is encouraged by their peers or friends to alter their behaviour, attitude and values. They are pressured to conform to the norm in the context of their peers. An athlete may be pressured by peers to take part in activities they would not choose; for example, drinking alcohol, excessive drinking, smoking or drug abuse. These activities will have negative effects.

- **Alcohol** – It is illegal to buy alcoholic drink under the age of 18. Over the age of 18, it is recommended not to drink regularly more than 3–4 units of alcohol a day for a man, and 2–3 units a day for a woman. One unit is equivalent to 25ml of a spirit such as whisky or vodka, a third of a pint of beer or 175ml glass of wine. Drinking can affect normal functions such as walking and talking and alter behaviour. Long-term effects of drinking include liver disease, liver cancer, mouth cancer, oral and digestive tract cancers and chronic pancreatitis. Mental health can also be affected resulting in anxiety, depression and even psychosis.

- **Smoking** – Cigarette smoke includes nicotine, carbon monoxide and tar containing lots of chemicals. In the short term, lung function may be affected, with further effects of smoking including lung cancer, chronic obstructive

pulmonary disorder, heart disease, many cancers and rheumatoid arthritis. Immediate effects for athletes include a reduced amount of oxygen absorbed, which causes an effect on respiration, resulting in an increase in airway resistance and heart rate.

- **Drugs** – Drug testing is common in sport for both social or **recreational drugs** and **performance-enhancing drugs**. Recreational drugs include cocaine, cannabis, ecstasy, LSD and amphetamines. Performance-enhancing drugs include stimulants, diuretics, beta blockers and anabolic steroids. A positive drugs test will most likely result in a long-term ban from sport, which may be indefinite. (See Table 11.1 for effects and side effects.)

However, in certain situations, peer pressure can have positive effects. If the athlete has peers who are ambitious, have a strong work ethos and have the drive to succeed, they will be pressured to follow their peers. These traits can only be of benefit.

Key term

Performance-enhancing drugs – drugs which are used to improve performance

Recreational drugs – drugs taken for recreational or social reasons, commonly known as street drugs

Socialising

Training, competition, work and education create many time pressures for athletes, leaving little time for socialising with their friends and family. Peers can create pressure for young athletes to socialise. This may divert their attention away from resting and recuperating, and have negative influences in unwanted activities. Friends who are supportive and understanding will have a positive influence, and be encouraging and supportive in terms of rest and relaxation. Time should be built into athletes' training regimes to include socialising in order to help reduce the pressure and tension from training and competition. Relaxation should be encouraged not only through socialisation but through other activities promoting health and well-being, such as yoga, Pilates or tai chi. This will enable the athlete to divert their attention from their sport and refocus their mind.

Table 11.1 Effects and side effects of performance-enhancing drugs

Drug	Effect	Examples of abuse in sport	Side effects
Anabolic steroids	• Increase power by increasing muscle strength and size • Used to help repair the body after training • Increase competitiveness and agression	• Power events such as shot put, javelin or weightlifting • Sprint events	• Liver disease • Certain forms of cancer • Fluid retention • Infertility • Hardening arteries increasing risk of coronary heart disease • Skin disorders
Beta blockers	• Used to steady nerves and hand tremors	• Snooker • Darts • Archery • Shooting events	• Tiredness • Lethargy • Low blood pressure • Fainting • Breathing problems
Diuretics	• Reduce body weight	• Horse racing • Boxing	• Dehydration • Muscle cramps • Kidney failure
Stimulants	• Improve performance through increased awareness • Athlete more physically aware • Reduce fatigue	• Endurance-based sport	• Increased blood pressure • Increased heart rate • Paranoid delusions • Anxiety • Shaking and sweatiness • Sleeplessness and restlessness

Staying away from home

Athletes will be required to stay away from home at times for training and/or competition. For athletes with family or job commitments this may create childcare issues or financial concerns because unpaid leave has to be taken. For younger athletes, the pressures may be greater as they are less experienced at being away from the support of close family and friends.

Employment

Having a supportive employer can reduce the pressures of balancing work and employment. Some employers facilitate flexible working time and support paid leave when required, but some employers are not as supportive which can create extra pressures. This may result in the athlete taking unpaid leave to participate in training and competition. Loss of income means that financial pressures may be created, particularly for those with mortgages or rent to pay and bills. For younger athletes, part-time employment may be difficult due to training commitments; this can lead to pressures as they are more financially dependent on their families.

Financial factors

Funding and sponsorship may be available for some athletes to ease the financial burden; however, sport can be expensive – some sports are considerably more expensive than others. Financial pressures are created through, for example, the cost of travel, equipment, clothing, nutritional intake, insurance and entry fees. Many athletes have to balance their sport with work commitments. For those who are professional or full-time athletes, careers may be short, or come to an abrupt end at any time; therefore it is important to save money for the future where possible.

Insurance

If athletes have invested money into equipment they should seek adequate insurance to cover the cost in case it is damaged or lost in transport, particularly if they are travelling abroad frequently. Health insurance should also be considered in order to reduce the waiting time should any medical advice be needed or investigations required.

Inappropriate behaviour

Athletes competing at a higher level may be exposed to media interest of varying levels. It is of the utmost importance that appropriate behaviour is conducted in an appropriate and professional manner at all times. Even those who attract little or no media interest should conduct themselves in an appropriate manner. This is important to avoid any negative images.

Stop and think

Ask one of your athletes to help you. Have a discussion on their lifestyle and identify five positive and five negative factors. Reflect on the negative factors and produce a mini action plan to reduce the negative impacts upon their lifestyle. You will need to draw on your skills, such as questioning to ensure all information is elicited and listening to ensure all information is recorded. You may also want to consult Chapter 8 (Psychology for coaches), to help you to formulate short-, medium- and long-term goals, as well as development strategies.

Nutrition terminology

It is useful to learn and understand the following terms about nutrition.

(RDA) Recommended daily allowance – this is the intake of nutrients deemed to be adequate on a daily basis to meet the nutritional needs of the majority of the healthy general population.

RDAs were first introduced in the 1940s to prevent nutritional deficiencies. RDAs were then reviewed by a panel of experts approximately 50 years later and then the Dietary Reference Values (**DRV**) emerged.

DRVs include RNI, EAR, LRNI and SI, and are a series of estimates of the amount of nutrients needed by different groups of the general healthy population. The needs of individuals will vary according to, for example, age, size and physical activity.

- **RNI** – Reference Nutrient Intake – is the amount of nutrients, vitamins and minerals deemed sufficient to meet the needs of the majority of the general healthy population (97.5% of the population).

- **EAR** – Estimated Average Requirement – is the amount of nutrients, vitamins and minerals deemed sufficient to meet the needs of 50% of the general healthy population. This means 50% of the population may need less and 50% of the population may need more than the EAR.

- **LRNI** – Lower Reference Nutrient Intake – is the amount of nutrients, vitamins and minerals deemed sufficient to meet the small percentage of the population (2.5%) with low needs. The majority of the population will need an increased amount.

To determine an athlete's Optimal Nutrient Intake (ONI) a series of biochemical analyses will have to be conducted by a nutrition scientist. This is a very complex process and is not routinely performed.

Individual nutritional requirement

Nutritional requirements are different for each individual due to variables such as age, gender, health and levels of physical activity. The general recommendation for health and to support physical performance is as follows.

Carbohydrate

This should provide approximately 50–60% of an athlete's total daily intake. However, if athletes are participating in regular intense training, it may need to be increased to around 65–70% of the total energy intake. This would apply to athletes such as marathon runners. This recommendation is compared to that for a sedentary individual who would source around 50% of their total energy intake from carbohydrates.

Carbohydrate intake should be based predominantly on complex carbohydrates and taken at regular intervals. Athletes who require a higher consumption may need to eat more frequently, and include a higher proportion of simple carbohydrates. Individual requirements can be calculated using Table 11.2 (see below).

Table 11.2 Carbohydrate requirements based on daily activity levels

Level of daily activity	Carbohydrate per kilogram body weight (g)
Less than 1 hour	4–5
1 hour	5–6
1–2 hours	6–7
2–3 hours	7–8
More than 3 hours	8–10

Protein

Protein should provide approximately 15% of an athlete's total daily intake. It is a misguided belief that increased protein consumption is required to facilitate the increase in muscle size for athletes, as the majority of people already consume more than the recommended protein requirement. Individual requirements can be calculated using Table 11.3 (see below).

Table 11.3 Daily protein requirements based on the type of activity.

Type of activity	Protein per kilogram of body weight (g)
Mainly sedentary	0.75–1.0
Mainly endurance	1.2–1.4
Mainly strength	1.2–1.7

Fat

Fat should provide around 25–35% of an athlete's total daily intake, with approximately 6–10% consumed from saturated fats. However, if an athlete needs to consume more carbohydrates, this should be allowed for by reducing the fat intake to around 20%.

Remember

1 gram of carbohydrate = 4kcal

1 gram of protein = 4kcal

1 gram of fat = 9kcal

Estimation of an individual's energy requirements

Ensuring an athlete consumes their optimal energy intake requires scientific support and referral to a sports nutritionist or dietician. However, an estimate of an athlete's energy requirement can be calculated as a guide. First, the basal metabolic rate (BMR) needs to be estimated using Table 11.4, and then multiplied against the physical activity level (PAL) using Table 11.5. PAL provides an estimation only of physical activity requirements.

Table 11.4 Calculating basal metabolic requirements (Schofield, 1985)

	Age (years)	Basal metabolic requirements in kilocalories per day (W = weight in kilograms)
Males	10–17	BMR = 17.7W + 657
	18–29	BMR = 15.1W + 692
	30–59	BMR = 11.5W + 873
	60–74	BMR = 11.9W + 700
Females	10–17	BMR = 13.4W + 692
	18–29	BMR = 14.8W + 487
	30–59	BMR = 8.3W + 846
	60–74	BMR = 9.2W + 687

Considerations when calculating BMR:

- BMR declines with age
- due to a male's increased muscle mass, their BMR is higher.

Table 11.5 Physical activity levels for three levels

Non-occupational activity	Occupational activity					
	Light		Moderate		Moderate /Heavy	
	Male	Female	Male	Female	Male	Female
Non-active	1.4	1.4	1.6	1.5	1.7	1.5
Moderately active	1.5	1.5	1.7	1.6	1.8	1.6
Very active	1.6	1.6	1.8	1.7	1.9	1.7

Activity

Use Tables 11.4 and 11.5 to calculate your own energy intake.

First calculate your BMR using Table 11.4. Use Table 11.5 to decide on your occupational activity – light, moderate or heavy – and then on your non-occupational activity – non-active, moderately active or very active. Use the figure where your columns cross to multiply to your BMR figure. You will have calculated your total energy intake. From here you can estimate your carbohydrate, protein and fat requirements.

Balanced diet

A **balanced diet** is just that – a balance of foods incorporating a variety of food groups in order to allow **healthy eating**. This is important to make sure the right quality and variety of foods are consumed and to ensure an intake of all the nutrients required for optimal health. When athletes are competing and training their energy expenditure increases, and so do their nutritional requirements. Athletes can, at times, find it difficult to consume the number of calories required to meet their energy expenditure. There are many reported studies and much advice on how to calculate energy requirements, and the proportions of pre- and post-event foods to

Key terms

Balanced diet – a healthy eating plan constituting the appropriate amount of nutrients for an individual's needs

Healthy eating – eating for health. In achieving a balanced diet, eating should support health and aim to reduce the risk of chronic disease, such as heart disease

be consumed to optimise performance. However, this is complex and a thorough understanding of nutritional science is required.

Food groups

This section is intended to facilitate your understanding of a balanced diet and how this can be achieved. In order to be able to guide your athletes to making appropriate food choices you need to understand the five food groups.

1. Bread, cereals and potatoes – these should be responsible for a large proportion of your meal. This group contains carbohydrates, mainly in the form of starch, for example potatoes, bread and cereal-based foods such as pasta, rice and cereals. This group also contains fibre. Fibre is very important for digestive function and can play a major role in preventing bowel disorders. To optimise healthy choices wholegrain foods should be chosen where possible, such as wholemeal or brown bread and rice.

2. Fruit and vegetables – you should consume a minimum of five portions a day of different colours. One portion of fruit and vegetables is approximately an 80g serving. Five portions a day equates to a minimum of 400g. These can be fresh, frozen, canned, dried or juiced. However, juice, beans and pulses only count as one portion each – regardless of how much you consume. Fruit and vegetables have a high content of vitamins, minerals and fibre, and provide a source of carbohydrate in the form of sugar. They are believed to play an important role in lowering the incidence of heart disease and some cancers.

3. Meat, fish and alternative sources of protein – these should be eaten in moderation. This group contains proteins in the form of meat, poultry, fish, eggs, nuts and pulses. Foods rich in protein contain minerals such as iron, zinc and magnesium, and vitamins such as vitamin B and B12. It is recommended that at least two portions of fish are consumed per week. These should be oily fish such as salmon, trout, sardines and mackerel. Oily fish is a good source of omega 3 oils which are beneficial to health. Canned oily fish is not included.

4. Milk and dairy – these should be eaten in moderation, although they make an important contribution to the diet. This food group provides a source of protein and is also rich in calcium. Foods included in this group include milk, cheese and yoghurts.

5. Foods and drinks high in fat and/or sugar – these should only be consumed occasionally. Fats should be limited in their consumption; they provide twice as much energy as carbohydrates and proteins and are generally over consumed. Some 'good' fats are essential to health and foods containing monosaturated and polyunsaturated fats actually contribute to lowering cholesterol levels. Foods high in polyunsaturated fats include nuts, seed, fish, avocados and olive oil. Foods high in saturated fat include biscuits, cakes, chocolates, butter, cheese and cream, and trans fats include hydrogenated vegetable oils and convenience foods. These should be avoided and consumed sparingly. As an approximate guide, when checking the nutritional label, foods containing a lot of fat will contain 20g or more of fat per 100g, foods with little fat will contain 3g or less per 100g. Foods high in sugar include fizzy drinks, jam, sweets and biscuits. These foods contain added sugar and should be consumed sparingly.

The Eatwell plate was originally generated by the Health Education Authority to simplify and communicate how to eat healthily. It has been adopted by the Food Standards Agency. The food plate represents the proportion of each food group that should be consumed: the larger sections, such as fruit and vegetables, should form the greatest proportion of food intake, while the smaller sections, such as foods containing fat and sugar, should be consumed sparingly.

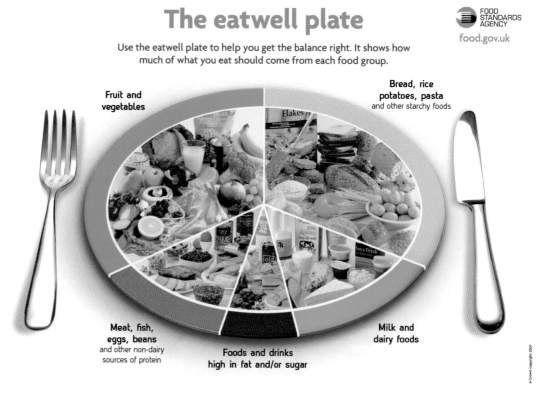

Figure 11.1 A healthy plate - the Eatwell plate

Table 11.6 provides further information about the foods contained within each food group, what constitutes a serving and how many servings are recommended daily. The last column shows the main nutrients supplied by each food group.

Stop and think

Write down everything you eat for one day, and compare it to Table 11.6 and Figure 11.1. Make a list of the changes you need to make to your own eating habits to ensure you consume a balanced diet.

Table 11.6 The five food groups

Food	What is a serving?	Recommended amount per day	Main nutrients supplied
Grains and potatoes			
Bread, rolls, muffins, bagels, crumpets, chapattis, naan bread, pitta, bread, tortillas, scones, pikelets, potato cakes, breakfast cereals, rice, pasta, noodles, couscous and potatoes	3 tbsp breakfast cereal, 1 Weetabix or Shredded Wheat, 1 slice of bread, ½ a pitta, 1 heaped tbsp boiled potato, pasta, rice or couscous	These should form the main part of all meals and snacks About a third of the total volume of food consumed each day	Carbohydrate, NSP (mainly insoluble), calcium iron and B vitamins
Vegetables and fruit			
All types of fresh, frozen, canned and dried fruits and vegetables (except potatoes) and fruit and vegetable juices	1 apple, orange, pear, banana, 1 small glass of fruit juice, 1 small salad, 2 tbsp vegetables, 2 tbsp stewed or tinned fruit in juice	At least five portions a day About a third of the total volume of food consumed each day	NSP (especially soluble), vitamin C, folate and potassium
Oils			
Butter, margarine, cooking oils, mayonnaise, salad dressing, cream, pastries, crisps, biscuits and cakes	1 tsp butter or margarine, 1 tsp vegetable or olive oil, 1 tsp mayonnaise	These should be eaten sparingly and lower-fat options selected	Fat, essential fatty acids and some vitamins
Dairy			
Milk, yoghurt, cheese, fromage frais	1/3 pint milk, 1¼ oz cheese, 1 small carton yoghurt or cottage cheese	Two or three servings per day About a sixth of the total volume of food consumed each day	Protein, calcium, vitamins A and D
Meat, fish and alternative proteins			
Meat, poultry, fish, eggs, pulses, nuts, meat and fish products (e.g. sausages, beefburgers, fish cakes, fish fingers)	2–3oz lean meat, chicken or oily fish, 4–5oz white fish, 2 eggs, 1 small tin baked beans, 2 tbsp nuts, 4oz Quorn or soya product	Two servings per day About a sixth of the total volume of food consumed each day	Protein, iron, zinc, magnesium and B vitamins Pulses provide a good source of NSP

Key tips to eating a balanced diet

- Reduce fat intake, particularly saturated fats, from sources such as chocolate, biscuits and cakes.

- Eat sugary foods sparingly.

- Do not add salt to your cooking or to food at the table.

- Reduce the amount of processed and convenience food consumed.

- Eat a wide variety of foods.

- Eat at least five portions of fruit and vegetables.

- Eat a high proportion of foods with a high starch and fibre content such as wholegrain rice.

Essential nutrients

Essential nutrients are referred to as macronutrients, micronutrients and water. They are classified into six groups.

- Carbohydrates – **macronutrient**
- Protein – macronutrient
- Fats – macronutrient
- Vitamins – **micronutrient**
- Minerals – micronutrient
- Water

> ### Key term
>
> **Macronutrient** – nutrients the body requires in large amounts such as carbohydrates, proteins and fats.
>
> **Micronutrients** – nutrients the body requires in small amounts such as vitamins and minerals.

Macronutrients

Macronutrients are required in large amounts every day, and provide the energy (glucose and glycogen) required to fuel the body.

Carbohydrates

Carbohydrates provide the body's main source of energy, in the form of glucose and glycogen (stored form of glucose). Carbohydrates are found in foods containing starches, sugars and cellulose, such as pasta and rice, as well as fruit, vegetables, lentils and nuts. Foods which are unrefined and rich in fibre should be the focus. One gram of carbohydrate contains 4kcal.

Carbohydrates are divided into two groups – simple and complex carbohydrates. A carbohydrate molecule is comprised of carbon (C), hydrogen (H) and oxygen (O). Simple carbohydrates are small molecular structures and are commonly known as sugars. The group includes monosaccharides (the simplest form), which are one sugar structures such as glucose, fructose and galactose, and disaccharides which are two sugar units (a pair of monosaccharides joined together, see Figure 11.2) such as sucrose (glucose plus fructose), and lactose (glucose and galactose). Simple sugars are sweet to taste, they metabolise quickly and provide a quick source of energy.

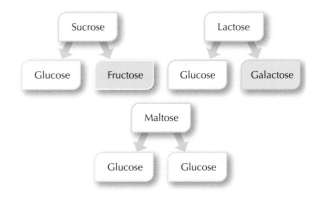

Figure 11.2 Disaccharides and their monosaccharides

Complex carbohydrates are larger molecular structures and commonly known as starches and fibre. This group includes polysaccharides, which are long chains of glucose molecules (these can be from several to hundreds or thousands). These have a much lower sweetness in taste, and take longer to metabolise, providing a longer source of energy. Food sources include those such as pasta, potatoes and rice. However, many foods contain a proportion of both simple and complex carbohydrates.

Table 11.7 Simple and complex carbohydrates

Simple	Complex
Sugar, syrup, jam, honey, marmalade, sugary fizzy drinks, boiled sweets, fudge, fruit juice, sports drinks, energy gels	Bread, bagels, crispbread, crackers, rice, pasta, noodles, couscous, potatoes, breakfast cereals, pulses, root vegetables

Glycaemic index (GI)

Carbohydrates are a fuel source that the body is reliant on for most types of exercise and activity. Carbohydrates are broken down to glucose which is readily available in the bloodstream, and the stored form of glucose known as glycogen is found in the muscles and liver, with approximately 80% stored in the muscles. During exercise, glucose and glycogen stores are depleted at varying levels; it is important therefore to consume a higher proportion of carbohydrates when exercising in order to facilitate the glucose supply. The glycogen stores hold approximately 375–475 grams on average (around 1500–2000kcals). Glycogen stores do adapt to training. The stores of elite endurance athletes will have adapted to hold an increased amount.

After exercise, carbohydrate needs to be consumed to ensure all glycogen stores are fully replenished. Depletion and recovery will be dependent on the intensity and duration of exercise. If glycogen stores are high, this will allow optimal training intensity and therefore optimal training effects. If glycogen stores are not fully replenished and are low, duration and intensity of training will be affected, combined with reduced power and strength and a

Remember

Training intensity and duration affects the amount of glycogen used and the rate at which it is used. Therefore more carbohydrates need to be consumed for those who exercise at a higher intensity for a longer duration. A runner competing in a 10km race would be exercising at a higher intensity for a longer duration, as opposed to a sprinter (short duration), or yoga practitioner (low intensity).

quicker onset of fatigue. Training effects therefore will be poor. However, excess consumption of carbohydrates is stored as fat within the adipose tissue.

GI

The glycaemic index (GI) is the measure of the effect of carbohydrates on blood sugar levels, compared to pure glucose. Carbohydrates which can be broken down quickly, releasing glucose rapidly into the bloodstream, are classified as having a high GI. Examples of these foods include white bread and rice, potatoes and confectionery items and refined bakery products, such as doughnuts and pastries. Carbohydrates which are broken down more slowly, releasing glucose at a slower rate into the bloodstream and providing a longer sustained energy source, are classified as low GI. Examples of low GI foods include wholewheat-based products (such as wholemeal bread, pasta and flour), nuts, chick peas, porridge and natural muesli. A balanced diet should comprise a large proportion of low GI foods.

Micronutrients are also found in macronutrient foods; therefore it is important to consume a wide variety of foods containing all the different nutrients.

Fibre

Foods that are high in fibre slow the absorption of nutrients and facilitate a steady blood sugar level. A diet high in fibre also has a variety of health benefits and reduces the risk of many diseases, such as bowel cancer. However, fibre intake for many people is lower than the recommended 15–30g per day. Foods such as wholewheat rice and bread, prunes and baked beans are good sources of fibre.

Protein

Protein is required for many body functions, including the growth, repair and maintenance of the body's cells, maintaining the structure of cells including red blood cells, tendons and internal organs, the function of antibodies against infection and the regulation of enzymes and hormones. In extreme cases protein is used as an energy source. Protein-rich foods include meat, fish, eggs, cheese, quinoa and soya. One gram of protein contains 4kcal.

Amino acids

Protein is metabolised to amino acids, which are used to make proteins in the body. There are approximately 20 amino acids: 12 of the amino acids are referred to as non-essential (although they are just as important to the body) but the body is able to synthesise these amino acids; the remaining eight amino acids are known as essential amino acids (EAA) because they cannot be synthesised by the body. Vegetables are a good source of essential amino acids. Foods containing all the EAAs such as meat, eggs, milk, cheese, poultry and soya, are referred to as first-class proteins or complete proteins. Second-class proteins or incomplete proteins do not contain all the EAAs and include foods such as lentils, nuts, cereals, pasta and noodles.

If insufficient protein is consumed, the body will utilise muscle protein. In certain cases, for example, during extreme events such as ultramarathon running, if there are not enough carbohydrates and fats available, the body will use protein as a secondary energy source. This means the body breaks down protein for energy; it is referred to as **catabolism**.

Excess protein cannot be stored so daily intake is required; excess intake will result in protein being converted to fat or carbohydrates and stored.

Fats

A diet high in fat has been linked to health problems such as atherosclerosis and therefore an increased risk of heart disease and stroke, cancer and obesity. However, not all fats are bad and some are actually essential to health. The main function of fats is to provide energy, structure of cell membranes, protection for vital organs, insulation of the body, production of hormones and absorption of fat-soluble vitamins. One gram of fat contains 9kcal, which is twice as much energy as one gram of carbohydrate. Fat-soluble vitamins such as A, D, E and K can be found in animal sources.

> ### Key term
>
> Catabolism – breaking down of molecules

Triglyceride is derived from one molecule of glycerol and three fatty acids, and is the main type of fat found in foods. When they are consumed, triglycerides are metabolised to glycerol and fatty acids, and provide energy at lower intensity and long durations. Fat becomes the main fuel source for activities such as long distance running and marathon running. Large fat stores are found in the adipose tissue and the liver. An infinite fat energy supply is provided by the body.

Saturated and unsaturated fats

Fats are divided into saturated fats (monosaturated) and unsaturated fats (polyunsaturated); the molecular structure of each type varies slightly. Fats are composed of carbon (C), oxygen (O) and hydrogen (H). A saturated fat depicts a molecular structure where all the carbons are associated with two hydrogen molecules, as opposed to unsaturated, where one or more carbons are lacking a hydrogen molecule.

Saturated fats are associated with disease and should be reduced in the diet. Foods containing saturated fats are usually solid at room temperature and include dairy foods such as cheese, butter, ghee, cream, lard, dripping, animal fats, prepared convenience foods and chocolate. Unsaturated fats are usually liquid at room temperature and are classified into monounsaturated fats and polyunsaturated fats. When taken in moderation they can contribute to lowering cholesterol levels in the blood, and therefore help to reduce the risk of heart disease. Monosaturated fats are found in foods such as avocados, olive oil, rapeseed oil, peanut oil, peanuts and some nuts. Polyunsaturated fats are found in foods such as oily fish, nuts and low-fat spreads which are labelled high in polyunsaturated fats.

Polyunsaturated fats include essential fats such as omega 6 and omega 3, which must be consumed through the diet as the body cannot produce them. Omega 6 and 3 play a vital role in brain function and in normal growth and development. Omega 6 food sources include nuts, seeds, chicken and lamb. Omega 3 food sources include oily fish such as salmon, herrings and sardines. It is advised that two portions of oily fish should be consumed per week.

Trans fats are modified fats used in the processing of manufactured foods, to increase their shelf life and the flavouring of foods. They are found in processed and convenience foods such as margarine, biscuits, cakes and fast food. These fats should be avoided, as their consumption contributes to health problems.

Table 11.8 Sources and types of fat in the diet

Saturated	Monosaturated	Polyunsaturated
Full-fat dairy products, butter, hard margarine, lard, dripping, suet, fatty meat, meat pies, pâté, cream, cakes, biscuits, chocolate, coconut, coconut oil	Olive oil, olive oil spreads, rapeseed oil, corn oil, peanuts, peanut butter, peanut oil	Soft margarine, low-fat spreads labelled high in polyunsaturated fats, sunflower oil, safflower oil, soya oil, oily fish, nuts

Micronutrients

Vitamins

Vitamins and **minerals** are essential to maintaining good health, for specific metabolic functions, immune function, function of the nervous system and in preventing disease; they are non-calorific nutrients. Each vitamin has a specific function. Vitamins are organic compounds required in tiny amounts, the majority of which need to be attained through the diet. They can be classified into two types: fat-soluble and water-soluble vitamins.

Fat-soluble vitamins include A, D, E and K; they are bound to lipids (fat) when absorbed. They are also stored within the adipose tissue and liver; excess intake can therefore cause toxicity. Water-soluble vitamins include vitamin C and the vitamin B complex and need regular replacement within the diet. Excess intake does not pose such a threat of toxicity as they can be excreted within the urine. However, vitamin D is an exception – the body is able to synthesise vitamin D from sunlight; while the bacteria of the large intestine can produce vitamin K.

Vitamin intake varies between individuals, depending on age, gender, health and levels of physical activity or exercise. Dietary reference values are available; however consuming a balanced and varied diet should ensure that all vitamin requirements are met naturally without the need for supplements.

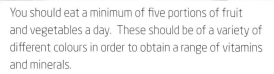

Key term

Vitamin – an organic compound required in tiny amounts such as vitamin A, C, D and K

Mineral – an inorganic compound naturally occurring in a solid chemical substance

Remember

You should eat a minimum of five portions of fruit and vegetables a day. These should be of a variety of different colours in order to obtain a range of vitamins and minerals.

Minerals

Minerals are inorganic compounds which are particularly essential to cell health and function and nerve function. They form components of your body such as bone, enzymes and hormones, regulate fluid balance and have an important function in muscle contraction. These are also a non-calorific nutrient.

Minerals are classified into major and trace minerals depending on their requirement for the body. Major minerals are required in amounts of more than 100mg and include calcium, sodium, magnesium, phosphorus and potassium; with trace elements requiring less than 100mg including chromium, copper, iodine, iron, manganese, selenium, zinc, boron and sulphur. The body regulates mineral levels, controlling the absorption and excretion, to ensure that excess build-up does not occur. You should maintain a varied and balanced diet to ensure your mineral requirements are met.

Salt

Foods high in salt should be avoided. Consuming too much salt can increase the risk of developing high blood pressure and consequently heart disease and the increased risk of a stroke. Nutritional labels may refer to sodium, as salt contains sodium. A high level is 0.5g or more per 100g, while 0.1g per 100g is a low level. Salt intake should not exceed 6g per day, which is comparable to 2.4g of sodium. Foods high in salt tend to be convenience and processed food and also take-away foods. You should limit the amount of salt you add during cooking and to your food at the table.

Hydration

Water constitutes approximately 50–60% of your body weight. However, the exact figure differs between individuals due to body composition, age and gender. Individuals with a higher proportion of muscle mass will have higher water content as muscle has a higher water content than fat.

Water provides the means for the main transport system in the body to suspend nutrients and waste products. Water also plays a major part in the digestive system, transporting food through your intestines, as well as regulating temperature. Water is lost by the body in a variety of ways, such as through sweating, urine, faeces and exhalation. It is therefore essential to maintain a constant water balance. If you lose 1% or more of your body weight due to water loss, this is classified as dehydration. The first sign of dehydration is thirst, lack of energy and early fatigue during exercise; this will be followed by other symptoms such as dizziness, headache, tiredness, nausea and dark concentrated urine.

In order to maintain an adequate water balance, the body needs 2–3 litres of fluid per day. However, depending on the intensity and duration of training, athletes will need to increase their fluid intake to replace lost water (and especially in hot temperatures).

Pre-event fluids

Athletes should be taking in plenty of fluid to ensure full hydration every day, ensuring they are fully hydrated before training and competition. It is recommended that 500–550ml of fluid should be consumed about 15–20 minutes before training or competition.

Inter-event fluids

During training or competition 150–200ml of fluid should be taken every 20 minutes; this is particularly important during endurance events.

Post-event fluids

After training or competition fluid loss should be replaced 1.5 times within the first two hours. To accurately assess fluid loss, getting weighed before and after exercise will provide an accurate guide. 1kg weight loss, therefore, is equivalent to 1 litre of fluid loss. If an athletes loses 2kg, they should consume an additional 3 litres of fluid to replace water lost during exercise. This is in addition to their normal fluid intake.

Urine is a good indicator: if pale in colour and plentiful in quantity this denotes good hydration but if dark in colour and less in volume this denotes dehydration. Severe dehydration may result in the inability to urinate, sunken eyes, low blood pressure, weak pulse, rapid heart beat, seizures and a low level of consciousness.

During fluid loss, the body also loses electrolytes; these are minerals such as calcium, potassium and sodium. It is essential that electrolytes are replaced. Sports drinks are a good way to replace fluid loss, electrolytes and carbohydrates. The carbohydrates are usually found in the simple form such as glucose, fructose and sucrose, so allowing for quick absorption from the body. There is often some sodium present in the sport drink, which facilitates the absorption of water and carbohydrate.

Hypertonic, isotonic or hypotonic sports drinks?

Hypertonic drinks – these have a high carbohydrate content and are absorbed slowly. They are recommended post-exercise as part of the recovery process.

Isotonic drinks – replicate the blood content in terms of glucose and fluid. As they contain sodium they are quickly absorbed. Isotonic drinks are recommended during warm weather or prolonged exercise to help replenish electrolytes and can also be taken pre event.

Hypotonic drinks – these have the weakest carbohydrate content. They encourage fluid replenishment due to the palatable taste and are easily absorbed.

Food labelling

Nutrition labels found on food products can help your athlete decide about choosing which products to consume. The majority of products display food labels (usually on the side or back of the packet) and contain information on calories, carbohydrate, protein and fat. In most circumstances, additional information is provided on saturated fat, sugar, fibre and sodium. Nutritional information is usually displayed per 100 grams and per individual serving of the food.

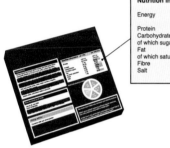

Nutrition information	per 100g	per half pizza
Energy	1027 kJ	1977 kJ
	244 kCal	470 kCal
Protein	11.5g	22.5g
Carbohydrate	30.4g	58.5g
of which sugars	3.5g	6.7g
Fat	8.5g	16.4g
of which saturates	2.9g	5.6g
Fibre	2.4g	4.6g
Salt	1.3g	2.4g

Figure 11.3 Food label on food packaging

Many manufacturers now also place highly visible labels on the front of food packaging highlighting key information such as calories, fat and saturated fat, sugars and salt. These labels may highlight the percentage that the food contributes towards the guideline daily amount (GDA). In the majority of cases, the information provided is comprehensive and allows for an informed decision to be made. The GDA information is a guideline to provide an approximation of the percentage that the product's nutrients will contribute to your GDA for a healthy diet. Remember that this is only an estimation and individual needs vary; your athlete may need more or less.

Sensible food choices include:

- products low in saturated fat
- products with no added sugar or salt

Remember

- **If a product is high in fat** it will contain 20g or more per 100g
  If a product is low in fat it will contain 3g or less per 100g
- **If a product is high in saturated fat** it will contain 5g or more per 100g
  If a product is low in saturated fat it will contain 1.5g or less per 100g
- **If a product is high in sugars** it will contain 12.5g or more of added sugars per 100g
  If a product is low in sugars it will contain 5g or less of total sugars per100g
- **If a product is high in salt** it will contain 1.5g or more per 100g, or if sodium is displayed it will be 0.6g or more
  If a product is low in salt it will contain 0.3g or less per 100g, or if sodium is displayed it will be 0.1g or less

- products low in salt
- wholegrain products
- minimum of five portions of fruit and vegetables every day.

Traffic light system

Many shop-bought products also follow the 'traffic light' colour-coding system. Red means high, amber means medium and green means low, which allows you at a glance to estimate the nutrient value as high, medium or low. In the main those products containing more green lights are a better choice for a healthy balanced diet. Those with mostly red lights are the products that should be kept to a minimum and consumed only occasionally. Amber light products are neither high nor low and can generally be consumed for the majority of the time, but less frequently than the green light products.

Case study (for recommended answers, see www.pearsonfe.co.uk/foundationsinsport)

Jonathan Cox is a 40-year-old male, who is 180cm tall, weighs 96kg and has a very physical job. He is married with four children aged 4, 8, 11 and 14 years old. His wife works full time, which means household chores and cooking are split equally. He has always enjoyed motor cross racing and understands the benefits of training to enhance his performance. He participates weekly in motor cross racing, and participates in three training sessions a week. Training incorporates a Pilates session for core stability training with two sessions working out at the gym. Gym sessions usually consist of 40 minutes of aerobic exercise, including a combination of treadmill (jogging), cross trainer (hill intervals) and a 1000m row, and 30 minutes of resistance training.

Questions

1. Calculate Jonathan's total energy requirement.
2. Discuss the carbohydrate, protein and fat requirements.
3. Calculate the carbohydrate, protein and fat requirements.
4. Identify the types of foods that should be consumed in each food group.
5. Discuss possible lifestyle factors that may affect participation in his training schedule.
6. Discuss the lifestyle strategies you would recommend to ensure optimal training and performance.

Check your understanding (for answers, see www.pearsonfe.co.uk/foundationsinsport)

1. Identify ten lifestyle factors which could impact upon an athlete.
2. Choose two lifestyle factors and describe their possible impact.
3. Define RDA and EAR.
4. Briefly describe the five food groups.
5. State the functions of carbohydrates, proteins and fats.
6. Briefly describe the glycaemic index.
7. State the difference between a macronutrient and micronutrient.
8. Briefly describe hydration.
9. State the difference between hypertonic, isotonic and hypotonic sports drinks.
10. State foods containing omega 3 essentials oils.

Time to reflect

Brainstorm all the possible lifestyle factors affecting your athletes.

Devise a group lifestyle session in order to address these factors.

Discuss the composition of a balanced diet.

Choose several of your athletes and calculate their energy intake.

Choose one of your athletes and identify realistic changes to their nutritional intake.

Useful resources

To obtain a secure link to the websites below, see the Websites section on page ii or visit the companion website at www.pearsonfe.co.uk/foundationsinsport.

- National Health Service Choices

- Food Standards Agency

- British Nutrition Foundation

- nutrition.gov

- patient.co.uk

Further reading

Barasi M.E. (2003) *Human Nutrition - A Health Perspective*. (2nd edition) London: Arnold.

Bean, A. (2010) *The Complete Guide to Sports Nutrition*. London: A & C Black publishers.

Burke, L.M. & Deakin V. (2006) *Clinical Sports Nutrition*. (3rd edition) Boston: McGraw Hill.

Burke, L.M. (2007) *Practical Sports Nutrition*. Champaign: Human Kinetics.

Hargreaves, M and Hawley, J. (2003) *Physiological Bases of Sports Performance*. Sydney: McGraw Hill.

Mann, J. and Truswell, A.S. (2002) *Essentials of Human Nutrition*. (2nd edition) Oxford: Oxford University Press.

Maughan, R.J. (2000) *Nutrition in Sport*. IOC Encyclopaedia Series. Oxford: Blackwell.

Maughan, R.J. and Burke, L.M. (2002) *Sports Nutrition*. IOC Handbook Series. Oxford: Blackwell.

Maughan, R.J., Burke, L.M. and Coyle, E.F. (2004) *Foods, Nutrition and Sports Performance II*. London: Routledge.

Powers, S.K. and Howley, E.T. (2006) *Exercise Physiology*. (6th edition) Boston: McGraw Hill.

Schofield, W.N. (1985) Predicting basal metabolic rate, new standards and review of previous work. Hum Niutr Clin Nutr 39: 5–41

Chapter 12

Analysis of sports performance

Introduction

Performance analysis is a newly developed sub-discipline of sport and exercise science that focuses on actual sports performance as opposed to laboratory-based investigations. It involves observational analysis of sports performance that often utilises audio-visual and information technology based equipment, particularly at the highest level of sport performance. At a grassroots level, performance analysis can be conducted through a more 'pencil and paper' method of analysis, but this method is generally limited by the accuracy of information that can be provided. Performance analysis can be completed using any methods that allow data from actual sports performance to be recorded and analysed; these include notational analysis, biomechanical analysis of technique, qualitative observation and the measurement of physiological and psychological variables during actual sports performance.

An understanding of the principles of performance analysis is crucial for the work of sports coaches. This is because performance analysis techniques are fundamental to understanding team and individual performances, to the development of team and athlete profiles, altering techniques where necessary and developing tactics or tactical awareness.

Learning outcomes

By the end of this chapter, you should:

- know the purposes of performance analysis at different levels of sport

- know the cycle of completing performance analysis in sport

- know the different performance criteria used in performance analysis

- know methods of performance analysis and the use of technology

- know how to provide feedback after analysing sport performance.

Starting block

In a game of basketball, player 1 has 15 successful shots at basket but player 2 has 20 successful shots at basket. Who has had the better game? Take it a stage further. Player 1 had the opportunity to shoot 30 times, but passed the ball 15 times which led to 15 more baskets; player 2 had the opportunity to shoot 40 times and he missed 20/40 when he could have passed 10 to a different player in a better position.

Who has had the better game now? What does this tell you about the use of statistics in performance analysis?

Purposes of performance analysis at different levels of sport

The overall role of performance analysis is to provide information that enhances the performance of individual athletes or teams. Performance analysis techniques that can be used after an event with players are important for sports coaches, as research suggests that sports coaches cannot often accurately recall what has happened during an event. For example, Franks and Miller (1986) found that football coaches were less than 45% correct in their post-game assessment of events during 45 minutes of a football game.

Within this over-arching aim of performance enhancement, there are a number of different purposes for performance analysis in sport, and these vary depending on the level of performance you are competing at and your role within the game (e.g. player, coach or official). The purposes of performance analysis are as follows:

- **technique development** (e.g. analysing a golf swing to identify faults and enhance driving distance)

- **tactical development** (e.g. analysing an opponent's on-court tactics in tennis to formulate a match plan)

- **injury reduction/management** (e.g. using a video of an incident that resulted in an injury during a game to treat an injury)

- **talent identification** (e.g. if a coach of an under-7 footballer recorded that the player scored 53 goals in a season, when the league average for a player is 20 goals, they would identify the player as talented and recommend them for a higher level of sport)

- **fitness assessment** (e.g. through completing fitness tests or time–motion analysis with players)

- **coach education** (e.g. to help coaches develop a greater knowledge of techniques and tactics used in their sport, and how to transfer this knowledge to their athletes)

- **athlete education** (e.g. giving athletes a greater understanding of their strengths and areas for improvement on a technical and tactical level)

- **modelling sport performance** (e.g. producing the 'perfect' model performance so that different elements of athlete's techniques can be compared against it)

- **squad selection** (e.g. providing coaches with performance statistics, such as successful passes against a particular team or total playing time, so that they can judge whether an athlete should play in the next game)

- **judging sports** (e.g. in sports, such as boxing, where points scoring is based on a boxer successfully landing punches with the knuckle part of the glove – a judge must analyse live performance to award points).

Sport development continuum

The different levels of sport are viewed on the sport development continuum (see Figure 12.1). The continuum starts with *foundation* level performance where novice athletes are introduced to sport. Novice athletes are generally young children at primary school through to late secondary school age, but can include older people who are new to a sport. The focus of the foundation stage of performance is fun and encouraging involvement in organised sport; and this is usually when the first stages of athlete development take place.

The *participation* stage of the continuum typically involves people taking part for fun, social reasons, health and fitness and to take part in organised sport. Normally at this stage, players will have a range of basic skills that they use in a competitive situation and tactics will be introduced into game play. Often, there will be a coach who will aim to develop the technique and tactical awareness of the player so that they are able to compete at a desired level. A local Sunday league sports player is an example of this level of participation.

Players who are at a higher level at the participation stage will often move onto the *performance* stage where they will compete in representative squads up to national standard. This level of the continuum usually provides access to a higher level of coaching staff and performance analysis and requires an increased commitment to developing as an athlete to be able to progress further.

Finally, the *excellence* stage of performance is the highest level of performance that encompasses the highest level athletes at the best clubs and international athletes. This stage provides access to the highest qualified coaches and the most specific level of performance analysis.

Figure 12.1: The sport development continuum. How do you think the purposes of, and resources required for, performance analysis will change at different levels of performance?

The purposes of performance analysis at different levels are the same, but the manner in which they are conducted is different. For example, at foundation level, the coach of a 9-year-old rugby player may count the number of passes that were successfully completed by a player and write this down on a piece of paper, whereas at excellence level, a team of performance analysts could use a specific IT programme to measure the successful

passes of the whole team. The purpose in both instances is the same (i.e. to see if players were able to successfully execute skills), but the method of completing the analysis is very different.

> ### Remember
>
> The purposes of performance analysis are broadly similar at each of the different stages of the continuum, but they will have different methods

Cycle of completing performance analysis in sport

Figure 12.2 shows the general cycle of performance analysis and how this progresses to interventions aimed at improving performance. Figure 12.2 demonstrates that performance analysis is an ongoing process in sport that starts and ends with the performance of an athlete. The performance analyst observes the athlete in their sport and records the necessary data from performance using one or more of the analysis methods (discussed later in this chapter). They will then analyse that data either qualitatively or quantitatively and interpret the data, extracting the key information that relates to the performance indicators in question. The next stage is feedback to the coach, athlete or team regarding the analysis that has taken place, before the coach and other members of the

Figure 12.2 The cycle of performance analysis

support staff (such as a sport scientist or strength and conditioning coach) will start planning and preparing the intervention that they are going to use to try to improve performance.

Different performance criteria used in performance analysis

Performance criteria are any aspects of performance that are used to analyse performance in sports. Performance criteria vary from sport to sport and can vary between different positions in different sports. For example, a striker in football would have different performance criteria from a goalkeeper. Common performance criteria used in sports include player movements, shots, passes, headers, saves, forced or unforced errors, dribbling attempts, crosses, strike rate and dismissal rate. Hughes and Bartlett (2004) offer an extensive list of performance criteria in a range of different sports.

When analysing performance criteria, a

Stop and think

Imagine you are coaching your favourite sport, or a specific position within that sport. Make a list of all of the different performance criteria that could be analysed.

performance analyst may need to take their analysis further. For example, if analysing the performance of a goalkeeper in football, the performance analyst may look at the number of successful or unsuccessful saves. However, to get a greater depth of analysis, they may examine the successful saves further and look at what happened after the save. For example, did the ball go out of play, did it remain in play and go to a teammate or did it remain in play and go to an opposing player?

Key term

Performance criteria – aspects of performance that are used to analyse performance in sports. These are also referred to as performance indicators or key performance indicators in some literature

Methods of performance analysis and the use of technology in sport

There are many methods of performance analysis that are used commonly in sport. They range from quantitative methods through to more qualitative-based methods and the method of analysis can sometimes be determined by the level of sport a coach is working in.

Analysing performance using notational analysis

Notational analysis is a method that provides a statistical account of the different performance indicators that have been targeted within a given analysis. With this in mind, there are five main applications of notational analysis (Hughes and Bartlett, 2008):

- tactical evaluation
- technical evaluation
- analysis of movement
- development of a database and performance modelling
- educating coaches and players.

Notational analysis can be conducted either by hand or through the use of specific software programmes. Given the extended use of performance analysis in elite sports in recent years, there are now specialised training courses designed for coaches and other support staff to help them understand some of the different commercially available methods of notational analysis. However, the cost associated with IT-based programmes for notational analysis means that their use is often limited to the higher end of the sport development continuum. Those at the lower end of the continuum will be more dependent upon hand-based notation systems because of lower costs and less experience of technical equipment required. Through this section, you will be introduced to the methods of notational analysis but are advised to see Hughes and Franks (2004) for a comprehensive account of notational analysis.

Developing a hand-based notational analysis system

Regardless of the sport involved, all hand-based notation systems are developed and used through similar stages. Essentially, the performance analyst will decide on the performance indicators under investigation and justify these; design the notational analysis layout, check the accuracy of the information gained and present the results of the analysis. When considering the performance analysis, the analyst should take into account the athlete and positional demands, and consider time frames or the sequencing of events during an activity. Data will normally be collected using tally marks and these will be converted to descriptive statistics, such as percentages or averages as part of the feedback process. Table 12.1 provides a hypothetical example of a simple hand-based notation system that indicates successful and unsuccessful performances of a centre midfield player in football during a 15-minute period.

Table 12.1 Example of a simple hand-based notation system

Performance criteria	Successful attempts	Unsuccessful attempts
Shots on goal	II	IIII
Passes	IIIIIIIIIII	IIIIII
Tackles	III	IIIII
Header	IIIII	IIIIII
Dribbles	IIII	II

More complex hand-based notation systems are sometimes used if a coach requires more complex information. For example, there may be a layout of a basketball court that is separated into segments so that positional play and ball transfer between court segments can be plotted. Another example comes through players and sporting actions being attached to different codes which are used to try to show which players attempted which actions and where (for example the Point Guard could be attached to the code 'PG', and a successful dribble could be attached the code 'DBL'). Predictably, this is a time-consuming approach and can be inaccurate. These limitations have led to the development of video and information technology-based notational analysis systems.

Activity

Using the performance criteria that you produced earlier, complete a hand-based notational analysis of a sporting event.

Video and IT-based notational analysis systems

Modern video and IT-based systems provide coaches with a quicker, more efficient and more detailed approach to notational analysis that can also be conducted 'real–time' if necessary. These systems allow the coach to use a recording of a particular event with their athletes and provide both qualitative and quantitative feedback, as well as allowing the coach to play and replay the video to provide more information to athletes if required. The use of digital video technology allows live footage to be downloaded and transferred to software packages for analysis and can then be transferred into visual forms of feedback such as graphs, charts or onto a simulated playing area (such as an animation of a football pitch to show the number of different runs a player makes).

Video and IT-based systems work by players and sporting actions being *coded* or *tagged* onto on-screen buttons so that, every time a particular action occurs, the performance analyst can press the button on screen and the system will store the number of actions or events ready to be viewed on that particular tag or button (see Figure 12.3 for an example). Other, more advanced systems can track players and reproduce match play based on this tracking which can be very useful in tactical analysis. In addition, systems are able to link videos of the events to a particular tag. So, if a player had scored three goals in a hockey game, the coach would be able to click on the tag for the third goal and the video file could be viewed at the same time. These systems can be altered to meet the needs of different sports, positions and players; hence they have made a big contribution to modern performance analysis in sport.

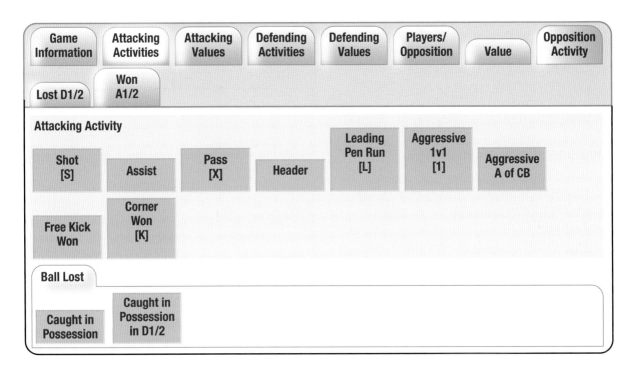

Figure 12.3 An example of a Dartfish tagging system used in football

Stop and think

Research popular performance analysis systems, such as Focus X2 from Elite Sports analysis and SportsCode Gamebreaker from Sportstec. How can they be used in notational analysis?

Analysing performance using motion analysis

Motion analysis has provided a wealth of information for coaches and athletes, including distance covered, speed of movements and the amount of time spent fulfilling activities in different sports. This has contributed greatly to the understanding of performance demands and fitness requirements of sport. The benefit of this contribution lies in knowing how coaches can shape their sessions to improve performance based on this information. For example, motion analysis literature (e.g. Carling et al., 2008; Carling et al., 2009) has found that elite footballers sprint an average of 20 metres during games and that the average sprint duration is four seconds. The implications of these findings are that acceleration may be more important for football players than maximum speed and so staff could use this information to plan sessions around developing these needs.

Remember

Motion analysis is important for coaches and sports scientists when trying to understand how to shape coaching and training methods around competition demands.

Bloomfield Movement Classification

The Bloomfield Movement Classification (BMC) (Bloomfield et al., 2004) was produced to allow analysts to measure the performance demands in sport and has since been adapted for use in a variety of team games (Bloomfield et al., 2007). This BMC involves 14 modes of timed-motion, 3 'other' non-timed movements, 14 directions, 4 intensities, 5 turning categories and 7 'On the Ball' activity classifications and is performed through video-based motion analysis (see Bloomfield et al., 2004 for full details).

The BMC has been used to analyse performance demands in different sports (such as soccer

[Bloomfield et al. 2007] and netball [Hale and O'Donoghue, 2007]), as well as injury risk in netball (Williams and O' Donoghue, 2005). Although there are advantages to using this approach because of the depth of information gained, the complexity of the method means that it can be difficult for some sports coaches to use.

Video-based motion analysis

Video-based motion analysis has been used in many sports and involves cameras being placed around the playing area that allow all of the athlete's movements to be recorded. Until recently, video-based analysis was recognised as the most accurate method for estimating distances; however, there are now some limitations that have come to light and challenged this notion (Edgecomb and Norton, 2006). While this method of analysis can track an athlete's movements, as well as using other information such as playing shirt colours and numbers, some systems do require manual data inputting by a performance analyst where lots of athletes may be in the same place (such as defending an indirect free kick in football). Where this type of analysis is used in professional sport, the number of cameras required is dependent upon factors such as the size of the playing area and (where applicable) stadium dimensions. The feedback from video-based motion analysis can take 24 hours, depending on the system that is being used, although the quality of information that can be gained from some tracking systems has been questioned (Carling et al. 2008; Edgecomb and Norton, 2006). Table 12.2 shows the different video-based tracking systems that are used in sport.

Table 12.2 Commercial video-based athlete tracking systems

Company	Software
Feedback Sport	Feedback Football
ProZone Holdings Ltd	ProZone
Sport – Universal SA	AMISCO

For websites for these companies, visit www.pearsonfe.co.uk/foundationsinsport

Activity

Using the websites in Table 12.2, compile a summary of each of the tracking systems and their uses.

Electronic tracking-based analysis

Electronic tracking-based systems (sometimes referred to as electronic automatic tracking systems or automatic tracking systems) allow data to be collected in real-time and allow for the recording of key performance indicators over one hundred times per second. This approach requires individual athletes to be 'tagged' and allows their movements to be tracked through radio transmitters and signal receivers located around the playing area.

More recently, Global Positioning Systems (GPS) technology has been used to analyse performance in a range of sports such as Australian Football (Aughey and Falloon, 2010) and court-based sports (Duffield et al. 2010). The use of GPS allows performance analysts to assess speed of movements, distances travelled, movement pathways, altitude and heart rate (although a heart rate transmitter must also be worn for this). GPS technology works by the receivers being located at a safe place on the athlete and the receivers locating signals that are sent at the speed of light by at least four satellites that are orbiting the Earth. When the receivers draw on these signals, they calculate performance-related data that are stored to be later downloaded onto a PC for use by the performance analyst or sports coach.

Various forms of electronic tracking systems (e.g. computer-based tracking systems and GPS tracking systems) have comparable capabilities when analysing motion. However, depending on the GPS device used, there have been reported errors in measurement ranging from 2 to 25% (Duffield et al. 2010) and there is currently little information available regarding the validity and reliability of GPS devices for high-intensity, intermittent sports activities (Coutts and Duffield, 2010).

Although various tracking systems are becoming more common in professional sport, there are issues to be considered, including electronic interference and poor signal strength (Edgecomb and Norton, 2006) and cost (Carling et al. 2009). Given that this type of analysis can require an athlete's kit to be fitted with electronic equipment (usually a small chip) its use in competition is against the rules of some sporting governing bodies (Carling et al. 2009) partly because there are concerns over player safety. For a comprehensive coverage of the use of motion analysis in sport, see Carling et al. (2008) and Carling et al. (2009). Table 12.3 (below) provides details of different electronic-based tracking systems that are commercially available.

Table 12.3. Commercially available electronic tracking systems

Company	Software
Catapult Innovations	Minimaxx
GPSports	SPI Elite
Trakus Inc	Digital Sports Information

For websites for these companies, visit www. pearsonfe.co.uk/foundationsinsport

Activity

Use the websites in Table 12.3 to compile a summary of each of the tracking systems and their uses.

Technique analysis

Technique analysis has often been used within coaching science to isolate differences in skill levels of performers, to enhance player performance or to identify injury risk. When analysing an athlete's sporting technique, video footage is usually taken from two dimensional or three dimensional perspectives, so that a performance analyst can highlight any faults in the technique when compared to the desired performance. When recording two-dimensional videos, the performance analyst must be careful with the camera placement ensuring that they take into account the **field of view**, and **perspective error**. When recording performance, it is also sometimes necessary to use **horizontal scaling** or **vertical referencing**.

Historically, this technique analysis can be done by 'an educated eye' (e.g. an experienced coach) subjectively analysing the technique against their ideal. With advances in modern technology, it

Key terms

Field of view – the area that the coach or sport scientist is recording that contains the sporting action

Perspective error – an error where objects appear larger or smaller than they actually are as they move towards or away from the camera; it is difficult to effectively judge their position

Horizontal scaling – providing a scale of measurement that will allow you to convert on-screen measurements to real-life measurements; for example, 1 metre 'real' = 1 centimetre 'screen'

Vertical referencing – as for horizontal scaling, but vertically

has become possible to get a more objective and holistic assessment of movements with reference to variables, such as joint angles, using analysis packages (e.g. Dartfish). For example, Judge et al. (2008) reported the use of Dartfish ProSuite to measure release height, release angle and support phase duration in their work with a female hammer thrower when analysing her technique. Modern analysis packages allow for several images to be viewed side-by-side, overlapped or sections of a technique to be selected to show how technique has developed. This will help the coach or the performance analyst to plan interventions to help athletes enhance their technique further. Figure 12.4 shows an example of the use of video analysis in swimming to isolate an element of technique to feedback to the athlete.

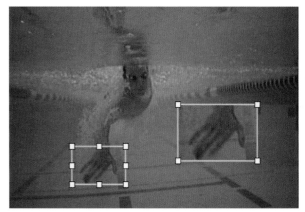

Figure 12.4 Using video analysis to isolate an element of technique. How can this level of analysis be used by sports coaches?

An athlete's performance will usually be measured against some form of standardised criteria for the particular technique, so that the coach has performance-related information that can be used with an athlete. In their study into tackling in collision sports, Gabbet and Ryan (2009) used the following technical criteria to analyse the tackling performance of the players.

1. Contacting the target in the centre of gravity
2. Contacting the target with the shoulder
3. Body position square/aligned
4. Leg drive upon contact
5. Watching the target onto the shoulder
6. Centre of gravity forward of base of support.

Using clear technical criteria to analyse the technique of athletes helps with the consistency, clarity and transparency of information that can be provided and can help when translating research findings into practice.

Providing feedback after analysing sport performance

Intrinsic feedback

Feedback is an essential part of the cycle of performance analysis and serves a number of important roles including enhancing motivation and helping athletes to detect errors. A lot of feedback that an athlete receives about their performance comes from intrinsic sources of sensory feedback, such as tactile, visual and auditory senses. The most obvious example of this is when an athlete sees a shot miss a target – the athlete then knows that they have to change something about performance to change the end result. As the athlete becomes more experienced, they will learn to detect feedback from their senses with a greater degree of sensitivity. For example, an experienced golfer can judge the success of the shot through the feel of their swing and hearing the sound of the club head on the ball without seeing where the ball lands. They will be able to make decisions about corrective action required to alter performance. A coach should encourage their athlete to concentrate on this **intrinsic feedback** as it is an essential element of skill acquisition.

Key terms

Intrinsic feedback – feedback that comes from the athlete's senses

Extrinsic feedback – feedback from an external source, such as a coach or sport scientist

Extrinsic feedback

Another important source of feedback is **extrinsic feedback**. This is feedback that comes from a source external to the athlete (such as a coach) and is an essential part of enhancing learning and performance. One of the biggest problems for coaches is to decide on what information to feedback to the athlete as there are often large amounts of data (either in print, video or digital versions) which would overwhelm an athlete if it was all given at the same time.

Typically, feedback should be prioritised in order of importance (i.e. the biggest area for improvement will need to be developed first so feedback on this will be provided first) in order to enhance performance. It will normally take the form of **Knowledge of Results (KR)** and **Knowledge of Performance (KP)**. KR and KP are both essential elements of the feedback process that complement each other – one is little use on a performance enhancement level without the other. For example, although it will be good for a young developing basketball player to notice that all of their shots keep bouncing off the backboard (KR), this is of little use to them if they do not know that their shots keep bouncing off the backboard because they are putting very little backspin on their free throws because of their poor shooting action (KP). Without KP, they will not be able to rectify the problem to improve the result. As well as highlighting the areas for improvement and providing **corrective feedback**, it is also important for the coach to provide a rationale for the identified areas and the methods for improvement (Mouratidis et al. 2010). As well as KP and KR, there are a number of different types of extrinsic feedback: **concurrent feedback**, **terminal feedback**, **positive feedback**, and **negative feedback**.

Knowledge of Results (KR) – feedback to the athlete about the outcome of an action or event

Knowledge of Performance (KP) – feedback to the athlete about the actions that have caused the result and how these must be changed to alter the result in future

Corrective feedback – statements that convey messages of how to improve after mistakes or poor performance

Concurrent feedback – ongoing feedback provided during an activity

Terminal feedback – feedback that happens after an event, rather than during the event

Positive feedback – feedback that occurs after successful completion of a task. This is used to reinforce performance

Negative feedback – feedback that happens after an unsuccessful attempt at a task. This is used to highlight and correct errors

Modes of feedback

Another key issue for coaches is how to present feedback to athletes. Feedback may be presented verbally to athletes or with different physical demonstrations. For example, when providing feedback to a young football player to explain why their shot has gone over the cross bar, a coach may tell the player that they need to make sure that they do not lean back too far when they kick the ball and that they should keep their head over the ball. This could be accompanied by a demonstration of the desired action. Using this verbal and demonstrative feedback allows the athlete to concentrate on the chief features that have been identified the next time that they attempt the skill and can result in enhanced skill learning and performance (Kernodle et al., 2001).

Emerging technologies mean that coaches have a range of videos, game reconstructions, statistics and computer-generated models that can be used and matched to the learning preference of the athlete. It is also possible to use a combination of different feedback methods to enhance performance. For example, Judge et al. (2008) showed how they combined video feedback, photograph

sequences and different statistics that related to key performance criteria in hammer throwing (release angle, height and support phase duration). These were used to develop an intervention to improve the technique of a female hammer thrower. They reported that the use of the range of feedback mechanisms, as well as the close work of the athlete, coach and sports scientist, were all combined and resulted in an American record being set for the women's hammer throw, despite the athlete not possessing what is considered to be an ideal physical make up for a hammer thrower.

Factors to consider when providing feedback

A number of factors should be considered when providing feedback to athletes (see Figure 12.5). As well as the mode of feedback, the coach should think about the depth and precision of feedback that they provide to the athlete. Generally, more precise feedback is beneficial for athletes, although this can be dependent upon the skill level of the athlete. If the feedback that a coach provides is too precise and technical for the athlete to understand, there is little chance that the feedback will have the desired effect of performance enhancement. In addition, the coach must decide on the amount of feedback required.

Greater amounts of feedback have been shown to enhance learning and development in novice athletes, but too much feedback later can be detrimental if it results in them trying to change their technique unnecessarily. In addition, too much feedback from the coach can lead to the athlete becoming dependent upon the feedback and prevents them from developing self-evaluative and reflective skills that are important for self-development as an athlete.

The timing of feedback is critical. If a coach provides concurrent feedback, the athlete will have to split their attention between performing the skill and listening to the feedback and is less likely to reflect on their skill development as they are constantly being guided by the coach. This is likely to reduce the performance of the skill as well as the athlete not being able to process the information from the coach.

Finally, the style of feedback is an important factor in its effectiveness. In their study of 337 adolescent athletes, Mouratidis et al. (2010) found that autonomy supporting feedback can still be motivating for an athlete, can encourage an athlete to persist with training and can enhance perceived well-being; even if the coach is delivering feedback that suggests they have a low level of competence.

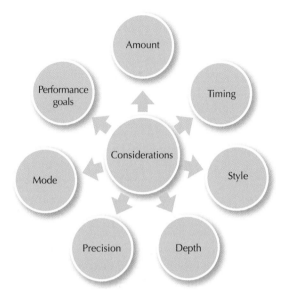

Figure 12.5 Factors to consider when providing feedback to athletes

Sandwich approach to feedback

A commonly used coach-led method of providing feedback to athletes is the sandwich approach. It is a useful method of providing feedback to an athlete based on the live, subjective type of performance assessment that coaches often go through at pitchside (e.g. when watching a player have a shot on goal in football where the ball rises steeply after it is struck, the coach must analyse this performance and produce feedback quickly). This approach has three stages.

1. The coach provides a positive opening statement about something that the athlete has done well (e.g. 'that was a great strike, well done!').

2. The coach then provides specific feedback to help the athlete to improve (e.g. 'next time, keep your head over the ball then you will keep the ball down').

3. The coach closes with a positive statement to encourage the athlete (e.g. 'keep up the hard work, the goal will come!').

One word that coaches should avoid using during the sandwich approach is 'but'. If it is used, the athlete will often forget everything that has preceded the 'but' which reduces the effect of the positive opening statement and places all of the emphasis on the corrective action – which could then potentially be seen as negative by the athlete.

Athlete-centred feedback

Effective coaches are those that are able to develop their athletes without simply giving them all of the answers. Coaches have an important role in helping athletes learn to think for themselves and to develop reflective and decision-making skills. This requires athlete-centred feedback.

Athlete-centred feedback is an important element of autonomy supportive coaching. An autonomy supportive environment is created when coaches offer their athletes opportunities for input and decision-making (e.g. choosing an appropriate tactic during a game), provide a sound rationale for tasks, and acknowledge athletes' feelings and perspectives (Stebbings et al. 2011). Athlete-centred approaches generally use questioning skills (such as open-ended and probing questions, for example 'what do you notice about your performance here?') where coaches deliberately engage athletes in the feedback process. By engaging with these questioning techniques, athletes are able to reflect on the positive elements of their performance, identify key areas for improvements and then discuss with their coach how their performance may be improved. The language used by both coach and athlete in this exchange should remain positive throughout.

Goal setting

Goal setting is an essential part of the feedback process as any corrective feedback will only be relevant to an athlete if it is linked to a performance goal (Liebermann et al. 2002). One of the issues with goal setting is that it can often be done incorrectly, resulting in ineffective goals. Using the

SMARTS principle (Smith, 1994) is one way to set effective goals. SMARTS stands for:

- **S**pecific – goals should show exactly what needs to be done

- **M**easurable – goals should be quantifiable

- **A**ction-orientated – the athlete should have to do something to achieve the goal

- **R**ealistic – goals should be within the athlete's reach

- **T**imed – there should be a reasonable time frame

- **S**elf-determined – there should be input from the athlete when setting the goals.

Types of goal

Goals are typically separated into subjective and objective goals. While subjective goals are general statements of intent, objective goals are more useful for coaches. Objective goals are defined as 'attaining a specific standard of proficiency on a task, usually within a specified time' (Locke et al. 1981, page 145). In addition to short- and long-term goals, there are three types of goals: outcome goals, performance goals and process goals; these are commonly viewed on a continuum (see Figure 12.6). As well as producing individual goals with athletes, team goals have been shown to be strongly associated with team success (Carron et al. 2009) and any barriers to goal achievement need to be identified (Karageorghis and Terry, 2011).

Outcome goals

Outcome goals focus on the result of an event, such as winning a race. This type of goal is often the least effective in enhancing motivation when it is used in isolation, as goal achievement is dependent on opposition as well as an athlete. For example, an athlete could run a personal best in a 1500-metre event but still finish last. If the outcome goal is always to win, their motivation could reduce due to constant failure. Spending too much time thinking about this type of goal before or during competition can increase anxiety and decrease concentration, which reduces motivation. However, this type of goal can improve short-term motivation.

Performance goals

Performance goals focus on an athlete's performance by comparing their current performance with previous performances. They are independent of other athletes and so provide a greater sense of control over the goal, helping to avoid negative social comparisons. Having greater control over goal achievement is beneficial for motivating an athlete. An example of a performance goal would be improving pass completion percentage in football to 85 per cent from 78 per cent.

Process goals

Process goals focus on improvements in techniques that need to be made to improve overall performance. An example of this type of goal would be a basketball player wanting to improve their jump shot accuracy by making sure they release the ball at the height of the jump. This type of goal is useful for improving motivation as it provides specific elements of performance to focus on, which facilitate learning and development.

Which goal to aim for?

The key to using outcome, performance and process goals successfully is knowing which to use and when. It is hard for an athlete to focus on achieving short-term process and performance goals without having a long-term outcome to aim for. Research (Weinberg and Butt, 2005) has shown that using a combination of all three types of goal is better than using any single type of goal when wanting to improve motivation, and that there should be a logical progression from short-term to long-term goals.

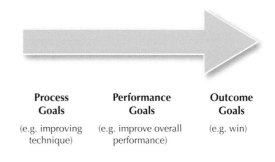

Process Goals	Performance Goals	Outcome Goals
(e.g. improving technique)	(e.g. improve overall performance)	(e.g. win)

Figure 12.6 Continuum of process – outcome goals

Principles of goal setting

The principles of goal setting (see Gould, 2010 for a detailed account) are important for designing an effective goal-setting programme. Some of the key principles from research and practice are summarised below:

- set specific goals
- set goals that are difficult but realistic
- set both short-term and long-term goals
- use a combination of performance, process and outcome goals
- set goals for both practice and competition
- record goals appropriately
- make sure the athlete knows how to achieve the goals
- provide support for achieving goals
- help the athlete to evaluate their goals
- provide appropriate feedback to the athlete.

Case study (for recommended answers, see www.pearsonfe.co.uk/foundationsinsport)

Nick is a sprinter who is part of the Olympic developmental squad and is aiming to succeed in the Olympic Games trials. He has a higher maximum speed than most of the other people that they compete against in races, a faster reaction time than most of the sprint team and is not suffering from any injuries. However, he rarely finishes first in competition. Nick's coach is at a loss as to why he doesn't win more races. Nick and his coach are both very receptive to feedback and are keen to improve.

Questions

1. What are the purposes of performance analysis in this case?
2. What techniques do you think you would use to analyse the performance of this athlete and why?
3. Which modes of feedback do you think would be useful for this athlete and why?
4. Using the answers to questions 1–3, analyse the performance of this athlete and use appropriate feedback techniques with a colleague, who can act as Nick in a role-play setting.

Check your understanding (for answers, see www.pearsonfe.co.uk/foundationsinsport)

1. What are the different purposes of performance analysis?
2. What are the different aspects of the sport development continuum?
3. What are performance criteria?
4. What are the applications of notational analysis?
5. What is the Bloomfield Movement Classification?
6. How does GPS tracking work?
7. What factors should a coach or sport scientist consider when filming techniques?
8. Why is it important to use established criteria when analysing techniques?
9. What are the different types of feedback?
10. What are the different factors to consider when providing feedback to athletes?

Time to reflect

1. How would the application of performance analysis techniques change with different levels of performance?
2. Why is it important for athletes to be actively engaged in the feedback process when their performance is being analysed?
3. What are the problems with a performance analyst being overly controlling when working with a client?
4. Do you think that performance analysis should be a stand-alone discipline within sport science or that it should be integrated with others?

Useful resources

To obtain a secure link to the websites below, see the Websites section on page ii or visit the companion website at www.pearsonfe.co.uk/foundationsinsport.

- Catapult Innovations
- Dartfish Video Software Solutions
- Dartfish.tv
- Elite Sports Analysis
- Feedback Sport
- GPS Navigation Intellectual Property
- GPSports
- International Association on Computer Science in Sport
- International Society of Performance Analysis of Sport (IACSS)
- Prozone
- Prozone Holdings Ltd
- Quintic
- Siliconcoach
- Sportstec
- Sport-Universal SA
- Trakus Inc

Further reading

Aughey, R.J., and Falloon, C. (2010). Real-Time vs. Post-Game GPS Data in Team Sports. *Journal of Science and Medicine in Sport*, 13, 348–349.

Bloomfield, J., Polman, R., and O'Donoghue, P.G. (2004). The Bloomfield Movement Classification: Movement Analysis of Individual Players in Dynamic Movement Sports. *International Journal of Performance Analysis in Sport-e*, 4, 20–31.

Bloomfield, J., Polman, R., and O'Donoghue, P.G. (2007). Reliability of the Bloomfield Movement Classification. *International Journal of Performance Analysis in Sport*, 7, 20–27.

Carling, C., Bloomfield, J., Nelson, L., and Reilly, T. (2008). The role of motion analysis in elite soccer: Contemporary performance measurement techniques and work rate data. *Sports Medicine*, 38, 839–862.

Carling, C., Reilly, T., & Williams, A.M. (2009). *Performance Assessment for Field Sports*. London: Routledge.

Carling, C., Williams, A.M., and Reilly, T. (2005). *Handbook of Soccer Match Analysis*. London: Routledge.

Carron, A.V., Burke, S.M., and Shapcott, K.M. (2009). Enhancing team effectiveness. In B. Brewer (ed.), *Handbook of Sports Medicine: Sport Psychology* (pp. 64–74). West Sussex: Wiley–Blackwell.

Coutts, A.J., and Duffield, R. (2010). Validity and reliability of GPS devices for measuring movement demands of team sports. *Journal of Science and Medicine in Sport*, **13**, 133–135.

Duffield, R., Reid, M., Baker, J., and Spratford, W. (2010). Accuracy and reliability of GPS devices for movement patterns in confined spaces for court-based sports. *Journal of Science and Medicine in Sport*, 13, 523–525.

Edgecomb, S.J., and Norton, K.I. (2006). Comparison of global positioning and computer-based tracking systems for measuring player movement distance during Australian football. *Journal of Science and Medicine in Sport*, 9, 25–32.

Franks, I.M. and Miller, G. (1986). Eyewitness testimony in sport. *Journal of Sport Behaviour*, 9, 39–45.

Gabbett, T., and Ryan, P. (2009). Tackling technique, injury risk and playing performance in high performance collision sport athletes. *International Journal of Sports Science and Coaching*, 4, 521–533.

Gould, D. (2010). Goal setting for peak performance. In J.M. Williams (Eds.), *Applied Sport Psychology: Personal Growth to Peak Performance* (6th edition, pp. 201–220). Boston: McGraw-Hill.

Hale, S.L. and O' Donoghue, P.G. (2007). Addressing turning and direction changes when using the Bloomfield Movement Classification. *International Journal of Performance Analysis of Sport, 7,* 84-88.

Hughes, M., and Bartlett, R. (2004). The use of performance indicators in performance analysis. In M. Hughes and I.M. Franks (eds.). *Notational Analysis of Sport: Systems for Better Coaching and Performance in Sport* (2nd edition, pp. 166–188). London: Routledge

Hughes, M., and Bartlett, R. (2008). What is Performance Analysis? In M. Hughes and I.M. Franks (eds.) *The Essentials of Performance Analysis: An Introduction.* London: Routledge, pp. 8-20.

Hughes, M., and Franks, I.M. (eds.) (2004). *Notational Analysis of Sport: Systems for Better Coaching and Performance in Sport (*2nd edition*).* London: Routledge.

Hughes, M., and Franks, I.M. (eds.) (2008). *The Essentials of Performance Analysis: An Introduction.* London: Routledge.

Judge, L.W., Hunter, I., and Gilreath, E. (2008). Using science to improve coaching: a case study of the American record holder in the women's hammer throw. *International Journal of Sport Science and Coaching, 3,* 477–488.

Karageorghis, C.I., and Terry, P.C. (2011). *Inside Sport Psychology.* Champaign, IL: Human Kinetics.

Kernodle, M.W., Johnson, R., and Arnold, D.R. (2001). Verbal instruction for correcting errors versus such instructions plus videotape replay on learning the overhand throw. *Perceptual Motor Skills,* 92, 1039–1051.

Liebermann, D., Katz, L., Hughes, M.D., Bartlett, R.M., McClements, J., and Franks, I.M. (2002). Advances in the application of information technology to sport performance. *Journal of Sports Sciences,* 20, 755–769.

Locke, E.A. , Shaw, K.N., Saari, L.M., and Latham, G.P. (1981). Goal setting and task performance. *Psychological Bulletin,* 90, 125–152.

Mouratidis, A., Lens, W., and Vansteenkiste, M. (2010). How you provide corrective feedback makes a difference: the motivating role of communicating in an autonomy – supporting way. *Journal of Sport and Exercise Psychology,* 32, 619–637.

Reilly, T., and Williams, A.M. (eds.) (2003). *Science and Soccer (*2nd edition*).* London: Routledge.

Smith, H.W. (1994). *The 10 Natural Laws of Successful Time and Life Management: Proven Strategies for Increased Productivity and Inner Peace.* New York: Warner.

Stebbings, J., Taylor, I., and Spray, C. (2011). Antecedents of perceived coach autonomy supportive and controlling behaviors: Coach psychological need satisfaction and well-being. *Journal of Sport and Exercise Psychology,* 33, 255 – 272.

Weinberg, R.S., and Butt, J. (2005). Goal setting in sport and exercise domains: the theory and practice of effective goal setting. In D. Hackfort, J. Duda and R. Lidor (eds.), *Handbook of Research in Applied Sport Psychology.* (pp. 129–146). Morgantown, WV: Fitness Information Technology.

Williams, R. and O'Donoghue, P. (2005). Lower limb injury risk in netball: a time-motion analysis investigation. *Journal of Human Movement Studies,* 49, 315–331.

Chapter 13

Athletic preparation for sports performance

Introduction

Individuals participate in sport and activity for many reasons, ranging from health to performance. This chapter discusses athletic preparation for sports performance. Athletic preparation and monitoring athletic improvement are vital in the field of performance sport. The difference between winning and losing is often determined by the smallest of margins. Therefore, the appropriate development of athletic potential is critical for individuals or teams to achieve their goals and compete at the highest level. A strength and conditioning coach's role is to develop the athlete from physiological and biomechanical perspective and should be guided by the technical coach's aims and objectives. The aim should be to a form a symbiotic relationship – working in partnership to achieve optimum results. In order for this to work effectively, both parties need a detailed understanding of the training principles to appropriately develop the athletic preparation of their athletes. This chapter discusses the main scientific theory that underpins your coaching practice in athletic preparation and training. This is focused towards improving some of the physical and motor fitness aspects of sports performance. Draw from your own experiences and try to link the topics within this chapter to your own practice.

Learning outcomes

After you have read this chapter you should be able to:

- understand the factors that influence performance
- understand the application of a needs analysis
- understand the contemporary training principles and the underpinning scientific theory that supports their use within the field of strength and conditioning
- understand the application of the training principles to speed, strength, endurance and power
- understand the application of the training principles to agility, balance and coordination.

The importance of appropriately loaded training weeks is often underestimated, with common misconceptions such as 'more is better' and 'no pain, no gain'. This may lead to burnout or unexplained 'under-performance syndrome' (overtraining). Work alone or in small groups who participate in sport and spend 10 minutes establishing the current format of your training week. (Please consider all forms of exercise you participate in during the week).

Use Table 12.1 as a template and consider the following points.
- How many sessions do you participate in?
- What is the modality of training? (Weights, plyometrics, game specific)
- The focus of the session? (Strength, speed, power, technical and tactical etc.)
- Total hours spent.

Table 12.1 Training diary

Day	Number of sessions (hours spent training)	Modality of training	Focus of the session
Monday			
Tuesday			
Wednesday			
Thursday			
Friday			
Saturday			
Sunday			

Understanding the factors that influence performance

In a training environment, you should be aware of the factors that you can influence when training your athletes. Considering this, you, as a coach, need to be aware that an individual's performance can be affected by the following factors:

- genetics (i.e. hereditary factors; influence of muscle fibre types and distribution – nature)

- environment (this includes time spent away from training, sociological factors – nurture)

- training (exercise prescription; in light of due consideration of genetics – nature – and environment – nurture).

You may be able to have a relatively small influence on an athlete from a performance perspective, as an individual's genetic potential is for the most part predetermined. Therefore, only a limited amount of adaptation can be induced by effective training. When considering training volume, an athlete may train for as much as 20 hours a week; however, this still forms only 12% of the total time in a week, i.e. the amount of time spent focusing on athletic preparation is relatively small. It is therefore important that you follow appropriate principles (see below) when delivering training sessions.

When considering the factors of environment and training, you need to be conscious that a large percentage of time is spent away from training; therefore, appropriate choices need to be made by the athlete between training sessions. While a coach is in a position to advise about factors outside training, it is important that coaches should be considerate of their role and responsibility as well as the boundaries they work within and try to avoid role conflict with other sports staff such as nutritionists, performance lifestyle advisers etc. Instead, support staff should attempt to complement each other's specialisations so that the athlete can develop appropriately. This form of coaching is often referred to as a 'humanistic approach'. Chapter 1 (Introduction to sports coaching) covers this approach in more detail.

Training

As genetics are predetermined by heredity (nature), and some of the environmental factors (nurture) arguably fall under lifestyle support, they are factors outside the area of training and, as such, are beyond the scope of this chapter. However, you can have an impact on training through the application of training principles and appropriate monitoring for improvement in performance, through the use of appropriate strategic testing.

Having identified training as the area that you can most influence, you can begin to establish the training landscape through a sequential approach using the following points:

- understanding a needs analysis (athlete and sport)
- understanding the physical and motor fitness components
- application of training principles
- application of appropriate monitoring.

Needs analysis

In the field of athletic training, a coach must first identify the desired outcome of the training undertaken and should establish whether the participants are training for improved performance or increased fitness and health. In order to determine the training an individual athlete should undertake, you need a clear understanding of the demands of the sport and the capabilities of the athlete (needs analysis). The sport can be analysed through **time–motion** characteristics, which encompasses the **bioenergetics** (energy systems) utilised, along with the mechanical movements made. Studying the mechanical movements allows you to understand both the muscles in use and the contraction characteristics through specific ranges of motion – which provides some judgement criteria which you can use for comparison with the individual athlete.

When analysing the athlete you should establish the training history of the individual and potential injury risk areas from participating in the sport as these could guide your application of training principles. You can identify the areas in need of development through appropriate application of field- or lab-based tests; the results of these may provide a baseline of data for future comparison. It is therefore vital that you choose and administer a valid and reliable test.

Stop and think

Megan and Emmie play netball; netball can be considered as an intermittent high intensity sport, involving walking, jogging, sprinting, jumping, catching and changing direction. Using a needs analysis, and referring to the further readings examining time-motion characteristics of different sports, identify the characteristics of a sport of your choice from a time–motion and bioenergetics perspective.

Key terms

Time-motion – duration of sports competition (i.e. 90 minute football match) and individual movement characteristics (walking, jogging, jumping, changing direction, sprinting and kicking; muscles utilised to perform these movements, linking to type of contraction: eccentric, concentric, isometric)

Bioenergetics – the energy system requirements of the sport based on information from the time–motion analysis (ATP-PC, fast glycolysis, slow glycolysis and oxidative)

Training principles and underlying theory

Within a training environment there is a distinct relationship between the different principles of terminology used, such as speed, strength and endurance etc. Understanding this interrelationship helps to ensure that you apply appropriate training methods, as it is important to train individual attributes and to integrate them. You will have come across acronyms such as SPORT (Specificity, Progression, Overload, Reversibility and Tedium) and FITT (Frequency, Intensity, Time and Type); while parts of these are appropriate, the field of strength and conditioning research has condensed the terminology into the following principles (Stone et al., 2002):

- **Specificity**
- **Overload** (Progressive overload)
- **Variation**

Key terms

Specificity – training principle: exercises should closely resemble the movements of the sport (dynamic correspondence)

Overload – training principle: the training intensity should be either of a stimulating, retaining or detraining level

Variation – training principle: exercises can be varied either through type (qualitative) or load (quantitative)

You can justify the exclusion of reversibility as this will only occur if one of two things happen: either you fail to apply progressive overload; or a player becomes injured, in which case you would apply the principle of variation to specificity and overload to accommodate the individual circumstances. The nature of training for performance sport will require elements of repetition that may be tedious but this cannot be avoided, instead this should be embraced as an opportunity for deliberate practice of common requirements to perform in your sport.

The purpose of the next section is for you to examine the underlying scientific theory supporting the training principles.

Specificity

Specificity is arguably the most important consideration when designing training programmes. You can link the concept to a needs analysis, which highlights that an understanding of mechanical movements and bioenergetics is important. The principles of specificity can be linked to the needs analysis, as any exercise prescription must be informed by your detailed understanding of the sport the athlete is training for. Subsequently, when considering the application of the training principle, you should consider the following components that link the mechanical aspects of movement to the training principle of specificity:

- **Movement patterns**
- **Force** application
- **Acceleration**
- **Velocity** of movement.

The degree of similarity between the *movement patterns* (jumping, running etc) within a sport or physical performance and the training exercise selected, the greater probability of transfer. A term that consists of an amalgamation of these areas has been put forward (Siff and Verkoshanski, 1999); '*dynamic correspondence*'. They argue that the basic mechanics, but not necessarily the appearance of the training exercise selected, must be similar to those of the performance. An example of '*dynamic correspondence*' would be the use of squatting and sprint performance. Strength and conditioning research by Wisloff et al., (2004) has established a positive correlation between the method of training (squatting) and performance (sprinting) in elite soccer players. This means that when you prescribe exercises to an athlete you should be aware of the *force* characteristics, i.e. how much is applied (maximal or sub maximal), the speed at which the force is applied, i.e. how quickly an object or body *accelerates*, and lastly the direction and magnitude in which it is applied, *velocity*.

> ## Key terms
>
> **Movement patterns** – movements made within the sport, (multijoint, jumping and running, encompassing, flexion, extension, rotation etc.) link to planes of motion and axis of rotation
>
> **Force** – force = mass x acceleration
>
> **Acceleration** – acceleration = force/mass OR (average) is the change in velocity/change in time
>
> **Velocity** – is a vector quantity and has both magnitude and direction, velocity (v) = s/change in time

Overload

Overload is concerned with the application of a training stimulus that leads to desired adaptations. Fundamentally this needs to be of an intensity or duration above the normal habitual levels of exercise. Therefore overload can be classified in the following format.

- Above the neutral zone = Stimulating
- Neutral = Retaining
- Below the neutral zone = Detraining

Classifying the training intensity into this format highlights that a coach does not always need to be prescribing training sessions that are of a high intensity in order to see performance gains in the athlete; i.e. the phrase 'no pain, no gain' becomes obsolete. In fact it is the cyclical application of appropriate intensity, using the training principles, which makes possible the performance adaptations. It highlights the importance of combining the concepts of specificity and overload in a format that is progressive in nature, as the athlete will adapt specifically to the imposed demands. This is the SAID principle – Specific Adaptations to Imposed Demands (Baechle and Earle, 2000).

Zatsiorsky (1995, page 4) also cites this law of adaptation:

> The adjustment of an organism (athlete) to its environment. If the environment changes, the organism changes to better survive in these new conditions.

Variation

The application of the training principle of variation is, in itself, an appropriate consideration of the factors discussed within specificity and overload. Manipulating specificity and overload accordingly can be achieved through changes that are both qualitative (exercise selection) and quantitative (volume, intensity). The large scale application of variation should be considered when designing training programmes over long time frames (Olympic cycle) as the appropriate sequencing can lead to superior improvement in performance.

Application of training principles to speed, strength, endurance and power

Having identified the training principles available to the coach, you need to examine their application to the attributes an athlete requires to perform. These are often broken down into the following subunits and key terms:

- physical fitness
- strength: ability to apply force
- speed
- endurance
- flexibility
- body composition
- motor fitness
- power
- agility
- coordination
- reaction time
- balance.

Although the subunits can be individually defined, within a sporting context they are often interlinked

within symbiotic relationships or performance hierarchies (see Figure 13.1). The aim of the following section is to highlight the complexity of issues that you should consider when applying the training principles to the physical and motor fitness components of sport.

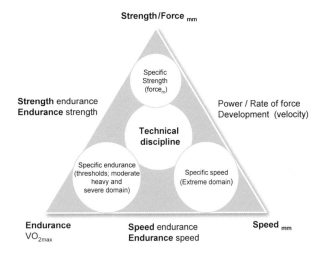

Figure 13.1 Strength, speed and endurance relationship (adapted from Figure 1.2, relationship among the main biomotor abilities, where strength, speed and endurance are dominant, Bompa, 1999)

Strength and speed

Strength is multifaceted and so it is useful to understand which aspect of strength is linked to performance. Strength is widely seen as the ability to exert force ($F=ma$). However, this does not provide the complete picture as sporting situations are not just interested in absolute strength i.e. maximum maximorum force (F_{mm}) production. They are interested in maximum force production through a sporting movement (F_m), and in the ability of the individual to generate force over a short period, i.e. rate of force development (RFD). This introduces the concepts of slow-speed strength and high-speed strength. During sports performance, force needs to be generated through specific movements. Perhaps a more appropriate explanation would be the maximal amount of force production at a specified velocity (Knuttgen and Kraemer, 1987). The incorporation of velocity (vector quantity) now means the force production has a magnitude and direction related to task (F_m). This can be easily displayed in a graphical format, (see below Figure 13.2).

Figure 13. 2 Force velocity relationship, overlaid with power output.

Power

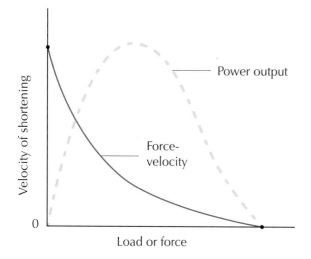

The motor fitness attribute of power is an essential element of performance. Power production needs to be trained appropriately to enhance performance; because of the factors used to calculate power (power = force × distance/time), it is often referred to as:

strength × speed.

This means that both aspects can be trained to improve power output. The emphasis of strength over speed, or vice versa, needs to be linked to the sporting environment. Figure 13.1 provides a diagrammatic explanation of this relationship. The point at which you decide to focus should be linked to the general and specific demands of the sport and can be viewed using the speed and strength points of the triangle in Figure 13.1 in a sliding scale relationship. You should find that the point chosen on the scale should be different depending on which point in the competition environment you are referring to.

The power output profile (see Figure 13.2) will change depending on the individual; often it is necessary to establish the optimum load when training to elicit maximum power output. This is an example of the application of the principle of specificity and should reflect the knowledge and understanding gained from the needs analysis. An example of this would be the use of timing mats when training weighted jump squats. Through examining the jump flight time, you can establish the load to apply to achieve optimum power output; Baker et al. (2001) suggest this may fall between 47% – 63% of 1RM when examining maximum power development from using jump squats.

With the complexity of issues highlighted, you should understand how you can manipulate training variables to improve both power output and rate of force development. This can be achieved through manipulating exercises to either work on the strength end of the spectrum, developing maximum force characteristics, or on the speed end of the spectrum, developing rate of force development.

The strength end of the spectrum could be developed by squatting (heavy resistant strength training, see Figure 13.3), the middle by squat jumps and speed end by repetitive countermovement jumps (explosive, ballistic strength training, see Figure 13.3). As a coach, you will have to decide which point of the spectrum is most important to train; often within sports it is about maximising rate of force development (speed strength or power) and subsequently training involves a blend of the training modalities to achieve optimum performance.

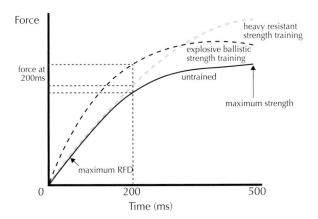

Figure 13.3 Force time curve showing effects of training. Baechle and Earle page 473 (Figure 20.1 Isometric force as a function of time, indicating untrained subjects (solid line), those who did heavy resistance training (dashed green line), and those who did explosive, ballistic training (dashed black line). Impulse is the product of force and time, represented by the area under each curve). Adapted from Hakkinen and Komi (1985)

Endurance

Considering the demands of sport using your needs analysis and the information in Figure 13.1, and unless the time characteristics of your sport mean it is completed within a matter of seconds, there will be an element of endurance involved. In fact, the 100m sprint, in athletics, is won by the person who decelerates the least in the closing stages of the race. Consequently, the relationship between strength and endurance – using the points of the triangle as a reference point (Figure 13.1) – can also be viewed on a sliding scale, as the tasks completed in the training sessions should reflect the strength/endurance characteristics of your sport.

As with the strength–speed scale, you should find that demands of the sport mean that the amount of strength or endurance that is required to perform is dependent on the context of the sport to which you refer. With this in mind, Zatsiorsky (1995, pages 213–214) goes as far as to suggest the following recommendations for training.

- If the sporting task requires ≥ than 80% F_m train maximal strength.

- If the sporting task requires < 80% or > 20% F_m train maximal strength and maximal endurance.

- If the sporting task requires ≤ 20% F_m train maximal endurance.

Endurance is multifaceted and incorporates both muscular and cardiovascular aspects. Therefore, you should identify which aspect of endurance is required in the sport under investigation. This can be linked back to the time–motion characteristics of the sport as it is possible to determine if the intensity of the sport is supra maximal, or sub maximal. If the sport is supra maximal, it is possible to focus towards the high intensity of the training spectrum encompassing strength and strength/speed endurance. If however, as with most sports, there is an element of cardiovascular endurance, you need to be able to differentiate between the intensities of training to ensure adaptation continues to take place. This is because of the complex relationship between endurance, speed endurance and speed. As most sports involve a combination of these physical fitness attributes, you have to be able to prescribe exercise appropriately to prepare your athletes for performance. Within the field of physiology, this has been the focus of research. For example, from the field of distance running, the work of Pringle et al. (2003) differentiates the intensities of exercise relating to lactate scores and VO_{2max}.

The thresholds are referred to as:

– lactate threshold 1 (LT_1); 1 mmol/dl rise in lactate above base levels. (Use to be 2mmol/dl, aerobic threshold or VT_1)

– maximal lactate steady state (MLSS); the maximal level of lactate the body can produce and clear without an exponential increase in lactate levels. (Use to be 4 mmol/dl, anaerobic threshold, onset of blood lactate accumulation (OBLA), ventilatory threshold 1 (VT_2) or lactate threshold 2 (LT_2))

– VO_{2max}; Maximal amount of oxygen uptake measured in ml/kg/min^{-1}.

There are four training zones in relation to these thresholds, see Table 13.2.

Table 13.2 Training zones, intensity domains and corresponding metabolic levels

Training zones	Exercise intensity domain	Metabolic level
Zone 1 (low lactate zone)	Moderate	≤ 1mmol/dl rise above base levels
Zone 2 (lactate accommodation zone)	Heavy	> 1mmol/dl rise above base levels ≤ MLSS
Zone 3 (lactate accumulation zone)	Severe	> MLSS ≤ VO_{2max}
Zone 4 (lactate accumulation zone)	Extreme	> VO_{2max}

Through appropriate testing (VO_{2max} test, lactate transition curve) it is possible to establish heart rates or work loads that correspond to metabolic levels below, above or between thresholds up to VO_{2max}. Because the nature of sport is multifaceted, training often takes place at intensities below VO_{2max} (sub maximal; moderate, heavy and severe domain); this encompasses an emphasis on endurance over

> ### Remember
>
> The intensities at which these thresholds occur is dependent on the modality of exercise undertaken; consequently coaches should not use heart rates established for running when using a bike or rower as the time–motion characteristics are different and will not correspond with each other. If you are unable to gather such data through testing, you can use a subjective scale such as rating of perceived exertion (RPE) – see Table13.3. The 6–20 rating of perceived exertion scale has been designed to correlate positively to heart rate.

speed, while training above VO_{2max} (supramaximal; extreme domain) encompasses an emphasis on speed over endurance.

Table 13.3 Rating of perceived exertion (RPE)

Rate of perceived exertion	Intensity	Heart rate equivalent
6		60
7	very, very light	70
8		80
9	very light	90
10		100
11	fairly light	110
12		120
13	somewhat hard	130
14		140
15	hard	150
16		160
17	very hard	170
18		180
19	very, very hard	190
20		200

Using the information within this section, you

should now be able to apply the principles of training to improve the physical fitness components of strength, speed and endurance.

Application of training principles to agility, balance and coordination

We have seen that there is a complex relationship between the physical (speed, strength and endurance) and motor fitness components of sport. By the end of this section, you should understand how to use the knowledge and understanding you have developed from the previous sections to improve the attributes of **agility**, **balance** and **coordination**.

The complex interrelationship between the attributes is key to addressing the concepts of agility, balance and coordination.

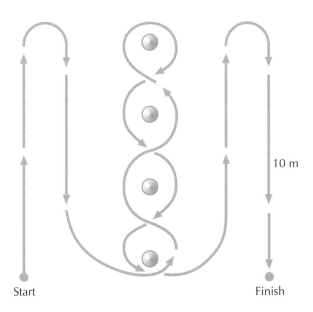

10 m

Start   Finish

Figure 13.4 The Illinois agility test

When administering a test, such as the Illinois agility test, it is important to see if the tests are linked through mechanical specificity to the sport and therefore may have positive transfer to performance.

You should therefore ask the following question: does the competitive environment challenge performers to move around fixed points? In the case of intermittent high intensity sports, the environment challenges the performers to move efficiently making responses in relation to their teammates and opposition. Consequently, does running around a cone actually reflect agility or is it more closely related to speed of acceleration and deceleration and therefore change of direction speed (CODS)? Referring to Figure 13.5 you can identify the differences in circumstances between CODS and agility. Identifying the complex factors enables a coach to apply the principles of specificity, overload (progressive) and variation. The complexity of athletic training and preparation may mean that cones are used in training environments to create boundaries or encourage changes in movement. However, as they do not completely replicate the sporting environment they should not be used as the sole training tool, but should be integrated with a training approach that develops the complexity of the training environment towards the game situation. This requires a good working relationship between the strength and conditioning coach and the technical coach. The effective manipulation of the variables in conjunction with the sound application of the training principles should develop an athlete who is truly agile.

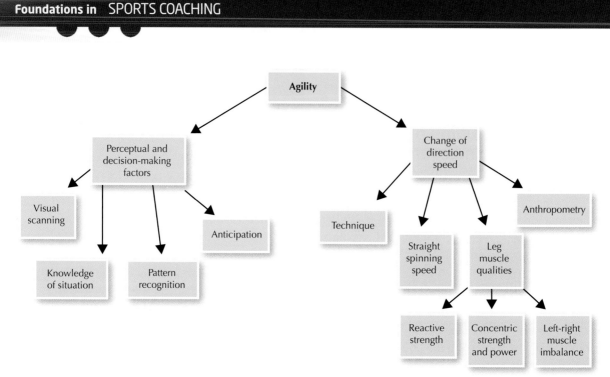

Figure 13.5 Diagram of review of agility Shephard and Young (2006)

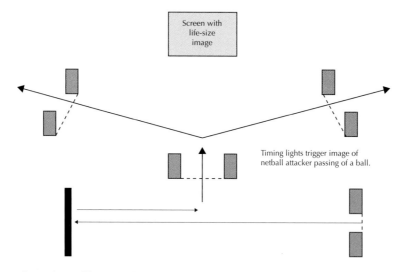

Figure 13.6 Diagram of reactive agility test (Shephard and Young, 2006)

A practical example

The following is an example of teaching agility using a process of increasing complexity of the task. You can initially use a cone set up (Illinois agility test) as a starting point, and then transition through to using live opponents to facilitate true agility using the concepts of dynamic correspondence and transfer to improve sports performance.

Consequently, the field of strength and conditioning research has now developed a reactive agility test, which combines the concept of CODS and reaction to a stimulus, forcing the athlete to become aware of perceptual cues that lead them to make movement decisions, as both an individual and team.

In order for an athlete to be able to demonstrate agility, they must have good coordination and demonstrate dynamic balance. While balance can be seen as the ability to retain the centre of mass of the body above the base of support, dynamic balance involves the ability of the body to adjust to a stimulus that has taken the body out of balance and then return to a state of balance. Consequently, balance is dependent on coordination between inner ear, brain, skeleton and muscles. Dynamic balance is, in fact, a whole body problem that requires the athlete to respond to the stimulus provided, process the information, action the movement and respond with the physical performance. The multifaceted nature of dynamic balance allows a constraints-led approach (constraints; task, performer or environment) to be adopted to apply the principles of training.

Remember

The use of abdominal workouts are commonplace to improve core stability, but should be combined with whole body exercises in order to truly develop dynamic balance. This may include slowing a movement down and taking the athlete through an extended range of motion (ROM), beyond that which usually takes place in their sport. This incorporates the elements of task and performer constraints,. i.e. ROM (task) and time under tension (performer)

In order to demonstrate efficient movement patterns and dynamic balance, the sports performer needs to move in a coordinated manner. The presentation of numerous pieces of information during sports performance means you will need to work closely with the technical coach in order to develop conditioning scenarios that provide your athletes with an opportunity to develop fitness and technical aspects within the same session. This requires the fitness sessions to have *dynamic correspondence* to the performance environment and the athlete to be presented with similar information (cognitive cues) thereby helping to develop transfer between training and sports performance. This encompasses the concept of mechanical specificity highlighted in the needs analysis section. When you apply the training principles appropriately to your athlete, considering the sport they participate in, efficient movement using agility, balance and coordination can be developed that positively impacts on sports specific reaction time. This means the athlete will reduce the time period between the presentation of a stimulus and the initiation of the response to the given stimulus.

Stop and think

When trying to side step an opponent in a game of rugby, how many different cues do you need to be aware of?

The successful understanding of the concepts covered in this chapter should enable you to establish the beginnings of a training programme and be able to justify your selection based on the underpinning scientific theory that supports their use within the field of strength and conditioning and technical coaching.

Case study (for recommended answers, see www.pearsonfe.co.uk/foundationsinsport)

Alex is a strength and conditioning coach tasked with developing a training programme for an international team in the build-up to the next Commonwealth games. The players are of an elite standard with a minimum of three years' playing at national level. They currently perform five technical sessions and five conditioning sessions per week. Consider the following areas, then establish and justify the content of the five conditioning sessions, and also establish how you have applied the training principles.

- Current training status of the athletes
- Needs analysis of the sport
- Motor and physical fitness components to be improved
- Application of training principles.

Time to reflect

1. Have you ever experienced consecutive training sessions that enforce a 'no pain, no gain' approach? How do you feel after the training sessions are completed?

2. Do training sessions you have experienced reflect a 'one size fits' all approach? Discuss why this might not be an appropriate method of training.

3. Working in pairs, explain the time–motion characteristics of your sport.

4. What are the variables in a constraints-led approach to athletic preparation? In pairs, consider the variables in relation to your sport and reflect on how they may be manipulated.

5. As an individual, reflect on your strengths and weaknesses in terms of the attributes required to perform in your sport.

6. In groups of four, consider the type of test you may administer to measure improvement in performance and how this links to the theory of 'dynamic correspondence'.

7. In groups of four, consider the training principles of specificity, overload and variation and establish how you can link them to a specific exercise.

Check your understanding (for answers, see www.pearsonfe.co.uk/foundationsinsport)

1. What are the three factors that influence performance?

2. What is a needs analysis composed of?

3. What are the three primary training principles?

4. What are the physical and motor fitness components of sports performance?

Useful resources

To obtain a secure link to the websites below, see the Websites section on page ii or visit the companion website at www.pearsonfe.co.uk/ foundationsinsport.

- American College of Sports Medicine
- UK Strength and Conditioning Association
- National Strength and Conditoning Association
- English Insititute of Sport

Further reading

Baechle, T.R., Earle, R.W. (Ed) (2000) *Essentials of Strength Training and Conditioning*. Human Kinetics: Champaign Illinois.

Baker, D., Nance, S., Moore, M. (2001) The Load That Maximizes the Average Mechanical Power Output During Jump Squats in Power-Trained Athletes. *Journal of Strength and Conditioning Research,* 15 (1), 92-97.

Bompa, T.O. (1999) *Periodisation training for sports*. Human Kinetics: Champaign Illinois.

Davids, K., Glazier, P., Araujo, D., Bartlett, R. (2003) Movement Systems as Dynamical Systems; The functional role of variability and its implications for sports medicine. *Sports Medicine,* 33 (4), 245-260.

Duthie, G., Pyne, D. and Hooper. S. (2005) Time motion analysis of 2001 and 2002 super 12 rugby *Journal of Sports Sciences,* 23 (5), 523-530.

Knuttgen, H. and Kraemer, W. (1987) Terminology and measurement in exercise and performance. *Journal of Applied Sports Science Research,* 1 (1), 1-10.

Noakes, T.D. and Durandt, J.J. (2000) Physiological requirements of cricket. *Journal of Sports Sciences,* 18, 191-929.

Pringle, J.S.M., Doust, J.H., Carter, H., Tolfrey, K., Campbell, I.T. and Jones. A.M. (2003) Oxygen uptake kinetics during moderate, heavy and severe intensity 'submaximal' exercise in humans: the influence of muscle fibre type and capillarisation. *European Journal of Applied Physiology,* 89, 289-300.

Seiler, S.K., Kjerland and G. O., (2006) Quantifying training intensity distribution in elite endurance athletes: is there evidence for an "optimal" distribution? *Scandinavian Journal of Medicine and Science in Sports,* 16, 49-56.

Shephard, R.J. (1999) Biology and medicine of soccer: an update. *Journal of Sports Sciences,* 17, 757- 786.

Shephard, J.M.and Young, W.B. (2006) Agility literature review: classifications, training and testing. *Journal of Sports Sciences,* 24 (9), 919-932.

Siff, M.C.and Verkoshanski, Y. V. (1999) *Supertraining*. (4th edition) Denver Colorado.

Spencer, M., Lawrence, S., Rechichi, C., Bishop, D., Dawson, B. and Goodman. C. (2004) Time motion analysis of elite field hockey, with special reference to repeated sprint activity. *Journal of Sports Sciences,* 22, 843-850.

Stolen, T., Chamari, K., Castagna, C. and Wisloff, U. (2005) Physiology of soccer: an update. *Sports Medicine,* 35 (6), 501-536

Stone, M., Plisk, S. and Collins, D. (2002) Training principles: evaluation of modes and methods of resistance training - a coaching perspective. *Sports Biomechanics,* (1), 79-103.

Wisloff, U., Helgrud, C., Castagna, J., Jones, R. and Hoff. J. (2004) Strong correlation of maximal squat strength with sprint performance and vertical jump height in elite soccer players. *British Journal of Sports Medicine,* 38, 285-288.

Zatsiorsky, V.M. (1995) *Science and practice of strength training*. Human Kinetics: Champaign Illinois.

Chapter 14

Ethics and good practice

Introduction

Sport offers players or coaches intrinsic and extrinsic benefits. These benefits include having fun and experiencing a positive and fulfilling activity. Chapter 1 looked at a humanistic approach to coaching, where the emphasis of coaching practice incorporates values such as personal development over winning. Your coaching philosophy may recognise the need for coaching actions and behaviours that facilitate and promote a positive experience. A coaching philosophy is often devised away from the fast-paced, dynamic and passionate atmosphere of the sporting contest, which means that it is constructed when you have time to reflect upon the things you value most in your coaching. In reality, when you are engrossed in the coaching experience, situations may arise that challenge your coaching philosophy and require you to behave in a manner that is socially appropriate. You should also ensure that your athletes behave responsibly and ethically and make the sporting experience enjoyable for them and their opponents. With the rewards that sport can offer for its victors, what price are coaches and athletes willing to pay to achieve victory?

Learning outcomes

After you have read this chapter you should be able to:

- understand and define the term 'ethics'
- appreciate how ethical issues arise in sport
- define and express the various approaches to ethics
- recognise why ethical practice is necessary in coaching
- understand why moral reasoning within the sport context may differ in comparison with other social situations
- apply ethics to the sport context to inform coaching practice, considering the role of violence in sport
- understand how coaches can adopt good practice principles in their coaching
- understand the key legislation that may impact on coaching practice
- appreciate the role of coach education in ensuring good practice
- understand the National Occupational Standards for coaching and how they benchmark good practice.

Examples of appropriate and inappropriate behaviour, from players and coaches, arise commonly in sport, and often receive significant coverage and attention in the media, particularly when they involve high-profile sportspeople or teams. Identify and list as many examples of such behaviours as you can that have arisen within the last six months.

- Are there more reported incidences of appropriate or of inappropriate behaviour?

- Are these issues related to 'on-field' or 'off-field' activity?

- What has been the reaction to these incidents from those within sport (e.g. National Governing Bodies; fellow players; coaches; etc.) and those more *external* to sport (e.g. fans; media; general public)?

Defining ethics

A useful way to understand and define the term **ethics** is to identify characteristics or behaviours that are attributed to somebody who is said to be acting ethically. An ethically acceptable act has been described as one that is both legal and aware of a shared standard of society (Boddy, 2005). While coaches need to act within legal boundaries, there are other elements of ethical action that coaches must consider. These include:

- knowing right from wrong

- making judgements on what behaviour is deemed appropriate

- being moral.

Morals

Morals are related to general principles about what behaviours are 'right' or acceptable in life. Your morals guide you to think that some actions, like telling the truth, are important and must be carried out at all times, in all situations and contexts. In addition, morals are usually socially agreed, in that there is often a consensus about what behaviour is appropriate (Lyle, 2002). In sport, your morals will influence your attitude towards such things as playing by the rules or demonstrating sportsmanship.

Ethics

Ethics refer to moral obligations or behaviours that relate to a specific context or environment. Therefore, you may adopt differing moral reasoning in different situations, where behaviour that is seen as appropriate in one setting (e.g. school) may be different from acceptable behaviour in another (e.g. sport). This may also mean that what is acceptable in sport in one country or culture may not be viewed positively in other countries or cultures.

Morals – deep-rooted personal beliefs that guide our behaviours and actions

Ethics – moral obligations and behaviours that are related to specific situations or contexts, such as within the context of coaching

Reasons why ethical issues arise in sport

There are different reasons why ethical issues arise in sport at various levels of participation.

Where there is a difference in the balance of power between coach and athlete, such as an age difference, the opportunity exists for exploitation. How might you need to adapt your coaching methods to minimise any power differentials?

These reasons could be categorised into the following issues.

- Sport is a site for power differentials – within the coaching environment there are several examples of an unequal balance of power between coach and athlete. For example, a coach is likely to possess more knowledge about specific techniques, or have greater experience of athlete preparation, than the people who they coach. There are often age differences between the coach and their athletes. These power differentials could be exploited by an unethical coach.

- Sport develops moral qualities – sport is often used to teach people, especially children, the wider values of society. It is seen as a good way to introduce positive values such as teamwork, communication, learning to win and lose, or playing by the rules. However, sport can also teach people how to break rules or to be solely focused on winning at all costs.

- Sport involves competition and reward – the recognition, prestige and rewards that are available to 'winners' in sport, particularly at elite levels, may encourage participants to employ dubious tactics or engage in 'sharp practice' to increase their chances of victory and receive the rewards offered to sports people.

- Sport success involves high levels of dedication – in order to be successful a sportsperson needs a significant amount of commitment and investment. This investment may be financial, emotional or involve investment of time. In some cases, such dedication may encourage athletes to employ deviant behaviour, such as drug taking (doping), to ensure that the investment pays off.

- Sport is played at various levels of participation – behaviour that is acceptable at elite levels of sport may not be acceptable at recreational levels of sport. However, deciding what behaviour is acceptable at different levels may be viewed differently by those involved.

- Different sports possess different levels of 'ethical practice' – each sport may have its own ethical guidelines. For example, many sports adopt the view that you should 'play to the whistle' and wait for the referee or umpire to make the decisions on fair play, while other sports, such as golf or snooker, are renowned for the players calling their own fouls or rule infringements.

- Role modelling – sports people are often viewed as heroes and role models for younger participants and you, as coach, may encourage your athletes to copy the skills and actions that the best performers display. However, sometimes the behaviour of leading sports stars may be negative but is also copied and reproduced – leading to unacceptable behaviour in sport.

Stop and think

Consider how these issues appear within your sport or influence your coaching practice, paying particular attention to the specific aspects of your sport and/or culture.

Approaches to ethics

An appreciation of the various approaches to ethics offers a useful framework for you to critically evaluate ethical behaviour. **Ethicists** recognise that there are three major approaches to the study of ethics: deontology, utilitarianism and virtue ethics.

Deontology: those who approach the study of ethics from a deontological perspective believe that ethical action is constrained by a number of **rights** and **entitlements** that are available in a given context. These rights and entitlements can be displayed in the form of a list that outlines actions that are inherently right or inherently wrong. Right and wrong actions within sporting contests are governed by written rules, which all participants in that contest agree to abide by. Similarly, within the sports coaching context, the rights and entitlements of coaches can be presented within a code of conduct. Consequently, from a deontological perspective, ethical behaviour would be present if the coach adhered to the rules and codes that are applicable to their coaching practice.

Utilitarianism: suggests that actions are appropriate if they benefit the recipient of that action. Therefore, provided that the coach's actions have an overall benefit for the athlete, then they could be considered appropriate and acceptable. An example of utilitarian ethics would involve a coach facilitating a physically demanding training session for an athlete, which may cause a degree of suffering for this individual but, ultimately, as a consequence the athlete may enhance their opportunity to attain their competition goals; and so it is deemed acceptable or ethical behaviour.

Virtue ethics: suggests that it is the individual's traits and dispositions (their virtues) that dictate whether actions are right and appropriate. Therefore, the coach who displays certain virtues within their practices will know, can identify, is sensitive to, can tackle and resolve issues that are wrong or immoral (Hardman and Jones, 2008). For example, a coach who adopts a virtues-based approach to their coaching ethics may decide to remove their stronger players to 'even up' a contest that their team is winning comfortably, in the knowledge that a comprehensive defeat may impact on the motivation and enjoyment of their opponents and hence their continued participation in sport.

Key terms

Ethicist – an individual who has an interest in studying the philosophy and ethics of a particular activity, such as sport or coaching

Deontology – an approach to ethics that states that ethical action is based on adherence to rules

Utilitarianism – an approach to ethics that states that ethical action is based on providing happiness or benefit for the recipient

Virtue ethics – an approach to ethics that states that ethical action is based on the characteristics or moral judgement of an individual, such as a coach

Rights – legal, social, or moral freedoms that permit or constrain certain actions

Entitlements – a guarantee of access to, or a belief that one is deserving of, a particular benefit

Ethical practice – why is this necessary in coaching?

In many fields or occupations, ethical practice is vital and often distinguishes professions from other work. For example, practitioners in the medical, legal or educational field call themselves professionals because of the ethical approach they adopt in providing their services. According to Chelladurai (1999), a professional can be defined as possessing four characteristics:

- an organised body of knowledge which can be gained through qualifications
- professional authority or a licence to provide their services or skills
- subject to a process of 'community sanction', whereby practitioners can be disciplined for unethical practice
- a regulative 'code of ethics' to guide professional practice.

Within sports coaching, the fact that coaches hold qualifications, have authority to provide their skills, can be disciplined for unethical practice and are subject to a code of conduct, may suggest that coaching possesses the necessary characteristics of a profession. However, it could be argued that it is adherence to the code of conduct that best defines whether or not an individual is acting professionally or displaying ethical practice (Koehn, 1994).

Codes of conduct

When looking for direction on how to act ethically in their practice, coaches may find it useful to turn to a code of conduct. A code of conduct provides a detailed list of actions which a coach must perform or avoid. In this country, sports coach UK have produced a code of conduct, which is designed to guide ethical behaviour in sports coaching and ensure that all coaches act with integrity, honesty and competence. The key principles of the sports coach UK code are outlined in Table 14.1.

Table 14.1 Coaches' code of practice (From sports coach UK, 2009)

Principle	Statement
Rights	Coaches must respect and champion the rights of every individual to participate in sport
Relationships	Coaches must develop a relationship with performers (and others) based on openness, honesty, mutual trust and respect
Responsibilities (personal standards)	Coaches must demonstrate proper personal behaviour and conduct at all times
Responsibilities (professional standards)	To maximise the benefits and minimise the risks to performers, coaches must attain a high level of competence through qualifications, and a commitment to ongoing training that ensures safe and correct practice

Codes of conduct help to guide the actions of coaches (McNamee, 1998). A written code of conduct can:

- offer **clarity** on the actions which may be permissible, prescribed (recommended), or proscribed (forbidden)
- provide expectations of the coach which are **consistent** over time
- offer a neutral framework for **resolving conflict**
- **allow exclusion** of those who do not conform to the code
- dissuade people from acting in pursuit of their own interests to the detriment of others.

Despite these benefits, codes of conduct, like all deontological approaches to ethics, possess inherent weaknesses. For instance, a situation could arise where a coach may be adhering to the code of conduct, but still be displaying unethical behaviour and action. McNamee (1998) proposes three main criticisms of codes of conducts and the deontological approach to ethics.

1. There is a tendency for codes of conduct to be negatively formulated or narrowly focused.

2. Rules, such as those outlined in deontological documents, cannot determine their own application.

3. That no rule book or code of conduct can anticipate all eventualities within a given context.

Negative formulation and narrow focus

Often the way in which a code of conduct is written only includes guidance about actions or behaviours that should be avoided or that are prohibited, rather than highlighting behaviours that should be encouraged. Because a code of conduct can be viewed as providing a definitive guide to what actions constitute ethical behaviour, there is an assumption that behaviour that conflicts with the code must be pre-determined and intentional. This narrow focus suggests that there is no scope for flexibility in deciding which actions are appropriate or ethical.

Rules cannot determine their own application

Ethics refers to standards of behaviour that are appropriate within a specific context. Similarly, a code of conduct is designed to offer guidance and regulate practice in a given context, such as sports coaching. However, sometimes it is difficult to determine at what point the coaching context begins and ends. For example, the sports coach UK, *Code of Practice for Sports Coaches,* states that coaches: 'must avoid sexual intimacy with performers either while coaching them or in the period of time immediately following the end of the coaching relationship'. While this would appear to be good practice, there may be situations, such as the case of Paula Radcliffe who is coached by her husband, where it may be problematic. Therefore, the rule is open to interpretation, with individuals having to decide where and when the coaching context, and the consequent ethics, applies.

No rule book can anticipate all eventualities

Because a code of conduct can be viewed as a universal or over-arching guide to ethical behaviour, it does not account for situations where a coach may be acting ethically, and practising in the best interests of their athlete, but is actually contravening an element of the code. This view implies that a coach could operate within the boundaries of what is deemed appropriate by the code, but is actually acting immorally.

Compliance with a code of conduct does not necessarily constitute ethical practice and a code, when viewed as an isolated document, offers limited value. sports coach UK recognise this perspective, and have adopted the following practices to ensure ethical coaching behaviour is ingrained into their practice.

- A focus on ethics is incorporated into governing bodies of sport or employer constitutions and governance documents.

- Ethics form a constituent part of a policy and procedure for dealing with allegations and complaints.

- The code is used as the definitive guide and benchmark measure of coaching practice, as well as determining any need for sanctions against a coach.

- The code is fully incorporated into the coach education process.

- The code is an assessed element of the coach accreditation process.

- Ethical concerns and the code of practice are supported by appropriate training and resources, such as being included in continuous professional development courses.

Moral reasoning in sport

Sport is often seen as a vehicle for developing moral behaviour, particularly in young people. Three arguments exist as to the moral educational value of sport (Carr, 1998). The first is that sport is morally positive and that engagement in sport has a significant impact on developing good moral characteristics. Secondly, and conversely, that sport can be viewed negatively, and that sport could teach morally undesirable behaviours. The final argument suggests that sport is neutral with no moral significance. However, as sport is a social activity, the third argument can be extended – that the people involved in sport can determine whether or not it is a moral educative pursuit.

Defining sport as an educational tool in this way suggests that the people involved in sport, most notably coaches, can influence the extent to which sport teaches moral reasoning. From a coaching perspective, you must be aware of the impact of your behaviour on those who learn from you, in terms of developing technical sports skills and in fostering moral reasoning. However, sport is often described as a 'moral contradiction', and there are numerous examples of sportspeople who display conflicting behaviour. For example, there are sportspeople and coaches who are renowned for their questionable conduct on the field, but demonstrate admirable off-field behaviour, underlining the view that sport has limited impact in developing moral reasoning. What is important for coaches to understand is how and why sport can influence individuals to adopt a slightly lower moral standard when they enter the sport arena, in comparison to situations which occur within their normal, daily activities.

Game reasoning and bracketed morality

Research by Bredemeier et al. (2003) indicates that sport can produce lower levels of moral reasoning than would be normally expected in other situations, but that this is temporary and only lasts for the duration of a sporting contest. This temporary, sport-specific morality is termed game reasoning or **bracketed morality**. Paramount within game reasoning is that sport requires its participants to adopt an **egocentric** or self-centred perspective whereby all decisions, moral or otherwise, are geared towards what is best for you or your team. Therefore, understanding why sport elicits egocentric behaviour may help coaches to facilitate moral development in their practice.

Key terms

Bracketed morality – the suspension of an individual's normal or everyday level of morality, which remains for the duration of a sports contest

Egocentric – having limited or no regard for the interests of others and focusing purely on our own

This may include the following issues.

- Often, the aim of sport is to beat your opponent. This requires the adoption of self-interest to ensure that the tactics employed optimally benefit you or your teammates to win. Therefore, if competition becomes less important, it could ensure that sport becomes more morally developmental.

- All sports are governed by rules or laws; therefore, sportspeople merely have to follow the rule book in order to be considered to be playing fairly or ethically. Consequently, sportspeople are not required to think about their moral actions, because the laws decide what actions are permissible. In this sense, rules restrict morality.

- As the moral responsibility for the enforcement of the rules of a sport rests with the officials, this may encourage athletes to try and bend the rules to their advantage and see what they can get away with. Any attempt to challenge the officials is undertaken with the intention of benefitting yourself or undermining your opponents.

- When playing sport, opponents are often de-humanised and treated as an object to overcome or defeat. You may make no attempt to understand opponents as a human being with feelings, emotions, or desirable characteristics – they are merely someone to be beaten.

- Sport is artificial and lacks any real life meaning. Once the final whistle is blown, whether you have won or lost, with the exception of a few circumstances, the result of a sporting contest has little bearing on other aspects of your life. Therefore, within the artificial world of sport, your actions have less impact on the real world – which permits you to act less morally.

Stop and think

Is it important that your coaching practice is aimed towards the moral development of your athletes, or focused on winning? Explain and justify your answer.

Ethics in context – violence in sport

The rules of many sports condone violent behaviour as a legitimate form of strategy. Is this ethical?

Many sports are based on physical domination of an opponent or physical contact between participants, suggesting that violent behaviour is frequently observed, but sanctioned, within the rules of the sport. However, many aspects of sport are viewed subjectively and consensus on what is legitimate or acceptable is difficult to determine. Violence is no exception, so what may be considered to be legitimate violence by one player may be interpreted differently by another – meaning that violence in sport is a subjective and contested aspect of sport.

Stop and think

A rugby player performs a strong but legal tackle on an opposing player, which forces the tackled player to leave the game with an injury to the ribs. Is this a legitimate use of violence? Why?

Causes of violence in sport

There may be many reasons why sportspeople resort to violent behaviour. These reasons may be strategic, to intimidate an opponent, or in response to an official who has lost control of the match. However, a major cause of violence in sport may be through a player or team becoming frustrated – either with themselves or something in the external environment.

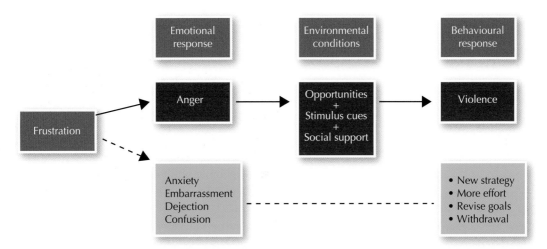

Figure 14.1 Model of frustration in sport (Source: Coakley, J. (2004) Sports in Society: Issues and Controversies 8E, McGraw Hill.)

The model in Figure 14.1 suggests that there are a variety of responses to frustration in sport, but if the response is one of anger within a player or team, then there is an increased probability that uncontrolled violence will be the behavioural response. The tendency for anger to lead to violence is affected by various factors within the sporting environment:

- Opportunities – in some cases, the nature of the sport provides opportunities for physical violence to be integrated into the players' actions. For example, the rules governing sports like rugby or combat sports encourage or permit physical violence as accepted strategies.

- Stimulus cues – many sports use equipment which could easily be used by players as 'weapons' should they experience frustration and anger. For example, ice hockey players could use their sticks, American footballers their helmets or footballers and rugby players the studs on their boots.

- Social support – violence is more likely to be the behavioural response if the culture surrounding a sport encourages physically aggressive behaviour. Contact sports frequently involve a culture of responding or retaliating to a violent act with another similar act.

Legitimate versus illegitimate violence

Given that violent behaviour is prevalent within sport, it is useful to distinguish between violent

Stop and think

How might anger lead to frustration in the sport you coach and how, as a coach, could you minimise the risks of violence or manage the environment?

acts that are acceptable and those that are not, as well as to identify what factors influence moral thinking on acceptable violence. Smith (2003) offers a framework to differentiate and classify acts of violence in sport (see Table 14.2).

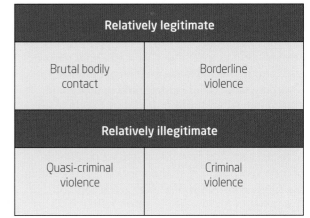

Relatively legitimate	
Brutal bodily contact	Borderline violence
Relatively illegitimate	
Quasi-criminal violence	Criminal violence

Table 14.2 Typology of sports violence (Smith, 2003)

At the legitimate end of this continuum, brutal bodily contact refers to acts that involve strong physical interaction between one or more participants but is justifiable and acceptable because it is permitted by the official written rules of a sport. For example, a punch to the head in boxing is legitimate violence, as would be a well-timed and well-directed tackle that forces an opponent to 'knock-on' in rugby.

At the other end of the scale, criminal violence refers to acts that occur in sport that are so ethically unacceptable that they not only contravene the written rules of a sport, but also the laws of a particular society. Thankfully, such violence is extremely rare.

These two extremes are simple to delineate, but the other two elements of Smith's typology are more complex. Borderline violence can be described as acts that breach the rules of a sport, but are accepted by the participants as they occur routinely and may be considered part of the game. A late tackle in football is a common occurrence and is often penalised by the referee (with a yellow card) but can be viewed as being unfortunate or unintentional and, therefore, accepted. In contrast, quasi-criminal violence violates both the written rules and the informal norms of player conduct. Examples may include an eye-gouge in rugby or the use of an elbow in football.

What distinguishes legitimate from illegitimate violence is the extent to which the act flouts the informal, unofficial conventions that are considered to be the norms of a sport. Such norms are termed the **ethos** of a sport (D'Agostino, 1981) and relate to how a specific subculture defines acts that are fair or otherwise. While ethos is being used in relation to violence in this instance, it can be applied to any situation in sport that challenges your morals and requires you to make an ethical decision regarding what is fair, appropriate or legitimate. Ethical behaviour in sport requires its participants, including coaches, to make moral decisions on the basis of how this decision relates to the formal rules of their sport, and how it will impact on the ethos of their sport. Actions that do not contravene either the rules or the ethos of a sport are acceptable and define moral behaviour in sport.

Good practice in coaching

For good coaching practice to occur, you, as coach, have to be aware of your legal and moral responsibilities. In recent years, this responsibility has magnified, as there is a greater emphasis on legal action being taken against people who have been deemed to have practised illegally or negligently. Therefore, an awareness of how a coach can safeguard their practice is fundamental to modern coaching practice.

Key terms

Ethos – the fundamental, unwritten values and norms that are specific to a particular culture (or sport)

Criminal Records Bureau Disclosure

In March 2002, in response to an increasing concern for the welfare of children, young people and vulnerable adults, legislation was introduced that required people working with these populations in either a paid or voluntary capacity to undergo a check to uncover whether or not they possessed a criminal record. The details of the checks, or disclosures, can be obtained by organisations responsible for providing services to children, young people and vulnerable adults, such as sports clubs and National Governing Bodies (NGBs). **CRB Disclosures** come in two forms.

Key terms

CRB (Criminal Records Bureau) Disclosure – a legal requirement for all individuals who have contact with children, young people and vulnerable adults in their work

- Standard disclosure: this disclosure is required for people who have regular contact with the specific populations highlighted above and provides details of any convictions and cautions that the applicant has received, along with details of whether they are banned from working with these populations. The majority of coaches would be required to complete this type of disclosure.

- Enhanced disclosure: this disclosure is required for people who have greater contact with children, young people and vulnerable adults, usually because they care for them, supervise them or train them. For example, school teachers would fall into this category. In addition to the information provided by the standard disclosure, the enhanced disclosure provides details from police files that may be relevant to assessing an individual's suitability to work with a specific population.

Key legislation for coaching

As a coach, you need to appreciate how various laws may impact on the coaching process and ensure that good practice is upheld. Table 14.3 outlines some legislation that relates to coaching.

Table 14.3 Key legislation for coaches

Act	Key information
Children Act 2004	Promotes awareness of the views and interests of children, including the implementation of '**Every Child Matters**'
Health and Safety at Work Act 1974	Outlines the general duties and responsibilities for employers, employees, persons in control of work premises and those who manage and maintain them
Activity Centres Young Person's Safety Act 1995	Outlines the regulations relating to the provision of facilities for adventurous activities

Coach education and good practice

As part of their remit, National Governing Bodies (NGBs) offer coach education courses to ensure that the people who coach their sport do so safely and in the best interests of their athletes. Crucially, by training qualified coaches, NGBs can ensure that their coaches are insured to coach and many NGBs (for example the England and Wales Cricket Board) cover their qualified coaches for Public Liability Insurance Cover and Personal Accident Cover.

However, as the content of coach education courses varies between sports, aspects of good practice may not translate across sports. So to standardise coaching practice, in particular with regard to safety and good practice, sports coach UK have implemented the United Kingdom Coaching Certificate (UKCC). This helps to ensure that good practice is shared across sports. The UKCC is an endorsement of an NGB coaching qualification, which means that it transfers between sports, ensuring that good practice exists irrespective of the sport being coached.

National Occupational Standards

To provide a benchmark for good coaching practice, a number of **National Occupational Standards** (NOS) for coaching have been embedded into the UKCC. These standards are as follows.

- Plan a series of sports coaching sessions. To attain this standard, the coach has to demonstrate that they can review the needs of their participants, ensure that all participants are able to take part safely, produce a series of coaching plans that specify the goals for the coaching and identify the resources that are needed for the sessions.

- Prepare the sports coaching environment. This involves conducting a risk assessment by checking the coaching environment and identifying particular hazards, checking equipment for poor repair, handling equipment in a way that prevents injury or damage, checking each participant for medical conditions or injuries that could be hazardous during the activity, and being alert to signs of abuse of children or vulnerable adults.

- Deliver a series of sports coaching sessions. To meet this standard coaches must be able to prepare their participants for activity by facilitating effective warm-ups, deliver their coaching sessions safely by being aware of potential hazards as they arise, develop the performance of their participants and conclude their session appropriately by integrating a cool-down activity.

- Monitor and evaluate sports coaching sessions. The final standard relates to the evaluation of the practices and activities undertaken during the coaching sessions to assess their suitability and appropriateness. This also involves an evaluation of each participant to ensure that they have benefitted from the session.

Chapter 4 and Chapter 9 cover the NOS in more detail. The following website also outlines the NOS in more detail. See the Skills Active for NOS link at www.pearsonfe.co.uk/foundationsinsport

Key terms

Every Child Matters – a government initiative design to ensure that every child has the support to be healthy; stay safe; enjoy and achieve; make a positive contribution; and achieve economic well-being

National Occupational Standards – nationally agreed standards of performance in a range of vocations, which offer benchmarks for good practice

Case study (for recommended answers, see www.pearsonfe.co.uk/foundationsinsport)

Paige is a coach for a high performance athlete, whom she has worked with for several years from junior level to their position now as a senior athlete who narrowly fails to meet the performance criteria set by UK Athletics. Consequently, neither Paige nor the athlete is eligible for funding to support the athlete's development, but a small increase in performance would ensure that both Paige and the athlete receive funding for their work. Paige has adapted several aspects of the athlete's preparation, ranging from improving techniques to altering the athlete's nutritional intake. None of these interventions appear to be having the desired results and impact on performance, and the athlete remains slightly below the standard for funding. The athlete remarks that they had been in conversation with a fellow competitor who had admitted to taking a performance-enhancing drug and

that they had noticed some improved results. Moreover, the person who had administered the drug had informed them that the drug could not be detected by current testing procedures.

Questions

1. How should Paige respond to the athlete's revelation?

2. What action, if any, should be taken against the fellow competitor, given their admission of taking a performance-enhancing drug?

3. How would the rules and ethos of athletics impact on the decisions and actions Paige should undertake?

4. What physical and psychological harm may Paige's actions do to the athlete as a consequence of the decisions she makes?

Time to reflect

1. Consider how your coaching practice attempts to develop the moral standards of your athletes, highlighting three examples of where your coaching has influenced moral development.

2. Is it important that your coaching practice is aimed towards the moral development of your athletes, or focused on winning? Explain and justify your answer.

3. 'Game reasoning' is advocated by many sports coaches in the pursuit of victory. How would you ensure that your athletes recognise when 'game reasoning' is suitable and when it is not?

Check your understanding (for answers, see www.pearsonfe.co.uk/foundationsinsport)

1. Give a definition of morals and ethics.

2. Outline how ethical issues may arise in the sports of netball and cricket.

3. List four reasons which outline the strengths of codes of conduct in sports coaching and three arguments as to why codes have limited utility.

4. Provide some arguments that explain why bracketed morality may occur in sport.

5. Discuss measures that a coach could introduce to ensure frustration does not translate to violence, using the examples of basketball and hockey.

6. How would you describe the ethos of your sport with regard to the following:
   a) accepting the official's decisions
   b) calling your own rule infringements
   c) using abusive language during a contest.

Useful resources

To obtain a secure link to the websites below, see the Websites section on page ii or visit the companion website at www.pearsonfe.co.uk/foundationsinsport.

- Journal of the Philosophy of Sport
- Sport, Ethics and Philosophy
- Criminal Records Bureau
- sports coach UK
- sports coach UK Workshop Finder
- Skills Active
- Skills Active for NOS
- Children Act 2004
- Health and Safety at Work Act 1974
- Activity Centres Young Person's Safety Act 1995

Further reading

Boddy, D., (2005). *Management: an introduction*. (3rd edition) London: Prentice Hall.

Boxill, J., Ed., (2003). *Sports ethics: an anthology*. Oxford: Blackwell.

Bredemeier, B.J., Shields, D.L., and Horn, J.C., (2003). Values and violence in sports today: the moral reasoning athletes use in their games and in their lives. In J. Boxall, eds. *Sport ethics: an anthology*. Oxford: Blackwell.

Carr, D., (1998). What moral educational significance has physical education? In M.J. McNamee and S.J. Parry, eds. *Ethics and sport*. London: E & FN Spon.

Cassidy, T., Jones, R. & Potrac, P., (2004). *Understanding sports coaching*. Abingdon: Routledge.

Chelladurai, P. (1999). *Human resource management in sport and recreation*. Leeds: Human Kinetics.

Coakley, J.J., (2003). *Sport in society: issues and controversies*. (8th edition) London: McGraw Hill.

D'Agostino, F., (1981). The ethos of games. *Journal of Philosophy of Sport,* 8, pp.7-18.

Hardman, A., and Jones, C., (2008). Philosophy for coaches. In R.L. Jones, M. Hughes and K. Kingston, (eds) *An introduction to sport coaching*. London: Routledge.

Koehn, D., (1994). *The ground of professional ethics*. London: Routledge.

Lyle, J., (2002). *Sports coaching concepts*. Abingdon: Routledge.

McNamee, M. (1998). Celebrating trust: virtues and rules in the ethical conduct of sports coaches. In M.J. McNamee and S.J. Parry, Eds. *Ethics and sport*. London: E & FN Spon.

McNamee, M.J., ed., (2010). *The ethics of sports: a reader*. London: Routledge.

McNamee, M.J. and Parry, S.J., (eds.) (1998). *Ethics and sport*. London: E&FN Spon.

Smith, M.J., (2003). What is sports violence? In J. Boxall, Eds. *Sport ethics: an anthology*. Oxford: Blackwell.

Chapter 15

Study skills

Introduction

Being able to take in new information, retain it and tackle assessments efficiently and effectively can be facilitated with the proper use of study skills. These are strategies which will help you to enhance your learning, improve achievement and ultimately to attain your foundation degree.

This chapter introduces different learning styles and will help you to identify the right one for you. If you are aware of your preferred learning style you can choose the most effective way to study.

Attention and time should be devoted to developing your study skills, in order to facilitate your understanding and learning and obtain the grades you deserve. Study skills covered in this chapter include the use of flash cards, listening skills, taking notes, reading skills and improving concentration.

This chapter covers skills to help you to prepare presentations, complete essays and revise for examinations.

Learning outcomes

After you have read this chapter you should be able to:

* identify and describe your learning style
* develop your study skills
* understand how to prepare for assessments.

Reflect on the last semester in terms of your modules and the information you have had to learn.

• What methods did you use to learn the information?

• Did you find you learned better with some methods as opposed to others?

• Which information did you remember: information you read, listened to or looked at visually?

Identify and describe your learning style

You will experience two types of learning throughout your foundation degree – pedagogy and andragogy. Pedagogy is teacher-led education; your lecturer will decide your learning content and best method of delivery. Andragogy is learner-focused education; this is where you are responsible for your own learning. This method is apparent in your self study and in your work experience module. To help you with your own studying you need to decide on your preferred learning style.

Table 15.1 Five learning styles (www.vark-learn.com, 2008)

Learning styles

One of the most widely used methods to identify different learning styles is the VARK model (Leite et al., 2009). It includes a series of questions and you choose the answer which best describes your preference. Your preferred learning style will be shown, and advice given about specific study strategies. Understanding your preferred learning style means you can use appropriate techniques to facilitate your learning.

To obtain a secure link to an online learning styles questionnaire, see the *Useful resources* list on page 235, or the Activity below.

Fleming (1995) suggests there are five learning styles, as shown in the table below.

● **Activity**

Using the website www.pearsonfe.co.uk/foundationsinsport, complete the questionnaire to identify your learning style. After identifying your learning style, reflect on the best methods you can use to learn.

Learning style	Tools and activities	Mini activity
Visual learners (learn best through seeing)	• Use visual images – diagrams, models, videos, flow charts, graphs and textbooks • Use different colours, highlight key information and underlining	• Select lecture notes and highlight key information in colour • Can you display the information in a visual manner such as a flow chart?
Aural learners (learn best through listening)	• Attend lectures • Record lectures using a dictaphone and replay • Active participation in discussions and tutorials • Explain information to others • Describe visual information • Read lecture notes aloud	• Ask permission from your lecturer to record a lecture using a dictaphone • Now replay the lecture and fill in any gaps in your lecture notes
Read/write (learn best through reading and writing)	• Read textbooks, journals and definitions • Write lecture notes up in full • Use headings, lists and definitions	• Read several journals in relation to a lecture topic
Kinaesthetic (learn best through experience)	• Focus on learning through moving, touching and doing • Visit medical school • Work experience placements • Shadowing other professionals	• Seek a placement in which you can shadow a sports therapist working
Multimodal	• Learn via a combination of two or more learning styles	• Use combinations of the strategies (above) to learn new information

Develop your study skills

Good listening

In order to maximise your performance you need to be a good listener. Taught programmes are heavily reliant on the delivery of information and your ability to listen. Listening is a cognitive act that requires you to pay attention, think about the information delivered and mentally process it.

There are numerous barriers to listening, including the following examples.

- Environmental distractions – these can include anything that may distract you, such as mobile phones, ipods, TVs and game consoles.

- Pride/self-centred attitude – people sometimes fail to listen to the other person because of what they think they have to offer or have already achieved. You may mistakenly think you have nothing to learn or fail to value what the other party has to say.

- Assumptions – assuming you know what the other party has to say and talking over them or finishing their sentences. You may interrupt them with your answer, assuming you know what they are going to say without letting them finish.

- Close-mindedness – having a closed mind and thinking you know the right way or you have the right answer. If you are not receptive or open-minded, you may miss an important point.

- Defensiveness – If you are close-minded you may feel you are being personally attacked by comments from the other party, particularly if you feel disrespected, threatened or misunderstood.

- Reacting to specific words – the speaker may unintentionally use words which provoke a reaction in you. You may become preoccupied or distracted, missing the explanation by creating the wrong context for the words used.

It is important that barriers to listening are identified and addressed with specific, individual strategies. This will help you to solve complex problems and understand complex information in order to learn and develop.

Figure 15.1 Key components to ensure you are a good listener. How can you achieve each of these?

To improve your listening skills you should do the following.

- **Be ready** – read any notes before the lecture. Consider how much you already understand about the topic that is due to be delivered. Make a conscious effort to find the topic useful and interesting.

- **Have clear objectives** – have a clear idea of what you expect from the lecture and the topic to be delivered. Ask questions if you are unsure of anything or if you think something has not been covered. Your lecturer may highlight that your question will be addressed in the next lecture.

- **Open your mind** – question what you are being taught but allow enough time for information to be covered. Your question may be answered as the lecture progresses. If it isn't, ask at a suitable interval, not in the middle of the lecture. Be receptive to new ideas and points of view. Allow your mind to be stretched when listening; look to acquire new ideas and theories as opposed to re-enforcing those you already know.

- **Be attentive** – turn off your mobile phone so you are not tempted to surf the internet or check for text messages. Focus, and maintain eye contact with your lecturer. Sit in a position where you can fully engage in the lecture and will not be distracted by others.

- **Do not be defeated** and stop listening when you feel challenged or find a topic hard. This is the time to increase your focus and listen very carefully while opening your mind. If you are struggling to understand, say so – others are probably feeling the same.

- **Monitor your environment** – if the room is too hot, sit by an open window and if you know the room is cold, wear extra clothing. Turn off mobile phones and remove game consoles. Be proactive and think how you can best cope with the environment to limit the distraction.

Activity

Brainstorm all the factors which you feel are a barrier to you listening. Devise strategies to overcome each barrier in order to improve your listening skills.

Make the most of lectures

Make the most of your lectures and you will gain a better understanding which could save you struggling later. Maximising your experience involves the following.

- **Preparation** –look on your university's virtual learning environment (VLE – your VLE may be referred to as a blackboard or moodle) and download the lecture notes and any required reading. Read them, reflect on the material and prepare questions. Take everything you need for making notes during the lecture.

- **Active participation** – make additional notes, listen attentively and ask questions to clarify where you are unsure. Try to understand the main message of the lecture and the links and ideas presented. Write key information quickly, particularly anything the lecturer has highlighted as important to your assessment or exam. If you know something requires further research, add a question mark to draw your attention to it after the lecture.

- **Closure after the lecture** – review your notes. Highlight information and rewrite, expanding on areas which need more clarification. Display information visually. Develop a system which works for you, and ensure you file all your notes in an organised way. Your notes will be a valuable resource when preparing for exams, assignments and further reading. Investing time now will save time during the assessment period and will develop your understanding of the subject. Complete any reading you are given to reinforce your understanding and make your notes more comprehensive.

Reading

Reading is an important part of your course, and can be time consuming. You need to identify your purpose for reading materials and ascertain what you want to find out.

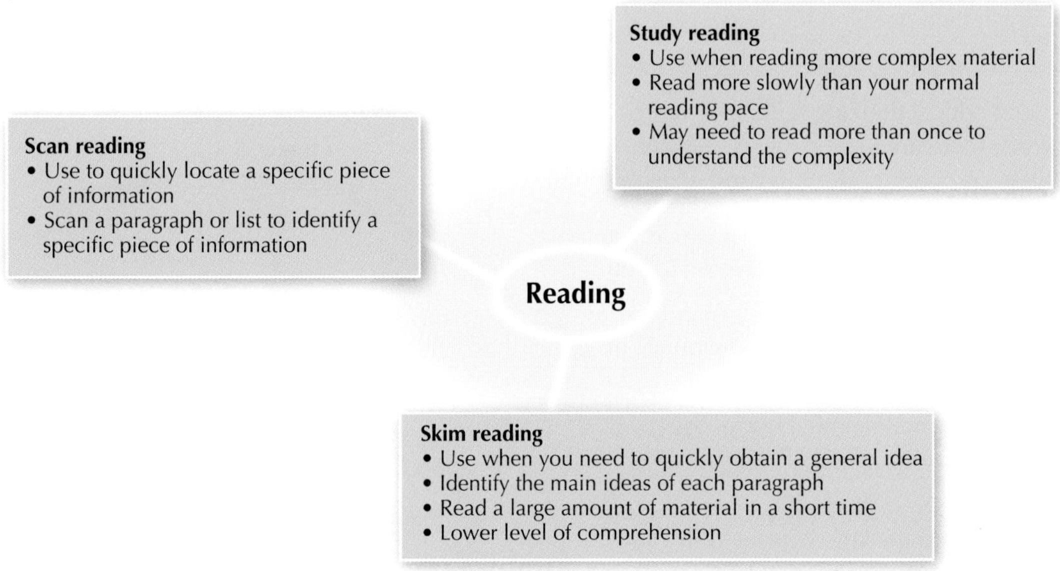

Study reading
- Use when reading more complex material
- Read more slowly than your normal reading pace
- May need to read more than once to understand the complexity

Scan reading
- Use to quickly locate a specific piece of information
- Scan a paragraph or list to identify a specific piece of information

Reading

Skim reading
- Use when you need to quickly obtain a general idea
- Identify the main ideas of each paragraph
- Read a large amount of material in a short time
- Lower level of comprehension

Figure 15.2 The three reading styles: study reading, skim reading and scan reading. Identify where you can use each of these reading styles in your study.

Active reading helps to keep the mind focused on the task in hand. If you own the book, or have printed out a journal, highlight or underline important details as you read. It will help to keep you focused. You may also wish to annotate the reading to reinforce information and make points for revision. If you have borrowed a reading source and find particular parts useful, take a photocopy so you can mark it.

Critical thinking and approach

Being critical is a skill you need to develop. A critical approach means you do not just accept ideas, information, opinions and research at face value. You will question the approach, research methodology, assumptions and attitudes and discuss them within your work.

Thinking critically involves understanding the strengths and weaknesses of an argument, drawing conclusions, identifying any parallel arguments and judging how sound the arguments are. When reviewing research think about the world view, the strategy taken, methodology and data as well as conclusions drawn. Within your work you will develop your critical thinking by making a claim; this will form the basis of your argument, progressing to flaws in the argument and analysing strengths and weaknesses in relation to the evidence. You will then question the evidence that is available.

Developing your critical thinking skills will improve your study skills. There are three main aspects to critical thinking – process, understand and analyse.

- **Process** – the taking in of information which you are reading, or which has been delivered to you.

- **Understand** – consolidate your understanding of the information by summarising key points or the evidence presented.

- **Analyse** – spend time thinking how all the components interrelate, and gain an in-depth overview.

You need to understand the key words within your assessment brief. Throughout your foundation degree you will encounter words such as **evaluate**, **synthesise**, **apply**, **justify** and **compare**.

Key terms

Evaluate – this is an assessment of the information with regard to your topic, the evidence it is based on and its relation to other ideas

Synthesise – drawing together information from a range of sources you have researched to support the assessment you are constructing. Logical connections should be made and presented in a logical format

Apply – the transference of information and knowledge you have gained to your topic, or application to practical aspects

Justify – the conclusion you have drawn or ideas you have formed will need to be justified. The information you have researched will allow you to support your work

Compare – addressing the similarities and differences presented in the information you have gathered

Flash cards

Flash cards can be very helpful; for example, when learning functional anatomy. You can buy anatomical flash cards, or make your own with reference to any subject.

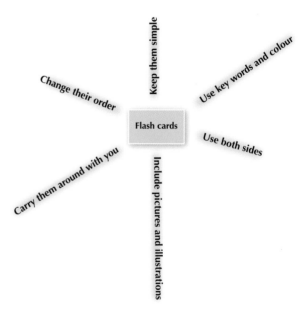

Figure 15.3 Key considerations when designing flash cards.

Design a set of flash cards for a subject you are finding challenging.

Flash cards are useful during group study. Take it in turns to randomly pick a card and then discuss subjects related to the flash card. This is a good method to practise for your viva voce (see page 232). You can also maximise your revision time when you have a spare ten minutes; for example, when travelling on buses or trains.

Time management

Time management is essential if you are to produce good quality work and achieve your grades. Your academic grades are a measure of your success, are rewarding and can provide you with the motivation to succeed. Poor time management often lets students down, resulting in poor grades.

A schedule reflecting the semester will help you to see the big picture. Your university will provide you with a course handbook or module handbook. This will tell you how many assessments you will have for the module, the types of assessment you will have (for example, presentation, essay, viva voce or examination) and the dates for submission. Develop a calendar for the semester and, for each module, list the type of assessment and the submission date. This will allow you to reflect on the semester ahead, consider what is expected of you and when you can expect a greater workload.

Planning a weekly schedule, reflecting on both academic and personal tasks, is invaluable in improving your time management. On a seven-day diary, from getting up to going to bed, document your typical week including:

- work commitments
- sports training and matches
- timetabled lectures
- travel to and from work, university and training
- social activities
- late morning rising

- surfing the internet, for example time on Facebook and Twitter
- studying.

Have you allocated sufficient time to your studies? You may need to sacrifice some less urgent activities in order to plan your study time effectively. You may also need to increase the time scheduled which leads up to a busy assessment period. To improve your time management consider:

- the time of day you study best
- studying difficult subjects first
- studying in an appropriate environment
- making use of a library when researching
- reviewing your schedule daily and weekly
- having clear objectives to achieve daily and weekly
- making a 'to do' list
- reflecting on your accomplishments.

If you are not achieving your 'to do' list, daily or weekly objectives, why not? Where is your time going? How can you manage your time more effectively?

Improve your concentration

Maintaining your concentration while studying can be a task in itself. There is always something to distract you – television, surfing the internet, phone calls, making snacks and drinks, etc. It is essential that you are able to concentrate and focus on the task in hand. Consider the following ideas to help improve your concentration.

- Remove all distractions and turn off your mobile phone – unplug the landline if necessary. Your environment should be quiet and at the right temperature. If you live in busy student accommodation it may be better to study in the library.

- Make a study plan. Confirm what you are trying to achieve in the study session and how long it will take you. If you have a complex task, break it down into smaller tasks which are easier to accomplish.

- Study at the time of day which is best for you.

- Ensure you are in the right mind set. If you are tired and hungry you will not have the energy to concentrate.
- Work for 20 to 30 minute interval periods and take regular breaks where you leave your study area.
- Ensure you have all the materials you require to study, including academic texts, journals and basic writing materials.

Motivation

Every student will find it difficult to motivate themselves at times. A lack of motivation will affect your concentration, focus and attitude. You may become negative and begin to feel the challenge is insurmountable. You can then find every excuse to avoid studying.

Motivation is the key to a positive attitude and believing you can achieve. Motivated students will find it easier to focus and improve their learning. Consider the following to improve your motivation.

- Use the 'concentration' list above to stay focused.
- Study with colleagues. Group study can be just as beneficial as individual study.
- Tick off aspects on your study plan when you accomplish them – this can be very rewarding.

- Focus on the long-term goal of achieving your foundation degree.
- Remember you have actually paid for this course. Pin your receipt somewhere obvious to remind you of the cost.
- The sooner you start, the sooner you will finish. If you spend time worrying about studying and avoiding the issue, you are losing valuable study time.

How to prepare for assessments

You will need to complete several assessments during your foundation degree. Read the assessment brief carefully and make sure you understand the task/s fully. If you are unsure, ask your tutor. Pay particular attention to the reading list on the assessment brief. Key readings will have been included to develop your understanding.

Preparing for a presentation

In sports coaching you must be able to communicate effectively with a range of people and explain and justify your decisions. At some point during your career you will be expected to present information. You need a good understanding of your presentation topic to be able to communicate effectively with your audience and answer any related questions.

Table 15.2 Top tips for an effective presentation

Preparation	Carry out research and understand your subject area thoroughly. Practise your presentation a number of times before your assessment. You could video yourself and reflect on your performance, or practise with colleagues and ask for feedback. Answer the task you have been given, and time yourself to ensure you stay within the time limit.
Presentation	Prepare your slides using a suitable IT package, for example PowerPoint® or www.Prezi.com. Ensure your material is presented with clarity, referenced and has visual aids. Do not overload your slides with lots of text which you are tempted to read word for word.
Your presentation	Dress appropriately. Present a positive attitude conveying enthusiasm and confidence.
Examples	Provide a range of examples to help explain aspects, ensuring they are related to the subject.
Additional aids	Use additional aids such as anatomical models, props or handouts to help support your explanation.
Audience	Connect with your audience by maintaining eye contact with them. Scan all participants in the audience.
Interesting	Make your presentation interesting by using visual aids. Ask questions to involve the audience (ensuring they are at an appropriate level). If you use video clips keep them short (20–30 seconds maximum) and clearly state their purpose or relevance.
Voice	Speak at an appropriate speed and vary the tone of your voice.

Exams

Give yourself plenty of time in order to prepare effectively for examinations. Implement good time management throughout the process, make a concerted effort and persevere through any difficulties.

You should first write down the exam date, time and location on your semester calendar and work out a realistic revision schedule to meet the exam deadline. When revising, refer back to the list on page 229 under 'Improve your concentration'.

> **Top tip**
>
> Remember KISS: **K**eep **I**t **S**imple and **S**traightforward. Start with the basics and progress to more complex information.

Maintain a routine before the exam, including regular meals to keep up your energy levels. If your exam is in the afternoon do not 'cram' in the morning – just refresh your memory with key points. Make sure you get a good sleep the night before a morning exam, and have a final read through of your revision notes. Ensure you have all your equipment and arrive in plenty of time for the start of the exam.

During the exam you should read the instructions carefully, and read *all* the questions first to identify those which are compulsory and those which are optional. Plan how much time you will allocate to each question, allowing a proportion of time to read through your answers. Clearly identify your answers within your answer book and start with the question you feel most confident with.

Use all your time effectively – never leave an exam early. Ensure you have answered the correct number of questions and your answer matches the question number. Read through your answers and edit where necessary, but remember that it is about the quality of your work, not the quantity. If you are running short of time, list the key information. Take care that your handwriting is legible – if the examiner cannot read your work they cannot mark it.

Writing an essay

An essay is structured through using coherent paragraphs which are connected in a logical way. An introduction is used to introduce the essay topic, with the main body developing an argument, linking point 1 to point 2, to point 3, etc. Always end your essay with a conclusion. This should conclude your argument and summarise the main points of the essay.

An essay takes time to develop. For a 2500 word essay allow a minimum of three weeks; for longer essays allow more time. You need this time not just to write the essay, but for researching, planning, drafting and redrafting, as well as editing and refining your work, paying particular attention to your spelling, grammar and referencing. The essay-writing process can be broken down into stages as shown below.

1. **Understand the topic** – ensure you fully understand the essay topic and the requirements of your work. Identify the key words within the essay title and make sure you understand their full meaning. You need a full grasp of the topic in order to ensure that all the information you include is relevant. You may decide to formulate your argument to the topic in question, in order to provide direction for the planning process. You can always amend your argument as your knowledge develops. Highlight key information on the assessment brief you have been given.

2. **Brainstorm** – this will allow you to put down all your ideas. Think laterally and document all information, even if something seems irrelevant (you may make a connection later on in your work). A brainstorm will help you to focus on your plan and reading.

3. **Essay plan** – produce a plan for your essay. Think about the structure and order, and which topics you are going to put where.

4. **Reading** – read a wide range of sources related to your essay topic and plan – use books as well as academic journals. The internet is a good source to develop thoughts and ideas and gain a quick understanding but should rarely be used as an academic reference. Academic references should form the basis of your research; these include books and journals.

5. **Amend essay plan** – on completion of your reading you will have a better understanding of the topic. Review your plan and make any amendments. Do you need to move or add a topic? Your plan should help you to write analytically. Consider the following and amend your plan as necessary:

   - clearly identified main proposal, hypothesis or argument

   - reasoned argument considering evidence, examples and research

   - reasoned opposing argument – again considering evidence, examples and research.

6. **Justification of your perspective** – address weaknesses and flaws in opposing arguments evidence, examples and research.

7. **Draft 1** – you need to write your essay based on your plan and the reading you have completed. If you feel there are gaps, or you do not have sufficient information, make a note and address these when you have completed the first draft.

8. **Additional information** – your first draft will have allowed you to ascertain weaker areas, and areas which require further understanding. Focus your additional reading on these areas.

9. **Draft 2** – amend your first draft to address any weak areas or gaps in your work.

10. **Break** – take a break from your work. Fresh eyes and thought will enhance the next stage.

11. **Final version** – review your work, focusing on the flow and logical structure. You may need additional sentences or paragraphs to improve the links. Is there any irrelevant information? Focus on each sentence. Could you write the sentence with fewer words or with a clearer structure?

12. **Proofreading** – this is the final read through, paying particular attention to details such as spelling, punctuation and referencing. A friend might be able to help with this stage of your essay. Referencing within the text as well as including a full reference list is often overlooked by many students. The section on referencing on page 233 includes full details.

Viva voce examinations

Viva voce exams (commonly known as a 'viva') are included as an assessment strategy in most foundation degree courses and are question and answer style spoken exams. With an essay or written exam you have access to many resources which you can collate, and you have time to reflect and amend your work. With a viva voce it is crucial you understand your subject area and are able to communicate information confidently and logically to your examiner. You will not pass by reciting information you have learned verbatim. You need to prepare thoroughly for your viva voce.

- Be logical. Start with the basics and progress to more complex information. For example, the practical may require you to demonstrate your planning, coaching and review skills. Your viva should be logical; you may start by addressing the planning stage justifying your preparation, explaining the coaching plan, and the short- and long-term goals, progressing to conducting the session, the delivery of the programme and the style you adopted and finally to the evaluation process.

- Understand the requirements of your viva voce and draft possible questions you may be asked – you can then verbalise your answers.

- Use anatomical models, game boards, protective equipment or sporting equipment to verbally explain information – this will allow you to confirm your understanding.

- Revise and practise with other students.

> ## Top tip
>
> - Be prepared and wear your sports coaching uniform – unless you are instructed to wear smart professional attire.
>
> - Stay calm and pleasant and maintain an appropriate manner and attitude.
>
> - Listen carefully to the question. Do not be afraid to ask the examiner to repeat it.
>
> - If you do not know the answer, do not bluff – acknowledge that you do not know.
>
> - Do not worry if parts of the viva voce were difficult. The examiner will ask a range of questions differing in complexity and difficulty in order to ascertain your knowledge and grade.

Referencing

In order to inform your assessment, your work needs to be based on academic sources. The material you read and research will form the substance of your work. Making reference to another author's work is known as citing (or citation) and you must give a full detailed list of all sources used in a reference list at the end of your work. You must fully reference your work; if you do not you may be guilty of plagiarism (see below).

Your university or college will have their own referencing guide which may differ slightly from the examples below. Pay particular attention to detail. This can be a time consuming process so on completion of your assessment, allow time in your planning.

When you are making direct reference to an author's original idea, or a study they have conducted, reference as follows:

> Mackay (2000) states that…

> Mackay and Cox (1996) propose that…

If there are more than two authors for the publication you should cite them as follows:

> Mackay et al., (2002) state that…

When you are not directly making reference to an author, although you have used their concepts or ideas, you should reference as follows:

> Sports massage has both physiological and psychological benefits (Pain, 2000).

If you have identified two sources which support this idea you should reference as follows:

> Sports massage has both physiological and psychological benefits (Sharma & Mafulli 1996; Pain et al., 2002).

The references at the end of your essay should be in alphabetical order. To reference a book, follow this format:

> Pain, T. (2000). The Complete Guide to Sports Massage. London: A&C Black.

To reference a journal, follow this format:

> Sharma, P. and Mafulli, N. (2005). Tendon Injury and Tendinopathy: Healing and Repair. Journal of Bone and Joint Surgery, Vol. 87, pp. 187–202.

Top tip

If you have two publications from the same author you should distinguish by placing an 'a', 'b' after each of the years. For example, Mackay (2010a) and Mackay (2010b).

Plagiarism

Plagarism is copying someone else's work or passing their work off as your own, or taking ownership of their original ideas. If you quote material and do not put it into quotation marks, or fail to reference the source, it is classed as plagiarism. This is taken very seriously and may lead to disciplinary proceedings. Most universities and colleges will provide you with access to plagiarism detection software called Turnitin. Turnitin is a tool you can use to gain feedback on the potential of plagiarism within your work and improper citation. It can be used at any stage of your work; for example, at first draft, second draft and your final version. Turnitin allows you to be proactive to avoid any plagiarism issues. You will find it on your college or university's VLE. All work is submitted electronically.

Taking responsibility

There is only one person responsible for your learning and achievement on your foundation degree, and that is you. It can be tempting to blame others or make excuses but you need to take responsibility for your learning, be proactive and find constructive solutions. Some of the following might sound familiar:

- 'I can't do it, it's too difficult…'
- 'it won't work… it's a waste of time… it's doing my head in…'
- 'it's not my problem… it's not fair…'

You might hear or say:

- 'they didn't explain it properly…'

- 'they should help me more…'
- 'it's their fault…'
- 'they have to do something about it…'

Take responsibility for a constructive outcome. Use positive phrases such as:

- 'I can do this…'
- 'I don't fully understand the lecture therefore I am going to…'
- 'I will take responsibility for…'
- 'it is my fault I did not do as I was asked so next time I will…'
- 'I have not completed the required reading so next time I will…'

Be positive, be proactive and plan to achieve. Universities have many support systems in place that you can use as much as you need to.

Time to reflect

1. Having identified your learning style, devise methods which will enable you to continue to learn.

2. Identify the learning styles of your athletes to enable to you to facilitate their learning.

3. Choose selected athletes and identify their barriers to listening, then devise strategies to improve their listening skills.

4. Develop three strategies in order to maximise your experience within lectures.

5. Reflect on your time management skills.

6. Use an online questionnaire to identify your learning style. Describe the methods that will help you to learn more effectively. To obtain a secure link to an online learning styles questionnaire, see the *Useful resources* list over the page.

7. Briefly describe two strategies which you could use to improve your listening skills.

8. Identify the three reading strategies and briefly describe why you would use each.

9. Choose two strategies which you could use to maximise the use of your lectures.

10. Consider two ways you could improve your concentration when studying.

11. Consider three aspects to consider when preparing for a presentation.

12. Consider why it is important to take responsibility for your own learning.

Useful resources

To obtain a secure link to the websites below, see the Websites section on page ii or visit the companion website at www.pearsonfe.co.uk/foundationsinsport.

- Directgov – Disabled Students' Allowances (DSAs)

- Dyslexia at College

- BRAINHE

- epax

- Learn Higher

- The Vark Questionnaire

- Study and Learning Centre – RMIT University

- Palgrave Macmillan – skills4study

Further reading

Boulay, D. (2009). *Study Skills for Dummies*. Chichester: John Wiley & Sons.

Cotterall, S. (2008). *The Study Skills Handbook*. Basingstoke: Palgrave Macmillan.

Cotterall, S. (2008). *How to Write Better Essays*. Basingstoke: Palgrave Macmillan.

Cotterall, S. (2008). *Critical Thinking Skills*. Basingstoke: Palgrave Macmillan.

Chapter 16

Work-based learning

Introduction

Work-based learning allows you to integrate theoretical knowledge with the practicalities of a workplace setting. Most universities will have a work-based learning supervisor, who will have a large portfolio of contacts and opportunities for you to view and apply for. Support will be given to develop your coaching skills to industry standards. This will prepare you for your industrial placement. Chapter 17 supports you through your industrial experience.

You are responsible for completing a minimum number of hours as documented in your university module specifications; the number of hours will differ between institutions. You are required to draw upon your Year 1 and Year 2 knowledge to competently execute a range of performance management tasks such as evaluating performance, assessing player strengths and weaknesses, encouraging and motivating players, execution of health and safety standards, planning coaching sessions with regards to technical, tactical and fitness aspects, as well as evaluating all aspects of the process.

This chapter clarifies employment opportunities and possible roles you may undertake in employment, as well as verbal and non-verbal communication skills. Personal skills will be addressed to further develop your knowledge and practice.

Learning outcomes

After you have read this chapter you should be able to:

- discuss employment opportunities for sports coaching
- explain the roles a sports coach may undertake within the industry
- demonstrate knowledge of appropriate verbal and non-verbal communication skills
- discuss personal skills essential for employment.

Employment opportunities for sports coaches

Sports coaching has been established as a career path for a number of years. However, over the past decade it has become increasingly popular – with new employment opportunities arising all the time. A proportion of sports coaches are self-employed, while others work as employees. At the start of your career, and for several years, you may have to work part-time and unsocial hours. Being self-employed means you work for yourself and are responsible for all aspects of your business, including seeking job opportunities, tax returns, paying national insurance and record keeping. You will not receive benefits such as sick pay and a private company pension. However, you do choose your own hours of work and the type of work you wish to undertake. Being able to secure a position as an employee, on the other hand, allows you the comfort of receiving a regular income and other possible benefits such as sick pay and a company pension.

Many sports coaches undertake voluntary work while studying and upon qualifying to ensure they have the relevant work experience to develop their personal profile and **curriculum vitae**. The disadvantage of voluntary work is that you will not be paid. However, reasonable expenses can usually be claimed. Volunteering is a good opportunity for you to network and gain valuable experience.

Key term

Curriculum vitae – document which provides an overview of your qualifications, employment and relevant life experience

Figure 16.1 Types of employment – how would your role as a sports coach differ between the employment opportunities?

Roles a sports coach may undertake

Your role as a sports coach will vary according to your chosen employment. You may decide to work within schools, within the community, with sports teams, individual athletes or with professional sports people. If you are working with schools, within the community or local league teams, or if you are self-employed, you may assume a wide variety of roles. These roles may include planning training programmes, delivery of training programmes or sports coaching sessions, reflecting on and evaluating sessions, monitoring short- and long-term athlete development, reducing injury risk, conducting evaluation tests and preparing for competitions or matches.

If you work for a larger organisation or a professional team, you are more likely to work as part of a multi-disciplinary team (MDT). Your role will be more specific and you will be expected to liaise with different colleagues who might include a sports therapist, a sports scientist, a strength and conditioning coach, a fitness coach, a nutrionist, a player development manager and a community liaison officer. Take time to ensure you clearly understand your role within your employment setting.

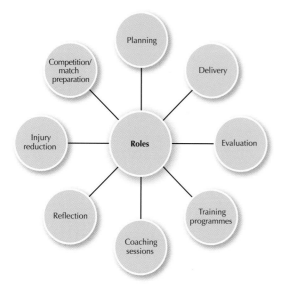

Figure 16.2 Examples of roles a sports coach may undertake

Your foundation degree will develop your portfolio of transferable skills. These are skills which can be applied to a range of jobs. Examples include communication, problem solving, leadership and time-management skills.

Stop and think

Investigate your local area and relevant organisations (such as the websites for sports coach UK, county sports partnerships and UK Sport) identifying all sports coaching jobs. What roles do the jobs include?

Verbal and non-verbal communication skills

Good communication skills are essential if you are to develop successful relationships with players, colleagues and employers. Good communication helps you to convey your message to the recipient clearly and unambiguously. It is also essential that you receive information clearly. Any distortion to, or from, the sender will cause confusion and affect the treatment process or relations between those involved. Poor communication may result in loss of players, loss of job opportunities and lead to a poor reputation.

Communication skills can be grouped into two main types – verbal and non-verbal.

Verbal communication

During all verbal communication you need to convey your message as clearly as possible to the recipient and avoid unnecessary jargon, such as complex medical terminology. You should speak clearly, concisely and at an appropriate speed. Words should be chosen which convey your intent and deliver succinct meaning in a logical manner. You should avoid creating resistance or a defensive mindset in your recipient. You should also try to avoid using words which are accusatory, judgemental, blaming or critical.

Non-verbal communication

Non-verbal communication, commonly known as body language, plays an important role in communication. Body language includes eye contact, facial expressions, gestures, posture, voice, touch and space – as discussed below.

Non-verbal communication is a powerful tool which you can use to help secure employment, build rapport with athletes, develop your client base and address challenging situations.

- **Eye contact** – to portray confidence ensure that you make frequent eye contact. When first approaching the recipient make gentle eye contact, and develop the gaze. Intense eye contact can be as detrimental as too little.

- **Voice** – think about the quality and projection of your voice, pace, expression and emphasis.

- **Posture** – move positively, adopting a confident posture. This will make you feel more self-assured and also help to make your client feel confident about you.

- **Facial expression** – your face is very expressive and communicates a wide range of emotions such as happiness, sadness, anger, fear and disgust. You should be aware of your emotional state and ensure you only show a positive, confident and pleasing expression.

- **Gestures** – many people talk with their hands; some more than others. Ensure that any hand gestures you make are not misinterpreted.

- **Touch** – used as a way of communicating. A clear distinction should be made between personal and professional communication. A firm handshake is a professional reassuring approach upon first meeting. A warm hug would be far too familiar and unprofessional within the work environment (although an appropriate way to greet a good friend).

- **Space** – the need for personal space differs from person to person. Invading a person's space can communicate signals for intimacy, aggression or dominance, all of which are inappropriate. Maintain your own personal space and respect the space of your client.

Effective and successful communication will depend on your ability to self reflect, to be emotionally self-aware and to critique your own non-verbal communication skills in relation to the message you are sending out. Pay attention and be attentive to your athletes to fully understand the message they are conveying. A good way to hone your skills is to observe yourself in action through a digital recording (ensure you have the consent of those you are videoing – if they are aged under 16 parental consent will need to be sought). Watch your performance while identifying your strengths and any areas for improvement. Reflective learning will be addressed in Chapter 17 (Industrial placement).

Personal skills required for employment

Chapters 1 to 14 focused upon the knowledge, understanding and practical requirements which you need to be a successful sports coach. This section addresses those additional personal skills required for employment within the industry. You should focus on implementing and developing these skills during your work-based learning so they are seamless during your industrial placement.

Figure 16.3 Additional personal skills required for employment

Listening

Listening is one of the most important skills that a coach can have. Your ability to listen to your players will have a major impact on how effective you are as a coach, as well as affecting the quality of the relationships that you form. Listening enables you to learn, understand and obtain information.

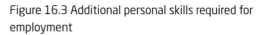

Stop and think

When you are listening during a team briefing, how much information do you really hear?

Research suggests that you remember 25 to 50 per cent of the information presented to you. During a 30-minute briefing, it might be that you will listen to between approximately 7.5 to 15 minutes only. Reflect on your ability to listen – how do you feel you could improve your listening skills, and therefore the amount of information you receive?

By developing your listening skills, you can improve your productivity and negotiation skills, as well as avoiding any misunderstanding and conflict.

Enthusiasm

Enthusiasm is paramount. It is the energy that you create to bring about a successful outcome. To have enthusiasm you need to have an interest in your subject and a knowledge and belief in yourself. Always be enthusiastic, but also realistic about what you and your athletes or team can achieve. People do not gravitate towards boring people.

Enthusiasm can act like a magnet, and people tend to be drawn to those who are enthusiastic because they are upbeat and positive. However, over-enthusiastic people can be too intense; they tend to invade the space of others and may even repel them.

Self-discipline

Self-discipline is an important tool whether you are employed or self-employed. It is the ability, regardless of emotional state, to take action. Actions will vary from being punctual, carrying out professional practice and thorough preparation to developing new behaviour and thought patterns. It is your ability to use your willpower to accomplish an objective, despite wishing you were doing something else. Self-discipline can be developed and trained.

Self-motivation

Self-motivation is your ability to motivate yourself. You will have a reason to accomplish an objective and find the strength to achieve without the need for persuasion or support from others. It is the ability to be able to motivate yourself to overcome setbacks, unfair criticism, overcome others' negative attitude towards you and general resistance and barriers in life and at work.

Organisation

Organisation is the ability to plan and coordinate your personal and professional schedules. Many professionals can help, for example:

- a life coach can help organise life issues
- a secretary can help with time management
- a psychologist can help to manage the mind.

However, you will be required to take responsibility for all organisational matters. Having good organisation skills will help to improve aspects such as productivity, success, creativity, efficient working practices and cost effectiveness.

Leadership

A leader is someone who guides and inspires, and sets a new direction and vision for others. This is important within the workplace, particularly if you are working as part of a multidisciplinary team. It is an essential component of your athlete or team relationship to lead you both to the intended goal. To be a good leader you need to make sure that the entire team understands their role, and is included when goals are being set.

Team building

Team building is an essential skill for any manager or leader. Building a strong relationship between team members improves productivity and therefore team success. To be able to do this you must understand each and every one of your team in terms of their strengths, weaknesses and personalities. You must draw upon your leadership and motivational skills in order to develop the ability to work as a team.

Equality and diversity

Equality and diversity should be embraced and embedded. Equality gives every individual the opportunity to achieve their potential. This should be done free from any prejudice and discrimination to develop a fairer society. Diversity is about recognising individual or group differences, treating people accordingly and valuing everyone positively. Equality and diversity is further addressed in Chapter 14 (Ethics and good practice).

Customer care

Customer care is fundamental in any business. It involves ensuring that systems are in place to maximise client satisfaction, and that everyone is trained to deal appropriately with customers. If you are self-employed this responsibility fundamentally lies with you. Excellent customer care is vital to the success of your business, for example, coaching session bookings, and links directly to profit. Profitability is dependent on customer service.

Stop and think

When have you received good customer care? Why was the care you received as a customer good? When have you received poor customer care and why was it poor? What would make you return as a customer?

Time to reflect

1. Considering all the information in this chapter, on a scale of 1 to 10 (1 being inexperienced and 10 being highly experienced) where do you feel you are?

2. Reflect on your verbal communication skills, identify your strengths and weaknesses.

3. Reflect on your non-verbal communication skills, identify your strengths and weaknesses.

4. Identify the roles you need to undertake as a self-employed sports coach.

5. Identify the roles you may undertake working as part of a large multi-disciplinary team.

6. Identify seven components of non-verbal communication. Consider four components.

7. Briefly consider eight personal skills a therapist needs to gain employment.

8. Consider the additional skill of listening.

9. Define equality.

10. Reflect on your own practice and identify six strengths.

11. Reflect on your own practice. Identify four areas needing improvement and set yourself actions for improvement.

Useful resources

To obtain a secure link to the websites below, see the Websites section on page ii or visit the companion website at www.pearsonfe.co.uk/foundationsinsport.

- Business Link

- Mind Tools

Further reading

Brounstein, M. (2001) *Communicating Effectively for Dummies*. Chichester: John Wiley & Sons.

Cassidy, T., Jones, R., Potrac, P. (2004) *Understanding Sports Coaching: The social, cultural and pedagogical foundations of coaching practice*. London: Routledge.

Cook, S. (2008) *Customer care excellence. How to create an effective customer focus*. Kogan Page.

Grodzki, L. (2000) *Building Your Ideal Private Practice: A Guide for Therapists and Other Healing Professionals*. W. W. Norton & Co

Jones, R. L., Armour, K. M., & Potrac, P. (2004) *Sports Coaching Cultures*. London: Routledge.

Jones, R.L., Armour, K.M. and Potrac, P. (2004) *The Cultures of Coaching*.London: Longman.

Leland, K. and Bailey, K. (2006) *Customer Service for Dummies*. Chichester: John Wiley & sons.

Lyle, J. (2002). *Sports coaching concepts: A framework for coaches' behaviour*. London: Routledge.

Smith, A. and Stewart, B. (1999) *Sports Management: A Guide to Professional Practice*. Oxford: Allen & Unwin.

Industrial placement

Introduction

Your industrial placement will allow you to put into practice the theoretical knowledge and techniques you have learned, along with the additional skills you explored in Chapter 16 (Work-based learning). The organisation in which you complete your industrial placement will expect you to perform to industry standards from the start, to be proactive and to have clear aims and objectives with regard to your personal and professional development – and to be able to reflect on your development.

Before you start any placement, your university or college will expect you to set targets, demonstrate the ability to engage in reflective practice throughout your placement using the Kolb learning cycle or Gibbs reflective cycle, and set new targets during your time in placement. It is particularly important that you develop your ability to reflect on what you have done and learnt whilst on your placement.

A key issue for you is to seek out opportunities to complete your work placement and to convince potential providers of the benefits they will gain by offering you an industrial placement.

This chapter will provide support when you are writing your letter of application and putting together your curriculum vitae. It will also help you to develop your knowledge and understanding of how to reflect upon your targets set and your experience of your placement.

Learning outcomes

After you have read this chapter you should be able to:

- write a letter of application
- write a curriculum vitae
- understand reflective practice
- describe Kolb's learning cycle
- describe Gibbs' reflective cycle.

Using the information you sourced in your starting block activity in Chapter 16, analyse which organisation you feel it is realistic to apply to in order to complete your industrial placement. Ensure that you consider:

- your ability to travel to the placement in terms of distance, location, transport and cost
- the hours of work you are able to fulfil
- the added value of the experience you will gain.

Writing a letter of application

Potential workplace providers will receive many requests from students for placements so you need to make sure your letter is noticed. See Table 17.1 for some key points to remember.

Table 17.1 Dos and don'ts when requesting work placements

Do	Don't
<ul><li>make your message clear</li><li>demonstrate a logical order representing your ideas and thoughts</li><li>proofread your letter for spelling and grammar</li><li>use the correct opening and closing phrase</li></ul>	<ul><li>use terms such as read now, urgent or help</li><li>provide too much information – this will overload the reader</li><li>use slang or abbreviations</li><li>be over familiar</li></ul>

When you write a letter of application you should:

1. put your address at the top right-hand corner

2. place the address of the person you are writing to on the left-hand side below your address

3. put the date below this on the right

4. always address your letter to somebody using their correct title, for example, Mr Cox or Ms Cox. Using first name terms to a person you do not know is over familiar and unprofessional. Using the title Mrs or Miss incorrectly can offend, therefore Ms is preferable. If you do not know the name of the person you are writing to you should address the letter Dear Sir or Madam

5. use your opening paragraph to convey the purpose of your letter; it is the most important element. Provide a clear, concise summary of your message, no longer than a couple of lines. Your letter should then go on to give information to support your message

6. structure your letter in a coherent manner. This is achieved by putting forward your ideas in structured sentences. These allow the reader to clearly understand each element of information being delivered. The sentences should be constructed in a logical order, allowing the reader to formulate a complete picture of the message you are delivering. Make sure you use accurate spelling and correct grammar and sentence structure. Read your letter out loud to ensure that it reads correctly and flows well. Get another person to proofread your letter

7. use the last paragraph of your letter to state what you would like the person to do as a result of your letter and thank them

8. end your letter correctly. Use 'Yours sincerely' if you know the name of the person to whom you are writing, or 'Yours faithfully' if you do not.

The Firs
10 Wintergreen Lane
Milford
Lancashire

Badgers Cottage
Lilliput lane
The Sidings
Little Harrowden
Bedfordshire
BE1 DG11   18 June 2010

Dear Mr Cox or Dear Sir or Madam

Text of opening paragraph should provide a clear summary.

The main body of your letter should be well structured and your last paragraph should state what you would like the person to do.

Yours sincerely or Yours faithfully

Your signature

Your name typed

Figure 17.1 Template for a letter of application

Writing a curriculum vitae (CV)

A CV, sometimes also known as a resumé, is a logical overview of your working life. It is important to ensure your potential work placement provider notices you. It must be concise and accurate and needs to be thorough to highlight all relevant information. You should view your CV as your chance to sell yourself to your potential work-placement provider. You are selling your skills, qualifications, experience and ultimately your ability to contribute to the organisation.

Many CV templates are available on the internet for free but there is no perfect one. CV format will differ from person to person and situation to situation. The CV you construct for your work placement will be different from that of someone who has more years of experience and qualifications than you and who is applying for a job.

Consider how relevant information is when you are constructing your CV, and whether or not it will help you to sell yourself to the prospective organisation. What you must not do is draw attention to your weaknesses. For example, if you have a valid driving licence then this could be an advantage so include it on your CV. However, if you do not have a driving licence or have failed your test twice, do not include the information and draw attention to weaknesses.

What to put in your CV

Essential details to include in your CV are listed below.

Personal details

- Name.
- Contact details – ensure these are personal details and not work details. Phone numbers included should be those which you are most accessible on. Email is a very accessible communication method.
- NB Nationality is not required.
- Marital status and family – this is optional.
- Date of birth – again, this is optional (age discrimination is illegal in the recruitment process under the Employment Equality (age) regulations 2006).

Education

- Include clearly the qualification and year of study (the institution is optional). Present the information starting with the most recent. For example:

  September 2008 – June 2011, FdSc Sports Coaching, Distinction, University name

- Include further education and school education. You may or may not wish to highlight GCSE grades.
- If you have additional qualifications which are vocationally-related, such as coaching, umpiring or first-aid qualifications, you may wish to include a heading 'Vocational qualifications', particularly if you have a strong educational background. This will further sell your skills and abilities. If your education is weak and you have not entered into too much detail, you should include other qualifications here. This will enhance your education section and appear stronger to the prospective organisation.

Experience

- List all relevant experience you have gained. Include all employment and be prepared to be questioned on any gaps in your employment.
- If you do not have an extensive employment history you should highlight experiences such as a gap year experience, part-time employment, voluntary work, charity work, summer camps, unpaid work, internships or association memberships. Provide a concise description of your experience for each.
- If your employment history is extensive and you have additional experiences to offer you may wish to use the headings 'Employment history' and 'Experiences' to strengthen your CV.

Additional information and sections you may want to include in your CV include the following.

Personal statement

This should grab the reader's attention. It should detail your attributes and goals and be no longer than 50 words. If you have a strong CV you could combine this section with your letter of application.

Skills

The skills you detail should be specific to the position for which you are applying and demonstrate that you would be a positive addition to the organisation. Provide a summary of job-related and transferable skills.

Job-related

These skills are related to the position for which you are applying and should be directly related to your industrial placement. For a summary, look at the title of the chapters within this book.

Transferable skills

All foundation degrees have a wide range of transferable skills embedded into the programmes. Transferable skills include teamwork, synthesis and analysing information, presentation, communication and problem solving.

Hobbies and interests

This section highlights you as a person. Your hobbies and interests can reflect your motivation, personality traits and personal skills. This section should still be related to the position applied for and sell you in a positive light. If it does not, then you should think about omitting it from your CV.

References

Do not provide any references on your CV. If the organisation wants this information they will ask you for it, or ask for it to be detailed on an application form. They should ask your permission to contact your referees either before an interview or upon appointment. You would not want your current employer to be approached for a reference when they do not know you have applied for another job – particularly if you are not appointed. For your industrial placement you may wish to put your supervisor's contact details here as an exception to the rule.

There are many CV templates available on the internet. You should consider which style is most appropriate to present the information you have. Here are two examples for you to consider:

- CV 1 – This format is appropriate for a person who has limited experience, but a strong educational background. It allows you to exploit your strengths, training, education and qualifications. The examples below are templates that you can adapt to your particular experience (editable versions are available at www. pearsonfe.co.uk/foundationsinsport)

Your name
Your address
Telephone number(s)
Email address

Profile
A brief, relevant description of you, including sector experience and your level of seniority.

Key strengths
- Item One – A sentence about your best skills
- Item Two – A sentence about your best skills
- Item Three – A sentence about your best skills
- Item Four – A sentence about your best skills
- Item Five – A sentence about your best skills

Employment history (most recent first)

Employer name   Date on right

Job title and description of job role.

Relevant key achievements
- 1st achievement (use active verbs wherever possible)
- 2nd achievement
- 3rd achievement

Employer name   Date on right
Job title and description of job role.

Relevant key achievements
- 1st achievement
- 2nd achievement
- 3rd achievement

Training, Education & Qualifications

Add relevant and notable items only with dates.
Mention your school or college if it is a recognised centre of excellence.
Recent substantial training courses.

Personal information
Marital status (optional), languages, relevant IT skills

- CV 2 – This format is ideal for a person who has a strong work experience background and can provide specific information about each placement.

Name
Address 1
Address 2
Postcode
Telephone number
Email address

Profile

Profile description Profile description Profile description Profile description Profile description Profile description Profile description Profile description Profile description Profile description Profile description Profile

Work experience

Dates | Job title
Employer name
Employer address

Key responsibilities
- Responsibility One
- Responsibility Two
- Responsibility Three
- Responsibility Four
- etc.

Key achievements
- Achievement One
- Achievement Two
- Achievement Three
- Achievement Four
- etc.

Dates | **Job title**
Employer name
Employer address

Key responsibilities
- Responsibility One
- Responsibility Two
- Responsibility Three
- Responsibility Four
- etc.

Key achievements
- Achievement One
- Achievement Two
- Achievement Three
- Achievement Four
- etc.

Dates | Job title
Employer name
Employer address

Key responsibilities
- Responsibility One
- Responsibility Two
- Responsibility Three
- Responsibility Four
- etc.

Key achievements
- Achievement One
- Achievement Two
- Achievement Three
- Achievement Four
- etc.

Qualifications

Dates | Qualification title
Details of qualification

References

Name of first referee
Job title of first referee
Appropriate contact details of first referee
Name of second referee
Job title of second referee
Appropriate contact details of second referee

Reflective practice

Reflective practice is about developing purposeful learning. It involves you looking at your experiences in more depth in order to learn for next time. It will develop your personal and professional growth and develop your ability to link theory and practice.

For your industrial placement, you will be required to set targets and reflect upon your progress in achieving your targets, and your experiences during your placement. Reflective practice is essential to help you learn from your experience, and to develop. This process should be continuous, both on a personal and professional level.

There are many academic theories to facilitate your reflective practice. The most popular used by universities and colleges within the industrial placement module are Kolb's learning cycle and Gibbs' reflective cycle.

Kolb learning cycle

In 1984 David Kolb published his learning styles model. This is known by various names, including Kolb's experiential learning theory, Kolb's learning styles inventory and the Kolb cycle. Kolb suggests four stages to his model which can be entered at any stage, although they must be followed in sequence thereafter to ensure learning takes place. The four stages are as follows.

1. **Concrete experience** – the '**doing**' phase. This is your experience while completing your industrial placement.

2. **Reflective observation** – the reflective process of your industrial experience. You will **self reflect** throughout the placement by keeping a log. You may also obtain feedback from your supervisor, colleagues, peers, players and

clients. These aspects can be drawn together to give an overall reflection of your industrial placement. Note that reflection on its own is not sufficient; you could complete this stage for the next 15, 20 or 30 years of your sports coaching career and not develop personally and professionally.

3. **Abstract conceptualisation** – this stage allows you to **review and draw conclusions** from your reflection. It is accompanied by you carrying out further research within the field of sports coaching and more input from your lecturers and other developmental activities. This will help you to plan what you would do differently next time.

4. **Active experimentation** – this is where you **implement your changes** within your industrial experience and therefore continue the cycle into the concrete experience stage. This cycle is continuous and ongoing throughout your industrial experience.

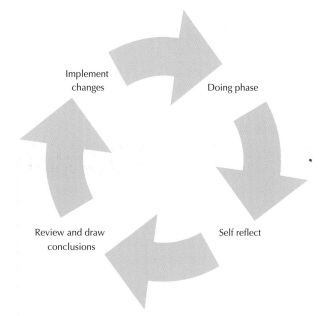

Figure 17.2 Kolb learning cycle

Kolb learning cycle reprinted from Kolb, David A., Experiential Learning: Experience as a Source of Learning & Development, 1st Edition, © 1984. Adapted by permission of Pearson Education, Inc., Upper Saddle River, NJ.

Gibbs' reflective cycle

Developed by Professor Graham Gibbs, the Gibbs' reflective cycle (1988) consists of six stages. It is one of the few models to take emotion into account.

1. **Description** – describe exactly what happened during your work placement. You should keep a detailed log of each day. Depending on the nature of your placement you may have a timetable to follow; for example, you may conduct coaching sessions on the hour every hour in a morning, or you may have a training session timetabled in the evening; if this is the case you may decide to describe each session individually rather than a whole day at a time.

2. **Feelings** – for each of your descriptions, document what you were thinking and feeling at the time. You may comment on how confident you felt – did you feel that you could not answer a question because of lack of knowledge or did you feel you could not communicate effectively with an athlete or parent?

3. **Evaluation** – for each experience you should list points (both good and bad). For example, it may be good that you were gaining experience coaching children aged under 9 years; but it was not very good when you witnessed an injury during the session, because you were unsure exactly what to do and had to look to others for guidance.

4. **Analysis** – analyse what sense you can make out of the situation. What does it mean? Using the example in point 3, you could analyse that your knowledge of dealing with injuries is poor and due to your lack of experience and the shock, you were unable to control the situation and deal with the injury.

5. **Conclusion** – conclude and document what else you could have done, or perhaps should have done, during that experience. Do you need to complete a first-aid course, or revise a course that you previously attended?

6. **Action plan** – if the situation arose again, what would you do differently, and how will you adapt your practice in the light of this new understanding? For example, if you witnessed an open fracture, you could set actions to include gaining more supervised pitch-side experience and attending a refresher first-aid course.

The cycle is only momentarily complete – should the situation arise again, you will have developed personally and professionally to deal with the situation and the new event will become a focus of the reflective cycle. Development is a continuous process.

Figure 17.3 Gibbs' reflective cycle (adapted from Gibbs, 1988). Use the cycle to reflect on a recent sports match you competed in or a training session.

Time to reflect

1. Explore the variety of CV templates and assess which template is most suitable for you.

2. Investigate five organisations where you could complete your industrial placement.

3. For each placement describe the skills you have to offer.

4. Write a letter of application for your chosen placement. Read the letter aloud and proofread it, making any changes as necessary. Now ask a peer, friend or family member to proofread the letter, marking any changes you need to make.

5. Discuss the headings which are fundamental to your CV.

6. Discuss the headings which are additional to your CV.

7. Construct a CV using an appropriate CV template from the internet.

8. Summarise Kolb's learning cycle.

9. Summarise Gibbs' reflective cycle.

10. Choose which reflective cycle you are going to use to facilitate reflection during your industrial placement and provide a justification.

11. Use your chosen cycle to complete a reflection for a chosen activity.

12. Using the learning cycle of your choice (e.g. Kolb or Gibbs) from chapter 17, monitor where you are now, the actions you have set yourself, and the development you have made over a set period of time.

Useful resources

To obtain a secure link to the websites below, see the Websites section on page ii or visit the companion website at www.pearsonfe.co.uk/foundationsinsport.

• Business Link

Further reading

Boud, D., Cressey, P. and Docherty, P. (eds.) (2005) *Productive Reflection at Work: Learning for Changing Organizations*. London: Routledge.

Brounstein, M. (2001) *Communicating Effectively for Dummies*. Chichester: John Wiley & Sons.

Field, S. (2010) *Career opportunities in the sports industry* New York: Ferguson.

Gibbs, G. (1988). *Learning by Doing: A Guide to Teaching and Learning Methods*. Oxford: Oxford Polytechnic.

Jones, R. (2006) *The Sports Coach as Educator*. Oxford: Routledge.

Jones, R., Armour, K., Potrac, p. (2004) Sports coaching cultures. London: Routledge.

Jones, R., Hughes, M. and Kingston, K. (2010*) An introduction to sports coaching. From science and theory to practice.* Oxford: Routledge.

Kolb, D. A. (1984) *Experiential Learning Experience as a Source of Learning and Development*. New Jersey: Prentice Hall.

Smith, A. and Stewart, B. (1999) *Sports Management: A Guide to Professional Practice*. Australia: Allen & Unwin.

Robinson, P. (2010) *Foundations in Sports Coaching*. Oxford: Routledge.

Chapter 18

Case study: sports coach

Context

The University of Bath is synonymous with academic excellence and sport. Over the last ten years, it has developed its sporting infrastructure to be one of the finest concentrations of sporting facilities in the country. The centrepiece is the £30 million Sports Training Village (STV), which was built with funding from the National Lottery, the Lawn Tennis Association, and the university. The STV is the home of the English Institute of Sport, South West. Facilities include:

- state-of-the-art fitness suite
- main sports hall (12 badminton courts or three netball courts in size)
- indoor tennis hall (eight courts)
- ten outdoor tennis courts (hard and clay)
- martial arts dojo
- 140m indoor athletics straight
- outdoor eight lane 400m athletics track
- indoor throws and jumps hall

- fencing salle
- pistol shooting hall
- 50m indoor swimming pool
- bobsleigh and bob-skeleton push-start track
- two astro pitches
- two beach volleyball pitches
- sauna, hydrotherapy pool and ice bath
- physiotherapy suite
- sports science laboratories.

More than 2000 children each week visit the university to participate in sporting activities. More than 4000 students participate in the dozens of sports and leisure clubs. These participants can then choose to engage in competitive sport through representing the university in its scores of teams that compete in the British University and College Sport (BUCS) Championships. It is the elite athletes who use the facilities that catch the media attention. These include: Amy Williams (bob-skeleton), Pamela Cookey (netball), and Ben Rushgrove (athletics).

Particular sports have had tremendous success: four Olympic medals for modern pentathlon and two for bob-skeleton, a netball programme that has produced 27 England senior or under-21 international players since 2006, and a badminton programme that produced three of the ten players that comprised the England Commonwealth Games team in Delhi in 2010.

At the centre of each of the categories of university sport is a coach. The STV is an employment hub for more than 40 full-time and more than 100 part-time coaches.

Meet Peter

Peter Bush, 43, began employment at the University of Bath in July 1998.

Peter Bush: Badminton England's High Performance Centre Coach at the University of Bath

Peter's qualifications include:

- BSc (Hons) Sports Science
- UKCC Level 1 and Level 2 Certificate in Coaching Badminton.

Continuous and Professional Development:

- working towards UKCC Level 3 Certificate in Coaching Badminton
- attendance at coaching conferences and workshops.

Background

Peter has been a professional badminton player and has developed into an expert coaching practitioner. As is the case for the majority of coaches who were formerly elite athletes, these experiences are not separate but occur simultaneously.

Playing experience:

- Senior England International player for ten years (1988–1998)
- 12 Senior caps for England
- represented England in three World Championships, European Championships and the 1996 Thomas Cup Finals
- highest world ranking of 32
- highest English senior ranking of 2
- National Junior Men's Singles Champion.

Coaching experience:

- High Performance Centre Coach (1998 to present day)
- England U17 National Age Group coach (2002–2006)
- International Badminton Federation (IBF) technician (1995–1998)
- Head Coach at the Östersundom IF badminton club (Finland) summer training camps (1995–1997)
- Head Coach at eight Danish badminton clubs. Senior and junior players from recreational to elite level (1991–1998)
- Head Coach at Kristiansand badminton club (Norway) for Junior players (1989–1991)
- Assistant Coach at the Andrew Ryan International Badminton Summer School (1986–1994).

Peter's development as a coach was symbiotic with his playing career. His first formal coaching appointment was working on the International Badminton Summer School, led by his coach and mentor Andrew Ryan. After completing his BSc (Honours) degree in Sports Science at Chelsea School of Human Movement in 1989, Peter relocated at the age of 21 to Norway to take up a role as Head Coach to the junior players at Kristiansand badminton club. To further his playing career, once again he relocated, this time to Denmark. Over a period of seven years, he coached at eight different clubs in Denmark, working with junior and senior players from recreational to elite level. To communicate with these players, Peter became fluent in Danish. During this time, he continued to represent England at badminton on the international stage, while competing in a range of domestic English and Danish tournaments. Peter remains, to date, the only player who has simultaneously been ranked in the top ten of the English and Danish men's singles rankings.

At the end of his playing career, Peter returned to England to take up his role as the Head Coach at the University of Bath. The University of Bath is one of only two High Performance Centres (HPCs) in Badminton England's structure. The other HPC is located at Leeds Metropolitan University. The primary function of the HPCs is to develop players to a level where they can become incorporated into the training set-up at the National Badminton Centre in Milton Keynes. Normally, this transition occurs on completion of their academic studies.

Coaching career highlights include the following.

- Chris Coles, HPC squad member, wins Individual Gold in the 2011 European Junior Championships

- Head badminton coach for the Great Britain team at the 2011 World University Games in Shenzhen, China

- numerous current and former HPC squad members are English Senior and Junior National Champions

- part of the England coaching team which won team gold in the 2007 European Junior Championships and Individual Gold in the men's doubles

- part of the England coaching team which won team gold in the under 17 six nations event. This was the first time that any team, apart from Denmark, had won the event in its 27-year history

- Coach to Richard Vaughn (Former World number 7, double Olympian, and European and Commonwealth Games medallist)

- Coach at the 1st Continental Coaching Camp (1997; Cape Town)

- Coach at the 1st World Badminton Academy (1995; Paris)

- Coach to the University of Bath's men's and women's teams which have won several BUCS Team Championships and Individual BUCS titles.

Peter feels strongly that his athletes should not only excel in their badminton development, but also focus strongly on their academic studies. He is proud that, in his thirteen years as Head Coach, he has seen the vast majority of his elite players achieve a high-class undergraduate degree or master's degree from the University of Bath. Although his players tend to pursue one of the sports-related degree programmes (BA in Coach Education and Sports Development, BSc in Sport and Exercise Science, or the FD in Sport (Sports Performance)), a number have graduated from studies in diverse subject areas such as Architecture, Mathematics, Pharmacy and Pharmacology.

Peter's responsibilities

Peter reports directly to Badminton England's Performance Manager and the Director of Sport at the University of Bath. As a sports coach, his responsibilities include:

- providing high quality badminton coaching to the following groups of players:

    1. full-time elite players on World Class Funding

    2. student athletes that are on World Class Funding

    3. student athletes on the Talented Athlete Scholarship Scheme (TASS)

    4. student athletes that represent the university in BUCS

    5. junior players that are part of the regional talent pool

- developing tournament and training programmes for his players

- managing all administration for his badminton programme

- liaising with support staff (physiotherapists, strength and conditioning coaches, doctors, nutritionists, and psychologists etc.)

- attending national and international tournaments in a coaching capacity.

A 'typical' working day

The main segments of Peter's day are the on-court sessions with his players. Normally, the World Class and TASS funded athletes will receive two on-court sessions of two hours in duration each day, and Peter will then do an evening session with the university BUCS players or the junior players who are part of the regional talent pool. These evening sessions usually run for four hours.

Before the first on-court training session of the day, with the World Class and TASS funded student athletes, Peter will spend an hour catching up on email communications with support staff, players, and parents. During this time, the athletes will arrive in the coaching environment and prepare themselves for the court session to come. Players are expected to arrive at the sports hall at least 20 minutes prior to the session in order to be ready for training. Peter works with men's and women's singles, doubles and mixed doubles players; therefore, the coaching environment is a complex work place. The different demands of each of the disciplines require specific drills and skills to be undertaken. Added layers of complexity emerge throughout the court session, such as injury, fatigue and illness, which require Peter to think on his feet and adapt the session accordingly.

At the end of the morning court session, players take responsibility for their post-training regime. Peter will use the time immediately at the end of the session to talk with players about any issues that they are experiencing. The break between court sessions is two hours, to allow for the players to rehydrate and refuel for the afternoon session. Peter spends this time preparing for the afternoon court session and in carrying out more administrative duties.

Even in group coaching situations, do you think that it is important for a participant to receive individual feedback?

The same expectations are in place for the afternoon session. The players arrive early and prepare for their training. The players who are injured or require specific physical development will depart for work in the gym or on the track. The afternoon session has three components; individual work with Peter, personal development work (self-directed developmental work), and match play. Once again, the end of session routine is observed.

More administrative duties follow in the time between the World Class/TASS-funded player sessions and the evening court session with the university BUCS players. This session requires Peter to change the emphasis of his coaching from one that is exclusively about developing the performance of his athletes, to one that is fundamentally about participation and enjoyment.

At times, Peter has to work unsociable hours – including weekends – and may sometimes work for several weeks without having a full day off, particularly during the competition season. However, he has a passion for his job and for badminton. He enjoys seeing his players develop their badminton proficiency, but also derives a great deal of satisfaction from the academic and social development he sees in his players during their time under his guidance.

Work ethic

Peter has transferred his strong work ethic from his playing career to his coaching career. Working as a sports coach can be hard and you have to be prepared to put in the hours. The work is not just about the time on court with players, it is about undertaking the multiple additional roles associated with running a high performance coaching centre, or indeed any coaching role. Peter draws an analogy of his coaching job being very much like an iceberg. The visible part is the bit that everyone can see and is typically used to describe what it means to be a coach. However, in reality, there is a considerable amount of work that goes on 'underneath the water line' to enable Peter to coach effectively. The paperwork in the office, establishing and maintaining relationships, continuous professional development, conversations with multiple stakeholders (players, parents, officials, sponsors, NGBs, physiotherapists, lifestyle advisors, academic tutors, and support staff etc.) among many other tasks, are all examples of the essential work undertaken by Peter behind the scenes.

Identify the skills and attributes that Peter must use in the coaching environment.

Activity

A player has come to Peter after a coaching session, asking to meet with him in private. During the conversation that followed, it transpires that the player has been going through a very tough time personally following a relationship breaking down. The result of this is that the player has put on a 'brave face' during the training sessions and found comfort through their badminton participation, but has hidden themselves away from other aspects of their life. The player explains that they have not been attending lectures for their academic programme. With assessment deadlines fast approaching, the player is very concerned that they will not be able to complete the assessments on time and maintain the same focus on their badminton participation.

Put yourself in Peter's shoes and describe how you would help this player in this context and situation.

Check your understanding (for answers, see www.pearsonfe.co.uk/foundationsinsport)

1. How do you think that Peter's playing career helped him to become an elite coach?

2. How important is it to communicate effectively with your participants and stakeholders? Do you think that it was essential that Peter became fluent in Danish when living, playing and coaching in Denmark?

3. Peter's typical working day includes working with participation, development and performance level participants. Consider these differences in and around the management of the coaching process and what this might mean for your own coaching practice.

4. Investigate how important universities are to Great Britain's Olympic medal aspirations.

5. Universities are a significant employer of sports coaches. Investigate the sporting and coaching infrastructure at a range of other UK universities.

6. Identify the multiple roles that Peter undertakes in his job. Think about your own multifaceted coaching role and consider how you can build on this in your own coaching practice.

7. Investigate the National Occupational Standards (NOS) that form the basis of coaching qualifications. Identify key areas that you need to develop and produce an action plan for enhancing your coaching skills and abilities.

8. Why is it important for the participants to take responsibility for sections of their coaching session? Consider how you can build this into your own coaching practice.

9. Consider what Peter's coaching philosophy statement might look like. How does this compare to yours?

10. Use the internet to investigate current job vacancies in sports coaching. Use the findings of your investigation to map out your coaching development journey.

Useful resources

To obtain a secure link to the websites below, see the Websites section on page ii or visit the companion website at www.pearsonfe.co.uk/foundationsinsport.

- Team Bath
- English Institute of Sport
- Badminton England
- UK Sport (Jobs in sport)
- sports coach UK
- Sport and Recreation Alliance

Further reading

Cassidy, T., Jones, R.L. and Potrac, P. (2009). *Understanding sports coaching: the social, cultural and pedagogical foundations of coaching practice* (2nd edition). London: Routledge.

Denison, J. (ed.). (1997). *Coaching knowledge: understanding the dynamics of sport performance*. London: A&C Black.

Jones, R.L., Armour, K.M. and Potrac, P. (2004). *Sports coaching cultures: from practice to theory*. London: Routledge.

Kidman, L. and Hanrahan, S. (2011). *The coaching process: a practical guide to improving your effectiveness* (3rd edition). Palmerston North: Dunmore.

Lombardo, B.J. (1987). *The humanistic coach: from theory to practice*. Springfield, Ill: C.C. Thomas.

Rynne, S.B., Mallett, C. and Tinning, R. (2006). High performance sport coaching: institutes of sport as sites for learning. *International Journal of Sports Science and Coaching*, 1 (3), 223-234.

Glossary

Acceleration – acceleration = force/mass OR (average) is the change in velocity/change

Achievement goals – personal definitions of the meaning of success

Activities of daily living – the things that you normally do in your daily life at home or at work

Aerobic – cellular respiration requiring oxygen

Agency – an organisation that is responsible for the promotion and administration of an activity, such as sport

Agility – the physical ability that enables a person to rapidly change body position and direction in a precise manner

Agonist – the muscle producing the action (movement)

Aim – something that you want to achieve (a goal) e.g. 'for everyone to be able to do a parallel turn in skiing by the end of the session'

Ambiguity – inexactness or being open to more than one interpretation

Anaerobic respiration – cellular respiration not requiring oxygen

Ankylosing spondylitis – an inflammatory arthritis affecting mainly the joints in the spine and the sacroilium in the pelvis. However, other joints of the body may also be affected as well as tissues including the heart, eyes, lungs and kidneys

Antagonist – the muscle opposing the action (movement)

Anteriorly – towards the front

Anticipation – the learned ability to make advance judgements in sport based on past experience in similar situations

Anxiety - a negative emotional state that is characterised by worry and apprehension in relation to perceived psychological threat or harm

Aponeurosis – a flat, broad tendon

Appendicular skeleton – all the parts that are joined to the head and trunk (axial)

Apply – the transference of information and knowledge you have gained to your topic, or application to practical aspects

Arousal – a general activation of our physiological and energy systems

Arteries – carry blood away from the heart, usually oxygenated

Arterioles – connect arteries to capillaries

Articular cartilage – (also known as hyaline cartilage) is smooth and covers the surface of bones

Articulation – the contact of two or more bones at a specific location

Asymmetric tonic reflex – the unconscious (automatic) muscular reaction linking head movement with arm movements like an archer pose

Athlete – a person who competes in organised sporting events

Athlete-centred – term applied to ensuring that the individual is at the centre of your considerations when coaching

Autocratic – an instructional and coach-centred style of coaching

Autocratic leader – in sport a leader who takes control of the athlete, dictating their actions and decisions. Autocratic leaders rarely consider the perspective of the athlete and their opinion of athletes is heavily influenced by successful or unsuccessful performances

Automaticity – expert performance of a learned skill where the action is executed with little conscious thought but in a mature and consistent manner

Axial skeleton – the head and trunk of the body

Balance – the ability to retain the centre of mass of the body above the base of support

Balanced diet – a healthy eating plan constituting the appropriate amount of nutrients for an individual's needs

Ballistic training – rapid and vigorous limb actions associated with the development of speed

Barrier to participation – a social factor that limits or blocks access to involvement in a particular organised activity

Bioenergetics – the energy system requirements of the sport based on information from the time–motion analysis (ATP-PC, fast glycolysis, slow glycolysis and oxidative)

Biological age – this will often be different from the actual age of a child as young people develop at different rates for lots of different reasons

Bottom-up approach – community-led sports development programmes that are better aligned to the specific needs of a local community

Bracketed morality – the suspension of an individual's normal or everyday level of morality, which remains for the duration of a sports contest

Capillaries – allow for gaseous exchange at the tissue cells and connect arterioles to venules

Career coaches – term applied to those coaches who are paid on a full-time basis for their coaching services

Catabolism – breaking down of molecules

Centrality – the exclusion of ethnic minorities from central positions of power and decision making in team sports and organisations

Chronological age – the age of the child in years and months. This is important to note as it may help you to assess how psychologically mature a child is and ready for intensity of coaching

Closeness – the emotional tone of the relationship

Coaching environment – the physical space in which sports coaching activities take place

Coaching philosophy – a set of values and behaviours that serve to guide the actions of a coach

Cognitive anxiety – the mental component of anxiety (e.g, worries and apprehension)

Cognitive appraisal – a mental evaluation that leads to an interpretation of a specific event (such as a sport injury)

Commitment – the degree of commitment to the relationship

Communities of practice – a group of people who share a common interest or profession. The group can evolve naturally over time or can be established specifically with the goal of developing knowledge or sharing good practice

Compare – addressing the similarities and differences presented in the information you have gathered

Compartmentalise – divide into separate and distinct sections or categories

Complementarity – the manner in which the roles of each party complement each other

Concentric contraction – muscle contraction generates force which causes muscle shortening

Concurrent feedback – ongoing feedback provided during an activity

Construct – it is thought that you cannot simply receive knowledge from a book or a teacher; in fact we take little bits from a wide variety of sources and create knowledge that is individual to us

Context – the situation within which something exists

Continuum – a continuous sequence [of teaching styles] in which adjacent elements are only slightly different to each other, but the extremes are quite distinct

Co-operative – offering leadership and involving athletes in decision making

Coordination – the ability to perform smooth and accurate motor tasks

Core stabilisation exercises – static exercises often using swiss balls, mats and medicine balls to strengthen abdominal muscles associated with postural control

Corrective feedback – statements that convey messages of how to improve after mistakes or poor performance

Costal cartilage – hyaline cartilage which connects the sternum to the ribs

CRB (Criminal Records Bureau Disclosure) – a legal requirement for all individuals who have contact with children, young people and vulnerable adults in their work

Culture – consists of the shared values of a group of people that guide specific behaviour

Curriculum vitae – document which provides an overview of your qualifications, employment and relevant life experience

Democratic – a problem-based and athlete-centred style of coaching

Democratic – coach cedes decision making responsibility to participants

Deontology – an approach to ethics that states that ethical action is based on adherence to rules

Development plan – using the feedback and assessment you receive as a coach can help create a development plan for future improvement

Diaphysis – main shaft of the bone

Dichotomy – the division of sports coaching into two non-overlapping theoretical traditions (science and art). Debate has existed about sports coaching comprising these two subsets that are mutually exclusive of one another

Disaffected – implies that an individual or group is alienated from the rest of society, and may be resentful or rebellious as a result

Discipline – a branch of learning or scholarly activity that is taught and researched at university level

Disempowerment – to deprive the athlete of power or influence

Domains – the term given to an area of knowledge

Dominant norms – the key values usually associated with a concept or identity. Values or ideas that inform your opinion relating to common issues in society such as gender, ethnicity and class

Dorsiflex – move the top of the foot towards the body, showing the sole of the foot

Duty of care – a legal obligation imposed on an individual, requiring that they adhere to a standard of reasonable care while performing any acts that could possibly harm others (such as the hazard of sport)

Eccentric contraction – the muscle lengthens due to the opposing force being greater than the force generated by the muscle

Effective – achieving the results that you want

Egocentric – having limited or no regard for the interests of others and focusing purely on our own

Empowerment – the control that athletes have over themselves to change things for the better

Endomysium – connective tissue encasing individual muscle fibres

Entitlements – a guarantee of access to, or a belief that one is deserving of, a particular benefit

Epimysium – connective tissue which encases all the fascicles surrounding the whole muscle

Epiphyseal growth plates – specific points at the end of long bones where the majority of physical growth occurs

Ethicist – an individual who has an interest in studying the philosophy and ethics of a particular activity, such as sport or coaching

Ethics – moral obligations and behaviours that are related to specific situations or contexts, such as within the context of coaching

Ethos – the fundamental, unwritten values and norms that are specific to a particular culture (or sport)

Evaluate – this is an assessment of the information with regard to your topic, the evidence it is based on and its relation to other ideas

Evert – move the sole of the foot away from the midline of the body

Every Child Matters – a government initiative design to ensure that every child has the support to be healthy; stay safe; enjoy and achieve; make a positive contribution; and achieve economic well-being

Exercise – activity that maintains or enhances fitness

Exercise referral scheme – the scheme that refers those who are sedentary (inactive) in order to help improve and manage health and activity

Exergaming – the term used for video games that also incorporate physical activity

Experiential learning – learning from direct experience

Extrinsic feedback – feedback from an external source, such as a coach or sport scientist

Extrinsic motivation – doing an activity because the activity is a means to an end

Facilitative – a relationship that allows for actions and processes to make things easy or easier

Fascia – fibrous tissue binding together or separating muscle

Fascicular arrangement – the arrangement of fascicles, which ultimately affects power output and range of movement

Fibrocartilage – this cartilage is very rich in type 1 collagen and is strong and durable. It can be found, for example, in the menisci of the knee and intevertebral disc

Field of view – the area that the coach or sport scientist is recording that contains the sporting action

Fixator – provides stabilisation at the proximal end of the limb

Force – force = mass x acceleration

Force transmission – impact forces transmitted through the body

Formative assessment – takes place informally and will support the development of a coach

Formative experiences – help you to develop or make sense of the things you see and experience. These formative experiences, such as playing sport or being an assistant coach, provide you with various contexts in which you can construct knowledge

Functionalism – a social theory used to understand society. Functionalism suggests that society contains many interrelated social systems that aim to promote balance in order to continue to operate efficiently

Gender – refers to characteristics of male/masculinity and female/femininity that are often used to define men and women

General Practitioner (GP) – often thought of as the family doctor, providing primary health care for patients in the community

Generic coaching knowledge – principles that can be applied to any learning context

Hazard – something with potential to cause harm

Health-related activities – activity aimed at improving the health and well-being of an individual

Healthy eating – eating for health. In achieving a balanced diet, eating should support health and aim to reduce the risk of chronic disease, such as heart disease

Horizontal scaling – providing a scale of measurement that will allow you to convert on-screen measurements to real-life measurements, for example 1 metre 'real' = 1 centimetre 'screen'

Humanistic approach to sports coaching – a person-centred approach focusing on the holistic development of an empowered individual

Imagery (in sport) – the use of mental rehearsal to improve physical performance by means of motivating pictures, visions and words

Inclusive coaching – changing your coaching practice to meet the needs of all the individuals in the group

Insertion – the attachment of a muscle usually via a tendon to bone. The insertion on the bone is moveable as a result of muscle contraction

Instrumentalism – a philosophy holding that what is most important about a thing or idea is its value as an instrument of action and its usefulness

Interactionist perspective – a sociological perspective that examines how roles are established through interaction between individuals and adherence to predetermined social values

Intervertebral disc – a fibrocartilage disc which lies between each adjacent vertebrae of the spine

Intrinsic feedback – feedback that comes from the athlete's senses

Intrinsic motivation – doing an activity because the activity is an end in itself

Invert – move the sole of the foot towards the midline of the body

Isometric contraction – force is generated by the muscle without changing length

Justify – the conclusion you have drawn or ideas you have formed will need to be justified. The information you have researched will allow you to support your work

Key factors – coaching points that are drawn from your sport's specific knowledge that will make up the key points of your coaching session. For example, if your session was designed for defending in football you might want to plan your sessions to allow you to coach some of these key factors

Knowledge – the sum of what is known

Knowledge of Performance (KP) – feedback to the athlete about the actions that have caused the result and how these must be changed to alter the result in future

Knowledge of Results (KR) – feedback to the athlete about the outcome of an action or event

Laissez-faire – often provides little direction and allows performers to learn from themselves and their sport

Learning – the activity of obtaining knowledge

Ligament – a band of tough fibrous tissue connecting bone to bone

Linear (traditional) **coaching** – drills and practices that assume learning is sequential

Lordosis – exaggerated curvature of the lumbar spine

Macronutrient – nutrients the body requires in large amounts such as carbohydrates, proteins and fats

Macro-sociology – the study of large-scale social phenomena, especially the comparison of whole societies with each other (Douglas, 1973)

Mastery – knowledge, ability and control in relation to specific learned situations in sport

Mastery climate – the environment sends signals suggesting success is synonymous with improvement and learning

Mastery goals – success is synonymous with learning, improvement and effort

Mediastinum – a mass of tissue between the lungs, extending from the sternum to the vertebral column

Mediated learning – learning directed by knowledgeable other

Mental staleness – a negative emotional state caused by undertaking too much or poorly balanced training of the same type

Mentor – an experienced and knowledgeable person who advises and guides a less experienced colleague early in their career

Method – the style of coaching adopted by the coach

Micronutrients – nutrients the body requires in small amounts such as vitamins and minerals

Micro-societies – smaller social groupings that are interrelated and help to make up the wider picture of society

Micro-sociology – the study of everyday behaviour and the face-to-face interaction of individuals within a particular social setting

Mineral – an inorganic compound naturally occurring in a solid chemical substance

Morals – deep-rooted personal beliefs that guide our behaviours and actions

Motivation – the intensity and direction of effort

Motivational climate – situationally induced psychological environment that influences achievement strategies of participants

Motivational climate – the way in which coaches structure the sporting environment in order to send signals to athletes about the meaning of success

Motor development – the normal pattern of movement progression throughout the early years and completed in adolescence involving growth, neural and mental changes in function

Movement patterns – movements made within the sport (multijoint, jumping and running, encompassing, flexion, extension, rotation etc), link to planes of motion and axis of rotation

Musculotendinous junctures – the point where muscles and tendons merge and a key site for over-use injury

National Occupational Standards – nationally agreed standards of performance in a range of vocations, which offer benchmarks for good practice

Negative feedback – feedback that happens after an unsuccessful attempt at a task. This is used to highlight and correct errors

Non-linear (non-traditional) coaching – problem-based, game play that leads to the learning of skills and technique as well as tactical understanding of sport

Normative ability – Your ability compared to another referenced norm

Objective – how a goal will be achieved e.g. 'introduce, demonstrate and develop the required techniques of the parallel turn'

Occipital condyles – kidney-shaped with convex surfaces. There are two occipital condyles located either side of the foramen magnum. They articulate with the atlas bone

Origin – the attachment site of a muscle to bone (in a few exceptions muscle). The origin is a fixed location

Osgood Schlatter's Syndrome – bony appositions which are pulled out from soft bone just below the knee by overtrained tendons before muscles fully develop

Ossification – the developmental process by which cartilage hardens to form bone

Over-learning – frequent and continued practice of key performance skills that have already been learned to prevent poor technique under the pressure of competition

Overload – training principle: the training intensity should be either of a stimulating, retaining or detraining level

Overtraining – training too hard and too frequently to adapt and improve. Often causing mental staleness and over-use injuries

Parietal layer – outer layer of the serous pericardium

Participant – a person who takes part or becomes involved in an activity

Participant management – the process of planning and organising the members of a group

Participation – involvement in an organised activity, such as sport

Pedagogical – strategies for teaching and learning

Pedagogy – the principles and practices designed to enhance learning in an individual

Performance – how well a person or team does an activity

Performance climate – the environment sends signals suggesting success is synonymous with demonstration of ability

Performance criteria – aspects of performance that are used to analyse performance in sports. These are also referred to as performance indicators or key performance indicators in some literature

Performance goals – success is synonymous with ability compared to others

Performance-enhancing drugs – drugs which are used to improve performance

Pericardial (serous) fluid – fluid found between the parietal and visceral layer

Pericardium – membrane surrounding the heart, containing two layers – fibrous and serous

Perimysium – connective tissue encasing fascicles

Perspective error – an error where objects appear larger or smaller than they actually are as they move towards or away from the camera; it is difficult to effectively judge their position

Philosophy statement – the written record of a coach's philosophy

Plantar reflex – reflex action naturally developed in infancy which controls the pointing of the toes

Plantarflex – point the toes away, pushing the sole of the foot away

Plyometric training – powerful jump, sprint and resistance training designed to improve dynamic or explosive movements in sport

Positive feedback – feedback that occurs after successful completion of a task. This is used to reinforce performance

Post-natal – the period directly after the birth, usually extending for approximately six weeks

Prehabilitation – joint and muscle specific exercises which strengthen limbs in preparation for certain sports, e.g. to prevent shoulder injuries sustained from practising the service action in tennis

Pre-natal – the period during the pregnancy before the birth of the baby when there are major physiological changes experienced by the mother

Reaction time – the shortest time taken for the body to start to produce movements following one physical signal to do so

Recreational drugs – drugs taken for recreational or social reasons, commonly known as street drugs

Relational – involving interaction with others

Relationships – the connections and bonds that are formed between you as a coach and the participants in your care

Responsibilities – you have legal, personal and professional standards to maintain in coaching so that those in your care are given the best opportunity to enjoy and progress in their chosen sport

Rights – legal, social, or moral freedoms that permit or constrain certain actions

Risk – the likelihood of a hazard occurring

Roles – a role often refers to the part played by an actor. A coach can be considered to 'play' a number of different roles and this will impact on the coaching process and how you plan for coaching

Sarcolemma – cell membrane of the muscle fibre

Science – knowledge gained from the systematic study of the physical world, especially through observation and experimentation, and the development of theories to describe the results

Self-confidence – the degree to which a person is confident about their ability to perform well in a given situation

Self-esteem – the value a young performer places upon themselves

Self-reflexive – the act of using individual experiences to guide future practice

Sexualisation – presenting a person, group or thing as sexual in nature. In sport this is usually conducted by the print and televised media focusing on the body image of female athletes to attract increased audiences and readers

Social cohesion – a group is united in the sense that it is 'socially close'

Social exclusion – a process where individuals or communities are prevented from accessing certain opportunities for social reasons, which results in being disadvantaged in some way

Socially constructed – society develops shared ideas or beliefs on different subjects. In the case of men and women this creates stereotypes in society that are played out in the media and in everyday actions

Society – a distinct collection of people who are bound together through the same political system and sense of self-identity

Socio-economic perspective – highlights the importance of using economics in the study of society

Sociology – the study of human life, observing how individuals interact and examining the cultural settings in which people live

Somatic anxiety – the physical accompaniment to cognitive anxiety (such as sweaty palms, butterflies in stomach or increased heart rate)

Special population – a population or group that shares particular needs, wants and similarities (physical, psychological, medical or genetic)

Specificity – training principle: exercises should closely resemble the movements of the sport (dynamic correspondence)

Spine curvature anomalies – structural abnormalities in the back (normally mild in nature) such as scoliosis or rounded shoulders which may prevent young people from training and competing

Sport compliance – the degree to which a young performer persists with and continues training for their chosen sport

Sport satisfaction – the pride and rewarding feelings associated with being successful at something you enjoy

Sport(s) science(s) – umbrella term for academic programmes that focus on the application of scientific principles and techniques with the aim of improving sporting performance

Stacking – the disproportionate representation of particular ethnic minority groups in specific positions in team sports

Stereotypes – a popular belief about a particular type of individual or specific social group based on prior assumption. Often stereotypes can be misleading and give an unfair or inaccurate representation of a particular individual, social group or culture

Strategy – the actions taken by the coach in response to identified priorities for coaching

Structural characteristics – social structures are comprised of the human interactions and relationships that are present within a society

Style – the way in which the coaching is performed

Sub-discipline – a field of specialised study within the discipline of sports sciences

Subjectivities – individual differences (for example, learning preferences, personality, experiences, values, morals, coaching philosophy)

Summative assessment – takes place formally and is normally an assessment of your competence or performance as a coach

Supinated – when the forearm is supinated the palm of the hand is facing forward when in the anatomical position

Sutural bone – extra piece of bone which appears in the suture in the cranium

Synergist – synergist muscles assist the agonist muscles and provide stabilisation to prevent any unwanted movement

Synthesise – drawing together information from a range of sources you have researched to support the assessment you are constructing. Logical connections should be made and presented in a logical format

Task cohesion – a group is united in its attempts to achieve group goals and objectives

Tendinitis – a type of overuse injury common in young performers when serious training is first undertaken. Normally found in the elbow, wrist, knee and ankle

Tendon – a band of inelastic tissue connecting a muscle to bone

Terminal feedback – feedback that happens after an event, rather than during the event

Thermogenesis – the process of heat production

Time–motion – duration of sports competition (i.e. 90-minute football match) and individual movement characteristics (walking, jogging, jumping, changing direction, sprinting and kicking; muscles utilised to perform these movements, linking to type of contraction: eccentric, concentric, isometric)

Top-down approach – externally-driven sports development programmes that are implemented by a centralised organisation who offer expertise and experience

Torso – the trunk or mid-section of the body

Training sensitivity – the amount of stress tolerance a young performer inherits and develops which helps them cope with heavy training phases

Trait anxiety – a personality disposition that predisposes individuals to higher levels of anxiety at a given moment

Underlying regularities or patternings – patterns of social behaviour and relationships that occur regularly within a particular social environment. These patternings or regularities help to build social structure

Urbanism – an analysis of the geographical, political, economical and social factors that impact upon and arise within urban areas

Utilitarianism – an approach to ethics that states that ethical action is based on providing happiness or benefit for the recipient

Variation – training principle: exercises can be varied either through type (qualitative) or load (quantitative)

Veins – carry blood to the heart, usually deoxygenated

Velocity – is a vector quantity and has both magnitude and direction, velocity (v) = s/change in time

Venules – connect capillaries to veins

Vertical referencing – as for horizontal scaling, but vertically

Virtue ethics – an approach to ethics that states that ethical action is based on the characteristics or moral judgement of an individual, such as a coach

Visceral layer – inner layer of serous pericardium, also known as the epicardium, surrounding the heart tightly

Vitamin – an organic compound required in tiny amounts such as vitamins A, C, D and K

Index